Productivity, Investment in Human Capital and the Challenge of Youth Employment

ADAPT LABOUR STUDIES BOOK-SERIES

International School of Higher Education in Labour and Industrial Relations

Series Editors
Tayo Fashoyin, University of Lagos (Nigeria)
Michele Tiraboschi, University of Modena and Reggio Emilia (Italy)

Guest Editors
Pietro Manzella, ADAPT Language Editor
Lisa Rustico, ADAPT Head of International Relations

ADAPT (www.adapt.it) is a non-profit organisation founded in 2000 by Professor Marco Biagi with the aim of promoting studies and research in the field of labour law and industrial relations from an international and comparative perspective. Our purpose is to encourage and implement a new approach to academic research, by establishing ongoing relationships with other universities and advanced studies institutes, and promoting academic and scientific exchange programmes with enterprises, institutions, foundations and associations. In collaboration with the **Marco Biagi Centre for International and Comparative Studies** (www.csmb. unimore.it), ADAPT set up the International School of Higher Education in Labour and Industrial Relations, a centre of excellence which is accredited at an international level for research, study and the postgraduate programmes in the area of industrial and labour relations.

ADAPT International Scientific Committee

Bertagna Giuseppe *(University of Bergamo, Italy)*, Bulgarelli Aviana *(ISFOL, Italy)*, Frommberger Dietmar *(Universität Magdeburg, Germany)*, Grisolia Julio Armando *(Universidad Nacional de Tres de Febrero, Argentina)*, Hajdù Jòzsef *(University of Szeged, Hungary)*, Kai Chang *(Renmin University, China)*, Ouchi Shynia *(University of Kobe, Japan)*, Quinlan Michael *(University of New South Wales, Australia)*, Raso Delgue Juan *(Universidad de la Republica, Uruguay)*, Ryan Paul *(King's College, University of Cambridge, United Kingdom)*, Sanchez Castaneda Alfredo *(Universidad Nacional Autonoma de Mexico, Mexico)*, Sargeant Malcolm *(Middlesex University, United Kingdom)*, Fashoyin Tayo *(University of Lagos, Nigeria)*, Tiraboschi Michele *(University of Modena and Reggio Emilia, Italy)*, Tucker Erick *(York University, Canada)*.

Productivity, Investment in Human Capital and the Challenge of Youth Employment

Series Editors
Tayo Fashoyin and Michele Tiraboschi

Guest Editors
Pietro Manzella and Lisa Rustico

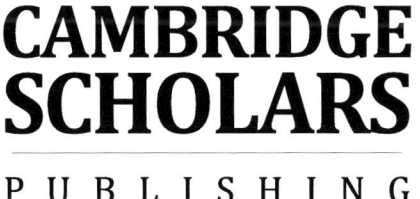

Productivity, Investment in Human Capital and the Challenge of Youth Employment,
Series Editors: Tayo Fashoyin and Michele Tiraboschi
Guest Editors: Pietro Manzella and Lisa Rustico

This book first published 2011

Cambridge Scholars Publishing

12 Back Chapman Street, Newcastle upon Tyne, NE6 2XX, UK

British Library Cataloguing in Publication Data
A catalogue record for this book is available from the British Library

ISBN (10): 1-4438-3174-3, ISBN (13): 978-1-4438-3174-1

TABLE OF CONTENTS

LIST OF ILLUSTRATIONS

LIST OF TABLES

FOREWORD

TAYO FASHOYIN AND MICHELE TIRABOSCHI

In an international and comparative perspective, access to the labour market on the part of young people is a complex issue with certain contradictory aspects reflecting the level of development of public policy, labour law and industrial relations in the respective countries.

In the most advanced economies there has been a steady increase in the age at which young people exit the educational system and enter the labour market, giving rise to significant economic and social problems. The increase in the levels of educational attainment is associated in some cases with an alarming rate of unemployment among those with academic qualifications, while employers encounter considerable difficulty in recruiting workers for unskilled and semi-skilled positions.

The economies of developing countries, on the other hand, are characterised by different trends, reminiscent of the early stages of modern labour law and their enforcement, resulting in large-scale exploitation of young workers and children. Many of such young entrants into the labour market join the flow of migrants towards the more highly developed regions of the world, with the consequent risk of impoverishing human capital in the country of origin.

In this connection, the *ADAPT LABOUR STUDIES BOOK-SERIES* has been set up with a view to advancing a better understanding of those issues in a global dimension through an interdisciplinary and comparative approach.

We wish to express our sincere thanks to Martina Ori, Barbara Winkler and Machilu Zimba for their editorial assistance.

YOUTH AND THE CHANGING WORLD OF WORK

PIETRO MANZELLA AND LISA RUSTICO

The labour market poses serious challenges in terms of youth employment, with this topic increasingly attracting the attention of many experts and policy-makers at an international level. Although from different perspectives, the provision of job opportunities to young people is deemed a priority in many countries. Far from being the direct result of labour reforms, adjustments in employment policies primarily stemmed from wide-ranging changes occurred in some production methods and work organisation, also considering the shift from an industrial-based to a service-based society. In this respect, by facing turbulent school-to-work transitions, unprofitable investments in education, joblessness and precariousness, the younger generations suffer the most from ineffective labour market dynamics and self-referential education systems, with such variables that are tightly intertwined, as shown, for instance, by the impact of the educational attainment levels on youth unemployment rates. When poorly educated, young people are more exposed to the effects of unemployment, even on the long run. Especially those who leave the school system without any formal qualification – dropouts – or those neither in employment nor in education and training – the NEETs – are at risk of suffering from bad economic conditions, social exclusion and lower participation in continuous training throughout their lives.

Young people still remain one of the weakest segments of the labour market, as particularly exposed to economic turmoil and changes, and this aspect is even more dramatic if we consider the increased dependency ratio, flowing from the ageing population. Moreover, while in employment, young people are often engaged in precarious jobs, therefore becoming more vulnerable to job loss than their adult counterparts. Besides facing employment instability, youngsters also lack adequate skills, and those qualifications the labour market longs for. In addition to formal qualifications, holding "the right skills for the right jobs" on the part of young people would represent a means to face such challenges and avoid risks of precariousness. However, matching labour demand and supply is regarded as a viable solution only through a dynamic and mutually supporting relationship between educational and training institutions and the labour market.

On the basis of these considerations, and in an awareness of the seriousness of the foregoing questions and consequences that ensue, the papers in this volume aim at providing some valuable insights into the issue, taking as a starting point initiatives, policies and legislative measures adopted in different national contexts to tackle young people unemployment.

THE CHALLENGE OF YOUTH EMPLOYMENT

THE YOUTH EMPLOYMENT CHALLENGE: AN INTRODUCTION

TAYO FASHOYIN

Recent data on global trends in employment clearly suggest that unemployment remains perhaps the most serious labour market policy challenge for most countries of the world. Specifically, recent publications of the International Labour Office (ILO) demonstrate that the number of unemployed people around the world has increased over the pre-crisis years, reaching 205 million during 2009-2010.[1] The actual increase in global unemployment was 27.6 million over the pre-crisis figure for 2007. This translates into a global unemployment rate of 5.6% at the onset of the economic crisis, which rose to 6.3% in 2009, and marginally fell to 6.2% in 2010.[2] Evidently, the global crisis has caused a contraction of employment, leading to joblessness across the globe.

In relation to the youth, defined as being between 15-24 years old, the unemployed youth accounted for about 81 million in 2009, which represented an increase of 7.8 million unemployed over the figure for the pre-crisis year of 2007.[3] Thus, while youth unemployment increased by 1.1 million between 2007 and 2008, the increase in the following year was 6.6 million.[4] This yielded a youth unemployment rate of 11.9% in 2007, which rose to 13% in 2009, nearly twice the size of the total increase in unemployment.[5] Accordingly, compared to global unemployment during the same period, it is evident that the impact of the crisis on the youth was far more severe. Taking account of the fact that most of the jobs being performed by young people are of inferior quality, the youth suffer comparatively poorer working conditions, such as long hours, short-term contracts or informal arrangements. Also, because they are comparatively

---

[1] International Labour Organization. 2011. *Global Employment Trends 2011. The Challenge of a Jobs Recovery*. Geneva: ILO, 12 and Table A4.
[2] Ibid., Table A2.
[3] ILO. 2010. *Global Employment Trends for Youth 2010*. Geneva: ILO, 4.
[4] Ibid.
[5] Ibid., Table A5.

low-skilled, they are found in unskilled and low-paid jobs, and virtually without social protection that they can fall back on.[6]

Poor employment prospects for the youth are in sharp contrast to the observable global recovery, as shown by a number of macroeconomic indicators, such as real global GDP, and world trade and investment.[7] In other words, while the global economic recovery is improving, the employment generating capacity of economic recovery has lagged, and, for several reasons, young people will likely feel the pinch much more than adult workers. As the ILO reports emphasise, not only does this situation represent a worsening of employment prospects for young people, but full recovery might not provide much relief to this group of labour market actors as well, due to systemic and institutional difficulties in many countries. In this brief introductory note, I draw attention to some of the key challenges faced by young people and the public policy direction that needs to take account of the unfavourable labour market experience of the youth, and so improve their long-term employment prospects.

1. Trends in Youth Employment

In the most advanced market economies, the available evidence indicates that the youth population appears to be a declining proportion of total population. In such economies, the youth share of the population was 12.57% in 2010.[8] In contrast, the youth accounted for about 20% of the population in the developing economies in 2010. In these economies, while the proportion of youth with respect to the overall population has declined marginally, it nevertheless ranged between 19.5% and 20.5% in 2010.[9] Significantly, the majority of the youth were in Asia.[10]

With regard to the employment situation of young people, a somewhat brighter picture is provided at a global level: the number of youth that was unemployed declined from 79.6 million to 77.7 million or by 1.9 million between 2009 and 2010.[11] However, this otherwise favourable prospect

---

[6] Ibid., 3. See also Weller, J. 2007. "Youth employment: characteristics, tensions and challenges," *CEPAL Review* 92: 73-74, Table 5.
[7] ILO. 2011. *Global Employment Trends 2011. The Challenge of a Jobs Recovery.* Geneva: ILO, 4-5.
[8] ILO. 2010. *Global Employment Trends for Youth 2010.* Geneva: ILO, 7.
[9] Ibid.
[10] Ibid., 8 Figure 2.
[11] ILO. 2011. *Global Employment Trends 2011. The Challenge of a Jobs Recovery.* Geneva: ILO. Table A4.

deteriorated rapidly as a result of the crisis. In other words, while the number of youth actively looking for employment decreased during this period, their employment prospects have not been as favourable. Most of the relevant literature enumerates the various reasons for this situation, including a lack of requisite education, skills and work experience, and discrimination of all sorts in the labour market.[12] For those youth who cannot afford not to work, this reality naturally pushes them to accept low-skilled and low-paying jobs, and often unremunerated employment in the informal sector.

In periods of high unemployment and job scarcity, young people are disadvantaged in the labour market, as their skills are low and their job search so frustrating that they tend to give up seeking employment much sooner than adults. Therefore, the youth labour market experience generally represents a particularly significant challenge to public policy-makers. This case emphasises the need for a mop up of unutilised or under-utilised human resources, but also the risk of dangerous social and political consequences resulting from an army of unemployed youth in society. I shall return to this issue later.

Disaggregated national data can be helpful in evaluating the particular challenge of unemployment among the young people. As a number of studies have shown, unemployment among the youth has been a major policy challenge even before the advent of the global crisis. For example, a study of youth unemployment in Latin America in the 1990s indicates that unemployment among them was prevalent well before the onset of the global recession. The study found that, compared to an unemployment rate of 31.1% for this group in 1990, the percentage of young people not in employment had risen to 39.2% by 2004.[13] Similarly, in South Africa, Mlatsheni and Rospabe show that unemployment among South African youth was twice as much of adults, at 50% in 2002.[14] This is comparable to another study in Burkina Faso, also in Africa. The study points out that in 2000, about 40% of urban male youth and as high as 55% of female

---

[12] The ILO report on youth employment documents in various context, the nature of the discriminatory practices against the youth in the labour market. See ILO 2010.

[13] Weller, J. 2007. "Youth Employment: Characteristics, Tensions and Challenges," *CEPAL Review* 92, 69, Table 5.

[14] Mlatsheni, C., and S. Rospabé. 2002. "Why is Youth Unemployment so High and unequally Spread in South Africa?" Development Policy Research Unit Working Paper No. 02/65, University of Cape Town.

youth were out of formal sector wage employment.[15] The study concludes that, over the 20-year period (1980-2000), unemployed youth had led to higher levels of informal employment. In East Asia and the Pacific, available information indicates that youth unemployment increased by 2.2% between 1998 and 2008.[16] The ILO projects an increase in the youth population in most of the developing countries by 2015.[17]

There has been an increase in the entry of young people into the labour force, which reflects several other realities of the labour market, including population, school enrolment and length of study. However, this structural change has not been followed by an increase in the demand for youth labour. The reasons for this include the rate at which jobs are being created, a general lack of skills and experience among young people, and a contraction of modern formal sector employment, particularly in the context of the current global economic crisis. As a result, when employers respond to a slump in demand, young workers are hardest hit.

Even though some youth might have gained work experience, such experience acquired in occupations requiring low levels of education or skills is not always the passport to better jobs in the formal sector, more so when specific attributes or skills are essential to perform in the labour market.[18] As is common among urban youth across countries, when they fail to find employment regarded as their first or preferred choice, normally in the modern wage employment sector, in the private or public sector, they naturally revert to the informal economy to earn a living. Available evidence and data reflect this tendency among the youth in the developing economies, and provide a picture of the challenges faced by public authorities across regions, and their need to find solutions and means of improving the labour market experience of their youth population.

---

[15] Calves, A-E., and B. Schoumaker. 2004. "Deteriorating Economic Context and Changing Patterns of Youth Employment in Urban Burkina Faso: 1980-2000," *World Development* 32, No.6.

[16] ILO. 2010. *Global Employment Trends for Youth 2010*. Geneva: ILO, 17, Table 3.

[17] See in particular Godfrey, M. 2003. "Youth Employment policy in Developing and Transition Countries—Prevention as well as Cure," *Social Protection Discussion Paper Series* No. 0320, Social Protection Unit, Washington: The World Bank; and O'Higgins, N. 2010. "Youth unemployment and employment policy: A global perspective," *Munich Personal RePEc Achieve, MPRA Paper* No. 23698.

[18] Weller, J. 2007. "Youth Employment: Characteristics, Tensions and Challenges," *CEPAL Review* 92, 74.

2. Gender and Regional Differences in the Youth Labour Market

Generally, there are fewer economically active women than men in the labour force, which is the result of many factors, including relatively lower educational attainment and skills, or episodes of discrimination in the labour market. In several societies, particularly in the developing economies, this state of affairs may also result from customs and traditions, and other social norms or realities that put women at a great disadvantage in terms of job opportunities. Available evidence confirms this view; as the data indicate, while global labour force participation rate among men was 58.9% in 2010, the corresponding rate for women was 42.4%.[19] This relativity between men and women is generally true across regions, with the only exception represented by areas in East Asia. Here, labour force among women (61.6%) outpaced men's participation rate (57%) in 2010.

However, the labour market experiences of men and women are very different. Some evidence suggests that, as a subgroup, women in the labour market do face some disadvantages when it comes to finding a decent job. Such differences might indicate that unemployment among young women is lower than that of young men, but this could also have been the result of other labour market factors. This might simply mean that young women tend to give up job search far much quicker than their male counterparts, and might exit from the labour market altogether.[20] Although several of the reasons given above are common to both young women and men, there could be a considerable number of differences in their resilience to paid job search.

That said, labour force participation among women is particularly low in the case of North Africa, and the Middle East. In these regions, the labour force participation rate among women was about one-half of the corresponding participation rate for men. Thus, while the labour force participation rate among men in these regions was respectively 52.5% and 50.3% in 2010, the corresponding participation rate for women was 22.9% and 21.5% in the same year.[21] In other words, either on account of unfavourable social and cultural norms, or of some social aspects, such as

---

[19] ILO. 2011. *Global Employment Trends 2011. The Challenge of a Jobs Recovery*. Geneva: ILO, Table A8.

[20] ILO. 2010. *Global Employment Trends for Youth 2010*. Geneva: ILO, 21, Table 1.

[21] Ibid., 9, Table 1.

education, women in some regions and societies are generally disadvantaged in the labour market.

3. The Effect of the Global Economic Crisis

As shown, prior to the global crisis there had been a decrease in unemployment among adults (particularly in the period 2006-2007) and a more significant decrease in youth unemployment, corresponding to 3.4 and 4.8 percentage points, respectively.[22] However, as the ILO estimates indicate, the number of unemployed among young people increased by 7.8 million, compared to an overall increase of 28 million. Unemployment among the youth rose from 11.9% to 13% between 2007 and 2009.[23] As data indicate, young women are far more adversely affected, as a result of the global crisis.

The effect of the crisis naturally led to a progressively loose labour market, where youth are generally disadvantaged. With low levels of education, little to no skills, young people are not competitive or attractive enough to operate in such labour markets. Accordingly, their employment prospects are worse in periods of contraction of employment opportunities. Apart from this, there are other labour market realities that might have accentuated unemployment among the youth during the current crisis. For example, the raising of the statutory retirement age and the re-entry of skilled workers into the labour market are bound to depress further the employment opportunities of young people, particularly when they are not employable for lack of education, skills and/or experience.

However, the consequences of the global recession vary across regions, with such impact producing different results even within the same region and usually being more relevant in the developed Western European countries. For example, the first full year of the crisis (2008-2009) produced unequal effects on the European regions. While the increase in youth unemployment was 4.6% in the advanced market economies, non-EU Member States and South-Eastern Europe countries reported a 3.5% increase over the same period.[24] Furthermore in 2007, that is before the crisis, young women were already experiencing high unemployment, and by 2009, unemployment among this group was even higher.

The situation is completely different as regards developing economies. In 2009, in Latin America, the Caribbean, and North Africa, the gap in

---

[22] Ibid., 31.
[23] Ibid., 28.
[24] Ibid., 63, Table A5.

unemployment rates between young females and males increased by as much as 7.3, 10.5 and 11.4 percentage points respectively, ostensibly because tighter labour market pushed back women jobseekers.[25] Despite the scarcity of employment opportunities in the formal economy, the absence of social protection normally induces young people to engage in informal and vulnerable employment. In Sub-Saharan Africa, for example, as a result of a high youth employment-to-population ratio, the proportion of young people actively engaged in work increased by 33.3% during the 1998-2008 period.[26]

However, such labour market activities were poverty-driven, undertaken in the informal economy out of desperation. These forms of employment are not necessarily "decent" in the sense that they provide meagre income, virtually without any form of social protection.[27] In other words, with low education, inexperience, little or no skills, the youth are not competitive or attractive enough to function in competitive labour markets. So their employment prospects are far worse in periods of contraction of employment.

In sum, and with special reference to developing economies, the global crisis slowly but steadily manifested in various forms, reversing, as it does, the economic development projections for poverty reduction, as anticipated in the Millennium Development Goals. The effect of the crisis is demonstrated, not only by the size of employment or unemployment, but perhaps by the corresponding increase in job opportunities that can be described—at best—as irrelevant to provide decent employment. This would obviously result in underemployment, that usually takes place in the informal economy, and various forms of atypical work in the modern sector.

4. Addressing the Youth Employment Challenge

In the future scenario of a post crisis recovery, there are prospects for a decrease in unemployment rates for young people over time. According to existing forecasts, the anticipated growth of GDP will lead to a decrease in the size of global unemployment. These estimates indicate a marginal decrease in youth unemployment rate from 13.1% in 2010 to 12.7% in

---

[25] Ibid., 29.

[26] Ibid., 14.

[27] Weller, J. 2007. "Youth Employment: Characteristics, Tensions and Challenges," *CEPAL Review* 92. Calves, A-E., and B. Schoumaker. 2004. "Deteriorating Economic Context and Changing Patterns of Youth Employment in Urban Burkina Faso: 1980-2000," *World Development* 32, No. 6.

2011.[28] But as studies show, there are various forms of discrimination which cannot be overlooked, particularly when explaining the unemployment dilemma faced by the youth. There is no doubt that disadvantaged young people risk marginalisation and social exclusion. Socially disadvantaged youth are more exposed to unemployment than others.

Obviously, existing evidence of the relatively poor employment status of young people calls for an integrated employment policy in which the promotion of youth employment represents a clearly defined element of the overall economic and social development agenda, with youth employment and employability that need to be regarded as key priorities. A considerable number of young people across regions are generally engaged in poor quality employment, including agricultural and casual employment in the informal economy, notably in the developing countries. The youth work long hours, usually on a short-term and informal basis, and under uncertain work arrangements characterised by decent work deficits, such as low pay, precarious working conditions and a lack of provisions in terms of social safety net.

The ILO report paints the following dilemma faced by the youth within the labour market, also explaining the perception of society at large, including policy-makers, when it comes to the youth employment challenge:

> An inability to find employment creates a sense of uselessness and idleness among young people that can lead to increased crime, mental health problems, violence, conflicts and drug taking…idleness among youth can come at great costs. They are not contributing to the economic welfare of the country—quite the contrary. The loss of income among the younger generation translates into a lack of savings as well as a loss of aggregate demand. Some youth who are unable to earn their own income have to be financially supported by the family, leaving less for spending and investments at the household level.[29]

Several years ago, the UN concluded that the social, economic and political consequences of youth unemployment represented a waste of valuable human resources and their potential contribution to social and economic development.[30] The document stated that failing to take decisive action was not an option for countries. Indeed, in countries where social

---

[28] ILO. 2010. *Global Employment Trends for Youth 2010*. Geneva: ILO, 46, Table 6.
[29] Ibid., 6, Box 2.
[30] United Nations General Assembly. 2005. *Global Analysis and Evaluation of National Action Plans on Youth Employment*. Report of the Secretary General Sixtieth Session. United Nations.

protection benefits exist, unemployment among youth represents a drain on national budget.

The impact is more significant where such facilities are not provided. It follows that it is a colossal waste of the potential contribution of manpower to the economic development at a national level. The UN went on to encourage Member States to undertake national reviews of the employment challenges affecting young people and develop action plans which espouse specific and concrete measures as part of the national development agenda.

As emphasised by relevant studies, the complexity of the issue of unemployment lies in the fact that aggregate labour demand and good macroeconomic policy and growth are critical to employment development, and are, in turn, favourable to youth employment. At the same time, the possibility for increasing youth employment is associated with or influenced by several factors, including aggregate demand, employment intensity of growth, and the lawmakers' willingness to set up employment policies, appropriate training, work experience and options for entrepreneurship.[31]

However, aggregate demand, although important, only explains part of the problem of young people; the issue is not limited to a lack of employment, but also to its low quality, as involving long hours and low remuneration, and low levels of social protection.[32] In this sense, skills development and employability are therefore at the heart of the quality of employment in terms of, say, well remunerated or compensated employment.

Lack of information also affects the awareness of employment opportunities, a point that is likely to be more severe in developing economies. Nevertheless, and in a similar context, the need for good and responsive policy that takes account of the number and quality of youth seeking employment, and that shoud be based on accurate labour market information that is critical for achieving school-to-work transition can hardly be overlooked. In the circumstances of a lack of favourable employment prospects for young people, the key public policy challenge is with regard to the provision of decent employment and their accessibility to such employment opportunities.

The employment challenge faced by young people is associated with the overall employment trends, but it requires concrete and specific attention for the development of sustainable and high-quality employment.

---

[31] For detailed policy proposals, see ILO. 2004a. *Conclusions of the Tripartite Meeting on Youth Employment: The Way Forward.* Geneva: ILO.

[32] O'Higgins, N. 2001. "Youth Unemployment and Employment Policy: A Global Perspective," Munich Personal RePEc Archive, MPRA Paper No. 23698.

Meeting this employment challenge calls for an integrated, comprehensive and coherent approach that combines macro and microeconomic policies and which addresses simultaneously demand and supply, both in quantitative and qualitative terms. The critical public policy challenge is how to improve the employment status of disadvantaged youth who are often poorly prepared for the labour market, and lack adequate education, skills and work experience potential employers are interested in. In other words, such a policy must focus on employability.

In several countries, these policies have formed part of the countries' Decent Work Country Programmes, which are developed by the government and the country's development partners and technically backstopped by the ILO.[33] At the national level, these programmes are basic elements of the United Nations Development Assistance Framework, UNDDAF. A key pillar of the Decent Work Country Programme is its emphasis of the essentiality of a favourable macroeconomic environment in meeting the full benefits of the achievement of decent work. As has been pointed out:

> Macroeconomic success is one of the primary determinants of employment growth. Both longer term growth and development and shorter term economic fluctuations have a major effect on the labour market.... macroeconomic policy is too important a determinant of employment to be ignored.[34]

Indeed, such a holistic approach is more than likely to capture or target specific growth sectors in the economy which have the largest possibility of employment generation.[35] It is hardly possible that a comprehensive decent work agenda at the national level ignores or fails to take into account the needs for improvement of labour market institutions, in particular the development of an active labour market policy as well as efficient labour market information and networks that will take on board the benefits accruable to the special needs of young people in the labour

---

[33] ILO. 2004b. *Improving Prospects for Young Women and Men in the World of Work. A Guide to Youth Employment.* Geneva: ILO. ILO. 2006. *Employment Strategies for Decent Work Country Programmes: Concepts, Approaches and Tools for Implementation of the Global Employment Agenda.* Geneva: ILO.
[34] ILO. 1999. *Decent Work.* Geneva: ILO, 22.
[35] Godfrey, M. 2003. "Youth Employment Policy in Developing and Transition Countries—Prevention as well as Cure," Social Protection Discussion Paper Series No. 0320, Social Protection Unit, Washington: The World Bank, 33.

market. In the event, these development programmes invariably address the issues of employability of youth in the labour market.

In the same vein, improvements in labour market institutions, in particular the development of an active labour market policy and effective labour market information and networks are more likely to work to the special benefits of young people entering the labour market. In the OECD, it has been shown that youth with upper secondary education report higher employment rates than those with no education. This suggests that public policy has some role in ensuring that students stay in school longer, in order to avoid early school dropout and allow them to acquire needed education which prepares them for decent employment.[36] Here again, the critical concern is the employability of the youth in the labour market. As stressed by the tripartite meeting, employability represents:

> a key outcome of education and training of high quality, as well as a range of other policies. It encompasses the skills, knowledge and competencies that enhance a worker's ability to secure and retain a job, progress at work and cope with change, secure another job if he/she so wishes or has been laid off, and enter more easily into the labour market at different periods of the life cycle.[37]

The strategy to incorporate the youth employment policy into national planning is a realistic approach to tackle the issue of unemployment among young people, because such a policy comprises human resource and manpower development, with entrepreneurship and the growth of the economy that are part of the constituent elements of the national economic development strategy. In the same context, company employment policies are often shaped or influenced by two direct parties in business, namely the employers and workers' organisations which are both concerned about the quality and size of employment.

Arguably, trade unions' primary preoccupation is the protection and advancement of the job interest of their members. To the extent that this impact on the size and type of employment makes it necessary to involve both employers and workers' organisations in building consensus on the

---

[36] OECD. "Tackling the job crisis: The Labour Market and Social Policy Response," Labour and Employment Ministerial Meeting, Paris, France, 28-29 September 2009.
[37] ILO. 2004a. *Conclusions of the Tripartite Meeting on Youth Employment: The Way Forward.* Geneva: ILO.

overall national employment strategy, particularly youth employment. This can provide a useful buy-in from the two direct actors in industry.[38]

Still on the issue of employability, the high tendency on the part of unemployed urban youth to seek conciliatory employment in the urban informal economy points to the critical need for public policy to strengthen the vocational and technical training content of school curricula so that the productive capacity of such youth is strengthened in job search. Such curricula might also include practical experience, such as work-study or a period of internship over the course of formal schooling. Such approach might make the transition to paid employment much easier.

However, the challenge includes enhancing the employability of the youth in the post-crisis period, which will make for the utmost use of their underutilised or unused talents by giving them a sense of worth and contribution to the socioeconomic development of their societies. In other words, to ensure that young people have access to quality employment, consideration needs also to be given to skills acquisition, most essentially as part of the educational policy and/or school curricula.

References

Calves, A-E., and B. Schoumaker. 2004. "Deteriorating Economic Context and Changing Patterns of Youth Employment in Urban Burkina Faso: 1980-2000," *World Development* 32, No. 6.

Godfrey, M. 2003. "Youth Employment Policy in Developing and Transition Countries—Prevention as well as Cure," Social Protection Discussion Paper Series No. 0320, Social Protection Unit, Washington: The World Bank.

International Labour Organization (ILO). 1986. *Youth. Report V of the 72nd Session of the International Labour Conference, June 1986.* Geneva: ILO.

—. 1999. *Decent Work.* Geneva: ILO

—. 2004a. *Conclusions of the Tripartite Meeting on Youth Employment: The Way Forward.* Geneva: ILO.

—. 2004b. *Improving Prospects for Young Women and Men in the World of Work. A Guide to Youth Employment.* Geneva: ILO.

---

[38] ILO. 1986. *Youth. Report V of the 72nd Session of the International Labour Conference, June 1986*, 136-7. Trade unions and employers' associations are normally active partners in the conception and formulation of the Decent Work Country Programmes. See also O'Higgins, N. 2001. "Youth Unemployment and Employment Policy: A Global Perspective," Munich Personal RePEc Archive, MPRA Paper No. 23698.

—. 2006. *Employment Strategies for Decent Work Country Programmes: Concepts, Approaches and Tools for Implementation of the Global Employment Agenda*. Geneva: ILO.

—. 2010. *Global Employment Trends for Youth 2010*. Geneva: ILO.

—. 2011. *Global Employment Trends 2011. The Challenge of a Jobs Recovery*. Geneva: ILO.

Mlatsheni, C., and S. Rospabé. 2002. "Why is Youth Unemployment so High and unequally Spread in South Africa?" Development Policy Research Unit Working Paper No. 02/65, University of Cape Town.

O' Higgins, N. 2001. "Youth Unemployment and Employment Policy: A Global Perspective," Munich Personal RePEc Archive, MPRA Paper No. 23698.

OECD. "Tackling the job crisis: The Labour Market and Social Policy Response," Labour and Employment Ministerial Meeting, Paris, France, 28-29 September 2009.

United Nations General Assembly. 2005. *Global Analysis and Evaluation of National Action Plans on Youth Employment*. Report of the Secretary General Sixtieth Session. United Nations.

Weller, J. 2007. "Youth Employment: Characteristics, Tensions and Challenges," *CEPAL Review* 92.

THE CHALLENGE OF YOUTH EMPLOYMENT IN THE PERSPECTIVE OF SCHOOL-TO-WORK TRANSITION

MICHELE TIRABOSCHI

1. Rethinking the Employment of Young People in the Global Market

In a comparative perspective, access to the labour market on the part of young people is a complex issue, and for some time now it has attracted the interest of labour market specialists.[1] In an awareness of this complexity, that is reflected in the relative lack of convincing proposals, even of an experimental nature, on the part of the academic community, and labour law scholars in particular, the analysis put forward in the present paper focuses on certain aspects of youth employment that are only apparently contradictory, not to say paradoxical.[2] These aspects are still in need of in-depth examination, at least in an international context and in the global workplace perspective, reflecting not only the various levels of economic and social development,[3] but also the stage of

---

[1] See, recently, ILO. 2010b. *Global Employment Trends for Youth 2010*. Geneva: ILO; OECD. 2010. *Economic Survey of China: a Labour Market in Transition*. Paris: OECD. Among the other authors, Bell, D. N. F., and D. G. Blanchflower. 2010. "Youth Unemployment: Déjà Vu?" IZA Discussion Paper No. 4705. Bonn: IZA.

[2] Or even "deeply ironic", as argued by the International Labour Organization. 2005a. "Youth Employment: From a National Challenge to a Global Development Goal," Background Paper contributed by the ILO to the G8 Labour and Employment Ministers' Conference, London, United Kingdom, 10-11 March 2005.

[3] Since the Industrial Revolution. Lansky, M. 1997 "Child Labour: How the Challenge is Being met," *International Labour Review* 136, No. 2. Malmberg-Heimonen, I., and I. Jukunen. 2006. "Out of Unemployment? A Comparative Analysis of the Risk and Opportunities Longer-term Unemployed Immigrant

development of labour law and industrial relations in the various countries considered in this study. Economists themselves show an increasing interest in youth employment, and in labour market dynamics more generally, as confirmed by the 2010 Nobel prize, that has been awarded to three economists who investigated labour market frictions, namely the imperfect matching between labour demand and supply.[4]

The most advanced economies are characterised, in general, by a progressive raising of the age at which young people enter the labour market, giving rise to significant social and economic problems in a context of overall ageing of the population. The high level of academic attainment and well-being is in some cases accompanied by a significant level of intellectual unemployment, together with difficulties on the part of enterprises in recruiting employees with the right skills for positions that tend to be rejected by young people among the local population. The same goes for the management of small or micro enterprises and for the numerous trades taken up by immigrant workers who are willing to learn and hand down trades that are essential for the national economy and that may now be seen as a kind of "endangered species". On the other hand, the economies and societies of the developing countries are characterised by the opposite trend, that may appear to be contradictory or paradoxical, bringing to mind the early stages of the Industrial Revolution and the emergence of modern labour law, marked by the large-scale and often

---

Youth Face when Entering the labour Market," *Journal of Youth Studies* 9, No. 5: 575-592.

[4] Diamond, P. A., Massachusetts Institute of Technology, Cambridge, MA, USA, Dale T. Mortensen, Northwestern University, Evanston, IL, USA, Aarhus University, Denmark, and Christopher A. Pissarides, London School of Economics and Political Science, UK. 2011. *The Prize in Economic Sciences 2010 - Press Release.* http://nobelprize.org/nobel_prizes/economics/laureates/2010/press.html. Their theory on markets with search frictions, shows how "unemployment, job vacancies, and wages are affected by regulation and economic policy. This may refer to benefit levels in unemployment insurance or rules in regard to hiring and firing. In fact, on many markets, buyers and sellers do not always make contact with one another immediately. This concerns, for example, employers who are looking for employees and workers who are trying to find jobs. Since the search process requires time and resources, it creates frictions in the market. On such search markets, demands of some buyers will not be met, while some sellers cannot sell as much as they would. Simultaneously, there are both job vacancies and unemployment on the labour market. One conclusion is that more generous unemployment benefits give rise to higher unemployment and longer search times". The theory has been applied to many other areas in addition to the labour market.

brutal exploitation of the young workforce and by child labour.[5] Extremely high levels of unemployment and underemployment lead to large-scale migrations towards the most developed regions,[6] that are characterised by a declining workforce, low birth rates, and an ageing population, giving rise to the risk of impoverishing the human capital in the country of origin.[7]

The question of youth employment has therefore become an extremely urgent matter which should be a priority on the agenda of political decision-makers and trade union leaders in all the regions of the world, including the most economically advanced ones. This holds especially true if one considers the financial downturn that affected the global economies during 2008/2009, with an impact particularly on younger people. In this connection, significant developments have been recorded in the countries of the Organisation for Economic Cooperation and Development (OECD). In these countries, although the younger age groups are less numerous and more highly educated than previous generations, there is increasing anxiety about their employment prospects, reflecting the alarming labour market statistics concerning young people in various countries, though these indicators are not necessarily the most appropriate[8] to explain unemployment (Fig. A) and in particular long-term unemployment, among young people (Fig. B). In addition, the issue of segmented labour markets or precarious employment, in the sense of work of a temporary nature and of low quality that is available to young people,[9] is of central importance

---

[5] The phenomenon of child labour exists nonetheless within developed countries as well, although in a lesser extent.

[6] United Nations. 2007. *World Youth Report 2007*. New York: Department of Economic and Social Affairs, United Nations.

[7] Docquier, F. 2006. "Brain Drain and Inequality Across Nation," in IZA Discussion Paper No. 2440. Bonn: IZA.

[8] See, for instance, Marchand, O. 1999. "Youth Unemployment in OECD Countries: How Can the Disparities Be Explained?" in *OECD Preparing Youth for the 21st Century—The Transition from Education to the labour Market* (Paris: OECD Publishing), 89-100, who argues that "the unemployment rate becomes less and less appropriate to describe their situation as the length of time they spent in school increases and the average age at which they start working increases". In similar vein see Rees, A. 1996. "An Essay on Youth Joblessness," *Journal of Economic Literature* 24, No. 2:613-28, who suggests using the parameter of joblessness instead of unemployment—undoubtedly more reliable, though not so easy to use in comparative terms—as the main indicator of youth employment problems.

[9] Booth, A. L., M. Francesconi, and J. Frank. 2002. "Temporary Jobs: Stepping Stones Or Dead Ends?" *The Economic Journal* 112, No. 480. Kalleberg, A. L.

in the domestic debate in many countries, with an impact on election campaigns both at national and local level.

2000. "Nonstandard Employment Relations: Part-Time, Temporary and Contract Work," *Annual Review of Sociology* 26.

Michele Tiraboschi

Fig. A. Youth Unemployment (age range 15- 24 years) in a Number of OECD Countries

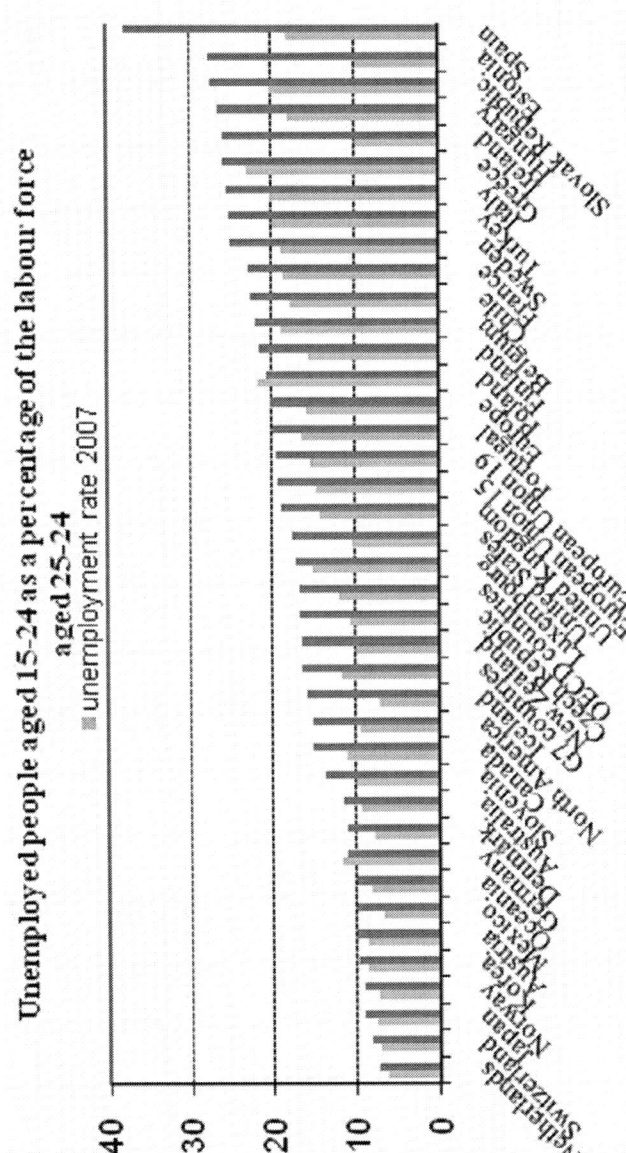

Source: OECD database on Labour Force Statistics.

The Challenge of Youth Employment in the Perspective
of School-to-work Transition

Fig. B. Incidence of Long-term Unemployment among Youth (1995 - 2009)

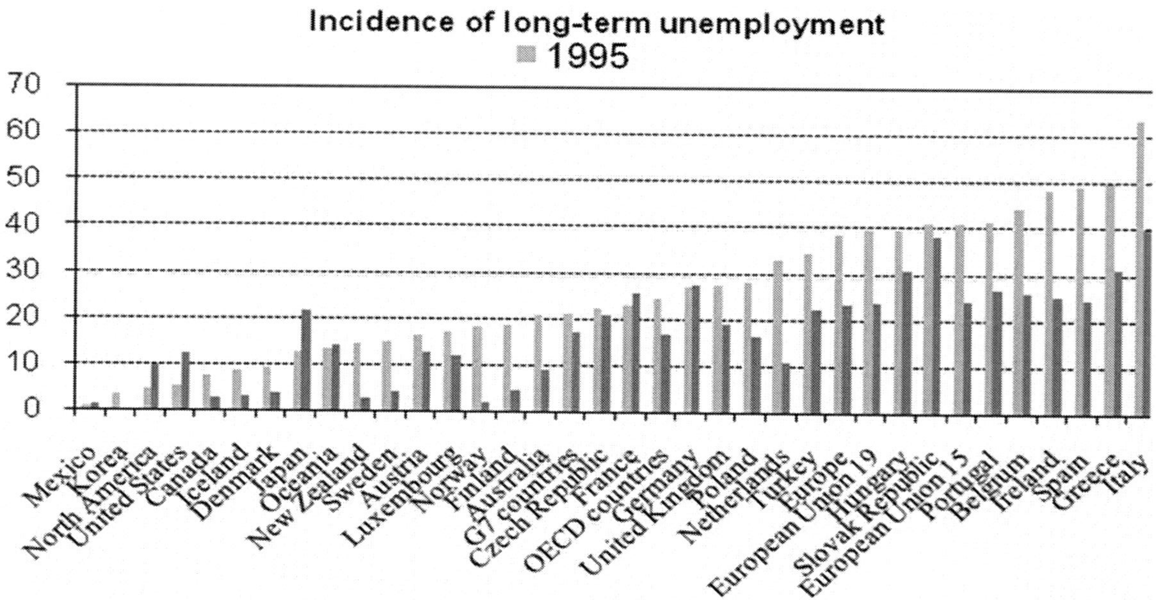

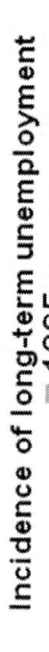

Source: OECD database on Labour Force Statistics.

The problem of youth unemployment takes a totally different form in other regions of the world, particularly Sub-Saharan Africa and South Asia, where the extremely high rates of poverty and low income levels are accompanied by a strong presence of young people, who account for 80% of the young people of the world (Fig. C).

The Challenge of Youth Employment in the Perspective
of School-to-work Transition

Fig. C. Half of the Global Youth Population Live in Low-income Countries

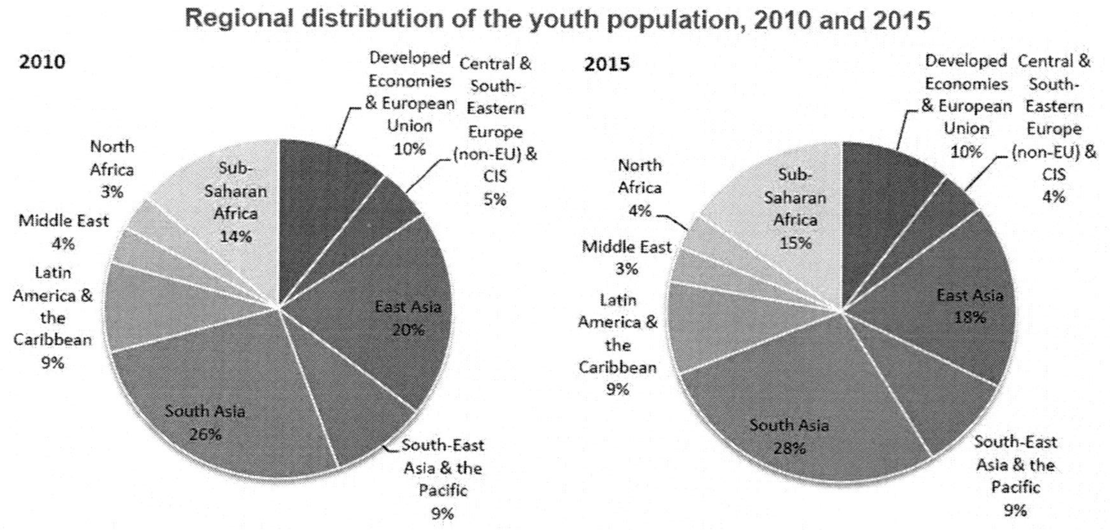

Regional distribution of the youth population, 2010 and 2015

2010

Developed Central &
Economies South-
& European Eastern
Union Europe
10% (non-EU) &
CIS
5%

East Asia
20%

South-East
Asia & the
Pacific
9%

Sub-
Saharan
Africa
14%

South Asia
26%

North
Africa
3%

Middle East
4%

Latin
America &
the
Caribbean
9%

2015

Developed Central &
Economies South-
& European Eastern
Union Europe
10% (non-EU) &
CIS
4%

East Asia
18%

South-East
Asia & the
Pacific
9%

Sub-
Saharan
Africa
15%

South Asia
28%

North
Africa
4%

Middle East
3%

Latin
America &
the
Caribbean
9%

Source: ILO—Regional Distribution of the Youth population, 2010 and 2015.

In the African countries, in particular, it is well known[1] that youth unemployment is closely linked with high levels of poverty, reflecting the apparently contradictory situation in which a low level of demand co-exists with the highest participation rates for young people in the world, with high rates of employment in the informal sector, and all the negative consequences that ensue in terms of unemployment, underemployment, lack of education, training and vocational skills.

The global dimension of the problem, arising from the irreversible interdependence between the economies of the world, is reflected in the migration of young people leaving their country of origin to seek better training and employment opportunities abroad (at times unsuccessfully) in what has been called the "battle for brains"[2]—which led analysts to examine the possibility of taking countermeasures on a transnational scale.

Significant steps have been taken in this direction by the International Labour Organization, the United Nations and the World Bank[3]: starting from a comparative study, they have gradually adopted measures to coordinate employment policies designed for young people. These initiatives, such as the *Youth Employment Programme* of the International Labour Organization, adopt measures of the type implemented in connection with the Employment Strategy of the European Union since the end of the 1990s, albeit with limited success. In particular, the approach is that of the Open Method of Coordination (OMC), consisting of the definition of common guidelines by a supranational body for the Member States, comparing the measures adopted by the various countries, providing for a periodic assessment aimed at identifying best practices, and where possible, their extension to other national settings (benchmarking).

However, the EU experience, together with the pressures exerted by the global economy on national systems, highlights the limits of an approach in which regulatory powers remain in the hands of the nation states, albeit with a certain amount of transnational coordination (that may be more or less strict), without calling this traditional function into question. The attention of institutions and scholars dealing with the legislative implications of economic internationalisation is now shifting

---

[1] International Labour Organization. 2006a. *Regional Labour Market Trends for Youth: Africa,* ILO Youth Employment Programme, Geneva: ILO.
[2] Blanpain, R. 2008. "The End of Labour Law?" in *The Global Labour Market. From Globalization to Flexicurity,* eds. Blanpain, R., and M. Tiraboschi, (The Hague: Kluwer Law International).
[3] Youth Employment Network, *Millennium Development, Global Employment Trends for Youth.*

from the external sphere of state sovereignty (the soft-law influence of transnational institutions) towards the internal sphere, concerning the national institutions, the actors in the industrial relations system, and the nature of regulatory provisions, based on the idea that in the context of globalisation, effective labour market policies require profound changes in terms of legal practice and fundamental legal principles.

2. Limits of the "Traditional" Approach to Labour Law and Shortcomings in Relevant Legislation. Investing in Human Capital and Increasing Productivity as an Alternative Perspective

When labour law and industrial relations scholars lose sight of the fundamental issues of labour productivity, investment in human resources, and the links between education, training and the labour market, then their main focus is on a formal, conceptual system that is in many cases largely self-referential. As a result, they can make only a limited contribution to labour market institutions and the work of the social partners (both national and international) in their efforts to implement an organic action plan, taking account of the insights provided by the economic disciplines relating to the improvement of employment conditions for young people.[4] Accordingly, it is possible to point to a plethora of international measures—such as the prohibition of child labour,[5] measures relating to decent and productive work,[6] and the definition of employment contracts as self-employment or salaried employment[7] —that are of great symbolic

---

[4] International Labour Organization. 2010b. *Global Employment Trends for Youth 2010*. Geneva: ILO.

[5] International Labour Organization. 1999. *Convention C182, Concerning the Prohibition and Immediate Action for the Elimination of the Worst Forms of Child Labour*. Geneva: ILO.

[6] See the several references to the concept of a "full, productive and freely chosen employment" included in the International Labour Organization Recommendations R122, *Employment Policy*, 1964; R169, *Employment Policy (Supplementary Provisions)*, 1984; R195, *Human Resources Development*, 2004.

[7] See the Green Paper released by the European Commission. 2006. *Modernising Labour Law to Meet the Challenges of the 21st Century, COM(2006) 708 final*. Brussels: European Commission, which puts into question the persistent relevance of such a distinction. For an outline of the debate developed throughout Europe on the issue see European Commission. 2007. *Outcome of the Public Consultation on the Commission's Green Paper "Modernising Labour Law to Meet the Challenges of the 21st Century", SEC(2007) 1373*. Brussels: European Commission.

value but largely ineffective in terms of their impact on the real economy, both in the advanced countries (that are characterised by high levels of employment protection) and in the developing countries (due to the brute force of circumstances and objective economic conditions).

An important point that could be made in this connection, with all the necessary provisos, is that employment safeguards and standards that are imposed in a mechanical way on developing countries may act as a brake on their economic growth to the benefit of the more developed regions of the globe which, in the course of their development over the centuries, have benefited from the implementation of modern labour law. As a result, though it may appear to be a paradox, bearing in mind the historical role played by labour law, it could be argued that standards of international competition that have been set are disadvantageous for enterprises in the less developed economies.

A paradigmatic case in this connection is that of the countries of East Asia, that have achieved record growth in recent years with the rapid expansion of the Chinese economy. Here, as underlined by the report of the International Labour Organization on *Global Employment Trends 2010,* the key cause of concern for the future is the development of human capital and labour productivity and the creation of employment with a high level of vocational skills. Further, it is crucial to prepare young people for the future through investment in their human capital, as low-cost labour will not continue to be the region's comparable advantage.[8]

The arguments put forward so far should contain all the elements to provide a general interpretation of the problem of youth employment, as indicated in the introduction. The analysis is based on a particular interpretation of the concept of "decent work", that of "employment opportunity", in the sense of employability, linked to the development of human capital.[9]

Of the four dimensions of the concept, as identified by the International Labour Organization (security, opportunities, basic workers' rights and representation),[10] this one appears to be the most appropriate in the context

---

See International Labour Organization. 2010a. *Global Employment Trends January 2010.* Geneva: ILO.

[9] See ILO. 2005c. *Resolution Concerning Youth Employment.* Geneva: ILO. The concept of employability "encompasses the skills, knowledge and competencies that enhance a worker's ability to secure and retain a job, progress at work and cope with change, secure another job if he/she so wishes or has been laid off, and enter more easily into the labour market at different periods of the life cycle."

[10] ILO. 2006b. *World Employment Report 2004/2005.* Geneva: ILO, chap. 2: "What society can achieve is to ensure that the worker has a smoother transition

of the global economy, in that it is the concept that is relevant to all the regions of the world, regardless of their specific characteristics. Whereas the imbalances between post-industrial and developing countries mean that it is unlikely that industrial relations can be coordinated on a global scale for instance in terms of trade union representation and fundamental rights (such as working hours and pay), for which it seems difficult to construct a shared platform, also in consideration of the extremely divergent levels of economic and social development, the problem of employment opportunities is a matter of common interest, as we have argued, for all the regions of the world. This includes the regions where there is a lack of skilled labour, engaged in the "battle for brains", and those with a surplus of young people which, in a global perspective, can transform the dramatic problem of youth unemployment into an unexpected resource for growth and development.

The argument put forward here is in keeping with the widely supported idea that the aim of "decent work for all" can only be achieved by raising productivity.[11] Studies on the relationship between productivity and the quality of employment, in line with the various stages of development that countries around the globe go through, have highlighted the fact that to achieve significant results in terms of long-term growth it may be necessary in the early stages of development to give lower priority to certain factors concerning quality employment.

In some cases, improvements in productivity may have detrimental effects on employment quality, especially in relation to fundamental rights. As shown in recent years by the Chinese experience,[12] the initial phases of development are characterised by factors that provide a competitive advantage, even when this means low labour costs and a lack of attention to labour protection. In these early stages, employment safeguards consist above all of the mental and physical qualities required to deal with the "turbulence" encountered on the way towards economic stability.

---

and protection in the form of security, opportunities, basic workers' rights and representation, the four main dimensions of decent work".

[11] ILO. 2006b. *World Employment Report 2004/2005*. Geneva: ILO. Preface: "Productive employment is the economic foundation of decent work".

[12] OECD. 2010b. *Economic Survey of China: a Labour Market in Transition*. Paris: OECD. Directorate-General for Employment, Social Affairs and Equal Opportunities, European Commission, The Institute of Population and Labor Economics, and Chinese Academy of Social Sciences. 2010. *New Skills for New Jobs: China and the EU. Shared Labour Market Experiences to Inform the Harmonious and Sustainable Society of the Future*. Brussels: European Commission.

Employment opportunities become therefore a priority, rather than a feature of decent work.

Due consideration should be given to the argument that the imposition of strict employment protection measures in the early stages of development of the economy may result in the competitive advantage shifting to the more developed economies, that in an earlier phase went through their own initial stages of development with low levels of employment safeguards, comparable to developing countries today. According to this argument the introduction of a high level of employment safeguards would be detrimental to the interests of workers in developing countries in the global economy.

With a view to considering this argument more fully, and to transfer it to a global economic context beyond national boundaries, reference may be made to the classic study *Industrial Democracy* by Sidney and Beatrice Webb (1897), in particular as regards their discussion of standard regulations for labour, with the preferences of individual workers and employers being subject to a "common rule" in the interest of both parties and the nation as a whole. The Webbs advocated the introduction of such regulation not *through* legislative intervention, but as an *alternative* to state intervention in employment relations, by means of a self-regulation of the market, based on collective bargaining as the essential method. In *Industrial Democracy* there are continual references to the regulatory role of collective bargaining, which is seen not as a mere economic tool for determining labour conditions, but as a social instrument aimed at furthering the "interests of Industrial Peace",[13] and promoting "the selection of the most efficient factors of production, whether capital, brains, or labour"; preventing the deterioration of the "capital stock of the nation"; stimulating "the invention and adoption of new processes of manufactures", while eliminating from the market "incompetent or old-fashioned employers", for the purposes of the "nation's productive efficiency" or "industrial efficiency". Just as emblematic are the pages of *Industrial Democracy* dedicated to "industrial parasitism", showing their strong faith in market self-regulation. On the one hand, they argue, the more extensive and effective the mechanism of the "common rule", the greater the proportion of the population protected from the devastating effects of speculation on the labour of others, whereas on the other hand, in cases in which minimum conditions for the use of the labour force are

---

[13] For this and the following quotations, see Webb, B., and S. Webb. 1897 and 1926. *Industrial Democracy*. London: Longmans, respectively p. 218, 703, 751, 724, 728, 732, 766 - 767, 759, 703.

stable and standardised, qualitative standards will tend to improve, both
for labour and the system of production as a whole, thus eliminating from
the market parasitic competitors who survive solely by speculating on the
cost of labour.

In considering the fundamental role of labour law in regulating the
competition between enterprises, it is evident that a mechanical and
historically decontextualised application of employment protection measures
would have a negative impact on developing economies and ultimately
also on the workers themselves, who would be expelled from the labour
market.[14]

The creation of employment opportunities, linked to the improvement
of human capital, may serve as the key objective for the governance of the
intermediate phases of economic development. It may be said that a close
match between an increase in productivity and an increase in decent
employment can be achieved only in the medium to long term. In the
intermediate phases, an increase in productivity, with a shift away from
labour-intensive systems of production, can result in a loss of jobs
(particularly in low-skilled occupations). Investment in human capital in
these circumstances is needed to cope with a fall in employment levels
that accompanies the increase in productivity, enabling workers to acquire
the skills needed for occupational mobility, both internal and external.

3. Global Perspectives for Future Actions

In the context of the global labour market, an interdisciplinary
perspective can turn the apparently insoluble problems of each country
into a great opportunity for development and growth in what is by no
means a zero-sum game, provided that an integrated and cross-disciplinary
approach is adopted.

As rightly argued by the International Labour Organization:

> the outflow of young migrants to the developed world presents a number of
> benefits for both receiving and sending countries. As regards the former,
> there is evidence that migrants have only slight negative effects on the
> wages of nationals, and tend to pay more taxes than they receive in tax-
> supported services. Conversely, little evidence exists that migration leads
> to a displacement of nationals in employment. Given the current
> demographic change, young immigrants are also likely to become part of

---

[14] A different argument could be developed for those multinational corporations
which settle in underdeveloped areas only to start activities intended for other
markets.

the solution to the employment and welfare problems raised by aging in developed economies. Young migrants can also be a source of funding for development in their countries of origin. Their remittances help cover family expenses and investment for job creation. When they return, they bring back human, financial and social capital, thereby contributing to the development of their home countries.[15]

The present paper, summarising the initial findings of a wider research project currently under way—resulting in a number of conferences and carried out by the International School of Higher Education in Labour and Industrial Relations set up by ADAPT (www.adapt.it)—promotes a global approach to analyse this phenomenon as the possible basis for rethinking institutional strategies for the labour market, and in particular the role of the actors in the industrial relations system. This paper will argue that the main limits to the "traditional" approach to labour law are the result of a "static" conception of labour markets on a global scale, whereas forward planning, in the sense of a complete rethinking of the transition and links between education and the world of work on the part of institutions and the social partners, could provide a dynamic contribution to achieve a better and more sustainable balance on a global scale.

For this purpose, it may be useful to adopt a school-to-work transition perspective, a concept that has until now been relegated to a secondary role by industrial relations and labour law scholars. This paper considers the reasons for the lack of attention that an approach of this kind has received. First of all, employment policies adopted so far have had a merely local and/or national application, whereas bridging the gap between the wealthiest and the poorest regions of the world requires a global approach, by strengthening the link between education and training, on the one hand, and the labour market, on the other. The school-to-work transition perspective, applied to industrial relations and labour law, seems particularly well suited to develop more effective policies and policy evaluation tools. This approach makes it possible to actively involve the various actors dealing with productivity issues, investment in human capital, youth unemployment and underemployment.

When applying the school-to-work transition concept to the legal and industrial relations methods in a comparative framework, it becomes clear that human capital improvement, work productivity and effective measures

---

[15] International Labour Organization. 2005a. "Youth Employment: From a National Challenge to a Global Development Goal," Background Paper contributed by the ILO to the G8 Labour and Employment Ministers' Conference, London, United Kingdom, 10-11 March 2005.

to deal with the problem of youth employment can be achieved only if policies are designed to cover the period before entering the labour market, i.e. the education and training phase. In general, labour market policies focus mainly on a given labour force, preventing the solution of the structural problems of youth employment, and particularly their impact on the gap between wealthy and poor regions. On the other hand, a method enabling us to tackle such problems at an earlier stage, dealing with how to design education and training to respond to the demands of the global labour market, might contribute to solutions for the governance of international flows of labour.

This strand of research will only develop its full potential if it succeeds in adopting a holistic vision linking the worlds of education and employment, moving beyond a traditional conception of labour law provisions and industrial relations, and education and training systems, that have until now been considered as two separate spheres, to be studied by specialised research groups who are separate from and not in communication with each other. A modern vision of the relations between education and training on the one hand, and socio-economic development on the other, leads to the development of policies and programmes that take account not only of the demand for labour, but also of the quality of the labour supply. It is only by means of integration between education and training, and the world of work, that it will be possible to deal in global and pragmatic terms with the problem of youth employment and promote a balanced development of human capital in all the regions of the world. It is undoubtedly the case that the availability of adequate education and vocational training is a key factor in the allocation of resources on the part of investors, and as a result of the quality of employment. Investors do not set up businesses of "good quality" (i.e. not aiming merely to exploit low-cost labour) in regions where there is a lack of personnel with the skills required to run the business. This means that the response to the problem of youth employment must be based on the construction of a system of education and vocational training. These are the real investment assets that generate income, productivity, development, social mobility and, last but not least, decent work.

In the new economy, the main source of the wealth of nations is their endowment with human capital. Indeed, human capital is the key factor for growth and development, and the engine for change. Compared to the European countries and the other western nations with a rapidly ageing population, developing countries and some of the poorest economies in the world are endowed with vast wealth. Therefore, in order to avoid wasting this precious resource, it is necessary to go well beyond a legal regulation that may or may not produce results, undertaking a reform of education and training systems on a global scale that should be entrusted to the social partners. This appears to be possible only if we are prepared to rethink the role and functions of industrial relations, in order to make a contribution to the true modernisation of education and training, closing the traditional gap between school and work.

In this connection, the report by the International Labour Organization on *Global Employment Trends for Youth,* published in 2010[16] provides supporting evidence for this argument. In this report, the ILO underlined that the indicators for youth employment currently available are sufficient to provide an analytical framework on the condition of young people on the labour market in the various regions of the world. In the words of the Report:

> for further expansion of the youth employment knowledge base, the need is not one of developing new indicators, but rather finding a way to make use of the indicators that already exist (labour force participation rates, employment ratios, unemployment rates, employment by status and sector, long-term unemployment, underemployment, hours of work and poverty).

4. A Different Legal, Institutional and Industrial Relations Perspective: Forward Planning and the School-to-work Transition Based on a Modern Conception of Education and Vocational Training

Recent studies have shown that in the debate on deregulation, following on from major developments in the English-speaking countries and from the authoritative recommendations over the past decade of the OECD,[17] there is a tendency to confuse employment policies and labour

---

[16] ILO. 2005b. *Resolution on Decent Work for Youth in Africa and the ILO Response, Document GB289/5.* Geneva: ILO.

[17] Relying upon the *Job Studies* started since 1992—which tended to show a relationship between high levels of unemployment and high standards of work protection—the OECD has set up an action programme (*Job Strategy*), addressed to governments and social partners, founded onto ten recommendations. Among those, particular reference should be made to the labour market deregulation for purposes of job creation. Along with the yearly *Employment Outlooks,* see OECD. 1994. *The OECD Job Study: Evidence and Explanations,* Paris: OECD. See also OECD. 1997. *Implementing the OECD Jobs Strategy: Lessons from Member Countries.* Paris: OECD, and OECD. 1999b. *Implementing the OECD Job Strategy: Assessing Performance and Policy.* Paris: OECD.

policies, that are taken to be one and the same thing.[18] Once the two concepts are confused, there appears to be an inevitable connection between high levels of unemployment (especially youth unemployment) and labour protection. In the same vein, simplistic claims are made that the opposite is also the case: lower unemployment levels in the United States, the United Kingdom, Australia and New Zealand are usually explained in the light of neo-liberal ideas.

The expressions "employment policies" and "labour policies" actually refer to two profoundly different concepts. Employment policies are intended to increase employment levels in a given socio-economic system, and to achieve this objective, they operate at another level in relation to the regulation of labour, by means of measures such as tax and contributions relief, credit and capital markets, investment in infrastructure, the reform of public spending and, of particular interest for the present study, investment in human capital and the modernisation of education and training systems.

Labour policies, on the other hand, are intended to promote jobs for certain groups (the long-term unemployed, those not in employment, workers lacking the skills required by the market, immigrants, women, young people) by means of employment services, schemes providing for alternation between training and work, the elimination of barriers to access to and exit from the labour market, as well as the various kinds of job creation mentioned above. As a result, they only have a marginal impact on total employment levels, while producing more significant effects on the duration and above all on the distribution of unemployment among different groups.

The most recent empirical studies have provided econometric evidence showing the lack of a clear correlation, in terms of cause and effect, between levels of employment protection and levels of unemployment. The OECD,[19] which over the past decade has advocated a neo-liberal approach to labour market policy, has come to the same conclusion that many researchers have also reached[20] in that the regulation of employment

---

[18] Biagi, M., and M. Tiraboschi. 2000. "The Role of Labour Law in Job Creation Policies: an Italian Perspective," in *Job Creation and Labour Law,* ed. Biagi, M., (The Hague: Kluwer Law International), 179-193.
[19] OECD. 1999b. *Implementing the OECD Job Strategy: Assessing Performance and Policy.* Paris: OECD, especially chapter 2: *Employment Protection and Labour Market Performance.*
[20] Regini, M., and G. Esping-Andersen. "The Effects of Labour Market De-regulation on Unemployment. A Critical Review of the Different Research

relations and the introduction of greater flexibility in the regulation of the workforce can, in the best possible case, contribute to creating the preconditions required to make employment policy effective.

The outcome of the current debate on deregulation is that it would be pointless to sacrifice labour law on the altar of employment. It would prove ineffective to assign to labour policy in the strict sense an ambitious role that it is well beyond its scope, especially with reference to the creation of new employment of good quality.

Rather, the route to be taken, also in relation to future research, is that of the modernisation and rethinking of labour law legislation, adopting a less formalistic approach, and assigning a larger role to industrial relations in order to provide a structural solution to the problem of youth unemployment.[21]

It would appear to be far more important to undertake the reform of education and vocational training, and to improve the functioning of the bodies intended to promote the employability of young people, by means of networks, whether formal or informal, between international and local institutions, educational and training bodies, employers' associations, undertakings or trade unions. In this connection particular attention needs to be paid to the alternation of periods of school and work, and especially apprenticeship schemes,[22] as well as institutional mechanisms aimed at promoting the placement of students and the transition from education to employment. As shown in the German and Japanese experience, "labor

---

Approaches and of Empirical Evidence," paper presented to the European Commission, Brussels, Belgium, 1998.

[21] Such an argument appears to be in line with the recent statements developed by the International Labour Organization, which draw a distinction between "good" and "bad" labour market institutions for the purposes of social development: Berg, J., and D. Kucera. 2007. *In Defence of Labour Market Institutions: Cultivating Justice in the Developing World.* Geneva: ILO.

[22] In the sense of programmes combining vocational education with enterprise-based training. See Axmann, M. 2004. "Facilitating Labour Market Entry for Youth through Enterprise-Based Schemes in Vocational Education and Training and Skills Development," SEED Working Paper No. 48. Geneva: ILO, par. XII. At a European level, the importance of apprenticeship for youth employability has been highlighted also by the European Parliament; see European Parliament. 2010. "Report on Promoting Youth Access to the Labour Market, Strengthening Trainee, Internship and Apprenticeship Status (2009/2221(INI))" Committee on Employment and Social Affairs.

market programmes come and go. Institutions develop, adapt and, for the most, endure".[23]

Once again, this strengthens the argument about human capital, which has so far been assigned a marginal role both by employment protection measures and by incentive measures.[24] The failure of job creation schemes and of employment protection measures based on non-negotiable conditions to produce the desired results provides reason to conceive the global governance of youth employment in a perspective of productivity and workforce employability.

It is therefore of considerable importance to identify regulatory techniques that are innovative both in terms of method and content. From the point of view of method, there is a need to recognise the limits of traditional techniques imposing norms from outside the employment relationship, that are not necessarily taking account of all the interests of the parties, nor of keeping up to date with changes taking place, and as a result they may not be capable of generating truly effective solutions. The need for "tailor-made regulations" should also be taken into account, especially for those categories of workers who "fall outside the pattern of the traditional employment relationship in a strict sense".[25] In this connection, more fluid and negotiated regulatory processes based on the

---

[23] See Ryan, P. 2001. "The School-to-work Transition: a Cross-national Perspective," *Journal of Economic* Literature 39, No. 1: 34-92. With regard to apprenticeships in Germany and school and university placement services in Japan, Ryan rightly notes that "those institutions have allowed Germany and Japan to avoid mass labour market programs and to concentrate instead on institutional development improving general education, vocational preparation and job placement, and making it easier for low achievers to participate. Although Japanese and German transition institutions have come under strain, they have adapted well and they continue—thus far at least—to function largely intact". For updated sources about Japan, see the *Japan Institute for Labour Policy and Training* http://www.jil.go.jp/english/reports/jilpt_01.html. Among the orthers, see Hisashi, T-O., K. Koichiro, I. Koh, H. Park, K. Reiko, S. Tomoki. 2010. "The Labour Issue of Youth: Looking Back over 20 Years," *The Japanese Journal of Labour Studies,* No. 602. For Germany, see Bundesministerium für Wirtschaft und Technologie. 2010. *Nationaler Pakt für Ausbildung und Fachkräftenachwuchs in Deutschland 2010—2014*. Berlin: BMWi.
[24] United Nations. 2005b. *The Economic report on Africa 2005—Meeting the Challenge of Unemployment and Poverty*. Addis Ababa: Economic Commission for Africa.
[25] Weiss, M. "Realising Decent Work in Africa," Keynote Speech at the Opening Ceremony of the Fifth African Regional Congress of the IIRA in Cape Town, South Africa, 26 March 2008.

active participation of the labour market actors might well be better suited to achieve greater policy coordination, that is essential in dealing with the issue of youth employment, which is of vital importance for every state and region of the world, since no region is immune from external pressures.

However, in terms of content, there is a need to focus more closely on the objectives of the policies to adopt, focusing on the areas where incisive action is required to deal with the structural problems that prevent the qualitative and quantitative growth of youth employment. These elements, in line with the role assigned to productivity as the key to decent work, may be linked to two principles: employability and stability. The first means that the individual is capable of playing a role on the labour market thanks to adequate cultural, vocational and social skills, dealing in a confident manner with transitional phases as they occur. The objective of stability is linked to the concept of productivity and to the level of turnover in the workforce of an enterprise. If there is any truth in the claim set forth in the *World Employment Report 2004/05* of the ILO,[26] that "there is substantial evidence that stability of employment (tenure) is positively related to productivity gains", the stability of the relationship between the employer and the employee should be safeguarded not so much by limits on termination, but rather by placing an emphasis, at the hiring stage, on matching the skills of job applicants to job descriptions.

In this respect, a central role is played by the school-to-work transition, in particular in the economic and sociological analysis, where it serves as an essential tool for gaining a better understanding of the problems of labour market entrants.[27] This concept, that could be used systematically also in the study of labour law and industrial relations, is particularly important as it:

> draws together in a common arena a previously disparate set of issues in such areas as vocational education and training, youth unemployment, and wage structure. It does so by emphasising process attributes, as individuals flow from full-time schooling to full-time permanent employment, through various intermediate conditions, including vocational education and apprenticeship, fixed-term and part-time employment, and labour market programmes.[28]

---

[26] ILO. 2006b. *World Employment Report 2004/*2005. Geneva: ILO, 183.

[27] 2010b. *Global Employment Trends for Youth 2010*. Geneva: ILO, 36-43.

[28] See Ryan, P. 2001. "The School-to-work Transition: a Cross-national Perspective," *Journal of Economic* Literature 39, No. 1: 34-92.

The ILO has itself resorted to this concept in examining certain youth employment indicators: the length of the transition from education and training to employment, the age of those entering the labour market, occupational status, the relation between the level of educational attainment and the position taken up in the labour market, income levels, employment sector, and gender inequality. At this point there is a need to complete the process, closing the gap between education, training and the labour market. With regard to the problem of youth unemployment and the quality and productivity of labour, the concept of the school-to-work transition can foster innovation in terms of both method and content, establishing a clear connection not just in theoretical but also in practical and operational terms between education, training and the labour market.[29] In terms of content, this concept enables us to focus on shortcomings in the "accumulation" of human capital in the phases leading up to the entry into the labour market. The key issues here are asymmetrical information and the mismatch between the supply and demand for labour, resulting in unemployment, underemployment and low-quality employment. Investing in productivity is the key to employment of good quality and means rethinking regulatory instruments (such as employment contracts), and perhaps also the principles underlying training and the interpretation of rules, with a view to improving the match between the supply and demand for labour.

In terms of method, the concept of school-to-work transition requires a highly institutionalised regulatory approach, not based on conditions imposed by an external authority, but on the participation of all the stakeholders (the public authorities, the social partners, education and training institutions). Only a strong institutional structure, actively involving all these actors, can strengthen the links between the various phases of the transition. These links are essential conditions for the development of human capital, leading to increased productivity and decent employment. This is because, on the one hand, they are the actors who are best placed to interpret the employment needs in a given economic situation; and on the other hand, because they play an essential role in monitoring and safeguarding the workforce against irregular practices (to prevent training schemes from being used solely as a means to supply low-cost labour, or as a means to replace adult workers with young people prepared to work for low wages). This could lead to a new

---

[29] United Nations. 2005b. *The Economic report on Africa 2005—Meeting the Challenge of Unemployment and Poverty.* Addis Ababa: Economic Commission for Africa. Aring, M., and M. Axmann. 2004. "Why Developing Countries Need a School-to-Work System, Now More Than Ever," RTI International.

concept of education and training, no longer considered as a self-referential world of its own, but rather as a resource closely linked to the world of work.

In an industrial relations perspective, and with a view to developing the above mentioned system, all the actors involved are required to provide a more decisive contribution in the design and implementation of education and training programmes in line with the needs of the global labour market, setting up networks and alliances with institutions and bodies in other countries, envisaging forward planning with a view to problem solving. For this purpose, the social partners must take a part in dealing with the school-to-work transition, integrating the formal system of education and training as a unified system of equivalent standing (with the option of taking interchangeable programmes of education to training from the secondary level onwards)—with the labour market (Fig. D) rather than maintaining the traditional division[30] between education and work (Fig. E).

Fig. D. Human Capital and the Labour Market: Our Proposal

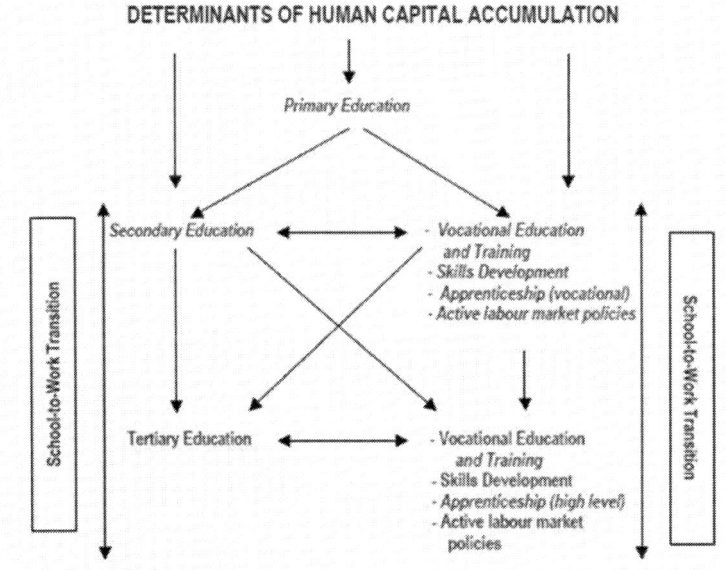

[30] See for example United Nations. 2005b. *The Economic report on Africa 2005—Meeting the Challenge of Unemployment and Poverty.* Addis Ababa: Economic Commission for Africa, 8.

Fig. E. Human Capital and the Labour Market: the Traditional Pathways

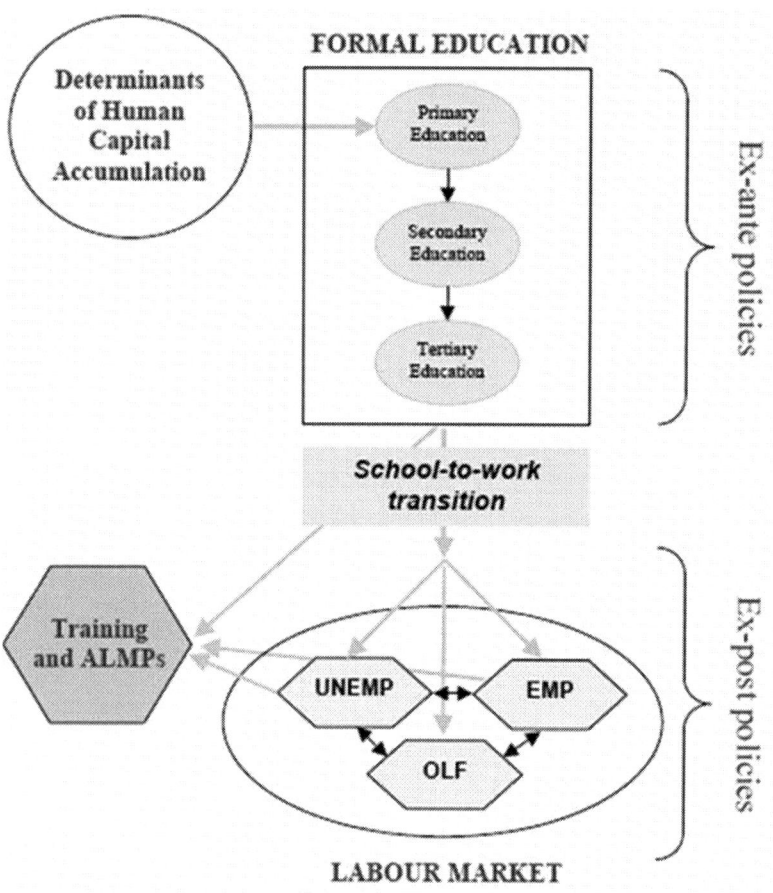

Source: United Nations—Economic Commission for Africa.

The importance of this pathway becomes evident only when taking account of the fact that many studies have concluded that the impact of interventions on future employment outcomes of disadvantaged young people diminishes with age.[31] In other words, as recently pointed out by

---

[31] See among others Martin, J., and D. Grubb. 2001. "What Works and for Whom: A Review of OECD Countries' Experiences with Active Labour Market Policies," IFAU Working Paper No. 14. Institute for Labour Market Policy Evaluation.

the World Bank in a major study on policies intended to support employment in Sub-Saharan Africa,[32] "addressing potential problems early has a greater return than when young people have left formal education". Also the OECD, in reviewing the evidence, has concluded that:

> the evidence from the evaluation literature suggests the biggest pay-off for disadvantaged youths comes from early and sustained interventions. Such interventions should begin before children enter the compulsory schooling system, and they should be followed by intensive efforts to boost their performance in primary and secondary schooling and reduce drop-out rates.[33]

It is not clear why, after recognising that "any policy advice on addressing youth employment problems should emphasise that prevention is more effective than curing",[34] legal scholars in general have not developed[35] a unitary approach to the relation between education and training and the labour market in a global perspective. It may perhaps be

---

Heckman, J. J., and L. Lochner. 2000. "Rethinking Education and Training Policy: Understanding the Sources of Skill Formation in a Modern Economy," in *Securing the Future: Investing in Children from Birth to Adulthood*, eds. Danziger, S., and J. Waldforgel, (New York: Russell Sage Foundation). Garces, E., D. Thomas, and J. Currie. 2000. "Longer-term Effects of Head Start," NBER Working Papers No. 8054. The National Bureau of Economic Research.

[32] See Rother, F. 2006. "Intervention to Support Young Workers in Sub-Saharan Africa," Regional Report for the Youth Employment Inventory. Washington: The World Bank, 3.

[33] See OECD. 2002. *Employment Outlook 2002. A Better Start for Youth,* Paris: OECD 32. See also the recent country-by-country and transnational programme of the OECD, Jobs for Youth. The European Commission is also addressing child care and early education, and intends to support specific measures to these policy areas, as declared in European Commission. 2011. "Tackling Early School Leaving: A Key Contribution to the Europe 2020 Agenda, COM(2011) 18," Communication From The Commission To The European Parliament, The Council, The European Economic And Social Committee And The Committee Of The Regions, Brussels: European Commission.

[34] See Rother, F. 2006. "Intervention to Support Young Workers in Sub-Saharan Africa," Regional Report for the Youth Employment Inventory. Washington: The World Bank, 3.

[35] With reference to youth employment in Sub-Saharan Africa see Rother, F. 2006. "Intervention to Support Young Workers in Sub-Saharan Africa," Regional Report for the Youth Employment Inventory. Washington: The World Bank, 3, that without going into detail refers to "practical grounds for limiting the inventory to post-formal-schooling interventions".

explained by the lack of interdisciplinary study bringing together, in a unified conceptual scheme, the various specific disciplinary competences. However, it is only by means of a reconsideration on the part of the institutions and the social partners of education and training pathways that a realistic integration with the world of work can be achieved in order to respond to the challenges of globalisation. An integrated system of education and vocational training, in a school-to-work perspective, as well as representing a step towards a solution to the problems of youth unemployment, could narrow the gap in education and training between developed and developing countries, bearing in mind that the expected duration of primary and secondary schooling is only 7.5 years in Africa compared with 12 years for Europe and the Americas.[36] Moreover,

> according to human capital theory, the education acquired by a young person will be remunerated in terms of earnings, with higher wages reflecting higher productivity resulting from more advanced levels of education. Education will also determine the ability to participate in the labour force, not just the level of wages.[37]

In addition, for developing countries and the African countries in particular, the crucial problem is to provide primary education for all. It seems to be unrealistic to maintain a formal traditional system for secondary and tertiary education when in a significant number of cases, the primary level is not completed.[38] In this connection, international experience provides a number of good practices that could be a suitable basis for experimental schemes in developing countries: *1)* a broadening of vocational programmes and qualifications (e.g. a broad construction trades programme rather than separate programmes in carpentry, painting and bricklaying); *2)* the creation of links between general and vocational education, and the combination of work-based learning with continuing school education (e.g. vocational options within upper secondary education, more general education content within vocational training, and a modular approach to general education and vocational training courses, making it possible to combine modules from both); *3)* the creation of pathways from secondary vocational education into tertiary education, consisting of "dual qualification" pathways (qualifying the individual

---

[36] United Nations. 2005b. *The Economic report on Africa 2005—Meeting the Challenge of Unemployment and Poverty.* Addis Ababa: Economic Commission for Africa, 9.

[37] Ibid.

[38] Ibid., 12.

either to start work with technical expertise or to continue into tertiary education) as in Austria, the Czech Republic and Hungary, and supplementary examinations and courses taken in parallel with or after vocational training qualifications, as in Australia, Austria, Norway and Switzerland.[39]

As highlighted by the OECD,[40] a wide variety of models exist for school-based workplace experience, ranging from unpaid work experience while still at school, to arrangements that combine schooling with half-day, or one-trimester-per-year, paid work. There is some evidence that school-based workplace experience has a positive impact on later labour market outcomes: some studies also suggest relatively good outcomes for students who take part-time or holiday jobs. It is well known that youth outcomes are generally good in countries like Germany and Denmark where a substantial proportion of young people enter work through apprenticeships that, in dual systems, provide an invaluable bridge between school and work. What these arrangements have in common is the benefit derived from contact with the world of work during education and training.

Measures can be taken to implement a major renewal of the systems of education and training that have so far been considered as two distinct spheres, and for this reason studied by separate research groups that are not in communication with each other. In most countries, young people are educated at school and then enter the labour market, with the transition from school to work being merely sequential. A modern vision of relations between education, training and socio-economic development calls for the design and implementation of policies and actions that take account not only of the demand for labour, but also of the quality of the supply. Only a real link between education, training and the world of work, by strengthening placement services and training schemes with an alternation of school and work, will enable us to deal in global and pragmatic terms with youth employment and balanced development of human capital all over the world. Clearly this perspective brings to mind the countries with a dual system (Austria, Denmark, Germany and Switzerland) that have relatively low youth unemployment rates and in which young people make the transition from school to apprenticeships, while they continue to spend one or two days a week in education.

It is well known that in countries such as Austria and Germany

---

[39] OECD. 2002. *Employment Outlook 2002. A Better Start for Youth,* Paris: OECD, 31-32.
[40] Ibid.

apprenticeship systems are built on several mutually dependent features.[41] Apprenticeship wages are low (initially about one-third of adult rates, rising to one-half in the final year), which makes apprenticeships attractive to employers. Apprenticeship qualifications have a high value on the labour market, and this makes apprenticeships attractive to young people and their parents. And the institutional basis for these systems is provided by strong and comprehensive industrial employer associations and industrial unions, which define apprenticeship qualifications and seek to maintain their value in the labour market. Hence the strategic role not only and not so much of public bodies, that can provide financial support for these schemes, but above all of the actors involved in the industrial relations system, who have a decisive role to play in relation to these schemes providing for an alternation between work and training.

Drawing on the disappointing results achieved by attempts to support apprenticeship schemes in the countries of Sub-Saharan Africa,[42] a complex problem arises when transposing such schemes from one country to another, that is well known to comparative law scholars, particularly in relation to apprenticeships that derive their strength from particular characteristics that are typical of the national systems in which they operate. It is however the case that only countries that use this tool efficiently have rates of youth unemployment in line with those of the adult population,[43] suggesting a link between apprenticeship schemes and stable employment of good quality.

Recent experience in countries such as Turkey, Malaysia, Tunisia and Egypt[44]—but also Uganda, Zambia and Kenya[45]—shows that, with

---

[41] Quintini, G., and S. Martin. 2006. "Starting Well or Losing their Way? The Position of Youth in the Labour Market in OECD Countries," OECD Social, Employment and Migration Working Paper No. 39. OECD, 22-25.

[42] See Rother, F. 2006. "Intervention to Support Young Workers in Sub-Saharan Africa," Regional Report for the Youth Employment Inventory. Washington: The World Bank, highlighting the fact that apprenticeships are one of the most significant policies in recent years.

[43] Axmann, M. 2004. "Facilitating Labour Market Entry for Youth through Enterprise-Based Schemes in Vocational Education and Training and Skills Development," SEED Working Paper No. 48. Geneva: ILO, 16-40.

[44] Mention should be made in particular of the Mubarak-Kohl initiative in Egypt (a summary is to be found in United Nations. 2005a. *Youth, Education, Skill and Employment.* Addis Ababa: Economic Commission for Africa, 25); see also El Zanaty & Associates. 2007. "School to Work Transition: evidence from Egypt," in *Employment Policy Paper*, No. 2 Geneva: ILO: according to the study "(...) Egyptian young people face significant challenges in finding decent employment after leaving school. The analysis of the collected data revealed that (in 2007) only

suitable adaptation, the chances of success are considerable.[46] At the same time, traditional vocational training schemes, as well as being particularly costly, have not been able to respond to the need for decent work of good quality, nor to the need for developing countries to invest in human capital by providing training for specific occupations.[47] There is a need to devise alternatives to traditional apprenticeship schemes.[48] However, it remains essential, in order to respond to the challenges of globalisation, to rethink traditional systems of education and training, that can no longer be designed and implemented in a self-referential manner, without strong links with the social partners and the labour market. Rather, the combination of practical training with additional theoretical training will increase the qualifications of trainees, and by meeting the needs of enterprises and employers, improve access to decent employment.

As underlined by recent studies[49]

> skills acquired in enterprises are mostly demand-driven as they respond to the needs of the enterprises for qualified workers. Young women and men that have gained working experience during training in enterprises have a good chance to be employed by the company that provided the training or by other companies working in similar branches. They are also much better prepared to start their own business […]. This approach will also have an impact on the productivity of the enterprise and the quality of the products

---

39% of respondents who were economically active (meaning either working or seeking work) or 17% of total respondents had attained employment that they were more or less satisfied with (more information on definitions of transition stages are provided below). The remaining 61% of economically active youth—more than one-quarter of total respondents (26%)—were still in a period of labour market transition, meaning they had not yet reached their desired goal for decent employment". With reference to Tunisia, see Stampini, M., and A. Verdier-Chouchane. 2011. "Labour Market Dynamics in Tunisia: the Issue of Youth Unemployment," Working Paper Series n. 123, African Development Bank, Tunisia.

[45] Grierson, J. 2002. *Enterprise-based Training in Africa: Case Studies from Kenya and Zambia*. Turin: ILO/ITC.

[46] Axmann, M. 2004. "Facilitating Labour Market Entry for Youth through Enterprise-Based Schemes in Vocational Education and Training and Skills Development," SEED Working Paper No. 48. Geneva: ILO.

[47] Ibid.

[48] Betcherman, G., M. Godfrey, S. Puerto, F. Rother, and A. Stavreska. 2007. "A Review of Interventions to Support Young Workers: Findings of the Youth Employment Inventory," SP Discussion Paper, No. 715. Washington: The World Bank.

[49] Ibid.

and services sold. At medium term, the competitiveness of the small enterprise sector will increase and create more and better jobs. It is also expected that improved skills and managerial capacity of the workforce in small enterprises, matched with a better insertion in market niches with higher value added and demand for labour will, jointly, lead to a sustainable expansion of the small enterprise sector.

Our proposal goes well beyond reforming education and training programmes at national level (though this is clearly an important objective),[50] and calls for the involvement of international organisations and networks of social actors at international and local level in taking a series of initiatives with a global dimension. This includes making provision for the exchange of students, with movement from the developing to the developed countries, in programmes designed at local level together with the institutions and the social partners in the various countries in order to meet training needs.

In the new economy, the main source of the wealth of nations is their endowment with human capital. Indeed, human capital is the key factor for growth and development, and the engine for change. From this point of view, compared to the European countries and the other western nations with a rapid ageing population, the African nations are endowed with enormous wealth. In order to avoid wasting this precious resource, there is a need to manage it not simply by means of legal regulation that may or may not produce results, but above all—in line with developments in many Asian economies in recent years[51]—by means of a reform of the education and training systems on a global scale that should be entrusted to the social partners. The active governance of this system could provide young people in Africa and other developing countries with a realistic alternative to unemployment, work in the hidden economy and migration as undocumented workers. This would require the training provided in the country of origin to meet the needs of the labour market in the most advanced countries, where there is a shortage of skilled workers. Alongside the modernisation of apprenticeship schemes, a decisive role can be played in developing countries by career guidance services, that

---

[50] Along this perspective, substantially limited to nationally-based actions and programmes, see the debate developed within the International Labour Organization and summarised in ILO. 2007a. "Informe y conclusiones de la undécesima Reuniòn Régional Africana," Addis Ababa, Ethiopia. April 24-28, 2007, and particularly Annex III and the Conclusions.

[51]See Yusuf, S., and K. Nabeshima, eds. 2007. *How Universities Promote Economic Growth*. Washington: The World Bank. For positive steps in Arabic Countries see http://www.tvet-portal.net/index.php?id=20&L=0.

need to be set up inside schools and universities, with the mutual recognition of vocational qualifications.

Bearing in mind that for many of these young people there is no real alternative to migration, as there is a lack of employment in their country of origin,[52] it should be noted that recent international economic studies,[53] have highlighted the fact that the temporary loss of human capital and skilled workers does not necessarily have a negative impact on the country of origin, but can serve as a step towards attracting capital and know-how and for the development of trade between the country of origin and the developed countries.

Today, in an increasingly global labour market, it may be argued that, provided it is properly governed,[54] the outflow of young migrants to the developed world can lead to a number of benefits for both receiving and sending countries.[55] Suffice it to consider the historical experience of many European countries, which after a long period of mass emigration, began to attract migrants from other countries, having benefited from migratory movements in the past.

Clearly, the solution that is proposed is not for the short term, nor is it easy to implement, but requires a considerable effort on the part of education and training, labour market and industrial relations actors, as there appears to be a lack of valid alternatives. There is an awareness among policy-makers "that productive employment for young people cannot be achieved and sustained through isolated and fragmented

---

[52] International Labour Organization. 2005a. "Youth Employment: From a National Challenge to a Global Development Goal," Background Paper contributed by the ILO to the G8 Labour and Employment Ministers' Conference, London, United Kingdom, 10-11 March 2005, 5.

[53] Ratha, D., and X. Zhimei. 2008. *Migration and Remittances Fact book 2008.* Migration and Remittances Team, Development Prospects Group, The World Bank. OECD. 2007. *International Migration Outlook.* Paris: OECD.

[54] Indeed, an ungoverned and not planned migration does not seem suitable for the purpose of providing solutions to this matter, since the lives of those leaving the countries of origin would be made difficult by the lack of integration into the countries of destination (Malmberg-Heimonen, I., and I. Jukunen. 2006. "Out of Unemployment? A Comparative Analysis of the Risk and Opportunities Longer-term Unemployed Immigrant Youth Face when Entering the labour Market," *Journal of Youth Studies* 9, No. 5: 575-592.

[55] International Labour Organization. 2005a. "Youth Employment: From a National Challenge to a Global Development Goal," Background paper contributed by the ILO to the G8 Labour and Employment Ministers' Conference, London, United Kingdom, 10-11 March 2005, 8.

measures".[56] Rather, it requires long-term, coherent and concerted action over a combination of economic and social policies (e.g. modernisation of labour legislation, labour market information, career guidance, education and training for employability in a global workplace).

The school-to-work transition, from this point of view, appears to be the most favourable area in which to work and invest in order to achieve structural results, dealing with the fragile growth of many of the African,[57] while respecting the reciprocal interests of all the regions and economies of the global market.

5. Final Remarks: Theoretical Implications of our Proposal in Terms of Future Developments in the Study of Labour Law and Industrial Relations

Clearly the perspective outlined in the present study requires more in-depth analysis and field work. However, in concluding this preliminary study, it may be said that the school-to-work transition can make a significant contribution to recent strands of research that call for a theoretical reformulation of labour law and industrial relations.

Although the present study is intended to be innovative, and is in need of further development, in theoretical terms it is in line with certain recent proposals by legal scholars aimed at extending and modifying the frame of reference of the study of labour law and industrial relations, in order to ensure that it continues to play a significant role, in spite of international trends that are tending to marginalise these disciplinary fields. Mention should be made of the strand of legal research calling for labour law to be recast as "the law of labour market regulation",[58] highlighting the fact that the dominant paradigm of labour law in the late twentieth century was

---

[56] Ibid. See also ILO. 2005b. *Resolution on Decent Work for Youth in Africa and the ILO Response, Document GB289/5.* Geneva: ILO.

[57] Arbache, J., D. S. Go, and J. Page. 2008. "Is Africa's Economy at a Turning Point?" The World Bank Africa Region, Policy Research Working Paper No. 4519. Angel-Urdinola, D. F., Semlali A., and S. Brodman. 2010. *Non-Public Provision of Active Labor Market Programs in Arab- Mediterranean Countries: An Inventory of Youth Programs.* Washington: The World Bank. ILO. 2007a. "Informe y conclusiones de la undécesima Reuniòn Régional Africana," Addis Ababa, Ethiopia. April 24-28, 2007, 5-10. ILO. 2007b. "The Decent Work Agenda in Africa: 2007–2015," Report of the Director-General to the Eleventh African Regional Meeting, Addis Ababa, Ethiopia, April 2007.

[58] Arup, C., P. Gahan, J. Howe, R. Mitchell, and A. O'Donnell. 2006. *Labour Law and Labour Market Regulations.* Annandale: The Federation Press.

lacking in "explanatory and normative power" in relation to the changing nature of the labour market (both within the enterprise and on a wider scale), to new economic theories concerning the labour market and its institutions, and to major changes in society arising from the globalisation of the economy and the markets. In this connection, mention should be made of the recent strand of labour law theory which, reflecting on the original paradigm of labour relations, as developed at the beginning of the twentieth century,[59] points to the need to considerable extend its field of observation beyond trade union issues in order to cover all the issues arising from labour relations. This development appears to be essential, if we are to avoid the risk of increasingly marginalising industrial relations in the context of the free market.

An important contribution in this direction could come from the proposal put forward in the present study, to govern the dynamics of supply and demand for labour by strengthening links on a global scale between education and training, and the labour market as a more effective and more realistic solution compared to a regulatory (or deregulatory) perspective, that is becoming weaker and less effective due to the loss of sovereignty on the part of nation states in the governance of the labour market. In this connection, it is not intended to turn away from the traditional protective function of labour law, but simply to highlight the fact that labour law concerns matters of production more than income distribution, in the sense that a lack of growth and development tends to have a negative impact on the potential of the labour market and on workers' protection. This confirms the decisive importance of the method of industrial relations, since no better tool has yet been invented for conciliating the protection of workers with the need for competitiveness on the part of enterprises.

---

[59] Kaufman, B. 2007. "*The Core Principle and Fundamental Theorem of Industrial Relations,*" Working Paper 07-01, Department of Economics, W.T. Beebe Institute of Personnel and Employment Relations. Georgia State University. An Italian translation was published in *Diritto delle Relazioni Industriali*, 2006, 4, *Il principio essenziale e il teorema fondamentale delle relazioni industriali.*

References

Online Resources

The following documents are available on the website of ADAPT, School for Advanced Studies in Industrial and Labour Relations (www.adapt.it):

A-Z Index, *Giovani e Lavoro*

Angel-Urdinola, D. F., A. Semlali, and S. Brodman. 2010. "Non-Public Provision of Active Labor Market Programs in Arab-Mediterranean Countries: An Inventory of Youth Programs," Working Paper. Washington: The World Bank.

Annan, K. 2004. "A Global Alliance for Youth Employment: Recommendations to the High-Level Panel on Youth Employment," Report to the Millennium Assembly of the United Nations. United Nations.

Aring, M., and M. Axmann. 2004. "Why Developing Countries Need a School-to-Work System, Now More Than Ever," RTI International.

Axmann, M. 2004. "Facilitating Labour Market Entry for Youth through Enterprise-Based Schemes in Vocational Education and Training and Skills Development," SEED Working Paper No. 48. Geneva: ILO.

El Zanaty & Associates. 2007. "School to Work Transition: evidence from Egypt," *Employment Policy Paper*, No. 2 Geneva: ILO.

Conventions and Recommendations Relevant to Work and Young Persons (list of)

Bell, D. N. F., and D. G. Blanchflower. 2010. "Youth Unemployment: Déjà Vu?" IZA Discussion Paper No. 4705. Bonn: IZA.

European Parliament. 2010. "Report on Promoting Youth Access to the Labour Market, Strengthening Trainee, Internship and Apprenticeship Status (2009/2221(INI))" Committee on Employment and Social Affairs.

Garces, E., D. Thomas, and J. Currie. 2000. "Longer-term Effects of Head Start," NBER Working Papers No. 8054. The National Bureau of Economic Research.

Ha, B., C. Mc Inerney, S. Tobin, and R. Torres. 2010. "Youth employment in Crisis," Discussion Paper. Geneva: International Institute for Labour Studies.

International Labour Organization. 2005a. "Youth Employment: From a National Challenge to a Global Development Goal," Background

Paper contributed by the ILO to the G8 Labour and Employment Ministers' Conference, London, United Kingdom, 10-11 March 2005.

International Labour Organization. 2006a. *Regional Labour Market Trends for Youth: Africa.* ILO Youth Employment Programme, Geneva: ILO.

—. 2006b. *World Employment Report 2004/2005.* Geneva: ILO.

—. 2008. *It is High Time to Rethink—Youth Employment in 2008.* Addis Ababa: Regional Office for Africa.

Martin, J., and D. Grubb. 2001. "What Works and for Whom: A Review of OECD Countries' Experiences with Active Labour Market Policies," IFAU Working Paper No. 14. Institute for Labour Market Policy Evaluation.

OECD. 2002. *Employment Outlook 2002. A Better Start for Youth,* Paris: OECD.

—. 2010a. *Off to a Good Start? Jobs for Youth.* Paris: OECD Publishing.

Quintini, G., and S. Martin. 2006. "Starting Well or Losing their Way? The Position of Youth in the Labour Market in OECD Countries," OECD Social, Employment and Migration Working Paper, No. 39. OECD.

Rother, F. 2006. "Intervention to Support Young Workers in Sub-Saharan Africa," Regional Report for the Youth Employment Inventory. Washington: The World Bank.

United Nations. 2005a. *Youth, Education, Skill and Employment,* Addis Ababa: Economic Commission for Africa.

—. 2005b. *The Economic report on Africa 2005—Meeting the Challenge of Unemployment and Poverty.* Addis Ababa: Economic Commission for Africa.

A-Z Index, Globalizzazione e lavoro

International Labour Organization. 2010a. *Global Employment Trends January 2010.* Geneva: ILO.

Further References

Arbache, J., D. S. Go, and J. Page. 2008. "Is Africa's Economy at a Turning Point?" The World Bank Africa Region, Policy Research Working Paper n. 4519.

Arup, C., P. Gahan, J. Howe, R. Mitchell, and A. O'Donnell. 2006. *Labour Law and Labour Market Regulations.* Annandale: The Federation Press.

Berg, J., and D. Kucera. 2007. *In Defence of Labour Market Institutions: Cultivating Justice in the Developing World.* Geneva: ILO.

Betcherman, G., M. Godfrey, S. Puerto, F. Rother, and A. Stavreska. 2007. "A Review of Interventions to Support Young Workers: Findings of the Youth Employment Inventory," SP Discussion Paper, No. 715. Washington: The World Bank.

Biagi, M., and M. Tiraboschi. 2000. "The Role of Labour Law in Job Creation Policies : an Italian Perspective," in *Job Creation and Labour Law,* ed. Biagi, M., (The Hague: Kluwer Law International), 179-193.

Blanpain, R. 2008. "The End of Labour Law?" in *The Global Labour Market. From Globalization to Flexicurity,* eds. Blanpain, R., and M. Tiraboschi, (The Hague: Kluwer Law International).

Booth A. L., M. Francesconi, and J. Frank. 2002. "Temporary Jobs: Stepping Stones Or Dead Ends?" *The Economic Journal* 112, No. 480.

Bundesministerium für Wirtschaft und Technologie. 2010. *Nationaler Pakt für Ausbildung und Fachkräftenachwuchs in Deutschland 2010— 2014.* Berlin: BMWi.

Diamond, P. A., Massachusetts Institute of Technology, Cambridge, MA, USA, Dale T. Mortensen, Northwestern University, Evanston, IL, USA, Aarhus University, Denmark, and Christopher A. Pissarides, London School of Economics and Political Science, UK. 2011. *The Prize in Economic Sciences 2010 - Press Release.* http://nobelprize.org/nobel_prizes/economics/laureates/2010/press.html

Directorate-General for Employment, Social Affairs and Equal Opportunities, European Commission, The Institute of Population and Labor Economics, and Chinese Academy of Social Sciences. 2010. *New Skills for New Jobs: China and the EU. Shared Labour Market Experiences to Inform the Harmonious and Sustainable Society of the Future.* Brussels: European Commission.

Docquier, F. 2006. "Brain Drain and Inequality Across Nation," in IZA Discussion Paper No. 2440.

European Commission. 2006. *Modernising Labour Law to Meet the Challenges of the 21st Century, COM(2006) 708 final.* Brussels: European Commission.

—. 2007. *Outcome of the Public Consultation on the Commission's Green Paper "Modernising Labour Law to Meet the Challenges of the 21st Century", SEC(2007) 1373.* Brussels: European Commission.

—. 2011. "Tackling Early School Leaving: A Key Contribution to the Europe 2020 Agenda, COM(2011) 18," Communication From The Commission To The European Parliament, The Council, The European Economic And Social Committee And The Committee Of The

Regions, Brussels: European Commission.

Grierson, J. 2002. *Enterprise-based Training in Africa: Case Studies from Kenya and Zambia.* Turin: ILO/ITC.

Heckman, J. J., and L. Lochner. 2000. "Rethinking Education and Training Policy: Understanding the Sources of Skill Formation in a Modern Economy," in *Securing the Future: Investing in Children from Birth to Adulthood*, eds. Danziger, S., and J. Waldforgel, (New York: Russell Sage Foundation).

Hisashi, T-O., K. Koichiro, I. Koh, H. Park, K. Reiko, S. Tomoki. 2010. "The Labour Issue of Youth: Looking Back over 20 Years," *The Japanese Journal of Labour Studies,* No. 602.

International Labour Organization. 1999. *Convention C182, Concerning the Prohibition and Immediate Action for the Elimination of the Worst Forms of Child Labour.* Geneva: ILO.

—. 2005b. *Resolution on Decent Work for Youth in Africa and the ILO Response, Document GB289/5.* Geneva: ILO.

—. 2005c. *Resolution Concerning Youth Employment.* Geneva: ILO.

—. 2007a. "Informe y conclusiones de la undécesima Reuniòn Régional Africana," Addis Ababa, Ethiopia. April 24-28, 2007.

—. 2007b. "The Decent Work Agenda in Africa: 2007–2015," Report of the Director-General to the Eleventh African Regional Meeting, Addis Ababa, Ethiopia, April 2007.

—. 2010b. *Global Employment Trends for Youth 2010.* Geneva: ILO.

Kalleberg, A. L. 2000. "Nonstandard Employment Relations: Part-Time, Temporary and Contract Work," *Annual Review of Sociology* 26.

Kaufman, B. 2007. *The Core Principle and Fundamental Theorem of Industrial Relations.* Working Paper 07-01, Department of Economics, W.T. Beebe Institute of Personnel and Employment Relations. Georgia State University.

Lansky, M. 1997 "Child Labour: How the Challenge is Being met," *International Labour Review* 136 No. 2.

Malmberg-Heimonen, I., and I. Jukunen. 2006. "Out of Unemployment? A Comparative Analysis of the Risk and Opportunities Longer-term Unemployed Immigrant Youth Face when Entering the labour Market," *Journal of Youth Studies* 9, No. 5: 575-592.

Marchand, O. 1999. "Youth Unemployment in OECD Countries: How Can the Disparities Be Explained?" in *OECD Preparing Youth for the 21st Century—The Transition from Education to the labour Market* (Paris: OECD Publishing).

OECD. 1994. *The OECD Job Study: Evidence and Explanations,* Paris: OECD.

—. 1997. *Implementing the OECD Jobs Strategy: Lessons from Member Countries.* Paris: OECD.

—. 1999a. *Employment Outlook,* Paris: OECD.

—. 1999b. *Implementing the OECD Job Strategy: Assessing Performance and Policy.* Paris: OECD.

—. 2007. *International Migration Outlook.* Paris: OECD.

—. 2010b. *Economic Survey of China: a Labour Market in Transition.* Paris: OECD.

Ratha, D., and X. Zhimei. 2008. *Migration and Remittances Fact book 2008.* Migration and Remittances Team, Development Prospects Group, The World Bank.

Rees, A. 1996. "An Essay on Youth Joblessness," *Journal of Economic Literature* 24, No. 2:613-28.

Regini, M., and G. Esping-Andersen. "The Effects of Labour Market De-regulation on Unemployment. A Critical Review of the Different Research Approaches and of Empirical Evidence," Paper presented to the European Commission, Brussels, Belgium, 1998.

Ryan, P. 2001. "The School-to-Work Transition: a Cross-national Perspective," *Journal of Economic* Literature 39, No. 1: 34-92.

Stampini, M., and A. Verdier-Chouchane. 2011. "Labour Market Dynamics in Tunisia: the Issue of Youth Unemployment," Working Paper Series n. 123, African Development Bank, Tunisia.

United Nations. 2007. *World Youth Report 2007.* New York: Department of Economic and Social Affairs, United Nations

Webb, B., and S. Webb. 1897 and 1926. *Industrial Democracy.* London: Longmans.

Weiss, M. "Realising Decent Work in Africa," Keynote Speech at the Opening Ceremony of the Fifth African Regional Congress of the IIRA in Cape Town, South Africa, 26 March 2008.

Yusuf, S., and K. Nabeshima, eds. 2007. *How Universities Promote Economic Growth.* Washington: The World Bank.

CHAPTER ONE:

YOUTH AND THE CRISIS

YOUTH UNEMPLOYMENT BEFORE AND AFTER THE CRISIS

ENRICO MARELLI
AND MARCELLO SIGNORELLI

1. Introduction

This paper focuses on the effects of youth unemployment before and after the recent crisis, particularly those taking place in the short run.[1] A review of the existing literature investigating the determinants of youth unemployment rates—at both theoretical and empirical levels—is firstly provided, with some of them (labour market institutions, educational systems, as well as processes of school-to-work transition) closely analysed. The review section also comprises a discussion on the impact of the economic crisis on youth unemployment: in general terms, the effects of a severe economic downturn on the labour market differ across countries, as depending on some specific factors (e.g. degree of flexibility and strictness of employment protection legislation), on the existence of a number of adjustment mechanisms (in terms of working hours, labour hoarding measures, internal flexibility) and on the adoption of specific policies (that are intended to preserve employment, at least on a temporary basis). As we shall see—in the post-crisis period—young people encounter considerable difficulty in both being hired as new entrants (as a consequence of hiring freezes) and in remaining employed, since they are

---

[1] The last crisis, originally affecting only the financial sector, began at the end of 2007, with the deepest impact on markets which was recorded in September 2008, when the real effects became apparent (e.g. the collapse of Lehman Brothers). However, production fell significantly in the first half of 2009 and translated into high rates of unemployment over the same year and also in 2010 in a number of countries. This aspect confirms that effects on the labour market (on production, income, and so on) resulting from financial crises are always lagged.

more likely to be laid off than workers with more seniority, also because young workers are often engaged in fixed-term jobs.

The empirical section presents data on youth unemployment before and during the global financial crisis and the Great Recession, also considering the subsequent recovery period, with a particular focus on the EU countries. In this respect, EU unemployment statistics for the 15-24 age group are provided and discussed, as compared with total unemployment rates reported over the last decade.

Findings revealed that youth unemployment in many European countries is a serious problem also in times of economic stability, and it is frequently associated with low participation rates. Indeed, many young people are "left behind" and are often trapped in a condition of "neither in employment nor in education or training" (the NEETs). Even when they find a job, they are usually employed on a temporary basis, and this results in job instability and low remuneration, with long-term consequences also on their retirement schemes.

Following the recent downturn, the labour market performance of young people reported a sharp decrease in several countries, because of the effects of significant reductions in labour demand, exacerbated by the age distribution of such reductions, which is actually the result of labour-hoarding strategies. It is also important to note in this respect that most vulnerable groups (see also the ILO reports)—that include those who have suffered the most from the consequences of the crisis—comprise young people, old workers, and the weakest segments of the labour force (e.g. migrants and informal labourers). Further, from a gender perspective, there are considerable differences stemming from industrial specialisations across regions (for instance, in some European countries, male workers have been more adversely affected than women).

In terms of policy implications, of first importance is the need to improve the effectiveness of those programmes which enhance the transition from school to work, and to promote active labour market policies, in order to favour a more "decent" integration of young people into the labour market. In this sense, the aim should also be to encourage youth labour market participation and to reduce the number of NEETs. Furthermore, in some European countries, it would be important to overcome "dualism" in the labour market. It follows that in the process of economic reform aimed at providing the labour market with higher levels of flexibility, attention should be paid to young workers, so as to ensure them more secure "employment paths".

It is also crucial, at the national and regional levels, that governments further implement existing European "best practices" and guidelines to build employment pathways for young people and reduce youth unemployment. It should be noted that the recent "Europe 2020" strategy gives priority to youth labour and educational issues, primarily aiming at the development of human capital,[2] the quality of which represents a key factor to favour—in both quantitative and qualitative terms—net job creation for young people.

This paper is structured in the following way: the first part of the review section (2) provides a definition of "young people" and a discussion about the key determinants of youth unemployment. An examination of recent literature on the impact of economic crises on youth follows. Section 3 presents the evolution of youth unemployment rates in the last decade, with particular reference to the EU countries, also analysing the consequences of the Great Recession. Implications that ensue in terms of policy are described in Section 4.

2. Review of Economic Literature

The first sub-section of this review is dedicated to a concise presentation of the several definitions of "young people" adopted in the literature and, particularly, to the growing body of economic literature on the specific determinants of youth unemployment rates (YUR). This is followed by a sub-section that focuses on a small set of studies concerning the behaviour of YUR during and after "major crises".

2.1. On the Definition of Young People and on the Determinants of Youth Unemployment

In the analysis of the youth labour market, official statistics tend to define young people as being between 15-24 years old, even though attention is also paid to the pros and cons of alternative definitions of "youth" and their consequences on the study of labour market performance and dynamics.[3] However, because of widespread data availability at an international level and in order to allow us to present empirical evidence,

---

[2] By the end of this decade, the percentage of 30-34 year olds having completed tertiary or equivalent education should reach at least 40%, while the drop-out rate should be reduced to less than 10%.

[3] Lefresne, F. 2003. "Les jeunes et l'emploi," *Collection Repères* Paris: La Découverte. O'Higgins, N. 1997. "The Challenge of Youth Unemployment," Employment and Training Papers No. 7. Geneva: ILO.

this narrow definition of young people (15-24 years) is also adopted in Section 3 of the present paper.[4]

The unemployment rate is usually much higher for young people than for adults. One reason for this might be a difference in labour market performance, which is usually related to lower levels (and/or different quality) of human capital and productivity which characterise the youth, and which, accordingly, makes employers opt for adult workers.

It has been noticed that among the several features characterising the transition of young people from school to the labour market—e.g. unemployment risks, performance at work, job quality and stability—human capital is the most prominent one. In particular, young people with low levels of human capital and skills are more exposed to long-term unemployment, to unstable and low-quality jobs and to social exclusion.[5] However, the educational level is only the most immediate variable used for measuring "human capital"; in fact, young people lack two additional and fundamental components in this respect, namely generic and job skills. From both a theoretical and empirical viewpoint, Carmeci and Mauro[6] have shown that, to ensure certain levels of productivity, educated youngsters need to acquire firm-specific knowledge by "schooling" human capital and through work experience.

As for the European context, Caroleo and Pastore[7] argued that the "youth experience gap" is the key factor explaining such a high level of unemployment among youth, especially when compared to adult unemployment. In addition, they classify the EU countries into five groups (North-European countries, Continental European countries, Anglo-Saxon countries, South-European countries and New Member States) on the basis of the institutional setting and considering several initiatives laid down to combat unemployment, such as policy measures (including various degrees and types of labour market flexibility), educational and training systems, passive income support schemes and fiscal incentives. To bridge

---

[4] For a more complete definition of "youth unemployment" and some evaluative aspects, see also International Labour Organization. 2009. "KILM9—Youth Unemployment," in *Key Indicators of the Labour Market* (KILM), Sixth Edition, Geneva: ILO.

[5] OECD. 2005. *Education at Glance*. Paris: OECD.

[6] Carmeci, L., and L. Mauro. 2003. "Long-run Growth and Investment in Education: Does Unemployment Matter?" *Journal of Macroeconomics*, No. 25:123-137.

[7] Caroleo, F. E., and F. Pastore. 2007. "The Youth Experience Gap: Explaining Differences across EU Countries," Università di Perugia, Quaderni del Dipartimento di Economia, Finanza e Statistica 41.

the gap, young people "experiment" and thus go through several labour market transitions[8] with significant differences[9] at a national level and in terms of market segmentation, which depend on the range of institutions implemented to enhance the school-to-work transition.[10]

The links between the "institutional framework" and policies to tackle youth unemployment are also widely discussed in the recent literature.[11] Further research on the issue analysed the role of institutional and policy settings with special reference to the youth, both focusing on specific aspects such as temporary jobs[12] or minimum wage regulation,[13] and

---

[8] Clark, K. B., and L. H. Summers. 1982. "The Dynamics of Youth Unemployment," in *The Youth Labour Market Problem: Its Nature, Causes and Consequences,* eds. Freeman, R., and D. Wise, (Chicago: University of Chicago Press). Freeman, R., and D. Wise, eds. 1982. *The Youth Labour Market Problem: Its Nature, Causes and Consequences.* Chicago: University of Chicago Press. Rees, A. 1986. "An Essay on Youth Joblessness," *Journal of Economic Literature* 24, No. 2: 613-628. Topel, R. H., and M. P. Ward. 1992. "Job Mobility and the Careers of Young Men," *Quarterly Journal of Economics* 107, No. 2: 439-479.

[9] Scarpetta, S., A. Sonnet, and T. Manfredi. 2010. "Rising Youth Unemployment During the Crisis: How to Prevent negative Long-Term Consequences on a Generation?" OECD Social, Employment and Migration Working Papers, No. 6. Paris: OECD.

[10] Ryan, P. 2001. "The School-to-work Transition: a Cross-national Perspective," *Journal of Economic Literature* 39, No. 1: 34-92. Caroleo, F. E., and F. Pastore. 2007. "The Youth Experience Gap: Explaining Differences across EU Countries," Università di Perugia, Quaderni del Dipartimento di Economia, Finanza e Statistica 41. Caroleo, F. E., and F. Pastore. 2009. "Le cause del(l'in)successo lavorativo dei giovani," *Economia & Lavoro* 3:107-31.

[11] Brunello, G., P. Garibaldi, and E. Wasmer. 2007. *Education and training in Europe*. New York: Oxford University Press. Checchi, D. 2006. *The Economics of Education.* Cambridge: Cambridge University Press. European Commission. 2008. *Employment in Europe 2008*. Brussels: European Commission, chapter 5. Perugini, C., and M. Signorelli. 2010a. "Youth Labour Market Performance in European Regions," *Economic Change and Restructuring*, No. 2. Perugini, C., and M. Signorelli. 2010b. "Youth Unemployment in Transition Countries and Regions," in *Economic Growth and Structural Features of Transition*, eds. Marelli E., and M. Signorelli, (London and New York: Palgrave Macmillan).

[12] Nunziata, L., and S. Staffolani. 2007. "Short-term Contracts Regulations and Dynamic Labour Demand: Theory and Evidence," *Scottish Journal of Political Economy* 54, No. 1: 72-104.

[13] Neumark, D., and W. Wascher. 1999. "A Cross-national Analysis of the Effects of Minimum Wages on Youth Employment," NBER Working Paper 7299. Neumark, D., and W. Wascher. 2004. "Minimum Wages, Labour Market Institutions, and Youth Employment: a Cross-national Analysis," *Industrial and Labour Relations Review* 57, No. 2: 223-247. Abowd, J., F. Kramarz, T. Lemieux,

providing a more comprehensive view of the possible institutional and policy interaction of those factors directly or indirectly related to the labour market.[14]

Quintini et al.[15] investigate changes in the transition processes between school and work in the OECD countries, also highlighting the persisting differences between youth and adult unemployment rates (the former is generally more than twice as high as the latter). As discussed earlier, Clark and Summers[16] analyse the determinants of the higher flows in and out of unemployment for young compared with adult people, while O'Higgins[17] examines trends in the youth labour market in developing and transition countries, highlighting significant difficulty in terms of integration of young people into "decent work". The persistence of youth unemployment[18] has been also investigated.

Another possible cause of high levels of youth unemployment and low quality employment—low entry wages, low quality jobs, spread of non-standard labour contracts—has been found in the mismatch between knowledge gained through formal education and the skills required by the labour market. In general, the difference between educational supply and labour demand lies in a stronger connection with the performance of local

---

and D. Margolis. 2000. "Minimum Wages and Youth Employment in France and the United States," in *Youth Employment and Joblessness in Advanced Countries*, 427-472. *NBER Chapters 6813*. National Bureau of Economic Research, Inc.

[14] Kolev, A., and C. Saget. 2005. "Understanding Youth Labour Market Disadvantage: Evidence from South-east Europe," *International Labour Review* 144, No. 2: 161-187. Bassanini, A. and R. Duval. 2006. "The Determinants of Unemployment across OECD Countries: Reassessing the Role of Policies and Institutions," *OECD Economic Studies*, No. 42:7–86. OECD. 2006. *Employment Outlook*. Paris: OECD.

[15] Quintini, G., J. P Martin, and S. Marti. 2007. "The changing nature of the school-to-work Transition Process in OECD Countries", IZA Discussion Paper No. 2582. Bonn: IZA.

[16] Clark, K. B., and L. H. Summers. 1982. "The Dynamics of Youth Unemployment," in *The Youth Labour Market Problem: Its Nature, Causes and Consequences,* eds. Freeman, R., and D. Wise, (Chicago: University of Chicago Press).

[17] O'Higgins, N. 2005. "Trends in the Youth Labour Market in Developing and Transition Countries," Labor and Demography WP 0507002.

[18] Heckman, J. J., and G. J. Borjas. 1980. "Does Unemployment Cause Future Unemployment? Definitions, Questions and Answers from a Continuous Time Model of Heterogeneity and State Dependence," *Econ* 47, No. 187: 247-283. Ryan, P. 2001. "The School-to-work Transition: a Cross-national Perspective," *Journal of Economic Literature* 39, No. 1: 34-92.

economies, rather than with the educational stock itself.[19] Many other factors can affect the youth labour market performance. It is a well known fact that either overall and youth unemployment mainly depend on macroeconomic cyclical conditions. Accordingly, even though the permanent effects—e.g. on potential output—of cyclical downturns can be evaluated,[20] the economic cycle can only explain some of the "persistent" employment difficulties faced by young people, especially when compared to adults.

2.2. On the Impact of Crises on Youth Unemployment

Scant attention has been paid on the part of the academic community to the impact of "economic crises" on youth unemployment.

It should be also recalled that the overall and specific impact of a crisis on the labour market is usually different across and within countries, as depending on many factors, such as: (i) the economic structure, (ii) the institutional framework (including institutions enhancing STWT and (iii) policy-makers' initiatives at different levels.[21] Such factors primarily affect the degree of (in)stability of the relationship between economic growth (or output decline) and unemployment rates, i.e. the so-called "Okun's law".[22] However, a decline in aggregate demand—as occurred in

---

[19] Rodrìguez-Pose A. "Human Capital and Regional Disparities in the EU," Joint Conference of the EC and the EIB on Human Capital, Employment, Productivity and Growth, Brussels, Belgium, September 2003.

[20] See, for instance in the case of the recent global recession, Furceri, D. and A. Mourougane. 2009. "The Effect of Financial Crises on Potential Output: New Empirical Evidence from OECD Countries," OECD Economics Department Working Paper No. 699. Paris: OECD. World Bank. 2010. *Global Economic Prospects. 2010 Foresees Long Road to Economic Recovery.* Washington: The World Bank.

[21] In many countries a number of policies are adopted—with different degrees of coordination and autonomy—at more than one level of government. See also Signorelli, M. 2008. "Employment and Unemployment in a Multilevel Regional Perspective," in *Mediterranean Europe*, ed. Petricioli M., (Brussels: P.I.E. Peter Lang).

[22] See Okun, A. M. 1962. "Potential GNP: Its Measurement and Significance," in *Proceedings of the Business and Economic Statistics Section* (Washington, D.C: American Statistical Association), 98-103. For a discussion on the stability (and main direction of causality) of the output-unemployment relationship, see Signorelli, M. 2005. "Growth and Employment: Comparative Performance, Convergences and Co-movements," Economic Department Working Paper, No. 8. Perugia: University of Perugia.

2008-09 in many countries—negatively affects labour demand, with different and immediate responses (also as a consequence of labour hoarding measures), different time lags (before the impact on employment indices becomes significant) and different degrees of persistence of the effects. Further, adverse effects can be partly mitigated by policy responses—both macroeconomic policies and *ad-hoc* measures for the labour market—and the development of a more effective institutional framework.

In considering young people, Scarpetta et al.[23] highlight that crises exacerbate a number of structural problems that affect the transition from school to work. In fact, during and after a crisis, be it financial or economic, the decline in GDP turns—after a number of months—into a reduction of labour demand.[24] Such state of affairs leads school-leavers to compete with more numerous jobseekers for fewer vacancies,[25] while the youth already in the labour market are generally among the first to lose their job, mainly due to the spread of temporary contracts,[26] which makes it difficult to find another position. Accordingly, the wide recourse to temporary contracts clearly explains the higher sensitivity to business-cycles on the part of the youth. However, many authors[27] also notice that

---

[23] Scarpetta, S., A. Sonnet, and T. Manfredi. 2010. "Rising Youth Unemployment During the Crisis: How to Prevent negative Long-Term Consequences on a Generation?" OECD Social, Employment and Migration Working Papers, No. 6. Paris: OECD.

[24] In terms of labour demand (at both firm and aggregate level) a distinction can also be made between "desired" and "actual" demand (see Signorelli, M. 1997. "Uncertainty, Flexibility Gap and Labour Demand in the Italian Economy," *Labour*, No. 1: 141-175), especially considering—together with other factors—the hiring and firing costs (also related to the labour hoarding strategies and to evidence of co-existence of vacancies and unemployment). In addition, somehow different dynamics of labour demand should be considered either in terms of "number of workers employed" or "overall number of hours worked".

[25] As mentioned in the previous section, the existence of a "youth experience gap" favours higher levels of employability among adults (with generic and sector/firm specific skills), particularly when compared to youngsters.

[26] The widespread use of temporary contracts to hire youngsters leads to the adoption of a sort of "last-in first-out" rule.

[27] Cockx, B., and M. Picchio. 2009. "Are Short-Lived Jobs Stepping Stones to Long-Lasting Jobs?" IZA Discussion Paper, No. 4004. Bonn: IZA. Scarpetta, S., A. Sonnet, and T. Manfredi. 2010. "Rising Youth Unemployment During the Crisis: How to Prevent negative Long-Term Consequences on a Generation?" OECD Social, Employment and Migration Working Papers No. 6. Paris: OECD.

many of them regard temporary contracts (especially apprenticeships) as a stepping stone to a permanent contract rather than as a "trap". The trap effect of temporary contracts seems to be more widespread in countries with a significant difference between permanent contracts (characterized by strict employment protection legislation, EPL) and temporary/atypical contractual arrangements, primarily when the level of stringency of such regulations is examined. Labour hoarding practices, especially in countries with the highest level of EPL on "permanent contracts", favour adult segments and can further aggravate the seriousness of the impact of the crisis on youth unemployment.

It should be noted that "educational matters" and consequences resulting from a financial crisis are usually more serious for low-skilled young people, as already being at a disadvantage in times of economic stability, since the downturn further increases their risk of long-term inactivity and exclusion.

Many authors found that negative effects on youth unemployment depend on overall labour market conditions, even though, significantly, young and disadvantaged workers are those who are most affected by such a situation.[28] In considering the definitions of Quintini and Manfredi,[29] the crisis is causing an increase in the number of youth—including those who reported good performance levels in good times—classified as "poorly-integrated new entrants" and "youth left behind". According to Scarpetta et al.[30] the size of the group of "youth left behind" can be proxied by the number of young people who are "neither in employment nor in education or training" (the NEETs). On average in 2007, such group represented 11% of those aged 15-25 years old by the OECD. In particular, Scarpetta et al.[31] highlight the risk to create a "lost generation" and the need to adopt effective (both active and passive) labour policies and STWT institutions for minimising the increase in the number of youth losing effective contact

---

[28] Bell, D. N. F., and D. G. Blanchflower. 2009. "What Should Be Done about Rising Unemployment in the UK," IZA Discussion Paper, No. 4040. Bonn: IZA.

[29] Quintini, G., and T. Manfredi. 2009. "Going Separate Ways? School-to-work Transitions in the United States and Europe," OECD Social, Employment and Migration Working Paper No. 90. Paris: OECD.

[30] Scarpetta, S., A. Sonnet, and T. Manfredi. 2010. "Rising Youth Unemployment During the Crisis: How to Prevent negative Long-Term Consequences on a Generation?" OECD Social, Employment and Migration Working Papers, No. 6. Paris: OECD.

[31] Ibid.

with the labour market and permanently damaging their employment prospects.

Verick[32] considers the effects on unemployment of the past "Big 5 Crises" (Spain 1977, Norway 1987, Finland 1991, Sweden 1991, and Japan 1992) in order to further investigate the impact of the recent crisis on the labour market, especially on young men and women.[33] The author argues that data on the five previous financial crises, as well as on the most recent one, reveal that young people are hardest hit and the impact persists long after the economy grows again;[34] the size and persistence of the impact on youth unemployment depend on: (i) the degree of economic contraction, (ii) the sectoral composition of employment prior to the crisis and (iii) the institutional structures. In particular, Verick[35] further confirms that—during and after a severe recession—it is increasingly difficult for young people to both find a job as a new entrant, especially as a consequence of hiring freezes, and to remain employed, since they are more likely to be laid off than workers with more seniority. As a result, youth unemployment rates are more sensitive to the business cycle than adult ones.[36]

Choudhry et al.[37] produced an econometric investigation for a large set of countries showing that (i) the impact of financial crises on youth unemployment rates is statistically significant and robust (although seeming more significant for high-income countries), (ii) adverse effects last up to five years after the onset of the crisis (though the most adverse effects are found in the second and the third year following the downturn).

---

[32] Verick, S. 2009. "Who Is Hit Hardest during a Financial Crisis? The Vulnerability of Young Men and Women to Unemployment in an Economic Downturn," IZA Discussion Papers No. 4359. Bonn: IZA.

[33] For an empirical investigation which compares the different impact on regional youth unemployment rates of two major Russian crises, see Demidova, O., and Signorelli, M. 2011. "The Impact of Crises on Youth Unemployment of Russian Regions: An Empirical Analysis," *China-USA Business Review*, no 6.

[34] Unlike the previous crises, the last one has affected mostly young men, mainly because of their high proportion in heavily impacted sectors.

[35] Verick, S. 2009. "Who Is Hit Hardest during a Financial Crisis? The Vulnerability of Young Men and Women to Unemployment in an Economic Downturn," IZA Discussion Papers, n. 4359. Bonn: IZA.

[36] OECD. 2008. *OECD Employment Outlook 2008*. Paris: OECD.

[37] Choudhry, M. T., E. Marelli, and M. Signorelli. "Financial Crises and Labour Market Performance," International Atlantic Economic Conference, Prague, Czech Republic, 24-27 March 2010.

Arpaia and Curci[38] presented a comprehensive analysis of the labour market adjustments in EU-27 after the 2008-09 recession (in terms of employment, unemployment, hours worked and remuneration) and they also highlighted that workers with weak contractual arrangements and lower qualifications and expertise have borne the brunt of the "great recession", with this aspect that has caused youth unemployment rates to increase considerably. In addition, in order to assess whether the rise in unemployment is due to an increase in job separations or to a decline in the job-finding rate, they also provided evidence of an asymmetric response over the cycle, with recession being characterised by higher rates of job destruction than job creation in the following recoveries (especially due to the interaction between wage dynamics and labour hoarding practices).

In considering the complex relationship between unemployment, employment and participation rates,[39] it should also be noted that—especially during and after a crisis—the increase in youth and total unemployment rates can undervalue the negative impact when the possible decrease, in both youth and overall participation rates, is not given attention. This phenomenon is known as "discouragement effect" (usually more relevant among women) that produces a reduction of the actual labour force and—especially in the case of young people—can partly lead to an increase in the duration of "education".[40]

3. Youth Unemployment Trends Before and After the Last Crisis

In financial terms, the last crisis began at the end of 2007 and the most significant consequences on markets—also due to Lehman Brothers' default—were reported in September 2008, when the downturn effectively took place (the most significant fall in production took place in the first

---

[38] Arpaia, A., and N. Curci. 2010. *The EU Labour Market Behaviour During the Great Recession.* Directorate General for Economic and Financial Affairs. Brussels: European Commission.

[39] See, for example, Perugini, C., and M. Signorelli. 2007. "Labour Market Performance Differentials and Dynamics in EU-15 Countries and Regions," *European Journal of Comparative Economics*, No. 2.

[40] We recall that, according to the ILO definition (but similar definitions are adopted by other national and international institutions), the unemployed are the persons who—during a reference period—are without work, but are currently available for work and, in addition, are actively seeking employment.

half of 2009) and led to increasing unemployment rates over the course of 2009, and—in some countries—2010.

In fact, the real effects (on production, income, and so on) of financial crises are always lagged. In the years to come, and similarly to past crises,[41] a certain degree of persistence of both overall and young unemployment is likely to be reported, due to so-called "hysteresis", that is an upward shift in structural unemployment.

The overall unemployment rate (UR) increased worldwide by about 0.6% (from 5.8% in 2008 to 6.4% in 2009), meaning that the number of those who are unemployed is equal to almost 23 million people. Such increase has been of a general nature, although with a number of differences arising among the various regions of the world. The developed economies, the EU and the other countries of Europe reported the highest level of UR with a further increase expected in 2010.[42]

The impact of the crisis has been heterogeneous not only across countries, but also between the various segments of the labour market. With regard to young workers, it should be noted that a decrease in labour demand implies fewer job openings, therefore young people—usually new entrants with no work experience—are particularly affected. Moreover, job destruction is also likely to disproportionately affect young workers, because the tendency to hire them on a temporary basis is more pronounced.

According to the ILO,[43] youth unemployment rates (15-24) increased from 12.1% in 2008 to 13.0% in 2009 (Tables 1-1 and 1-2), corresponding to an increase of more than 6 million people, with significant differences across world regions. However, the impact on youth, as evidenced by the ILO,[44] is well beyond the unemployment indicator. Further evidence is presented in Appendix (Table 1-6).

---

[41] Choudhry, M. T., E. Marelli, and M. Signorelli. 2011. "Youth Unemployment and the Impact of Financial Crises," preprint, submitted to International Journal of Manpower.

[42] See for example ILO. 2010a. *Global Employment Trends*. Geneva: ILO, and ILO. 2010b. *Global Employment Trends for Youth. Special Issue on the Impact of Global Economic Crisis on Youth*. Geneva: ILO.

[43] ILO. 2010b. *Global Employment Trends for Youth. Special Issue on the Impact of Global Economic Crisis on Youth*. Geneva: ILO.

[44] Ibid.

Table 1-1.Youth Unemployment Rate, by Sex and Region, 1998, 2008 and 2009 (percentage rates)

	Total			Male			Female		
	1998	2008	2009	1998	2008	2009	1998	2008	2009
World	12.4	12.1	13.0	12.3	11.9	12.9	12.6	12.3	13.2
Developed Economies & EU	14.0	13.1	17.7	14.1	13.8	19.5	13.9	12.2	15.6
Central and South-Eastern Europe (non-EU) & CIS	23.0	17.3	20.8	22.5	16.8	20.6	23.7	17.9	21.1
East Asia	9.1	8.6	8.9	10.6	10.0	10.3	7.6	7.2	7.4
South-East Asia & the Pacific	12.2	14.5	14.7	12.1	13.9	14.0	12.4	15.2	15.7
South Asia	8.9	10.0	10.3	8.9	9.7	10.1	8.9	10.6	10.9
Latin America & the Caribbean	15.6	14.3	16.1	12.9	11.7	13.2	20.1	18.2	20.4
Middle East	22.8	23.3	23.4	20.6	20.3	20.4	29.1	30.8	30.9
North Africa	26.5	23.3	23.7	23.7	20.2	20.3	32.6	30.3	31.7
Sub-Saharan Africa	13.5	11.9	11.9	12.7	11.5	11.6	14.5	12.3	12.4

Source: ILO (2010b).

Table 1-2. Total (15+) and Youth (15-24) Unemployment and Unemployment Rates

	2007	2008	2009	2010p	2011p
Annual real GDP growth (%)	5.2	3.0	-0.6	4.2	4.3
Total unemployment (millions)	177.8	184.0	206.7	209.0	204.9
Total unemployment rate (%)	5.7	5.8	6.4	6.4	6.2
Youth unemployment (millions)	72.9	74.1	80.7	81.2	78.5
Youth unemployment rate (%)	11.9	12.1	13.0	13.1	12.7

Source: ILO (2010b); ILO, Trend Econometric Models, April 2010; IMF, World Economic Outlook, April 2010. p = projection.

The impact of the crisis on the youth UR is now discussed with reference to EU data. First of all, it is useful to point out that, from the third quarter 2008 to the third quarter 2010, considerable and different increases in total unemployment rates took place within EU-27 countries (Table 1-3). Total UR increased in EU-27 to 9.4% in the third quarter 2010 with respect to 6.9% in the third quarter 2008, with the final level being similar to the one reported in the US (9.7%).[45] Surprisingly, Germany reported the most significant decrease (from 7.2% to 6.8%), followed by Luxembourg (from 5.5% to 3.9%), Austria (from 3.8% to 4.5%), Belgium (from 7.8% to 8.7%) and Italy (from 6.2% to 7.7%), while the highest increases were recorded in Latvia (from 7.5% to 18.2%), Estonia (from 6.3% to 15.7%), Spain (from 11.4% to 19.9%), Ireland (from 6.9% to 14.0%), Greece (from 7.3% to 12.6%) and Slovakia (from 8.9% to 14.2%).

In the same period, youth UR (15-24) increased from 15.7% to 20.5% in EU-27, with extremely high rates in the last period in Spain (40.7%), Lithuania (35.5%), Slovakia (34.3), Greece (32.5%) and Latvia (32.4%).

---

[45] These data refer to March 2010. In 2011, however, unemployment rates decreased below 9% in US.

Table 1-3. Unemployment Rates (total and youth) (third quarter) 2008 versus (third quarter) 2010

	Total UR (%)			Youth UR (%)	
	2008 (third quarter)	2010 (third quarter)		2008 (third quarter)	2010 (third quarter)
Belgium	7.8	8.7		22.7	22.5
Germany	7.2	6.8		11.1	10.3
Ireland	6.9	14.0		15.1	27.7
Greece	7.3	12.6		21.3	32.5
Spain	11.4	19.9		24.2	40.7
France	7.3	9.1		18.0	22.5
Italy	6.2	7.7		19.5	24.7
Cyprus	3.7	5.9		8.4	13.0
Luxembourg	5.5	3.9		23.0	12.5
Malta	5.8	6.9		11.2	10.0
Netherlands	2.4	4.3		4.9	8.3
Austria	3.8	4.5		8.2	9.6
Portugal	8.2	11.5		17.1	23.4
Slovenia	4.2	7.2		9.1	13.0
Slovakia	8.9	14.2		19.4	34.3
Finland	5.6	7.4		11.2	14.2
Euro area	7.3	9.8		15.5	20.0
Bulgaria	5.2	9.6		11.4	21.4
Czech Rep.	4.3	7.1		10.3	18.4
Denmark	3.4	7.4		8.7	14.8
Estonia	6.3	15.7		14.7	28.0
Latvia	7.5	18.2		12.2	32.4
Lithuania	6.0	18.0		15.0	35.5
Hungary	7.8	10.9		20.8	26.7
Poland	6.7	9.2		16.1	23.4
Romania	5.7	7.2		19.2	22.9
Sweden	5.7	7.9		16.2	20.9
U.K.	6.1	8.0		16.6	19.9
EU-27	6.9	9.4		15.7	20.5
US	6.2*	9.7***		13.4*	18.8***
Japan	4.0*	4.8**		-	-

Source: Eurostat, online database (March 7, 2011), for EU-27 countries and aggregates; Eurostat (April 30, 2010) for US and Japan [* September 2008; ** February 2010; *** March 2010].

At this point, it would be interesting to discuss the impact of the crisis on youth unemployment in the EU countries resulting from the structural problems that affect young people, that is particularly significant in some countries. To this end, data over a longer period are needed. Table 1-4 shows the unemployment rate of young people (15-24 years) in the EU-27 countries, for the 1998-2009 period.[46] For the EU-27 aggregate, indicators reveal a steady situation until 2005, then an improvement in employment prospects was reported in 2006-07—prior to the global crisis—and a rise in 2009 (19.6%, the highest level of all decades).

Higher than average figures are shown by different groups of countries: (i) some Mediterranean countries (Spain, Italy, Greece) plus France and Belgium; (ii) many Nordic countries (Sweden, Finland, the Baltic states); (iii) some NMS (Poland, Hungary, Slovakia); on the other hand, in Romania and Bulgaria the situation improved over time[47] (and now the two countries are close to or below the EU average). The crisis has caused a deep worsening—from 2008 to 2009—in the Baltic states, in Spain and Greece, in Hungary and Slovakia, but also in Sweden, Finland, France and Italy. The pattern further deteriorated in 2010.[48]

A possible question that now arises is whether the increase in youth unemployment rates is the result of a period of economic instability—as shown by the total unemployment rates—or a negative trend concerning young people. Many studies[49] have argued that the most vulnerable segments of the labour market include young people, old workers, vulnerable employees in general and (in many world regions) women.

---

[46] Unfortunately, data for the whole year (2010) are still not available (and quarterly data are highly unstable).

[47] Also in the Baltic States, the situation had improved in the years preceding the crisis, then worsening sharply; conversely, youth unemployment in Sweden was getting worse since the mid decade.

[48] For example, in Italy it was equal to 25.3% for 2009 on average, but it reached almost 30% at the end of 2010 and again at the beginning of 2011.

[49] See for instance ILO. 2010a. *Global Employment Trends*. Geneva: ILO, and ILO. 2010b. *Global Employment Trends for Youth. Special Issue on the Impact of Global Economic Crisis on Youth*. Geneva: ILO.

Table 1-4. Unemployment Rate of Young People (15-24 years) (%)

	1998	1999	2000	2001	2002	2003	2004	2005	2006	2007	2008	2009
Belgium	**22.1**	**21**	16.7	16.8	17.7	21.8	21.2	21.5	**20.5**	**18.8**	**18**	**21.9**
Bulgaria		17.7	**33.7**	**38.8**	**37**	**28.2**	**25.8**	**22.3**	**19.5**	15.1	12.7	16.2
Czech Republic	12.8		**17.8**	17.3	16.9	**18.6**	**21**	**19.2**	**17.5**	10.7	9.9	16.6
Denmark	7.3	9.1	6.2	8.3	7.4	9.2	8.2	8.6	7.7	7.9	7.6	11.2
Germany	9.1	8.1	7.5	7.7	9.1	9.8	11.9	14.2	12.8	11.1	9.9	10.4
Estonia			24.4	**23.2**	**17.6**	**20.6**	**21.7**	15.9	12	10	12	**27.5**
Ireland	11.3	8.5	6.7	7.2	8.4	8.7	8.7	8.6	8.6	8.9	13.3	**24.4**
Greece	**29.9**	**31.5**	**29.1**	**28**	**26.8**	**26.8**	**26.9**	**26**	**25.2**	**22.9**	**22.1**	**25.8**
Spain	**33.1**	**27.3**	24.3	**23.2**	24.2	**24.6**	**23.9**	**19.7**	**17.9**	**18.2**	**24.6**	**37.8**
France	**25.1**	**22.9**	**19.6**	**18.9**	**19.3**	**19.2**	**20.6**	**21.1**	**22.1**	**19.6**	**19.1**	**23.3**
Italy	**29.9**	**28.7**	**27**	**24.1**	**23.1**	**23.7**	**23.5**	**23.9**	**21.7**	**20.3**	**21.2**	**25.3**
Cyprus			10.1	8.1	8.1	8.9	10.5	13	10.5	10.1	8.8	13.8
Latria	**26.8**	**23.6**	**21.4**	**22.9**	**22**	**18**	**18.1**	**13.6**	12.2	10.7	13.1	**33.6**
Lithuania	**25.5**	**26.4**	**30.6**	**30.9**	**22.4**	**25.1**	**22.7**	15.7	9.8	8.2	13.4	**29.2**
Luxembourg	6.9	6.9	6.6	6.2	7	11.2	16.4	14.3	15.8	**15.6**	**17.3**	17.5
Hungary	15	12.6	12.4	11.3	12.7	13.4	15.5	**19.4**	**19.1**	**18**	**19.9**	**26.5**
Malta			13.7	**18.8**	17.1	17.2	16.8	16.2	16.5	13.8	11.9	14.3
Netherlands	7.6	6.8	5.7	4.5	5	6.3	8	8.2	6.6	5.9	5.3	6.6
Austria	6.4	5.4	5.3	5.8	6.7	8.1	9.7	10.3	9.1	8.7	8	10

Youth Unemployment Before and After the Crisis

Poland	**22.5**	**30.1**	**35.1**	**39.5**	**42.5**	**41.9**	**39.6**	**36.9**	**29.8**	**21.7**	**17.3**	**20.6**
Portugal	10.4	8.8	8.6	9.4	11.6	14.5	15.3	16.1	16.3	**16.6**	**16.4**	**20**
Romania		**20.4**	**20**	**18.6**	**23.2**	**19.6**	**21.9**	**20.2**	**21.4**	**20.1**	**18.6**	**20.8**
Slovenia	17.8	17.6	16.3	**17.8**	16.5	17.3	16.1	15.9	13.9	10.1	10.4	13.6
Slovakia	**25.1**	**33.8**	**36.9**	**39.2**	**37.7**	**33.4**	**33.1**	**30.1**	**26.6**	**20.3**	**19**	**27.3**
Finland	**23.5**	**21.4**	**21.4**	**19.8**	**21**	**21.8**	**20.7**	**20.1**	**18.7**	**16.5**	**16.5**	**21.5**
Sweden	16.1	12.3	10.5	14.9	16.3	17.3	**20.4**	**22.5**	**21.5**	**19.1**	**20**	**25**
United Kingdom	13.1	12.7	12.2	11.7	12	12.2	12.1	12.8	14	14.3	15	19.1
EU (27 countries)	*18.4*	*17.8*	*17.3*	*17.3*	*18*	*18.1*	*18.5*	*18.3*	*17.1*	*15.3*	*15.4*	*19.6*

Source: Eurostat on-line data base.
Note: *EU-25 for 1998 and 1999. In bold the values higher than the EU average.

Table 1-5 shows the ratio between the youth unemployment rates (15-24 years) and the total unemployment rates (all ages) for the EU-27 countries. A first consideration is that—for the EU as a whole—despite the development of the European Employment Strategy and Lisbon's Agenda goals, there has been no improvement of employment prospects for young people over the last decade.

The ratio has been pretty close to 2, slightly deteriorating even before the crisis. The real figure is probably higher, because the "discouraged worker effect" is more pronounced among young people, who can continue studying or simply live with their families (meaning that they are less motivated to find a job).

If figures for each countries are examined, what is striking is that higher-than-average ratios can be found for the same countries with higher-than-average unemployment rates (the bold cells in Table 1-5 roughly correspond to the bold cells in Table 1-4). Spain and by the Baltic States represent the clearest exceptions, as here the ratios are close to the European average (which is around 2) with the highest levels of unemployment—as emphasised before— that are also a consequence of the dramatic labour market situation. On the other hand, the labour market exhibits specific problems concerning young people—with youth/total ratios around or close to 3—in Italy, Greece, some NMS, in the Belgium-Luxembourg-France zone and, rather surprisingly, also in Sweden and the UK.

Austria, Denmark, Germany, and the Netherlands have been able to cope with the labour market problems more effectively and, in general terms, to keep the unemployment levels under control. Is this the revenge of the flexicurity model or, from a different viewpoint, a successful attempt to make some labour market institutions more flexible, also safeguarding the basic elements of the pre-existing "social model" (exemplified by the past German experience)? The German case, also favoured by the "dual" educational system, high R&D investment and a competitive manufacturing sector, shows that it is possible—in a cooperative and participative system of industrial relations—to benefit from internal flexibility measures (in terms, say, of working time) and also wage flexibility, to safeguard both employment levels (during recessions) and also human capital investments, thus creating the conditions for prompt economic recovery.

Youth Unemployment Before and After the Crisis

Table 1-5. Ratios of Youth Unemployment Rate vs. Total Unemployment rate

	1998	1999	2000	2001	2002	2003	2004	2005	2006	2007	2008	2009
Belgium	2.4	2.5	2.4	2.5	2.4	2.7	2.5	2.5	2.5	2.5	2.6	2.8
Bulgaria			2.1	2.0	2.0	2.1	2.1	2.2	2.2	2.2	2.3	2.4
Czech Republic	2.0	2.1	2.0	2.2	2.3	2.4	2.5	2.4	2.4	2.0	2.3	2.5
Denmark	1.5	1.8	1.4	1.8	1.6	1.7	1.5	1.8	2.0	2.1	2.3	1.9
Germany	1.0	1.0	1.0	1.0	1.1	1.1	1.2	1.3	1.3	1.3	1.4	1.4
Estonia			1.8	1.8	1.7	2.1	2.2	2.0	2.0	2.1	2.2	2.0
Ireland	1.5	1.5	1.6	1.8	1.9	1.9	1.9	2.0	1.9	1.9	2.1	2.1
Greece	2.8	2.6	2.6	2.6	2.6	2.8	2.6	2.6	2.8	2.8	2.9	2.7
Spain	2.2	2.2	2.2	2.3	2.2	2.2	2.3	2.1	2.1	2.2	2.2	2.1
France	2.3	2.2	2.2	2.3	2.2	2.1	2.2	2.3	2.4	2.3	2.4	2.5
Italy	2.6	2.6	2.7	2.6	2.7	2.8	2.9	3.1	3.2	3.3	3.2	3.2
Cyprus			2.1	2.1	2.3	2.2	2.2	2.5	2.3	2.5	2.4	2.6
Latvia	1.9	1.7	1.6	1.8	1.8	1.7	1.7	1.5	1.8	1.8	1.7	2.0
Lithuania	1.9	1.9	1.9	1.9	1.7	2.0	2.0	1.9	1.8	1.9	2.3	2.1
Luxembourg	2.6	2.9	3.0	3.3	2.7	2.9	3.3	3.1	3.4	3.7	3.5	3.2
Hungary	1.8	1.8	1.9	2.0	2.2	2.3	2.5	2.7	2.5	2.4	2.6	2.7
Malta			2.0	2.5	2.3	2.3	2.3	2.3	2.3	2.2	2.0	2.1
Netherlands	2.0	2.1	2.0	2.0	1.8	1.7	1.7	1.7	1.7	1.8	1.9	1.9
Austria	1.4	1.4	1.5	1.6	1.6	1.9	2.0	2.0	1.9	2.0	2.1	2.1

Poland	**2.2**	**2.2**	**2.2**	**2.2**	**2.1**	**2.1**	**2.1**	**2.1**	**2.1**	**2.3**	**2.4**	**2.5**
Portugal	**2.1**	2.0	2.2	**2.3**	**2.3**	**2.3**	2.1	2.1	2.0	2.1	2.1
Romania		**2.9**	**2.7**	**2.7**	**2.7**	**2.8**	**2.7**	**2.8**	**2.9**	**3.1**	**3.2**	**3.0**
Slovenia	**2.4**	**2.4**	**2.4**	**2.9**	**2.6**	**2.6**	**2.6**	**2.4**	**2.3**	2.1	**2.4**	**2.3**
Slovakia	2.0	2.1	2.0	2.0	2.0	1.9	1.8	1.8	2.0	1.8	2.0	**2.3**
Finland	**2.1**	**2.1**	**2.2**	**2.2**	**2.3**	**2.4**	**2.4**	**2.4**	**2.4**	**2.4**	**2.6**	**2.6**
Sweden	2.0	1.8	1.9	**2.6**	**2.7**	**2.6**	**2.8**	**3.0**	**3.1**	**3.1**	**3.2**	**3.0**
United Kingdom	**2.1**	**2.2**	**2.3**	**2.3**	**2.4**	**2.4**	**2.6**	**2.7**	**2.6**	**2.7**	**2.7**	**2.5**
EU27	2.0	2.0	2.0	2.0	2.0	2.0	2.0	2.1	2.1	2.2	2.2	2.2

Source: Eurostat on-line data base

Note: *EU-25 for 1998 and 1999. In bold the ratios higher than the EU average.

4. Conclusions

In the empirical section of this paper, we have seen that youth unemployment is a long-lasting issue, since youth UR has been persistently higher than total UR—at least three times higher in some countries (probably underestimating the real figures because of the "discouraged worker" and other effects)—even in times of economic stability, e.g. in the last decade before the global crisis. Therefore, notwithstanding the goals set up in the Lisbon Agenda, persistent effects have been reported within the EU, although with some exceptions (e.g. Germany). The impact of the crisis on labour markets has been delayed, yet persisting. The deepest impact affected the weakest segments of the labour force, especially young people. This was due not only to unstable jobs, usually concerning young workers, but also to the consequences of "labour hoarding" phenomena regarding adult workers in a situation of low labour demand.

Public policies in response to the crisis have generally adopted two key approaches: (i) providing huge fiscal incentives to sustain, consumption, aggregate demand and production; (ii) adopting "passive" labour market policies, to financially support the unemployed (or workers being at risk to be dismissed).

As for the first approach, the timing of exit strategies will be crucial (see also World Bank 2010), although a rapid reduction in public deficit is required by the policy adopted by many EU countries in fiscal terms (that has increased the risks arising from sovereign debts in 2010).

With regard to the second point, effective improvements in active labour market policies should accompany the adoption of passive measures, in order to help the weakest segments of the labour market—particularly young people—usually the most affected by the crisis. However, passive policies are not always adequate: most young workers are not fully covered by unemployment insurance schemes (because of their precarious and temporary jobs), with unemployment benefits that are—in many countries—totally lacking for new entrants in the labour market.

Appropriate "active" policies are regarded as a matter of urgency, especially in countries where youth performance was awful even before the crisis. In addition to reforms in the labour market institutions and industrial relations system aiming—in the context of flexible labour markets and cooperative industrial relations—at ensuring more certain and stable "employment paths" for young people and overcoming the "dualism" in labour market (that is typical of some countries, especially in

Southern Europe), more specific measures are needed in other spheres. In particular, the setting up of effective STWT institutions and placement services, and the provision of more adequate training should be given priority; as for the educational system, in some countries, a gradual shift from a "sequential and rigid" system towards the "dual and flexible" system seems appropriate. Otherwise, the NEET generation will continue to expand, with tremendous economic and social consequences.

References

Abowd, J., F. Kramarz, T. Lemieux, and D. Margolis. 2000. "Minimum Wages and Youth Employment in France and the United States," in *Youth Employment and Joblessness in Advanced Countries*, 427-472. *NBER Chapters 6813*. National Bureau of Economic Research, Inc.

Arpaia, A., and N. Curci. 2010. *The EU Labour Market Behaviour During the Great Recession*. Directorate General for Economic and Financial Affairs. Brussels: European Commission.

Bassanini, A., and R. Duval. 2006. "The Determinants of Unemployment across OECD Countries: Reassessing the Role of Policies and Institutions," *OECD Economic Studies*, No. 42:7–86.

Bell, D. N. F., and D. G. Blanchflower. 2009. "What Should Be Done about Rising Unemployment in the UK," Bonn: IZA Discussion Paper, No. 4040.

Belot, M., and J. C. Van Ours. 2001. "Unemployment and Labor Market Institutions: An Empirical Analysis," *Journal of Japanese and International Economics*, No. 15:403-418.

Blanchflower D. G., and R. Freeman. 2000. *Youth Employment and Joblessness*. Chicago: University of Chicago Press.

Brunello, G., P. Garibaldi, and E. Wasmer. 2007. *Education and training in Europe*. New York: Oxford University Press.

Carmeci, L., and L. Mauro. 2003. "Long-run Growth and Investment in Education: Does Unemployment Matter?" *Journal of Macroeconomics*, No. 25:123-137.

Caroleo, F. E., and F. Pastore. 2007. "The Youth Experience Gap: Explaining Differences across EU Countries," Università di Perugia, Quaderni del Dipartimento di Economia, Finanza e Statistica 41.

—. 2009. "Le cause del(l'in)successo lavorativo dei giovani," *Economia & Lavoro* 3:107-31.

Checchi, D. 2006. *The Economics of Education*. Cambridge: Cambridge University Press.

Choudhry, M. T., E. Marelli, and M. Signorelli. "Financial Crises and Labour Market Performance," International Atlantic Economic Conference, Prague, Czech Republic, 24-27 March 2010.

Choudhry, M. T., E. Marelli, and M. Signorelli. 2011. "Youth Unemployment and the Impact of Financial Crises," preprint, submitted to International Journal of Manpower.

Clark, K. B., and L. H. Summers. 1982. "The Dynamics of Youth Unemployment," in *The Youth Labour Market Problem: Its Nature, Causes and Consequences,* eds. Freeman, R., and D. Wise, (Chicago: University of Chicago Press).

Cockx, B., and M. Picchio. 2009. "Are Short-Lived Jobs Stepping Stones to Long-Lasting Jobs?" IZA Discussion Paper No. 4004. Bonn: IZA.

Demidova, O., and M. Signorelli. 2011. "The Impact of Crises on Youth Unemployment of Russian Regions: An Empirical Analysis," *China-USA Business Review*, no 6.

Elhorst, J. P., and A. S. Zeilstra. 2007. "Labor Force Participation Rates at Regional and National Levels of the European Union: An Integrated Analysis," *Papers in Regional Science* 86, No. 4:525-549.

European Commission. 2008. *Employment in Europe 2008.* Brussels: European Commission.

Freeman, R., and D. Wise, eds. 1982. *The Youth Labour Market Problem: Its Nature, Causes and Consequences.* Chicago: University of Chicago Press.

Furceri, D., and A. Mourougane. 2009. "The Effect of Financial Crises on Potential Output: New Empirical Evidence from OECD Countries," OECD Economics Department Working Paper No. 699. Paris: OECD.

Heckman, J. J., and G. J. Borjas. 1980. "Does Unemployment Cause Future Unemployment? Definitions, Questions and Answers from a Continuous Time Model of Heterogeneity and State Dependence," *Econ* 47 No. 187: 247-283.

International Labour Organization. 2009. "KILM9—Youth Unemployment" in *Key Indicators of the Labour Market* (KILM), Sixth Edition, Geneva: ILO.

—. 2010a. *Global Employment Trends.* Geneva: ILO.

—. 2010b. *Global Employment Trends for Youth. Special Issue on the Impact of Global Economic Crisis on Youth.* Geneva: ILO.

International Monetary Fund. 2009. *World Economic Outlook. Sustaining the Recovery.* Washington: IMF.

Jacobsen, J. P. 1999. "Labor Force Participation," *The Quarterly Review of Economics and Finance* 39, No. 5:597-610.

Kolev, A., and C. Saget. 2005. "Understanding Youth Labour Market Disadvantage: Evidence from South-east Europe," *International Labour Review* 144, No. 2: 161-187

Lefresne, F. 2003. "Les jeunes et l'emploi," *Collection Repères* Paris: La Découverte.

Marelli, E., and M. Signorelli, eds. 2010. *Economic Growth and Structural Features of Transition*. London and New York: Palgrave Macmillan.

Neumark, D., and W. Wascher. 1999. "A Cross-national Analysis of the Effects of Minimum Wages on Youth Employment," NBER Working Paper 7299.

—. 2004. "Minimum Wages, Labour Market Institutions, and Youth Employment: a Cross-national Analysis," *Industrial and Labour Relations Review* 57, No. 2: 223-247.

Nickell, S. 1998. "Unemployment: Questions and Some Answers," *The Economic Journal*, No. 108: 802-816.

Nunziata, L., and S. Staffolani. 2007. "Short-term Contracts Regulations and Dynamic Labour Demand: Theory and Evidence," *Scottish Journal of Poltical Economy* 54, No. 1: 72-104.

O'Higgins, N. 1997. "The Challenge of Youth Unemployment," Employment and Training Papers No. 7. Geneva: ILO.

—. 2005. "Trends in the Youth Labour Market in Developing and Transition Countries," Labor and Demography WP 0507002.

OECD. 1994. *The OECD Jobs Study*. Paris: OECD.

—. 2005. *Education at Glance*. Paris: OECD.

—. 2006. *Employment Outlook.* Paris: OECD.

—. 2008. *OECD Employment Outlook 2008*. Paris: OECD.

Okun, A. M. 1962. "Potential GNP: Its Measurement and Significance," in *Proceedings of the Business and Economic Statistics Section* (Washington, D.C: American Statistical Association), 98-103.

Perugini, C., and M. Signorelli. 2007. "Labour Market Performance Differentials and Dynamics in EU-15 Countries and Regions," *European Journal of Comparative Economics*, No. 2.

—. 2010a. "Youth Labour Market Performance in European Regions," *Economic Change and Restructuring*, No. 2.

—. 2010b. "Youth Unemployment in Transition Countries and Regions," in *Economic Growth and Structural Features of Transition*, eds. Marelli, E., and M. Signorelli, (London and New York: Palgrave Macmillan).

Quintini, G., and T. Manfredi. 2009. "Going Separate Ways? School-to-Work Transitions in the United States and Europe," OECD Social, Employment and Migration Working Paper No. 90. Paris: OECD.

Quintini, G., J. P Martin, and S. Marti. 2007. "The changing nature of the school-to-work Transition Process in OECD Countries," IZA Discussion Paper No. 2582. Bonn: IZA.

Rees, A. 1986. "An Essay on Youth Joblessness," *Journal of Economic Literature* 24, No. 2: 613-628.

Rodrìguez-Pose, A. "Human Capital and Regional Disparities in the EU," Joint Conference of the EC and the EIB on Human capital, Employment, Productivity and Growth, Brussels, Belgium, September 2003.

Ryan, P. 2001. "The School-to-work Transition: a Cross-national Perspective," *Journal of Economic Literature* 39, No. 1: 34-92.

Scarpetta, S., A. Sonnet, and T. Manfredi. 2010. "Rising Youth Unemployment During the Crisis: How to Prevent negative Long-Term Consequences on a Generation?" OECD Social, Employment and Migration Working Papers, No. 6. Paris: OECD.

Signorelli, M. 1997. "Uncertainty, Flexibility Gap and Labour Demand in the Italian Economy," *Labour*, No. 1: 141-175.

—. 2005. "Growth and Employment: Comparative Performance, Convergences and Co-movements," Economic Department Working Paper, No. 8. Perugia: University of Perugia.

—. 2008. "Employment and Unemployment in a Multilevel Regional Perspective," in *Mediterranean Europe*, ed. Petricioli, M., (Brussels: P.I.E. Peter Lang).

Sperl, L. 2009. "The Crisis and its Consequences for Women," *Development and Transition*, No. 13, United Nation Programme and London School of Economics and Political Science.

Topel, R. H., and M. P. Ward. 1992. "Job Mobility and the Careers of Young Men," *Quarterly Journal of Economics* 107, No. 2: 439-479.

Verick, S. 2009. "Who Is Hit Hardest during a Financial Crisis? The Vulnerability of Young Men and Women to Unemployment in an Economic Downturn," IZA Discussion Papers, No. 4359. Bonn: IZA.

World Bank. 2010. *Global Economic Prospects. 2010 Foresees Long Road to Economic Recovery*. Washington: The World Bank.

Appendix

Table 1-6. Global Labour Market Indicators for Youth (15-24) and Total (15+), 1998, 2008 and 2009

	Total			Male			Female		
Youth (15-24)	1998	2008	2009	1998	2008	2009	1998	2008	2009
Labour force (millions)	577.8	614.4	619.2	340.6	364.7	368.5	237.2	249.7	250.6
Employment (millions)	505.9	540.4	538.5	298.6	321.3	321.0	207.2	219.1	217.5
Unemployment (millions)	71.9	74.1	80.7	41.9	43.4	47.5	30.0	30.6	33.2
Labour force participation rate (%)	54.7	50.8	51.0	63.2	58.8	59.1	45.9	42.5	42.5
Employment-to-population rate (%)	47.9	44.7	44.4	55.4	51.8	51.4	40.1	37.3	36.9
Unemployment rate (%)	12.4	12.1	13.0	12.3	11.9	12.9	12.6	12.3	13.2
Total (15+)									
Labour force (millions)	2689.0	3166.7	3212.9	1624.3	1898.7	1928.1	1064.7	1268.0	1284.8
Employment (millions)	2517.5	2982.7	3006.2	1525.3	1791.7	1807.8	992.2	1191.0	1198.4
Unemployment (millions)	171.5	184.0	206.7	99.0	107.0	120.2	72.5	77.0	86.4
Labour force participation rate (%)	65.5	64.7	64.7	79.3	77.7	77.7	51.8	51.7	51.6
Employment-to-population rate (%)	61.3	61.0	60.5	74.5	73.3	72.9	48.2	48.6	48.2
Unemployment rate (%)	6.4	5.8	6.4	6.1	5.6	6.2	6.8	6.1	6.7

Source: ILO (2010b).

YOUNG WORKERS AND THE RECESSION

BARBARA GRANDI AND MALCOLM SARGEANT

1. Introduction

The purpose of this paper is to consider some of the issues concerning employment and unemployment of young workers and to examine the effect of the current recession in this regard. We are also concerned with the regulatory measures that governments take in order to reduce unemployment amongst such workers. Apart from a consideration of the subject at EU level, we also provided for comparative purposes the situation in Italy and the United Kingdom (UK).

There are, of course, problems in such an analysis, especially when comparing how young people are treated in the two countries. Some of the differences can be explained in cultural terms. In Italy, the employment rate for the population aged 15-64 is 58.7%, compared to 71.5% in the UK.[1] The employment rate for those aged 15-24 is 24.4%, again compared to the figure of 52.4% in the UK. These differences are not to be explained just by bald statistics. They reflect perhaps a difference in attitude towards family and the position of young people. This is further emphasised when one looks at the differences in employment rates by gender. In Italy, there is a large difference between the employment rates for males aged 15-24 (29.1%) and females of the same age group (19.4%). In the UK, the difference is much less pronounced with 53.8% for males and 51% for females. Unemployment rates amongst young people show a really interesting difference between the two countries. In Italy, a much higher percentage of young women are unemployed (25.7%) than young men (18.9%). In the UK, this pattern is reversed with unemployment amongst young men being much higher (17%) than young women (12.9%).

In addition, we know that there are other important issues such as, firstly, the geographical divide between the north and south of Italy and that national averages may hide the disparities in figures between the two

---

[1] European Commission. 2009. *Employment in Europe 2009*. Brussels: European Commission.

parts of the country (see below for further discussion of this); secondly, the size of the informal economy is also an important issue. Although such figures must be unreliable, one estimate puts the size of the informal economy in Italy as being up to 8 times the size of that in the UK.[2] This is not to say that these are not important issues in the United Kingdom also. Unemployment is higher in the north of England, compared to the south, e.g. the proportion of families in which no one is working is 17.8% in the north east, compared to 9.9% in the south east.[3]

In comparing two national systems, it is also important to focus on the definition of young worker. One problem with studying employment amongst young workers is that many of them are deliberately excluded from the labour market, as a result of being in full-time education, or enter it only on a part-time or temporary basis during their studies. Although compulsory schooling terminates at the same age, of 15/16 years, in Italy and the UK the actual numbers that progress into higher education will depend in part on the incentives to stay out of the labour market resulting from government policy. In the UK, one of the major goals of the government elected in 1997 was to increase the proportion of young people who went to university to 50%. This may have been reversed by the current government which has announced plans to charge students up to £9000 per year in fees for attending university.

A second definitional issue concerns age statistics. At what point does a person start and stop being a young worker and not require, perhaps, special measures of assistance. In the UK, for example, there is a statutory national minimum wage (NMW) and the full adult rate is reached at the age of 21 years.[4] Statistics available are for age bands up to the age of 25 years and, of course, connected to this issue is the importance of ensuring that any comparison uses the same approach to age bands in statistics. We propose therefore to accept that young workers are those in full-time employment, or actively seeking employment, between the age of 15 and 25 years.[5] This is also the definition adopted by the ILO in its report on global trends for youth.

---

[2] Vermeylen, G. "Informal Employment in the European Union," paper prepared for WIEGO Workshop on Informal Employment in Developed Countries, Harvard University, November 2008.
[3] Data from the Office for National Statistics (ONS) http://www.statistics.gov.uk/statbase/product.asp?vlnk=15150.
[4] Until October 2010 this age level was 22 years; the NMW is considered further below.
[5] According to ISTAT, the measurement of unemployment rates means including many people who are still investing in improving their own capabilities and skills,

A final factor to be taken into account when considering this issue is that unemployment rates have traditionally been much higher amongst younger workers than the working population in general.[6] Our hypothesis is that this has been accentuated by the current recession as fewer training and development opportunities become available and employers are, perhaps, less willing to invest in inexperienced employees. In this connection, employer's views of young people should also be taken into consideration, and one of the aim of this paper is to discuss the extent to which stereotypical attitudes affect the chances of young people in the employment market.

2. International Perspectives

According to an ILO report,[7] countries in general proceed through three stages of demographic shifts. Firstly, the proportion of the young in the population rises; then the proportion of young people declines and that of the older population increases modestly and most importantly, the proportion of adults (aged 25-64 years) increases sharply; finally, in the third stage, the proportion of adults falls while that of older people rises. In all regions of the world (but not in all countries) the ILO reports that the proportion of young people in the population is decreasing and concludes that this is "a clear sign that the developing world is nearing the final stage of the demographic transition". The conclusion that one might draw from this is that young workers are likely to be in greater demand as their numbers fall as a proportion of the population. This has not happened, partly because of the increasing numbers of young people in education.

---

thus they are not really looking for a job despite the fact that they match the unemployed position. ISTAT figures include those interviewed who are aged from 15 to 74 having acted at least once in the four weeks before the considered period in order to seek for a job, and who are "available to work" within the two forthcoming weeks.

[6] According to the ILO, in *Global Employment Trends for Youth: Special Issue on the Impact of the Global Economic Crisis on Youth*, "Youth unemployment rates were on a downward trend prior to the economic crisis but were still nearly three times higher than adults. The youth unemployment rate stood at 12.1 per cent in 2008 compared to 5.8 per cent for the overall global unemployment rate and 4.3 per cent for the adult unemployment rate. Compared to adults, youth are almost three times as likely to be unemployed; the ratio of the youth-to-adult unemployment rate was 2.8 in 2008, up from 2.6 in 1998".

[7] International Labour Office. 2010. *Global Employment Trends for Youth: Special Issue on the Impact of the Global Economic Crisis on Youth*. Geneva: ILO.

From a global perspective, youth unemployment appears to have risen during the recession. The ILO reported that, at the end of 2009, there were an estimated 81 million unemployed young people in the world and this was 7.8 million more than in 2007.[8] Youth unemployment "rose sharply during the economic crisis—more sharply than ever before—from 11.9 to 13.0%". It predicted a continued increase in the youth unemployment rate in 2010 to 13.1%, followed by a decline in 2011. The consequences of this are described in the report as follows:

> In developed and some emerging economies, the crisis impact on youth is felt mainly in terms of unemployment and the social hazards associated with joblessness and prolonged inactivity. Numerous studies show how entering labour markets during recession can leave permanent scars on the generation of youth affected and, recently, fears have been expressed regarding a possible crisis legacy of a "lost generation" made up of young people who detach themselves from the labour market altogether.

This report also describes how certain groups of young people are likely, from a global perspective, to find it more difficult to access and remain in the labour market. These groups are young women, the less educated, ethnic minorities and those that come from poorer families. This is an important piece of analysis because it shows the need not to treat young workers as a homogenous group. Within the age group of 15-25 there is the same diversity as in the labour force in general and it is important to take this into account.

3. EU

One of the headline targets from Europe 2020[9] is that, by the year 2020, some 75% of the population aged 20-64 should be employed. This is one of the targets that will help the Community achieve "the three priorities of smart, sustainable and inclusive growth". Two of the seven "flagship initiatives" that are meant to "catalyse progress" towards the achievement of the headline targets are "Youth on the move", which is about enhancing education systems to facilitate the entry of young people into the labour market; and "An agenda for new skills and jobs", whose aim is to modernise the labour market and:

---

[8] European Commission. 2010a. *Communication from the Commission COM(2010) 2020: Europe 2020, A Strategy for Smart, Sustainable and Inclusive Growth.* Brussels: European Commission.
[9] Ibid.

empower people by developing their skills throughout the lifecycle with a view to increase labour participation and better match labour supply and demand, including through labour mobility.

This is not the first time that the EU has set itself grand targets in relation to employment levels. Such objectives were an important aspect of the Lisbon Strategy, which set employment targets[10] and called for an increase in the total employment rate within the EU to 67% by 2005 and 70% by 2010; a 60% employment rate for female workers, and an employment rate of older workers of 50% by 2010. Despite a re-launch in 2005,[11] the Lisbon Strategy failed to achieve its objectives. It was replaced by Europe 2020 that, however, only includes a general commitment to achieving an overall employment rate of 75% by 2020. The new strategy lays down objectives concerning the percentage of people in tertiary education, but there are no specific targets for youth unemployment (or indeed any other age group). This only makes sense if there is an acceptance that such targets could not be met and that in fact there is a limit to how much the EU can influence employment statistics within the Member States.

4. Employment Rates in the EU

Eurostat[12] provided the following figures for the overall employment rate in the EU (Table 1-7). Here are extracted just those figures for a selection of the larger Member States.

---

[10] Further information can be found at http://ec.europa.eu/archives/growthandjobs_2009/.

[11] Barroso J. M., and G. Verheugen. 2005. COM(2005) 24 "Working Together for Growth and Jobs. A New Start for the Lisbon Strategy," *Communication to the spring European Council.*

[12] http://epp.eurostat.ec.europa.eu/tgm/table.do?tab=table&plugin=1&language=en&pcode=t2020_10.

Table 1-7. Total Employment Rate (%)

Place	2000	2001	2002	2003	2004	2005	2006	2007	2008	2009
EU27	66.6	66.9	66.7	67.0	67.4	68.1	69.1	70.0	70.5	69.1
Germany	68.8	69.1	68.8	68.4	68.8	69.9	71.6	73.4	74.6	74.8
France	67.8	68.5	68.7	69.7	69.6	69.4	69.3	69.9	70.4	69.6
Italy	57.4	58.5	59.4	60.0	61.5	61.6	62.5	62.8	63.0	61.7
UK	74.0	74.4	74.5	74.7	75.0	75.2	75.2	75.2	75.2	73.9

It is noticeable that, in all the Member States, the overall employment rate increased until the end of 2008/09. In this year the overall employment rate dropped everywhere except in Germany. The European Commission reported in 2010:[13]

> Overall, young people account for one fifth (21.3%) of the total increase in unemployment since 2008, although youth unemployment as a share of total unemployment decreased slightly from around 25% in 2008 to just below 24% in January 2010.

Further on, the Commission states:

> The marked increase in the youth unemployment rate since spring 2008 has been driven mainly by a very sharp rise in the rate for young men, who account for more than two thirds of the increase in youth unemployment since then.

Thus, unemployment rates for those aged 15-24 years have increased significantly from an already high level during the current recession. In particular, there has been a "sharp" rise in the unemployment rate for young men, much higher than that for young women. As a result, the proportion of 15-24 year olds not in employment, education or training (NEETS) increased to 13% by the first quarter of 2009 compared to the previous year, and this "risks becoming a significant problem as the recession continues".[14]

---

[13] European Commission. 2010b. *EU Employment Situation and Social Outlook, March 2010*. Brussels: European Commission.
[14] European Commission. 2009. *Employment in Europe 2009*. Brussels: European Commission.

5. Italy

Italian statistics concerning the total labour force need to be read with care. There are significant geographical differences within the country when compared to other jurisdictions such as the UK. The informal sector (and informal agreements) plays an important part in the economy of the south. The size of the informal sector has an impact on the effect of any public ruling on the labour market as well as on the respect of any labour rights. It may also have an impact on national employment statistics.

The following figures concerning employment and unemployment rates refer to all types of employment and working activity, thus meaning that self-employment and independent contracting are also included.[15]

The employment rate of the active population (age group 15-64) has slightly reduced during the period 2007-2010, whilst the youngest group dropped from 24.7% to 20.5%. It is clear that it is the youngest generation that has suffered the most in terms of employment from the recession; this might explain why they are sometimes referred to as the "baby loser generation".[16]

---

[15] It is useful to recall that in Italy the "employment rate" concerns the percentage of employed persons as related to the considered overall population, while the "unemployment rate" concerns the percentage of unemployed people (those actively seeking for a job) as related to the so-called "active population" (that refers to the considered overall population but does not include those who are not seeking for any job). While the employment rate gives us the perception of how much the economic system matches the demand of work in general, the unemployment rate gives us the perception of the incapability of the economic system of matching the demand of those who are actively asking for a job.

[16] See the various terminologies as used to define the particular position of the youths in the social context as recalled by Ponzellini, A. M. 2009. "Il rapporto tra generazioni nel lavoro. Disuguaglianza senza conflitto?" in *Diritto delle Relazioni Industriali* No. 3: 538. The Author puts the issue of why such a differential in the social position of young workers does not rise a proper conflict against older generation, especially when considering the huge cost that young generations are asked to pay in term of loss for their social security. A possible answer, together with a change of social perspectives and needs is to be found in the so-called complicity of the youths with the older generation of parents and tutors (see also Cavalli, A. 2004. "Generation and Value Orientation," in *Social Compass* 51, No. 2).

Table 1-8. Employment Rate (%)

Year	15-64 years	15-24 years	25-34 years
2007	58.65	24.7	70.1
2008	58.67	24.4	70.1
2009	57.55	21.7	67.5
2001 (July)	57.00	20.5	65.9

Statistics from 2007 to 2010 reveal that the highest increase in the unemployment rate took place amongst young workers compared to the overall active population (15-64 years). The increase reached 27.71% in 2010 (July), to be compared with the total unemployment rate that rose up from 6.16% to 8.47%.

Table 1-9. Unemployment Rate (%)

Year	Overall active population	15-24 age group
2007	6.16	20.35
2008	6.75	21.53
2009	7.79	25.4
2010 (July)	8.47	27.71

Particular attention must be paid to unemployment rates when it comes to long-term policy-making. The table below shows clearly how the figures concerning the south of the country are far from the average of the national territory as a whole (bearing in mind that those numbers may be affected by the thousands of informal agreements that people can be tempted to hide, in order to be still eligible for unemployment benefits).

Table 1-10. Long-term Unemployment Rates by Age Group (%)

Age group	2007		2008		2009	
	South	Italy	South	Italy	South	Italy
15-24	16.1	8.1	16.2	7.9	18.4	10.0
25-34	8.3	3.8	9.0	3.9	9.6	4.5
35-54	4.0	2.0	4.5	2.3	4.6	2.6
55+	1.8	1.1	2.0	1.5	2.0	1.5
Total	5.9	2.8	6.4	3.0	6.6	3.4

Previously, the highest point for long-term unemployment of young workers was reached in 2005 with a long-term unemployment level of 10.4%. Thereafter, the figure declined until the recessionary year of 2008/09, when it reached double digits, some three times the average of the total labour force. It is noticeable that the likelihood of long-term unemployment lessens with age, so that young workers are much more likely to be impacted than other age groups. The figures for the south of Italy are consistently much higher than the rates for the country as a whole.

6. United Kingdom

The number of people in employment aged 16 and over increased by 178,000 to August 2010 to reach 29.16 million. Employment has increased by 241,000 over the previous year, but it is still 270,000 lower than two years before. The number of men in employment increased by 132,000 on the quarter, to reach 15.62 million, while the number of women in employment increased by 46,000 on the quarter to reach 13.54 million. The unemployment rate for the three months to August 2010 was 7.7%. Male unemployment fell by 56,000 on the quarter to reach 1.44 million, but female unemployment increased by 36,000 on the quarter to reach 1.01 million.[17] Although employment rates in the UK are relatively high compared to other countries, we do have an issue over the next four years with the coalition government making significant cuts in public spending leading to the loss of some 500,000 public sector jobs. The government appears confident that the private sector will fill the gap, but this remains to be seen, especially with the recruitment of young inexperienced workers. Indeed, graduate unemployment, affecting mostly young new university graduates, is reported as being at its highest level for 17 years, with one graduate in 11 (some 21,000 people) still being without work 6 months after finishing at university.[18]

---

[17] Labour Market Trends October 2010; the figures are for June to August; Office for National Statistics www.statistics.gov.uk.

[18] Shepherd, J. 2010. "Graduate Unemployment at Highest Level for 17 Years," *Guardian Newspaper* 1 November 2010

http://www.guardian.co.uk/business/2010/nov/01/graduate-unemployment-highest-for-17-years (accessed November 9, 2010).

7. Employment and Unemployment

Although in the recession young people fared worse than people aged 25 and over, the labour market position of 16-24 year olds started to deteriorate long before the beginning of the crisis. In general, the employment rate of young people has been falling and the unemployment rate rising since 2001. However, the speed of deterioration has increased during this recession.[19] Nearly half of young workers are employed in either retail or hospitality, with these sectors being an important source of work for young people. Research has found that the use of age-related pay continued to be widespread in the fast food, restaurant and pub sector, where around 80% of the companies surveyed used the youth rates associated with the national minimum wage. In the retail sector, 57% of companies surveyed had an age-related pay structure, although most employers start paying the adult rate from age 18 onwards. Many unions, youth organisations and age equality bodies, according to the Low Pay Commission Report 2010, called for the removal of the youth rates. They argued that varying the minimum wage by age was discriminatory. Some suggested that the youth rates be phased out while others said they should be abolished as soon as possible.[20]

Young people and those with no qualifications have been most affected by the recession. Therefore, young people not in full-time education (FTE) are particularly vulnerable.

> The employment rate of 16-17 year olds not in FTE has fallen sharply, while the unemployment rate has risen sharply. [...] The labour market performance of 18-20 year olds not in FTE has been in general decline since 2001. Employment had started to increase after the middle of 2007, but since the start of the recession the employment rate of 18-20 year olds not in FTE has fallen sharply.[21]

Employment statistics for the UK reveal a decline in the employment rate of young people in the period of the current recession,[22] with the employment rate falling from 33.4% to 25.9% for the youngest cohort and from 63.5% to 59.0% for the 18-24 age group, between 2008 and 2010.

---

[19] Secretary of State for Business, Innovation and Skills. 2010. *National Minimum Wage Low Pay Commission Report 2010*. Cm 7823.

[20] Ibid.

[21] Ibid.

[22] Labour Market Trends October 2010 and October 2009; the figures are for June to August; Office for National Statistics www.statistics.gov.uk.

Table 1-11. Employment Rate for 16-17 Year Olds

Year	Total employed	Employment rate (%)
2008	530,000	33.4
2009	412,000	26.5
2010	391,000	25.9

Table 1-12. Employment Rate for 18-24 Year Olds

Year	Total employed	Employment rate (%)
2008	3,638,000	63.5
2009	3,454,000	59.5
2010	3,446,000	59.0

The steepest decline was recorded in the period 2008-2009, with a subsequent levelling off which may reflect the optimism of the European Commission (see above). It is clear that the biggest falls in youth employment took place during 2008/09 with the rate of decline falling rapidly in the following period.

Table 1-13. Employment Rate by Age Group

Year	18-24	25-34	35-49	50-64	65+
2008	63.3	80.3	82.2	65.5	7.2
2009	59.5	77.9	82.1	65.1	7.8
2010	59.0	78.7	81.1	64.9	8.6

If one looks at the declining employment rates by age group, the really interesting result is that there appears to be a direct correlation between the decline of employment rates and age. Those over the age of 35 years have hardly suffered from a decline at all and the oldest age group has actually increased its employment rate during the period in question. The 25-34 year age group has shown an increase over the last year and it is only the youngest group that continues to decline, albeit at a slower rate.

One reason given for this increase in the employment rate for older workers is that the UK, which still has a statutory retirement age, has created a flexible and contingent workforce which is available to work on temporary or fixed-term contracts, as employers show a reluctance to take on permanent employees in uncertain times.[23] One question is, therefore, why this same logic does not apply to younger workers who may also work on temporary and/or part time contracts, and why they have suffered disproportionately compared to other age groups.

In gender terms, it is the young male workers, as in Europe generally, who have been most affected, with employment rates falling more rapidly. It is difficult to know whether this difference is of significance or not.

Table 1-14. Employment Rate (%) for 16-17 Year Olds by Gender

Year	Male	Female
2008	32.4	35.5
2009	23.9	29.3
2010	23.6	28.3

Table 1-15. Employment Rate (%) for 18-24 Year Olds by Gender

Year	Male	Female
2008	65.8	61.1
2009	60.7	58.2
2010	60.7	57.3

For the youngest cohort the unemployment rate has been declining through the recession, but there has been a more than 10% increase in the inactivity rate, which consists of those who have opted out of the labour market. For the older group, the unemployment rate has increased more significantly, with a much lower rate of increase in those who are opting out.

---

[23] Bisom-Rapp, S., A. Frazer, and M. Sargeant. 2011. "Older Workers and the Recession: a Global Perspective," in *Employee Rights and Employment Policy Journal*, No. 15, forthcoming.

Table 1-16. Unemployment and Inactivity Rates (%) for 16-17 Year Olds

Year	Overall rate	Inactivity rate[24]
2008	33.3	54.7
2009	33.0	60.2
2010	31.1	62.4

Table 1-17. Unemployment and Inactivity Rates (%) for 18-24 Year Olds

Year	Overall rate	Inactivity rate
2008	13.2	26.8
2009	17.5	27.9
2010	17.7	28.3

The comparison of these unemployment rates with other age groups points out that (see Table 1-18) the percentage increase for some of the older groups is actually much higher than for the 18-24 year group, e.g. the rate for the 35-49 group increased by about 50% during this period. This is not to say that the increase for the youngest group was not significant and, of course, the absolute levels are much higher at the beginning and end of the period.

Table 1-18. Unemployment Rates by Age Group (%)

Year	18-24	25-34	35-49	50-64	65+
2008	13.2	5.3	3.8	3.3	2.3
2009	17.5	8.0	5.4	4.7	2.6
2010	17.7	7.3	5.6	4.8	2.3

The long-term unemployment rate has increased in all age groups, especially over the last year. It is a depressing picture, but the younger age group is at a lower level than the others listed here.

---

[24] The economically inactive are people who are neither in employment nor unemployed. This group comprises those who want a job but who have not been seeking work in the last four weeks, those who want a job and are seeking work but not available to start and those who do not want a job. For example, students not working or seeking work and those in retirement are classed as economically inactive.

Table 1-19. People in Unemployment for 12 Months and over (%)

Year	18-24	25-49	50+
2008	20.0	28.4	36.9
2009	22.0	26.7	31.5
2010	28.0	37.1	42.7

It is young men that are more affected by long-term unemployment than young women. For men in the 18-24 year age group the unemployment rate has increased from 22.7% in 2008 to 33.7% in 2010, whereas women unemployment rate increased from 15.3% in 2008 to 19.8% in 2010.

8. Comparisons

In both countries, as elsewhere in Europe, young people have consistently had lower employment rates than other age groups. Useful comparisons, however, are very difficult to make. In 2008, for example, the employment rate for young Italians was 24.4% and by mid 2010 it had fallen to 20.5%. This age group includes the very youngest, most of whom will still be in education. However, it is still a lower rate than that for 16-17 year olds in the UK, where the employment rate in 2008 was 33.4% falling to 25.9% in mid 2010. The comparable figures for 18-24 year olds in the UK are 63.5% and 59.0%. There are clearly other, perhaps cultural factors, which influence at what age young people enter the job market. These figures suggest that the number of people in the UK entering the labour market at an earlier age is much greater than in Italy.

Whatever issues are raised by this, one can see that in both countries the employment rate has reduced for younger workers more than for any other age group.

In terms of unemployment statistics, figures from the EU (Table 1-20) for the EU27 and for Italy and the United Kingdom[25] show that the Italian rate has always been much higher than the EU and UK average, which are very similar to each other.

---

[25] European Commission. 2009. *Employment in Europe 2009*. Brussels: European Commission. The percentages here are those of the workforce aged 15-24, thus excluding those who are not available for work.

Table 1-20. Unemployment Rates of Young People (15-24) (%)

	2000	2004	2008
EU27	17.3	18.4	15.4
Italy	27.0	23.5	21.3
UK	12.2	12.1	15.0

It is interesting to see how the situation changed since the beginning of the recession. Eurostat figures[26] show that by July 2010 the figures were (Table 1-21):

Table 1-21. Unemployment Rate of Young People during the Recession (%)

	2009	2010[27]
EU27	20.3	20.2
Italy	25.0	26.8
UK	19.6	19.7[28]

These two sets of figures are not intended to be sequential, but indicative of the difficulties that young people face while seeking a job.

Furthermore, some 10% of the 15-24 year olds in Italy experienced long-term unemployment in 2009 compared to 22% in the UK for the 18-24 year age group. Italian figures include the very youngest, many of whom could not have been in the labour market long enough to be long-term unemployed. This will obviously make the overall percentage reflect a lower rate than if it was just for the older age group.

---

[26] According to Eurostat the unemployment rate represents unemployed persons as a percentage of the labour force based on the International Labour Organization (ILO) definition, which here refers to the total number of employed and unemployed persons aged 15 to 24. Unemployed persons comprise here those aged 15-24 who are without work; are available to start work within the next two weeks; and have been actively seeking work in the last four weeks or have already found a job to start within the next three months. Data are presented in seasonally adjusted form.

[27] As at month 8 2009 and month 7 2010.

[28] Month 5 for the UK.

9. Why Do Young People Suffer a Detriment when Seeking Work?

If a comparison is difficult and, indeed, questionable in its usefulness, it is clear that young people as a group, in both countries, have a disadvantage when compared to other age groups when looking for full-time open-ended contracts of employment. There is little research done on how employer's perceptions of young applicants influence their decision-making in the job selection process. This raises the question as to whether employers adopt stereotypical attitudes that could negatively affect young people when they compete against other age groups for jobs.

Of course, young people are assumed to have less work experience and probably less "life experience" than their older colleagues. This is not always true, however, as there can be inexperienced individuals in all age groups. Certainly, as it is also the case with much older workers, their age can count against them in recruitment. One UK analysis[29] revealed that, in its sample, some 10% of establishments which had recruited in the previous five years confirmed that age affected selection for the largest occupational group. This was particularly true for process, plant and machine operatives, drivers, skilled trade staff and caring, leisure and personal service staff. The analysis also stated that

> At the same time, 11% said that there were some ages which counted against applicants and three per cent said some ages counted in favour of applicants. Those most often disadvantaged were the young and the old, with those over 60 (and, especially those over 65) and those under 22 (and, especially, those under 18) most likely to find recruiters holding their age against them.

There is a tacit admission by governments that, somehow, the state should sometimes apply different rules to young people in order to help overcome the disadvantages they suffer in the job market. There have, for example, been two cases, one from Austria[30] and one from Germany,[31] at the European Court of Justice concerning state employer rules not counting service under a certain age as relevant for length or continuity of

---

[29] Metcalf, H., and P. Meadows. 2010. "Second Survey of Employers' Policies, Practices and Preferences Relating to Age," *Employment relations research series* No. 110. Sponsored by the Department for Business, Innovation and Skills and the Department for Work and Pensions.

[30] Court of Justice of the European Communities 2009. *Case C-88/08.*

[31] Court of Justice of the European Communities 2010. *Case C-555/07.*

service. It is an attitude that states that it is permissible to take away, or lessen, individual rights to employment protection to make individuals more attractive to the employer than others who retain these employment rights.

The most obvious exchange of rights for work opportunities is the apprenticeship system that operates in both countries.

In Italy, the apprenticeship system provides the main way of transit for youths into the labour market. Such a contract basically allows the employer who wishes to hire a young worker to pay him a lower salary or wage. Such a lower salary is supposed to be compensated by the training activity that the employer must provide to the worker, in order to help him or her achieve the required skills. So, this formative support, as well as the encouragement costs for the hiring, are the arguments that justify, whenever the equality principle comes into consideration, the detrimental treatment as accorded to any apprentice in term of balance and proportionality.[32]

The employer is also in the position to pay lower social security contributions for his or her apprentices (while the rest of the contribution is covered by the state). The employer of an apprentice also joins some so-called "normative benefits". As there are a number of laws only applicable to enterprises with a low number of employees, the system is meant to facilitate the entry of young workers by not counting them as employees strictly speaking for the purpose of applying such laws (as an example, the Italian law on unfair dismissals provides the dismissed employees with a higher compensation when the enterprise has more than 15 employees).

The Reform of 2003 (Legislative Decree No. 276/2003, Artt. 47-53) has deeply affected the law on apprenticeships. Government policy stresses the intention of enhancing the interaction between the education system on the one hand and the necessary training and work experience on the other, in order to shorten the distance that exists between these two worlds.[33] Such a distance is blamed as the main cause for Italian youth unemployment.

---

[32] On the possible arguments against the application of the equality principle, see Peruzzi, M. 2009. "Politiche sociali e differenze di trattamento fondate sull'età, il giudizio di appropriatezza della Corte, nota a CGCE 18 giugno 2009," in *Rivista critica di diritto del lavoro*, No. 3:649.

[33] Senatori I., and M. Tiraboschi. 2008. "Ricerche: lavoro decente e valorizzazione del capitale umano—la sfida della disoccupazione giovanile nel mercato globale tra produttività del lavoro e capitale umano," in *Diritto delle Relazioni Industriali*, No. 3: 648.

From a strictly legal point of view, the weakness of the apprenticeship system currently in force lies in the fact that its implementation requires a coordinated action involving different entities (regions, enterprises, social partners, educational institutions and so on) that is far from being simply realised. Although being a contract without a fixed-time limit, it cannot last more than a certain time depending on the type and the age limit of the apprentice. It is at the end of the training, during which the worker can be dismissed only for justified reasons, that the employer will be free to terminate the contract.[34] However, incentives to transform the apprenticeship into a regular contract are also possible.

The UK also has an apprenticeship system which relies on the exchange of rights for training. The UK is one of those EU countries which has a national minimum wage. There is a lower rate payable to those aged 18-20 years (£4.92 per hour) and an even lower rate for 16 and 17 year olds (£3.64 per hour). Until recently, apprenticeships were not covered by the national minimum wage legislation. From 1 October 2010 this policy has changed and the government has introduced a minimum wage for apprentices of £2.50 per hour.

There seem to be three main reasons why those under the age of 21 years receive a lower rate than "adults".[35] Firstly, there is concern with the balance between education and work and a desire not to make work more attractive than continuing in education. Secondly, there is the issue of making young people more attractive to employers. The government has said that, for example, "younger workers are typically less skilled and productive than older workers".[36] This somehow justifies a lower rate, but some research[37] has found that most companies employing young workers in low-skilled roles did not think they were less productive than older workers. Thirdly, there has been a general concern that the national minimum wage should be neutral as regards its impact on employment.[38] The government states that it has been successful in this objective.

---

[34] On the termination of the apprenticeship see Trib. Milano 17.6.2005 in D&L, 2005, 751.

[35] Sargeant, M. 2010. "National Minimum Wage and Age Discrimination," in *Policy Studies* 31, No. 3: 351-364.

[36] Department for Trade and Industry. 2006. *Government Evidence to the Low Pay Commission on the National Minimum Wage*. Department of Trade and Industry.

[37] Neathey, F., H. Ritchie, and M. Silverman. 2005. *The Employment of Young People in the Retail and Hospitality Sectors. Report for the Low Pay Commission.* Brighton: IES.

[38] See statement by Margaret Beckett MP, President of the Board of Trade, on the first LPC Report, Thursday 18 June 1998; http://www.berr.gov.uk.

Lower rates for young people are *prima facie* examples of discrimination on the grounds of age, and governments, if challenged, would have to show that such measures had a legitimate aim and that the lower rates of pay were a proportionate means of achieving that aim. It may be that this is possible but it is a wider context that should be viewed, perhaps in terms of making adverse treatment of younger workers more acceptable. Therefore, further research is required in this area.

References

Barroso, J. M., and G. Verheugen. 2005. COM(2005) 24 "Working Together for Growth and Jobs. A New Start for the Lisbon Strategy," *Communication to the spring European Council.*

Bisom-Rapp, S., A. Frazer, and M. Sargeant. 2011. "Older Workers and the Recession: a Global Perspective," in *Employee Rights and Employment Policy Journal*, No. 15, forthcoming.

Cavalli, A. 2004. "Generation and Value Orientation," in *Social Compass* 51, No. 2.

Court of Justice of the European Communities. 2009. *Case C-88/08 David Hütter v Technische Universität Graz.* European Court reports 2009.

—. 2010. *Case C-555/07 Seda Kücükdeveci v Swedex GmbH and Co. KG.* European Court reports 2010.

Department for Trade and Industry. 2006. *Government Evidence to the Low Pay Commission on the National Minimum Wage.* Department of Trade and Industry.

European Commission. 2009. *Employment in Europe 2009.* Brussels: European Commission.

—. 2010a. *Communication from the Commission COM(2010) 2020: Europe 2020, A Strategy for Smart, Sustainable and Inclusive Growth.* Brussels: European Commission.

—. 2010b. *EU Employment Situation and Social Outlook, March 2010.* Brussels: European Commission.

International Labour Organization. 2010. *Global Employment Trends for Youth: Special Issue on the Impact of the Global Economic Crisis on Youth.* Geneva: ILO.

Metcalf, H., and P. Meadows. 2010. "Second Survey of Employers' Policies, Practices and Preferences Relating to Age," *Employment relations research series* No. 110. Sponsored by the Department for Business, Innovation and Skills and the Department for Work and Pensions.

Neathey, F., H. Ritchie, and M. Silverman. 2005. *The Employment of Young People in the Retail and Hospitality Sectors. Report for the Low Pay Commission*. Brighton: IES.

Peruzzi, M. 2009. "Politiche sociali e differenze di trattamento fondate sull'età, il giudizio di appropriatezza della Corte, nota a CGCE 18 giugno 2009," in *Rivista critica di diritto del lavoro*, No. 3:649.

Ponzellini, A. M. 2009. "Il rapporto tra generazioni nel lavoro. Disuguaglianza senza conflitto?" in *Diritto delle Relazioni Industriali* No. 3: 538.

Sargeant, M. 2010. "National Minimum Wage and Age Discrimination," in *Policy Studies* 31, No. 3: 351-364.

Secretary of State for Business, Innovation and Skills. 2010. *National Minimum Wage Low Pay Commission Report 2010*. Cm 7823.

Senatori I., and M. Tiraboschi. 2008. "Ricerche: lavoro decente e valorizzazione del capitale umano—la sfida della disoccupazione giovanile nel mercato globale tra produttività del lavoro e capitale umano," in *Diritto delle Relazioni Industriali*, No. 3: 648.

Shepherd, J. 2010. "Graduate Unemployment at Highest Level for 17 Years," *Guardian Newspaper,* 1 November 2010
http://www.guardian.co.uk/business/2010/nov/01/graduate-unemployment-highest-for-17-years (accessed November 9, 2010).

Vermeylen, G. "Informal employment in the European Union," Paper prepared for WIEGO Workshop on Informal Employment in Developed Countries; Harvard University, November 2008.

The Changing Nature of Youth Employment in Australia: How Can this Be Understood?

Erica Smith

1. Introduction

This paper uses Australia as a case study of youth employment in an advanced industrial nation, examining the way in which youth employment has changed over the past two decades. The particular emphasis of the case study is on the increased incidence of part-time working while studying, and the far-reaching effects of this change. It needs to be noted that Australia has survived the global financial crisis with very few ill effects and the present research needs to be read with that in mind; unemployment among young people in Australia is quite low, although still higher than the average for all workers. Some other countries (e.g. the United Kingdom) exhibited similar characteristics pre-2008, but their situation may be somewhat different now.

2. Background

This section discusses the youth employment issue under two headings: part-time working while studying and the Australian schooling system and its relationship with workplaces.

3. Part-time Working while Studying

In Australia, as in many other countries, the majority of school students of working age are in the formal part-time workforce, many from the age of 14 or 15, and continue in that workforce during their periods of senior secondary and tertiary education.[1]

There are several motivations for working while being a student: financial, social, resume-building and a wish to establish independence. While the student working phenomenon was commonplace in the US early in the second half of the 20th century,[2] it has only recently become widespread in Australia, and in other countries such as Germany.[3] The context for part-time working and the links with other areas of students' lives, especially school and university[4] has received some attention in the literature, yet with reference to the potential adverse effects on studies, as Patton and Smith[5] maintain in their summary of literature on working by secondary school students. Young students' part-time jobs *per se* (as opposed to their effects on other aspects of young people's lives such as their grades while studying) have rarely been studied. And yet part-time work while studying is now the manner in which most young Australian people first enter the workforce. Most workers now have a lengthy part-time work history before leaving full-time education and this work history is likely to take place in industries which may not be the site of their eventual "career jobs".

During most of the twentieth century, early working experience in a full-time job was the major stepping stone for Australian young people to adult life, but this pathway is no longer utilised by most young people. By 2003, the proportion of people aged 15-19 years in full-time employment had fallen to 15% with an increase in part-time employment between 1983

[1] Vickers, M., S. Lamb, and J. Hinkley. 2003. *Student Workers in High School & Beyond: The Effects on Part-time Employment on Participation in Employment, Education & Training.* Longitudinal Surveys of Australian Youth Research Report, No. 30. Melbourne: Australian Council for Educational Research.

[2] Greenberger, E., and L. Steinberg. 1986. *When Teenagers Work: The Psychological and Social Costs of Teenage Employment.* New York: Basic Books.

[3] Winkler, I. 2009. "Term-time Employment: Exploring the Influence of Self-identity, Motivation and Social Issues," *Education + Training* 51, No. 2:124-138.

[4] In the Australian literature see Smith, E., and A. Green. 2001. *School Students' Learning from their Paid and Unpaid Work.* Adelaide: NCVER. Billett, S. 2006. *Informing Post-school Pathways: Investigating School Students' Authentic Work Experiences.* Adelaide: National Centre for Vocational Education Research (NCVER).

[5] Patton, W., and E. Smith. 2009. "Part-time Work of High School Students and Impact on Educational Outcomes," *Australian Journal of Guidance and Counselling.* 19: 2, 216-224.

to 2003 from 28% to 68% of employed people in that age group[6] and it has remained at this level since then.[7] About two-thirds of Australian students in the final three years of school (roughly ages 15-18) work at any one time[8] and the average number of hours worked by school students per week has been consistently found to be around 9 or 10,[9] which also tends to be the standard working week for student-workers employed by several major Australian companies.[10] Full-time university students who are recent school-leavers work longer hours; the Australian average is around 15 hours.[11] Figures on the average number of hours worked mask considerable differences among groups of young people. While it is normally assumed that working-class school students work more frequently and for longer hours than better-off students, and this has been shown to be the case in some US studies,[12] there is also contradictory evidence; for example an Australian study shows above-average engagement in paid work by school students from self-reported high as well as low socio-economic status (SES) backgrounds, with lower engagement by middle-range SES students.[13]

Student-working is likely to continue as a mass phenomenon, partly because students need jobs, and this need will increase as university students are increasingly being required to make a financial contribution towards their education through Australia's HECS scheme (Higher Education Contribution Scheme), choosing either to pay up-front or to incur substantial tax debts if they do not pay as they go along. But it is also embedded in the Australian way of life because the jobs need students. The shift in the balance of industries within the Australian and other economies from primary and secondary to tertiary industries means an

---

[6] Australian Bureau of Statistics (ABS). 2004. *The Labour Force*. Canberra: ABS.

[7] ABS. 2008. *Yearbook 2007, Series 1301.0*. Canberra: ABS.

[8] Smith, E., and A. Green. 2001. *School Students' Learning from their Paid and Unpaid Work*. Adelaide: NCVER.

[9] See Robinson, L. 1999. *The Effects of Part-time Work on School Students. Longitudinal Surveys of Australian Youth, Research Report No 9*. Melbourne: Australian Council for Educational Research.

[10] Smith, E., and A. Green. 2001. *School Students' Learning from their Paid and Unpaid Work*. Adelaide: NCVER.

[11] James, R., E. Bexley, M. Devlin, and S. Marginson. 2007. *Australian University Student Finances 2006*. Canberra: Universities Australia.

[12] For instance Nelson, I., and B. Gastic. 2009. "Street Ball, Swim Team & the Sour Cream Machine: A Cluster Analysis of out of School Time Participation Portfolios," *Journal of Youth and Adolescence* No. 38: 1172-1186.

[13] Smith, E., and A. Green. 2001. *School Students' Learning from their Paid and Unpaid Work*. Adelaide: NCVER, 47.

increasing need for people available during non-standard working hours and for short shifts. In addition, it is becoming particularly important for students to work while studying so that they can show they have employment experience and employment-related skills.

Historically, there have been few regulations to impede Australian companies from taking on school students or that restrict their hours of work. In the United States, by contrast, school student working has for many years been highly regulated particularly with regard to hours of work and special safety regulations.[14] However, in Australia there is an increasing amount of legislative interest in adolescent workers,[15] who are primarily student-workers. Five States and Territories have introduced Child Employment Acts in the six years since 2003. Regulations cover such issues as the number of hours worked in school weeks (e.g. Queensland, 12 hours), banning work within school hours (Western Australia), minimum age for formal work (below the age of 13, except for newspaper delivery, Victoria) and working split shifts (New South Wales).[16]

Despite these massive changes, there is still a tendency in the Australian educational and labour market literature to talk about the school-to-work transition, ignoring the fact that most young people are working at the same time as studying. The significance of this early move into the labour market has been little discussed; it is as though young people's participation in work remains invisible until they finally leave full-time education, whether it be after the end of secondary school or after the end of university studies. Students' jobs are part-time and usually in the service industries, particularly retail and hospitality. One reason for the seeming lack of interest in students' jobs may be an undervaluing of the worth both of part-time jobs *vis-a-vis* full-time work, and of service sector

---

[14] Committee on the Health and Safety Implications of Child Labor, Board on Children, Youth and Families, Commission on Behavioral and Social Sciences and Education National Research Council and Institute of Medicine. 1998. *Protecting Youth at Work: Health, Safety and Development of Working Children and Adolescents in the United States.* Washington, DC: National Academic Press.
[15] Mourell, M., and C. Allan. 2006. "Regulating the Health and Safety of Young Workers in Australia," *Journal of Occupational Health and Safety,* 22, No. 2: 115-125.
[16] Smith, E., and W. Patton. 2009. "Part-time Working by School Students: Workplace Problems and Challenges," *Youth Studies Australia*, 29, No. 3: 21-31.

jobs, which are often depicted as low-skilled.[17] Whatever the reason, it is an area that needs further inquiry.

4. The Australian Schooling System and its Engagement with Workplaces

A brief overview of the secondary school leaving situation and school-mediated engagement with workplaces in Australia follows. In Australia, students complete 12 or 13 years of schooling: Years 1 to 12, with a preliminary year in most States and Territories. Approximately 75% of students complete schooling at the end of year 12[18] while a substantial minority completes it at the end of Year 10, with a small number leaving school "early"—before the end of Year 10. Years 11 and 12 are regarded as "post-compulsory" and have a separate curriculum from the earlier years. About 30% of Year 12 leavers proceed directly to university; in Australia, there are many opportunities to enter university later on.

As Woods[19] points out, the safe transition of young people from school to work has been a concern of governments throughout the world for many decades. Increasingly in many countries, including Australia, there has been an emphasis on "readying" students for the workplace through a focus on the development of employability skills and also through the provision of explicit vocational training as part of the curriculum; as well as initiatives in several states to raise the school-leaving age unless evidence is provided of engagement in jobs that have associated training. This proceeds at the same time as most students also have part-time jobs gained independently. All Australian secondary schools have work experience programmes. These programmes were introduced to give the school student a taste of the workplace before leaving school, generally in the context of sampling a career area of interest. Students may undertake one or sometimes more periods of work experience, during Year 10 and/or Year 11, usually of one or two weeks duration. They are designed less for skills development than for learning about workplaces and about a particular type of work. More formal Vocational Education and Training (VET) in schools programmes is more recent, having been introduced

---

[17] Korczynski, M. 2002. *Human Resource Management in Service Work.* London: Palgrave.
[18] ABS. 2008. *Yearbook 2007, Series 1301.0.* Canberra: ABS.
[19] Woods, D. 2008. *The Role of VET in Helping Young People's Transitions into Work.* Adelaide: NCVE.

during the 1990s[20] and provides training in a vocational area that normally leads to a competency-based VET qualification or Statement of Attainment (part-qualification), usually at Australian Qualifications Framework level II or III. These programmes are generally undertaken in the post-compulsory years and count towards the senior secondary certificate[21] although sometimes they require extra academic tasks in order to "count" for university entrance scores. In VET in schools programmes, students may be trained at school or may attend TAFE, the public provider of VET, or to another Registered Training Organisation (RTO) for their VET in schools classes. Such programmes generally include periods of vocational placement in workplaces, where students practice skills learned at school or sometimes develop new skills. A number of studies by writers such as Polesol and Teese[22] have examined VET in schools programmes in some depth. VET in schools has been found to be particularly beneficial for students of lower academic achievement, those disengaged with school, and those at greater risk in the post-school labour market,[23] but having become increasingly "mainstreamed", the programmes serve multiple and complex purposes within schools and for individual young people.[24] By 2004, 50% of Years 11 and 12 students were enrolled in VET in schools programmes.[25] School students may also commence or even complete school-based apprenticeships and traineeships; these have been available for the past decade. They constitute a combination of independent part-time work and VET in schools as they involve paid part-time work and a

---

[20] National Board for Employment, Education and Training (NBEET) Schools Council. 1994. *The Role of Schools in the Vocational Preparation of Australia's Senior Secondary Students: Discussion Paper.* Canberra: AGPS.

[21] Smith, E., and L. Keating. 2003. *From Training Reform to Training Packages.* Tuggerah Lakes, NSW: Social Science Press.

[22] For example Polesel, J., S. Helme, M. Davies, R. Teese, T. Nicholas, and M. Vickers. 2004. *VET in Schools: A Post-compulsory Education Perspective.* Adelaide: NCVER.

[23] Woods, D. 2008. *The Role of VET in Helping Young People's Transitions into Work.* Adelaide: NCVE. Polesel, J. 2008. "Democratising the Curriculum or Training the Children of the Poor: School-based Vocational Educational Training in Australia," *Journal of Education Policy* 23, No. 6: 615-632.

[24] Smith, E. 2004. "Vocational Education and Training in Schools in Australia: What are the Consequences of Moving from Margins to Mainstream?" *Journal of Vocational Education & Training* 56, No. 4:559-578.

[25] Woods, D. 2008. *The Role of VET in Helping Young People's Transitions into Work.* Adelaide: NCVE.

formal VET in schools qualification that is part of the formal apprenticeship or traineeship.[26]

5. Data Sources and Findings

The analysis in this paper is based on the findings of five research projects carried out between 2000 and 2005. Table 1-22 shows these projects and their methods.

Smith[27] has used the findings from these studies to develop six "types" of young people following different pathways through school, further study, and entry to full-time work. These are:

- the vocationally certain (young people who leave school and enter an apprenticeship in an area which they have long wanted to enter);
- the diverted career path (those who have diverted from their original career goal to take up full-time work in an industry in which they have worked part-time as a student);
- the early school leaver (those who leave school at an early age without clear goals, often continuing, at least initially, in the part-time jobs they had while at school);
- the school-based apprentice (those who continue after secondary school in the part-time apprenticeship commenced while at school);
- the "nerd", or academically-inclined student (those who have not worked at school due to academic or cultural commitments and therefore find it hard to get part-time work while at university); and
- the multi-option individual (those who use their part-time school jobs to work through university, juggling career options in the part-time jobs as well as their area of university study).[28]

---

[26] Andrew, P., S. Kenman, and L. Smith. 2000. *An Evaluation of School-based Apprenticeships and Traineeships.* Brisbane: Queensland Department of Employment, Training and Industrial Relations.

[27] Smith, E. 2009. "New Models of Working and Learning: How Young People are Shaping their Futures Differently," *Research in Post Compulsory Education*, 14, No. 4: 436.

[28] Ibid. 438-440.

Table 1-22. Five Australian Research Studies of Young People and Workplaces

	Participants	Research method	Location
Study 1 (Smith 2000)	Full-time workers in their first year after leaving school	Qualitative year-long study of 11 new workers and significant adults associated with their work, educational and home life.	New South Wales
Study 2 (Smith and Green 2001)	School students in Years 10, 11 and 12	Survey of students in 13 schools in Years 10-12 (1451 responses), and six school case studies. School case studies involved interviews with teachers, careers advisers, students, and local enterprises.	New South Wales and South Australia
Study 3 (Smith and Wilson 2002)	School-based Australian apprentices ("SBNAs")	Survey of a large sample of school-based apprentices, 641 responses	Queensland, Victoria & South Australia
Study 4 (Smith and Comyn 2003)	Novice workers in full-time and part-time jobs	Case studies in 12 enterprises in different industry areas. Interviews with student workers, co-workers, supervisors and senior managers.	Queensland, Victoria & South Australia
Study 5 (Smith and Green 2005)	Participants from Studies 2 and 3, two to three years after leaving school	Survey sent to those young people from studies 2 and 3 who had agreed to take part in a follow-up study. 126 responses. Telephone interviews with 16 of the respondents.	New South Wales, Queensland, Victoria & South Australia

In most of the types, the part-time jobs undertaken while at school and/or university feature to a large extent. This is why the proportion of young people working while at school is so high. About two-thirds of students in the final three years of school work at any one time.[29] There are no firm figures on the proportion of young full-time university students

---

[29] Smith, E., and A. Green. 2001. School Students' Learning from their Paid and Unpaid Work. Adelaide: NCVER.

who work, but it is thought to be around 70%. The remainder are probably eligible for a government living allowance due to their family's income. Thus part-time working is a normal and important part of most young students' lives. The research projects showed evidence of a strategic approach to their part-time working careers; for example young people recognised the need to work while at school in order to ensure that they could get a job while at university to support their living costs. Sometimes this took considerable planning and commitment. For example, one interviewee at a university, whose family lived in a rural area, recounted that while she was at school, her parents drove her 100km each way each Saturday morning for a four-hour a week job and waited in town while she worked.

What are these part-time jobs like? Table 1-23 shows the following positives and negatives of student-working, derived from the research projects listed in Table 1-22.

Table 1-23. Positives and Negatives of Working While a Student: Findings from the Five Studies

Positives of part-time working while a student	Negatives of part-time working while a student
• Most enjoy their jobs at least somewhat; • Jobs provide self-esteem, social contact and the development of employability skills; • Holding down a job ensures the development of time management skills; • Managers positively enjoy developing student-workers; • Employers like McDonalds have systems to develop novice (13-14 year old) workers; • Major service sector employers provide supervisory paths while still at school/university and fervently hope that their student-workers become future senior managers; • Some evidence that career decision-making improves because of part-time work.	• Jobs are rarely discussed in school, even with friends; • Students occasionally struggle to balance their jobs and school requirements, although many employers provide time off for exams etc; • Sometimes employers put pressure on students to do too many extra shifts; • Small and medium employers tend to provide less favourable working conditions than major employers; • The preponderance of student-working may discriminate against those who do not or cannot work.

In Australia, young people are therefore increasingly adopting dual identities—as worker and learner—during the long transition from full-time student to full-time worker. This period may last until the mid-twenties or even beyond. The research projects listed above have shown that while the part-time jobs that are undertaken during this working career may not—but sometimes do—lead to full-time careers in the same industry area, they nevertheless pave the way for transition to full-time work and learning about work. At the same time, those who enter full-time work directly, either at minimum school-leaving age or having completed their senior secondary schooling, are increasingly likely to be doing so through an apprenticeship or traineeship that involves part-time study. In some cases, full-time students, particularly at universities, undertake part-time jobs in the form of apprenticeships or traineeships in areas that are unrelated to their primary field of study, and thus have a "triple identity": university student, worker, and vocational student.

Fig. 1-1. Young People's Working and Learning Aged 15-25

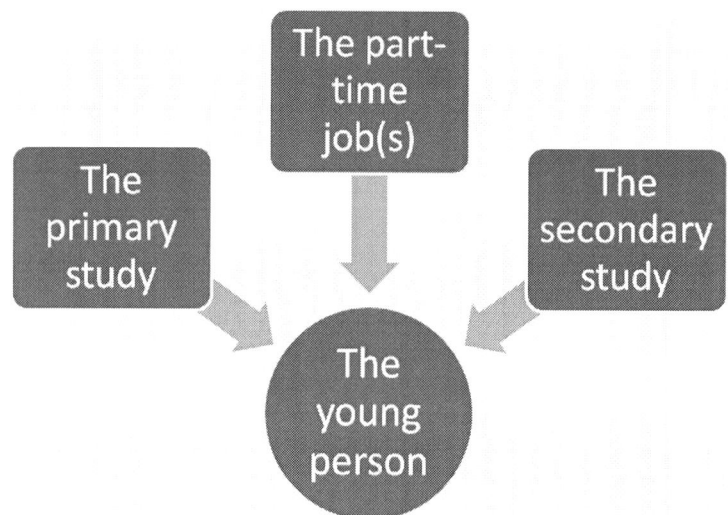

Fig. 1-1 illustrates the ways in which the different parts of the young person's life contribute to their lives as a whole. The "secondary study" in this diagram refers to a part-time apprenticeship or (more frequently) traineeship, which may be associated with the part-time job.

These changes have been apparent among the student-workers that I have interviewed over the years, but also, increasingly, among the managers that I have spoken to. More and more managers report that their current senior positions have grown from the part-time jobs that they had while they were school or university students. In many cases they enjoyed these jobs, typically in retail or hospitality, so much that they chose to stay with their employing company when they left school or university, even though their original career goals were in different industries or occupations. Employers of part-time students often set out very deliberately to entice their better student-workers to stay with them, offering incentives such as transfers among towns, university scholarships, promotion opportunities while still students, and so on to retain them.[30]

6. Conclusion and Discussion

It is clear that changes in labour markets, both internal and external, that have taken place have been radical and deep, and their significance extends well beyond what happens to individual young people during their years of study. The complex and often under-planned arrangements for combining work and study may well be redefining how young people think about education and jobs and how they conceptualise their movement into the full-time workforce.

Changes to education and training policy, for example the availability of VET qualifications as part of schooling and increased access to apprenticeships and traineeships for part-time workers, have had some effects on these changes; but beyond this it is evident that in Australia young people now have an intimate and self-driven knowledge of the workplace, which begins at an early age. Schools and training providers can no longer expect to introduce the workplace to children, either through work experience programmes, through advice from careers teachers, or even through enrolling students in VET qualifications. While there certainly remains a place for programmes arranged by education providers, there is also much independent activity by young people as early and busy participants in the labour market. Such engagement has positive sides that may also be seen as "negative". There is a sense of urgency to engage with work which, it might be argued, has made the life of young people less leisurely and more pressured. Moreover, lack of engagement with workplaces at an early age can be argued to lead to later disadvantage,

---

[30] Smith, E., and W. Patton. 2007. "A Serendipitous Synchronisation of Interests: Employers and Student-working," Evolution, revolution or status quo? The new context for VET. 10th Conference of the Australian VET Research Association, Victoria University, Footscray Park, Vic, 11-13 April.

which could be cumulative as it is often through workplaces that young people hear about other options. It can be affected by variables such as geographical location, socio-economic status or ethnicity. However, on the positive side, our young people are now developing employability skills earlier in life and acquire valuable knowledge that can be drawn upon in subsequent careers and educational experiences. These include time management skills and the ability to negotiate with employers about their needs. In addition, they become used to working "unsocial hours" and therefore more open to a wider range of careers than those that fall within the "nine to five" spectrum. They may also develop a service orientation which carries over into subsequent careers and makes them critical consumers, forcing service industries to improve their performance.

The response of the scholarly community to these changes, as reported earlier, has been quite mixed. Some literature tends to view the jobs that young people undertake part-time as being relatively menial, and their employers as exploitative.[31] Other literature is more balanced.[32] Much of the response seems to be affected by attitudes of some scholars to the industries in which students work; many feeling that the service industries lack prestige and are "low-skilled". Many industrial relations scholars seem to assume that since the student-workers are employed casually, they will naturally not be treated properly nor given opportunities to advance. The research projects outlined above have indicated that most major employers, on the contrary, treat their student-workers well, partly because of the need to attract other young people as potential workers and also as customers. As discussed, much literature on part-time student-working focuses on the effects upon education, ignoring, perhaps, the fact that it would be impossible to "turn back the clock" to a time when young people did not work whilst studying. Still, other scholars continue to focus on the so-called "school-to-work transition", preferring to cling to the old notion that young people enter the labour market, or perhaps the "real" labour market only upon completing formal education.

This paper has provided data from empirical research to describe and explain the labour market entry experiences of the majority of the Australian workforce. It has provided some initial analysis of these data

---

[31] Tannock, S. 2001. *Youth at Work: The Unionized Fast-food and Grocery Workplace*. Philadelphia: Temple University Press.

[32] For example Bailey, T., and L. Bernhardt. 1997. "In Search of the High Road in a Low Wage Industry," *Politics and Society* 25, No. 2:179-201. Allan, C., G. Bamber, and N. Timo. 2005. "McJobs, Student Attitudes to Work and Employment Relations in the Fast Food Industry," *Journal of Hospitality & Tourism Management* 12, No. 1:1-11.

and a conceptual model for representing young people's working and learning lives. Much further research remains to be done in this area. What effects does labour market entry through part-time work have upon the eventual career destinations of young people? While these projects have provided some insight into this question, much more research on a larger scale needs to be carried out. What are the benefits and challenges to individuals, the economy and society of these changes and who needs to be involved in these discussions? Importantly, what happens to those left behind—those who leave school and/or university without part-time working experience, for whatever reason? And finally, an important question is whether the Australian system is a suitable model for other countries to consider.

References

Andrew, P., S. Kenman, and L. Smith. 2000. *An Evaluation of School-based Apprenticeships and Traineeships.* Brisbane: Queensland Department of Employment, Training and Industrial Relations.

Australian Bureau of Statistics (ABS). 2004. *The Labour Force.* Canberra: ABS.

—. 2008. *Yearbook 2007, Series 1301.0.* Canberra: ABS.

Allan, C., G. Bamber, and N. Timo. 2005. "McJobs, Student Attitudes to Work and Employment Relations in the Fast Food Industry," *Journal of Hospitality & Tourism Management* 12, No. 1:1-11.

Bailey, T. and L. Bernhardt. 1997. "In Search of the High Road in a Low Wage Industry," *Politics and Society* 25, No. 2:179-201.

Billett, S. 2006. *Informing Post-school Pathways: Investigating School Students' Authentic Work Experiences.* Adelaide: National Centre for Vocational Education Research (NCVER).

Committee on the Health and Safety Implications of Child Labor, Board on Children, Youth and Families, Commission on Behavioral and Social Sciences and Education National Research Council and Institute of Medicine. 1998. *Protecting Youth at Work: Health, Safety and Development of Working Children and Adolescents in the United States.* Washington, DC: National Academic Press.

Greenberger, E., and L. Steinberg. 1986. *When Teenagers Work: The Psychological and Social Costs of Teenage Employment.* New York: Basic Books.

James, R., E. Bexley, M. Devlin, and S. Marginson. 2007. *Australian University Student Finances 2006.* Canberra: Universities Australia.

Korczynski, M. 2002. *Human Resource Management in Service Work*. London: Palgrave.

Mourell, M., and C. Allan. 2006. "Regulating the Health and Safety of Young Workers in Australia," *Journal of Occupational Health and Safety* 22, No. 2: 115-125.

National Board for Employment, Education and Training (NBEET) Schools Council. 1994. *The Role of Schools in the Vocational Preparation of Australia's Senior Secondary Students: Discussion Paper*. Canberra: AGPS.

Nelson, I., and B. Gastic. 2009. "Street Ball, Swim Team & the Sour Cream Machine: A Cluster Analysis of out of School Time Participation Portfolios," *Journal of Youth and Adolescence* No. 38: 1172-1186.

Patton, W., and E. Smith. 2009. "Part-time Work of High School Students and Impact on Educational Outcomes," *Australian Journal of Guidance and Counselling* 19: 2, 216-224.

Polesel, J. 2008. "Democratising the Curriculum or Training the Children of the Poor: School-based Vocational Educational Training in Australia," *Journal of Education Policy* 23 No. 6: 615-632.

Polesel, J., S. Helme, M. Davies, R. Teese, T. Nicholas, and M. Vickers. 2004. *VET in Schools: A Post-compulsory Education Perspective*. Adelaide: NCVER.

Robinson, L. 1999. *The Effects of Part-time Work on School Students. Longitudinal Surveys of Australian Youth, Research Report No 9*. Melbourne: Australian Council for Educational Research.

Smith, E. 2000. "Young People's Learning about Work in their First Year of Full-time Work," PhD diss. Sydney: University of Technology.

—. 2004. "Vocational Education and Training in Schools in Australia: What are the Consequences of Moving from Margins to Mainstream?" *Journal of Vocational Education & Training* 56, No. 4: 559-578.

—. 2009. "New Models of Working and Learning: How Young People are Shaping their Futures Differently," *Research in Post Compulsory Education* 14, No. 4: 429-440.

Smith, E., and A. Green. 2001. *School Students' Learning from their Paid and Unpaid Work*. Adelaide: NCVER.

Smith, E., and A. Green. 2005. *How workplace experiences while at school affect career pathways*. Adelaide: NCVER.

Smith, E., and L. Keating. 2003. *From Training Reform to Training Packages*. Tuggerah Lakes, NSW: Social Science Press.

Smith, E., and W. Patton. 2007. "A Serendipitous Synchronisation of Interests: Employers and Student-working," Evolution, revolution or status quo? The new context for VET. 10th Conference of the Australian VET Research Association, Victoria University, Footscray Park, Vic, 11-13 April.

—. 2009. "Part-time Working by School Students: Workplace Problems and Challenges," *Youth Studies Australia* 29, No. 3: 21-31.

Smith, E., and L. Wilson. 2002. *Learning and Training in School-based New Apprenticeships.* Kensington: NCVER Publication.

Smith, E., and P. Comyn. 2003. *The Development of Employability Skills in Novice Workers through Employment.* Adelaide: NCVER.

Tannock, S. 2001. *Youth at Work: The Unionized Fast-food and Grocery Workplace.* Philadelphia: Temple University Press.

Vickers, M., S. Lamb, and J. Hinkley. 2003. *Student Workers in High School & Beyond: The Effects on Part-time Employment on Participation in Employment, Education & Training.* Longitudinal Surveys of Australian Youth Research Report No. 30. Melbourne: Australian Council for Educational Research.

Winkler, I. 2009. "Term-time Employment: Exploring the Influence of Self-identity, Motivation and Social Issues," *Education + Training* 51, No. 2:124-138.

Woods, D. 2008. *The Role of VET in Helping Young People's Transitions into Work.* Adelaide: NCVE.

CHAPTER TWO:

HUMAN CAPITAL, PRODUCTIVITY AND NEW FORMS OF WORK

SOFT SKILLS: A TOOL FOR GROOMING HIGH-PERFORMING MANAGERS

THAYYULLATHIL ASOKAN AND MOHAMMED PARAKANDI

1. Introduction

Soft skills are regarded as crucial to enhance workers' ability to achieve high levels of performance. Relevant studies pointed out that business and industry representatives were profoundly dissatisfied with the overall levels of qualifications of new labour market entrants. It was found that more than 50% of young people leave school without the required level of knowledge to find and maintain a good job.[1] In this sense, employers have provided a list of specific soft skills which are said to be essential for employees, *inter alia* recognising the importance of:

> knowing how to learn; competence in reading, writing, and computation; effective listening and oral communication skills; adaptability through creative thinking and problem solving; personal management with strong self-esteem and initiative; people skills; the ability to work in teams or groups; leadership effectiveness; and technology skills.[2]

According to Wentling,[3] employers do not doubt the skills base of high-school leavers, expressing, however, reservations when it comes to their non-technical abilities. Mastery of non-technical skills on the part of new entrants is a matter of serious concern because this deficiency might

---

[1] Alpern, M. 1997. *Critical Workplace Competencies*. Canadian Vocational Journal 32, No. 4:6-16.

[2] Clagett, C. 1997. *Workforce Skills Needed by today's Employers.* Market Analysis, Prince George's Community College, Office of Institutional Research Analysis.

[3] Wentling, R. 1987. "Teaching Employability Skills in Vocational Education," *Journal of Studies in Technical Careers* 9, No. 4:354

affect their performance and their ability to stay on at work. Beach[4] indicates that 87% of persons who lose their jobs or fail to be promoted were found to have "improper work habits and attitudes" rather than inadequate job skills or knowledge. Beach also highlights the fact that there is increasing demand for employees with technical and soft skills on the part of companies, and it is up to the educational bodies to develop such soft skills. Therefore, priority should be given to the strengthening and refinement of their abilities.

In the context of this paper, the concept of "soft skills" refers to a combination of three components, notably self-management skills, interpersonal skills, and technology skills. Self-management skills comprise the ability to deal with a given situation and to improve individual performance through intrapersonal competences, such as: attitude, emotions, personality, perception, and so on. Interpersonal skills are mainly those needed to interact with individuals and to influence people's behaviour and performance. Finally, soft skills also include technical skills which are now regarded as essential, although generic, such as the capability of handling technical devices, computers, mobile phones, presentation tools and so on.

2. Scope and Methodology

At an international level, much research has been carried out in a number of sectors (construction, health, retailing, Information Technology - IT, education, and hospitality) on the relationship between skill levels and performance at work, with the research focus that has been primarily on a few skill components. As a result, the purpose of the present paper is to provide a comprehensive list of soft skills (generic competences), to identify the main components of soft skills, deemed to be important for both individuals and teams in service management, and to examine the role and importance attached to soft skills by executive staff members.

The study was conducted with a sample of 360 senior managers in the service sector in India, considering their daily activities and related skills, which have been analysed for three days. On the basis of common features, the skills identified to perform specific duties were grouped into three categories, namely Self-Management, Interpersonal, and Technology. The association between skills proficiency and managerial performance has been also investigated.

---

[4] Beach, D. 1982. "A Training Program to Improve Work Habits," *Journal of Epsilon Pi Tau* 8, No. 2:69-74.

3. Related Work

In the analysis of major industry sectors, Hager, Garrick and Crowley[5] pointed out some of the main issues arising from the lack of soft skills, also identifying those which are basic to improve performance: teamworking, communication, and management skills.

Furthermore, a great deal of research has examined critical skills for project managers, with Richard N. Bolles[6] who grouped them into three categories: skills with data, people, and things. For project managers, people are second only to data, although some members of the academic community believe that people skills should be given priority.[7] However, according to Mulcahy,[8] communication is the most valuable skill for this category of workers, as they spend 90% of their time communicating, and their aim should be to gain expertise in all forms of communication (formal and informal writing style, private and public speaking and so on).

Listening skills are implicit in highly qualified people: in order to be successful, it is basic to express concepts in a clear way, but also to listen and interpret other people's ideas, and to explain them to different audiences. Communication is not a direct and hierarchical process, but it is somehow implicit in people skills. A study carried out by Alex S. Brown[9] on project managers revealed the importance of people skills that might be applied to project management and help to succeed in their career.

Haskel et al.[10] attempted to answer the following questions:
- do businesses with higher levels of productivity employ high-skilled workforce?
- If so, which skills matter in terms of productivity?
- To what extent variations in productivity are a reflection of different levels of qualifications?

---

[5] Hager, P., S. Crowley, and J. Garrick. 2000. *Soft Skills in a Hard Industry: How Developing Generic Competencies may Assist the Learning of the Small Building Contractor.* Australia: UTS Research Centre Vocational Education and Training.
[6] Bolles, R. N. 2002. *What Color Is Your Parachute?: A Practical Manual For Job-Hunters & Career- Changers.* Berkeley, CA: Ten Speed Press.
[7] Ibid.
[8] Mulcahy, P. R. 2000. *PMP Exam Prep, Second Edition.* Edina: Beaver's Pond Press.
[9] Brown, A. S. 2002. *Project Management Personality & Skill Types.* http://www.alexsbrown.com (accessed February 2, 2009).
[10] Haskel, J. D. H. 2003. *Skills and Productivity in the UK Using Matched Establishment, Worker and Workforce Data.* London: Queen Mary University of London, Centre for Research into Business Activity.

The outcomes of the present analysis confirmed that highly productive firms employ highly qualified workers and that the attempt to classify them in accordance with the framework of formal qualifications is insufficient in drawing the picture of workforce skills within the company. In this light, human capital—especially if highly qualified—and the "human factor" play a pivotal role, particularly due to the significant correlation between skills and firm-level productivity.

For instance, in the manufacturing sector, there is evidence that plants with higher levels of productivity usually hired highly qualified workers. Furthermore, they found that factors such as skill assessment based on qualifications (hard skills) and people facing double-fixed effects in wage regressions (hard and soft skills) affect productivity. Finally, they demonstrated that the skills gap between top and bottom firms can be explained in terms of productivity.[11]

Abowd et al.[12] developed a system to evaluate skills by providing a wage equation that assesses the effects on both people and company, and also using such effects to measure skills within the company. Unlike the more traditional and formal assessment, such procedure captures skills and identifies the strong correlation between employees' skills and organisational productivity.

Prasad Kaipa et al.[13] carried out a survey on the extent to which soft skills development affects entrepreneurial achievements, singling out the most significant ones: leadership, decision-making, conflict resolution, negotiation, communication, creativity and presentation skills. It emerged that soft skills are crucial to successful management, as they represent a key instrument to maximize human capital within the enterprise. Research findings also emphasised the importance of hiring people with the most adequate set of skills. Prasad Kaipa et al. described soft skills as a stepping stone to success, with effective leadership implying refined "soft skills". Some of them are behaviour-related, while others are the result of some processes, or associated with awareness, self-control, and team building. In this sense, researchers observed that nearly 25% of executives in high-tech positions face management difficulty because of low levels of soft skills, meaning that "technical skills get you at the door, but soft skills keep you at the job".[14]

---

[11] Ibid.

[12] Abowd, J. C. 2002. *Computing Person and Firm Effects Using Linked Longitudinal Employer-Employee Data*. Edina: Speed Press.

[13] Prasad Kaipa, T. M. 2002. *Soft Skills are Smart Skills*. www.selfcorp.com (accessed December 12, 2009).

[14] Ibid.

As firms develop alternative forms of organisation, further adjustments in terms of job structure are needed to support new competitive strategies. Changes in job structure are basically organisational changes designed to deliver services or produce goods in a different way. Even though innovative technology is required to play a supportive role, such technology is not usually considered as a main driver for change in job structure, nor the most relevant factor defining that. Thus, adjustments in "hard" technical skills are not as significant as those affecting learning capacity (e.g. the ability to acquire multiple job skills through training and/or on-the-job learning), soft skills development, and the strengthening of social "character" attributes.[15]

Tamkin et al.[16] tried to assess whether higher skill levels among the workforce helped high-performing firms to better perform. In general terms, the relationship between a highly skilled workforce and organisational performance is of a positive nature, with the study which also revealed that higher productivity is associated with higher levels of qualifications and results in better organisational outcomes. Further, mention should be made of other interesting findings. For instance, a lack of communication skills was found among those applying to perform administrative and secretarial tasks, and to fill vacancies in sales and customer service. Managers and staff employed in personal service and even elementary occupations were also lacking in such ability.

In addition, in considering the same set of occupations, it emerged that customer handling skills were particularly difficult to obtain from applicants. Team-working skills were developed among professionals, but not among managers, those engaged in housewares, customer service and elementary occupations. Problem solving was the preserve of managers, senior officials, administrative and secretarial staff, whereas management skills characterised managers and senior officials. The study concluded with an examination of the employment situation in the years ahead. In this sense, employers' demand for skills, as well as the importance of an investigation of "sector" skill development across the UK is evident throughout this research report.[17]

---

[15] Salzman, H. 1998. *The New Corporate Landscape and Workforce Skills*. U.S. Department of Education, Office of Educational Research and Improvement (OERI), Publication Number NCPI-2-07.

[16] Tamkin, P. G. 2004. *Skills Pay: The Contribution of Skills to Business Success*. SSDA. www.ssdamatrix.org.uk (accessed December 12, 2009).

[17] Ibid.

Spilsbury[18] found that 65% of employers in England who provided their employees with training over the previous 12 months, argued that such training resulted in a rise in productivity. Some 47% of employers in the private sector considered that training led to an increase in profit. From the employer's standpoint, productivity benefits the most from four types of training activity in terms of performance. Spilsbury also pointed out that generic soft skills and off-the-job training produced greater returns than firm specific training.

Studies on IT professionals, including management, technical staff, and consultants, revealed that communication, people, and business skills, hands-on experience, troubleshooting, project management, analytical skills, and integration are the most "in-demand" skills. Some 75% of the respondents are of the opinion that colleges and universities do not prepare students adequately to compete for IT jobs in the years to come. However, employers did not complain about the level of technical skills of entry-level employees.[19]

4. Soft Skills for Managerial Performance

Tables 2-1, 2-2, and 2-3 show the list of requirements in terms of managerial skills and the existence of such skills among the respondents. In this connection:

- Table 2-1 provides the number of respondents whose working activity required them to resort to certain self-management skills;
- Table 2-2 shows the number of those whose job required them to gain a number of interpersonal skills;
- finally, Table 2-3 examines the number of respondents whose working activity required them to use technology skills.

For an easier comparison, skills have been sorted by frequency.

---

[18] Pilsbury, D. 2002. *Learning and Training at Work.* Nottingham: DfES.
[19] Hoffman, T. G. 2003. *Preparing Generation Z.*
www.computerworld.com/printthis/2003/0,4814,84295,00.html
(accessed December 1, 2009).

Table 2-1. Self-management Skills for Managers

Self-management skills	Skill needs (Number of respondents)	Percentage of respondents
Conformity to work ethics	312	86.67
Self-confidence	308	85.56
Self-discipline	307	85.28
Presence of mind	304	84.44
Positive attitude	303	84.17
Time management & punctuality	294	81.67
Self-esteem	289	80.28
Self-awareness	289	80.28
Adaptability/ Flexibility	282	78.33
Motivating self	279	77.50
Decision-making/ Problem solving	279	77.50
Acceptance	277	76.94
Initiative	271	75.28
Managing non-verbal behaviour	266	73.89
Stress management	262	72.78
Assertiveness	258	71.67
Conformity to trends/ norms	258	71.67
Emotional consciousness	256	71.11
Control over temper	252	70.00
Managing own perception	248	68.89
Managing non-verbal behaviour	243	67.50

Source: Primary data.

Table 2-2. Interpersonal Skills for Managers

Interpersonal skills	Skill Needs (Number of respondents)	Percentage of the respondents
Building trust and rapport	291	80.83
Creating relationship	286	79.44
Socialising skill	285	79.17
Maintaining relationship	284	78.89
Impressive speaking skill	278	77.22
Presentation skills	277	76.94
Motivating others	275	76.39
Team player skill	275	76.39
Decision-making (group)	274	76.11
Agreeableness	273	75.83
Leadership	273	75.83
Courtesy	271	75.28
Listening and comprehension	270	75.00
Delegation with respect	269	74.72
Generosity	269	74.72
Empathy	268	74.44
Forgiveness	266	73.89
Persuasiveness	266	73.89
Mentoring/ coaching skills	264	73.33
Negotiation skill	264	73.33
Promoting change	263	73.06
Appropriate use of power	261	72.50
Affectionate	260	72.22
Managing expectations	255	70.83
Counselling skills	252	70.00
Sensing other's non verbal behaviour	250	69.44

Managing other's perception	245	68.06
Conflict management	244	67.78
Managing remote relationships	244	67.78
Tolerance to criticism	241	66.94
Sensitivity to cultural/ gender diversity	233	64.72

Source: Primary data.

Table 2-3. Technology Skills for Managers

Technology skills	Skill Needs (Number of respondents)	Percentage of the respondents
Computer skills	298	82.78
Mobile phones	294	81.67
Email etiquette	279	77.50

Source: Primary data.

5. Association between Managerial Performance Index and Soft Skills

Soft-skills, such as self-management, interpersonal and technology skills, have been assessed and then compared considering the performance index among managers. A chi-square test has been implemented to verify the relationship between soft skills inventory and managerial performance.

The test has been made on the assumption of a close association between managers' soft skills and performance index (H:1).

Furthermore, and with the aim to verifying the association of each component of soft skills with the performance of managers, H:1 has been further divided into three sub-hypothesis such as, H:1.1, H:1.2, and H:1.3. More specifically, in considering the category of managers:

- there is a close relationship between their self-management skills and their performance index (H:1.1);
- their performance index and interpersonal skills are closely connected (H:1.2);
- there is no significant relationship between their technology skills and their performance index (H:1.3).

Table 2-4. Association between Self-management Skills and Managerial Performance Index: the chi-square Test

Details	Value	Df	Asymp. Sig. (2-sided)
Pearson Chi-Square	31.126a	8	.000
Likelihood Ratio	33.639	8	.000
Linear-by-Linear Association	22.026	1	.000
N of Valid Cases	360		
a. 4 cells (26.7%) have expected count less than 5. The minimum expected count is 1.33			

Source: Primary data.

With reference to managers, the chi-square test in Table 2-4 reveals statistical evidence of a significant association between their self-management skills and their performance index. The test also confirmed hypothesis H:1.1 that there is a significant relationship between managers' performance index and their self-management skills. Thus, it can be stated that self-management skills have a high impact on the performance index.

Table 2-5. Association between Interpersonal Skills and Managerial Performance Index: the chi-square Test

Details	Value	df	Asymp. Sig. (2-sided)
Pearson Chi-Square	38.103a	8	.000
Likelihood Ratio	33.556	8	.000
Linear-by-Linear Association	15.372	1	.000
No. of Valid Cases	360		
a. 1 cells (6.7%) have expected to count less than 5. The minimum expected count is 3.83.			

Source: Primary data.

Chi-square test in table 2-5 provides statistical evidence of a significant association between performance index and interpersonal skills, with the confirming hypothesis H:1.2 which states that there is significant relationship between performance index of managers and their interpersonal skills. Thus, it can be inferred that interpersonal skills have a high impact on the performance index.

Table 2-6. Association between Technology Skills and Managerial Performance Index: the chi-square Test

Details	Value	df	Asymp. Sig. (2-sided)
Pearson Chi-Square	34.741a	8	.000
Likelihood Ratio	33.891	8	.000
Linear-by-Linear Association	21.490	1	.000
N of Valid Cases	360		
a. 3 cells (20.0%) have expected to count less than 5. The minimum expected count is 2.50.			

Source: Primary data.

In statistical terms, the chi-square test in table 8-6 provides evidence of a significant association between technology skills and performance index among managers, as also upheld by hypothesis H:1.3. Thus, it can be stated that technology skills have a high impact on the performance index.

6. Conclusion

The findings above demonstrate that managerial positions require a widespread use of soft skills, which are generally classified into three broad categories, namely, self-management skills, interpersonal skills, and technology skills. This paper also provided evidence of a significant association between soft skills of managers and managerial performance index. This suggests that current managers and ideal candidates should further develop their soft skills in order to provide better performance at work.

7. Future Work

The results of this study are encouraging. At present, our research focus is on factors enhancing the development of soft skills—and the role of training in this connection—which have been examined also through an investigation of the impact of soft skills on the relationship index.

References

Abowd, J. C. 2002. *Computing Person and Firm Effects Using Linked Longitudinal Employer-Employee Data*. Edina: Speed Press.

Alpern, M. 1997. "Critical Workplace Competencies," *Canadian Vocational Journal* 32, No. 4:6-16.

Beach, D. 1982. "A Training Program to Improve Work Habits," *Journal of Epsilon Pi Tau* 8, No. 2:69-74.

Bolles, R. N. 2002. *What Color Is Your Parachute?: A Practical Manual For Job-Hunters & Career- Changers*. Berkeley, CA: Ten Speed Press.

Brown, A. S. 2002. *Project Management Personality & Skill Types*. http://www.alexsbrown.com (accessed February 2, 2009).

Clagett, C. 1997. *Workforce Skills Needed by today's Employers*. Market Analysis, Prince George's Community College, Office of Institutional Research Analysis.

Hager, P., S. Crowley, and J. Garrick. 2000. *Soft Skills in a Hard Industry: How Developing Generic Competencies may Assist the Learning of the Small Building Contractor*. Australia: UTS Research Centre Vocational Education & Training.

Haskel, J. D. H. 2003. *Skills and Productivity in the UK Using Matched Establishment, Worker and Workforce Data*. London: Queen Mary University of London, Centre for Research into Business Activity.

Hoffman, T. G. 2003. *Preparing Generation Z*. www.computerworld.com/printthis/2003/0,4814,84295,00.html (accessed December 1, 2009).

Mulcahy, P. R. 2000. *PMP Exam Prep, Second Edition*. Edina: Beaver's Pond Press.

Pilsbury, D. 2002. *Learning and Training at Work* . Nottingham: DfES.

Prasad Kaipa, T. M. 2002. *Soft Skills are Smart Skills*. www.selfcorp.com (accessed December 12, 2009).

Salzman, H. 1998. *The New Corporate Landscape and Workforce Skills*. U.S. Department of Education, Office of Educational Research and Improvement (OERI), Publication Number NCPI-2-07.

Tamkin, P. G. 2004. *Skills Pay: The Contribution of Skills to Business Success*. SSDA. www.ssdamatrix.org.uk (accessed December 12, 2009).

Wentling, R. 1987. "Teaching Employability Skills in Vocational Education," *Journal of Studies in Technical Careers* 9, No. 4:354.

COMBINATORIAL APPROACHES TO INFORMAL SECTOR HUMAN CAPITAL INVESTMENTS AND YOUTH EMPLOYMENT IN SUB-SAHARAN AFRICA

BENJAMIN A. OGWO

1. Background

Globalisation has increased the ease, scope, and intensity of international relationships, the nature of which reflects the counterproductive results of the "beggar-my-neighbour" policy regimes of many developed countries. The thrust of these policies clearly illustrates the proverbial "hen coming home to roost", since their negative impacts on the beggar countries generate boomerang effects on richer countries. Conversely, the inclusive and systemic policies now advocated by regional unions and international agencies tend to promote mutual neighbourly co-existence. For example, issues relating to sourcing and outsourcing of human capital are now shared concerns among nations at both investment and utilisation phases. However, the ongoing global re-orientation towards "friend-my-neighbour" policies is not without political-economic rancour in balancing national survival instincts and sustainable global symbiotic relationships. In the final analysis, persistent international solidarity is required to sustain emerging perceptual re-orientation since the new world order cannot withstand the perils of perpetuated impoverishment of beggar countries.[1]

In Sub-Saharan Africa (SSA), another dimension of "beggar-my-neighbour" policies includes national policies designed to alienate some tribes or ethnic groups for the gains of others. In many SSA countries, these policies were pursued by colonial governments but sovereign

---

[1] Ogwo, B. A., V. C. Onweh, and S. C. Nwizu. 2010. "Globalized Workforce Development and Responsible Global Citizenship through E-literacy Capacity Building Programs for Low Income African Countries," in *E-agriculture and E-government for Global Policy Development: Implications for Future Directions*, eds. Maumbe, B. M., and V. T. Owei, (Hershey: IGI Global Publishers).

governments, after 50 years of independence in some cases, have continued to pay lip service to abolishing them. In another respect, "beggarly" policies are reflected in the dichotomous conceptualisation of education: the mainstream (formal) and an estranged sub-system (informal). In the educational sector, for example, the gentry are educated in the formal sub-system while the poor are left to grapple with the neglected informal sector. Informal sub-systems have persisted in many SSA countries as a consequence of non-inclusive governance leading to parallel economies, sectors and divisions named formal and informal.

In policy circles, there are three distinct schools of thought regarding the nature of the informal and formal sector relationship. The three schools of thought are the dualists, structuralists and the legalists.[2] Dualists describe the informal sector as distinct, marginal and not directly linked to the formal sector[3] but providing income or a safety net for the poor. Structuralists perceive the sector as being subordinated to the formal sector, while the legalists view informal sector activities as unregistered businesses that are the rational response of micro-entrepreneurs to the over-regulation within formal government bureaucracies.[4] Policy-makers at different times tend to be guided by the principles underlying these three schools of thought. The differences between these ideas explain the controversies and misconceptions surrounding understandings of the informal sector.

The concept of the informal sector entered academic discourse for the first time at the beginning of the 1970s as included in the reports on Ghana and Kenya prepared by the International Labour Organization (ILO) World Employment Programme.[5] It is an essential part of the private sector,[6] including individuals or groups of people engaged in legitimate enterprises, some of which may be regulated by the state but the vast

---

[2] Chen, M. A., R. Jhabrala, and F. Lund. 2002. "Supporting Workers in the Informal Economy: A Policy Framework," Working Paper on the Informal Sector, No. 2. Geneva: Employment Sector, International Labour Office.

[3] Soetan, R. O. 1996. *Technology and Female-owned Business in the Urban Informal Sector of South-west Nigeria.* Nairobi: ATPS.

[4] De Soto, H. 1990. *The Other Path.* London: I.B.Tauris and Co.

[5] Liimatainen, M. 2002. *Training and Skills Acquisition in the Informal Sector: A Literature Review.* Geneva: International Labour Office.

[6] Aluko-Olokun, I. 1997. "Institutional Building for Effective Capacity Development," in *Realizing National Vision by the Year 2010: The Human Resource Development Imperatives,* ed. ITF, (Jos: Industrial Training Fund), 69-76.

majority operating outside the legal framework of the state.[7] The informal sector has been characterised as being unregulated, and unrecognised by the government,[8] with unstructured apprenticeship training programmes[9] and employing low-productivity activities.[10] As already mentioned, informal activities are often characterised by low levels of capital, skills, access to organised markets and technology; low and unstable incomes and poor or unpredictable working conditions (vulnerable employment). In SSA the informal sector is heterogeneous, vast, difficult to operationalise and its size is not easy to quantify.[11] According to the ILO,[12] informal sector activities are often outside the scope of official statistical enumeration and government regulations, and beyond formal systems of labour and social protection. On average, the informal sector economy in 2000 accounted for 42% of GDP in 23 African countries and provided employment for a significant number of people.[13] Estimates suggest that, depending on the measure used, the informal sector generates between 10 and 20% of the aggregate output in developed countries and more than a third of the aggregate output in developing countries, reaching levels of more than 50% in some countries.[14]

The informal human capital investment pattern was the only mode for skills development in SSA before the advent of colonialism. Despite

[7] Kent, D. W., and P. S. D. Mushi. 1995. *The Education and Training of Artisans for the Informal Sector in Tanzania, Serial No. 18.* London: Overseas Development Administration.

[8] Odetola, T. 1993. "The Informal Sector and National Development: Contributions, Problems, Prospects and their Implications for Human Resources Development—An overview," in *12th National Training Conference proceedings,* ed. ITF, (Jos: ITF press), 1–30.

[9] Ogwo, B. A. 1994. "Transactional Analysis on the Activities of the Nigerian Technicians on the Nation's Technological Growth," in *Vocational/Technical Education and Technological Growth,* eds. Anyakoha, E. U., and E. C. Osuala, (Nsukka: Nigerian Vocational Association), 55-61.

[10] Ekpenyong, D. B., and M. O. Nyong. 1992. *Small and Medium-Scale Enterprises in Nigeria: Their Characteristics, Problems and Sources of Finance, RP16.* Nairobi: African Economic Research Consortium (AERC).

[11] Liimatainen, M. 2002. *Training and Skills Acquisition in the Informal Sector: A Literature Review.* Geneva: International Labour Office.

[12] International Labour Organization. 2000. *Employment and Social Protection in the Informal Sector.* Geneva: ILO.

[13] Adams, A. V. 2008. *Skills Development in the Informal Sector of Sub-Saharan Africa.* The World Bank.

[14] Schneider, F., and D. Enste, 2002, "Shadow Economies: Size, Causes and Consequences," *Journal of Economic Literature,* Vol. 38:77–114.

colonial and later on national neglect, the informal sector remained the major setting for skills training in SSA. The resilience of informal human capital investment practices is explained by the social cohesion and economic returns they engender in human capital development for the region. In their primordial form, informal human capital investment practices have focused on transmitting family-based knowledge in traditional medicine, agriculture, construction, arts and so on from one generation to another. In this situation, family ties automatically guarantee social and labour justice between the apprentice and the teacher. With the increasing expansion of the informal sector, apprentices are not always members of the teacher's family and the natural familial engagement is considerably reduced. The social injustice inherent in the system is akin to what is referred to as modern slavery. Apprentices serve their masters for three to five years at work, home and anywhere their masters want them to work. There are literarily no boundaries to what activities the apprentices can be involved in, whether that work relates to the business or to their master's personal life. This arrangement is in line with the socio-economic understanding that the apprentice would be "settled" (establish a similar business) after some years of service and training. In some cases, apprentices pay for the training they receive. In other arrangements, they not only pay for their training, but for services rendered as well. These types of investment practices seem incapable of meeting the demands of best practices in human capital development. Particular changes experienced in the SSA informal sector are listed below:

1. The presence of organised trade unions.
2. Higher education qualification of apprentices.
3. Marginal training programmes offered by national and international agencies.
4. An increased use of modern communication technology.

In some trades like auto-mechanics, there have been attempts to develop training guides to assist the master craftsman in conducting various training programmes.[15] A number of international agencies like the United Nations Development Programme (UNDP), the United Nations Educational, Scientific and Cultural Organisation (UNESCO) and the United Nations International Children's Fund (UNICEF) have at different

---

[15] Ogwo, B. A., and E. O. Ede. 2009. "Training and Continuing Education Program in Nigeria's informal Sector Automobile Industry," *International Journal of Vocational Education and Training* 17, No. 1:60-73.

times and in different countries promoted various capacity building programmes for practitioners in the informal sector. In Europe, there are different initiatives to accredit informal learning[16] and similar efforts are undertaken also in South Africa. These paradigm shifts in thought and the demographic composition of the informal sector provide the impetus for more interventions to be sustained so that there may be an increase in youth employment rates as well as enhanced productivity in SSA.

The global economic crisis has prompted economists to evaluate certain measures that were hitherto considered trivial such as addressing issues relating to the informal sector of SSA. Neglect of human capital investments in the informal sector by SSA governments despite the sector employing over 50% of the workforce is obvious economic negligence. Master craftsmen or teachers are lords unto themselves and apprentices are not afforded the best training in their trades. The international community has shown insufficient commitment towards integrating human capital investments in the informal sector onto the national workforce grid. Notably, many criminal activities such as illegal migration, piracy, human trafficking, and prostitution committed by SSA youth can be explained by the lack of gainful employment due to insufficient human capital investments in the informal sector. In a number of cases these young people are given skills that are not transferable. The resulting scenario is gross underemployment, low productivity, and many labour-related injustices. Even when other areas of the world are recognising informal learning, and indigenous knowledge/technology in SSA, these are undervalued, and their potentials are untapped. The formal technical and vocational education is separated from the informal equivalent. Foreign agencies as well as governments in SSA do not work to optimise human capital potential in the informal sector. Doing this would reduce the migration of many youth to other regions of the world.

There is hardly one single approach that can tackle the complex issue of productive utilisation of human capital in the informal sector to boost the economy of SSA countries. A combination of approaches promises to be a suitable response to challenges in the sector. The first step is to encourage policy-makers to accord the sector significant recognition attracting scholars' interest on how best to remediate the sector's shortcomings. Several economic models have been developed to address the issues related to formal sector human capital investment. This type of

---

[16] European Centre for the Development of Vocational Training (CEDEFOP). 2009. *European Guidelines for the Validation of Non-formal and Informal Learning*. CEDEFOP. http://www.cedefop.europa.eu/EN/Files/4054_en.pdf (accessed December 03, 2010).

attention should be directed to the informal sector as well. Educators should invest more of their interest and time in developing training packages suitable for the informal sector. In this connection, multidisciplinary studies should be encouraged to identify optimal solutions for the informal sector economy. It is commendable to note the efforts made in recognising traditional medicine in the health care system in many SSA countries. This recognition has improved the status and practice of traditional medicine as complementary to orthodox medicine in treating certain ailments.

Given the size of the informal sector's economic activity, no country in SSA can continue to neglect it without severe consequences. Asian countries remain an outsourcing destination for developed countries because their workforce is able to cope with the skills required by the outsourced companies. Besides the outsourcing issue, SSA countries should create novel ways of tapping into indigenous knowledge in the informal sector, gathering it and exporting it to other countries as part of their contribution to globalisation. It is only through the optimisation of this sector that these expectations could be realised. When this is properly articulated, the SSA countries would be on their way to earning recognition as real players in globalisation.

2. Objective of the Paper

On the basis of these considerations, this paper will further examine different combinatorial approaches to promote human capital investments in the informal sector for sustainable youth employment. These approaches include but are not limited to the development of new models (cf. combinatorial optimisation) for sustainable human capital investment or utilisation in the sector, synergistic international initiatives carried out by training agencies (ILO, UNESCO, UNDP, WHO and so on), use of customizable ICT, recognition of prior informal learning/indigenous knowledge by the formal education system and provision of compensatory international trade regimes for SSA are needed. The paper is organised under three major subheadings; Youth employment and productivity in SSA, Combinatorial Approaches for Sustainable Human Capital Investments in SSA, and Re-engineering SSA Informal Sector and Human Capital Investments for Youth Employment.

3. Youth Employment and Productivity in Sub-Saharan Africa

The global recession has brought to the fore issues relating to youth employment around the world. As expected, some countries have high employment rates while others are experiencing an array of social problems associated with youth unemployment and underemployment. According to the ILO,[17] poverty and lack of viable alternatives within the education system remain the main motivation for the majority of working youth in SSA. This can be explained by the failing and low returns-on-investment in formal education. The diminishing returns-on-investment in formal education due to the high unemployment rate of graduates explains why especially males, who are expected to reach early economic stability in order to bear the economic headship, were tacitly allowed to drop out of schools.[18] The informal sector is perceived as providing ready employment for the youth that have "failed" within the formal school system. Given the human capital investment pattern where the apprentice is "settled" (establishing a similar business) by their teacher or master on graduation, many parents tended to prefer informal sector training to the formal alternative that cannot guarantee employment. Table 2.7 below provides a very interesting insight into youth employment according to world regions.

Table 2-7 shows an appreciable increase in the percentage (between 1998 and 2009) of employed youth in SSA when compared to other regions. SSA has the second highest youth employment-to-population ratio and deserves special attention because of both the extent and nature of youth employment in the region.[19] A high youth employment-to-population ratio is not necessarily commendable, given the fact that most of these jobs are either unskilled or semi-skilled. It can clearly be related to the higher incidence of child labour, vulnerable employment and working

---

[17] ILO. 2010b. *Global Employment Trends for Youth*. ILO.
http://www.ilo.org/empelm/what/pubs/lang--en/docName--WCMS_143349/index.htm (accessed August 16, 2010).
[18] Ogwo, B. A., G. C. Oranu, and R. N. Oranu. "Application of ICT-based Open Learning Principles for Market/Mechanic Village Schools in South Eastern Nigeria," Paper presented at the IST-Africa 2008 Conference, Windhoek, Namibia,7-9 May 2008.
http://www.ist-africa.org/Conference2008/default.asp?page=my-page.
[19] ILO. 2010b. *Global Employment Trends for Youth*. ILO.
http://www.ilo.org/empelm/what/pubs/lang--en/docName--WCMS_143349/index.htm (accessed August 16, 2010).

Table 2-7. Youth Population, Employment and Unemployment, by Sex and Region, 1998, 2008 and 2009.

	Total			Male			Female		
	1998	2008	2009	1998	2008	2009	1998	2008	2009
Youth population (millions)									
WORLD	1056.5	1208.5	1214.0	539.2	620.5	624.0	517.3	588.0	590.0
Developed Economies & European Union	129.9	128.9	128.3	66.3	65.9	65.7	63.6	62.9	62.6
Central & South-East Europe (non-EU) & CIS	61.7	64.3	63.0	31.2	32.7	32.0	30.5	31.7	31.0
East Asia	212.1	243.8	243.0	109.3	128.0	128.0	102.8	115.8	115.0
South-East Asia & the Pacific	100.4	109.1	109.3	50.6	55.4	55.6	49.8	53.7	53.8
South Asia	263.4	313.9	317.8	136.5	162.9	165.0	126.9	150.9	152.8
Latin America & the Caribbean	98.6	104.8	105.0	49.5	52.7	52.8	49.1	52.1	52.2
Middle East	34.1	42.8	42.7	17.5	21.9	21.9	16.6	20.9	20.8
North Africa	35.8	42.7	42.6	18.1	21.6	21.6	17.7	21.0	21.0
Sub-Saharan Africa	120.6	158.4	162.2	60.2	79.4	81.3	60.4	79.0	80.9
Youth employment (millions)									
WORLD	505.9	540.4	538.5	298.6	321.3	321.0	207.2	219.1	217.5
Developed Economies & European Union	59.1	56.8	53.1	31.7	30.2	27.9	27.3	26.7	25.2
Central & South-East Europe (non-EU) & CIS	20.8	22.1	20.8	12.1	12.9	12.1	8.6	9.1	8.7
East Asia	134.8	130.5	131.2	67.1	64.8	65.6	67.7	65.7	65.6
South-East Asia & the Pacific	48.0	47.9	48.2	27.2	28.1	28.4	20.8	19.8	19.7
South Asia	117.4	131.6	132.8	82.8	94.3	95.6	34.6	37.4	37.3
Latin America & the Caribbean	45.7	47.4	46.1	29.3	29.2	28.4	16.3	18.1	17.7
Middle East	9.7	11.8	11.9	7.3	8.7	8.8	2.4	3.1	3.1
North Africa	10.4	12.2	12.4	7.4	8.8	9.1	3.0	3.4	3.3
Sub-Saharan Africa	60.1	80.1	82.1	33.7	44.3	45.2	26.5	35.9	36.9
Youth unemployment (millions)									
WORLD	71.9	74.1	80.7	41.9	43.4	47.5	30.0	30.6	33.2
Developed Economies & European Union	9.6	8.5	11.4	5.2	4.8	6.7	4.4	3.7	4.7
Central & South-East Europe (non-EU) & CIS	6.2	4.6	5.4	3.5	2.6	3.1	2.7	2.0	2.3
East Asia	13.6	12.3	12.8	8.0	7.2	7.5	5.6	5.1	5.3
South-East Asia & the Pacific	6.7	8.1	8.3	3.7	4.5	4.6	3.0	3.5	3.7
South Asia	11.4	14.6	15.3	8.0	10.2	10.7	3.4	4.4	4.6
Latin America & the Caribbean	8.4	7.9	8.8	4.3	3.9	4.3	4.1	4.0	4.5

Middle East	2.9	3.6	3.6	1.9	2.2	2.3	1.0	1.4	1.4
North Africa	3.7	3.7	3.8	2.3	2.2	2.3	1.5	1.5	1.5
Sub-Saharan Africa	9.4	10.8	11.1	4.9	5.7	5.9	4.5	5.0	5.2

Source: ILO 2010b: Global Employment Trends For Youth.

poor that are widespread in the region. These figures relate only to the formal sector, but it could be argued that "vulnerable" employment is even higher in the informal sector, since a number of people lost their jobs in the formal sector during the global recession, and moved to the informal sector as last resort.

In comparison, the formal and informal sector productivity quotient could be measured by the volume and quality of work as well as working conditions in each sector. In this paper the focus is placed on labour productivity, which is defined as output per unit of labour input, measured either in terms of the number of persons employed or in terms of the number of hours worked.[20] No doubt there is considerable technological learning occurring in the informal sector but there is insufficient record and dissemination of these innovations. The equation developed by Nnadi[21] to analyse the developed and developing countries' knowledge divide illustrates a similar relationship between formal and informal sectors. Increased knowledge derived from various productive activities in the formal sector is well documented providing for considerable high-quality knowledge density leading to further improvement. The same cannot be said of the informal sector. The advances made in the informal sector are scanty and far behind. Many of these specialised skills are located in sometimes remote locations where there is often a "skills glut", while other areas of the same country lack the same expertise. Given the increasing attention accorded to traditional medicine, there have been appreciable advances in the identification of more active ingredients in the herbs used by traditional "medicine men/women". In this sector, it is necessary to promote a closer collaboration between the formal and informal sector in order to enhance productivity. The formal educational process should develop programmes that could bridge the knowledge gap between the two sectors.

---

[20] ILO. 2008. *Skills for Improved Productivity, Employment Growth and Development.* ILO. http://www.ilo.org/public/libdoc/ilo/2008/108B09_54_engl.pdf (accessed August 23, 2010).
[21] Nnadi, I. 2010. "Knowledge-Centred Capacity Building Imperative In the Context of Industrial Raw Material Development," (lecture, 13th Herbert Macaulay Memorial Lecture, Faculty of Engineering University of Nigeria, Nsukka, July 24, 2010).

Fig. 2-1. Knowledge Divide between Formal and Informal Sectors (adapted from Nnadi 2010)

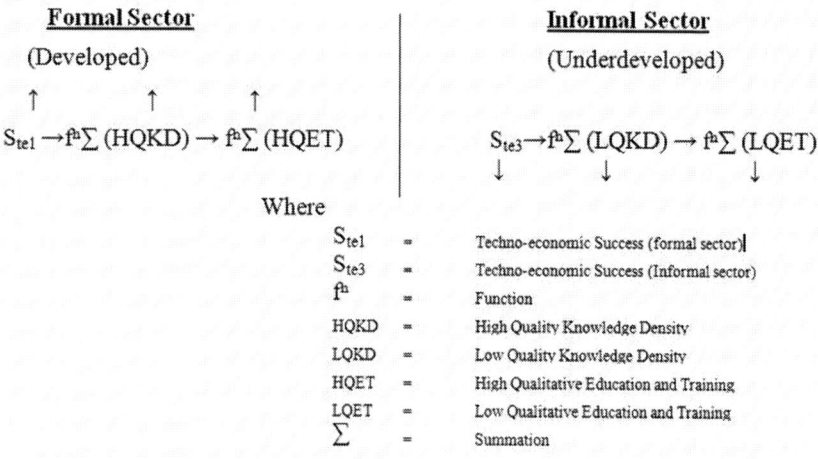

As the global economic crisis gets a firmer grip on the SSA region, more of those displaced from the formal sector inevitably resort to the informal sector. The position of this paper is not about formalising the informal sector, but to increase its productive potentials while retaining its fundamental characteristics of flexibility, fluidity and indigenous nature. There are many skills, techniques, knowledge in the SSA informal sector that can contribute to the global economy. Oriental medicine and the Chinese "all you can eat" restaurants are becoming increasingly popular in the United States' health and food industries without imitating their western equivalents. There will be more options in a globalised world if every region's best is made available to all. More machines should be introduced in the production processes in the informal sector in order to reduce man-hours spent on certain activities. A lot can be achieved by listening and comparing experiences among practitioners operating in two sectors in the similar trades, thereby bridging the existing divide and connecting the formal and informal sectors of the economies of SSA countries.

4. Combinatorial Approaches for Sustainable-Human Capital Investments in the Informal Sector in Sub-Saharan Africa

Human capital is regarded as the aggregate of human traits that could provide economic benefits to both the individual and society. In many countries, these human attributes are nurtured by parents and society in order to derive maximum benefits. These various forms of nurturing are regarded as education as well as investments that increase raw human capital. In the formal educational system, governments of many SSA countries provide compulsory basic education. In other situations, scholarships are offered to brilliant students. In addition, other incentives are provided for students to travel overseas and study certain disciplines. These calculated policy thrusts aim at enhancing the human capital accumulation in SSA countries. Unfortunately, similar policy interventions are not extended to the informal sector. The predominant human capital investment practices in the informal sector include family-oriented apprenticeship, journeymanship, self-learning and community/group learning.

There are some challenges with regards to intervening in the informal sector. Many of the craftsmen/women consider almost all of their activities as trade secrets and hardly allow anyone to understand the tenets of their practice. In some cases, an apprentice who is regarded as a threat or unruly would not be allowed into many of the trade secrets by the master or teacher. There is hardly any provision for continuing career development programmes[22] unless in instances where the apprentice gets employed as journeyman to another master craftsman. The current situation in relation to human capital investments in the informal sector cannot engender sustainable youth employment unless similar measures taken at the formal sector are extended to the informal sector. It is against this background that some combinatorial approaches are suggested, namely the combinatorial optimisation model of development, use of information communication technology to improve human capital investment practices in the informal sector, linking formal and informal human capital investments in SSA (National vocational qualification framework) and an introduction of compensatory Trade Regimes for SSA.

---

[22] Ogwo, B. A., and E. O. Ede. 2009. "Training and Continuing Education Program in Nigeria's informal Sector Automobile Industry," *International Journal of Vocational Education and Training* 17, No. 1: 60-73.

Combinatorial optimisation models are often referred to as *integer programming* models where programming refers to "planning". Since these models are used in planning where some or all of the decisions can take on only a finite number of alternative possibilities.[23] This is the process of arriving at one or more optimal answers to defined discrete research questions. According to Boorman,[24] historically, there has been the tendency to associate informal social/economic structure with non-rational human behaviour. This trend has limited the number of rigorous academic initiatives designed to address the problems that have been identified in the informal sector. In the bid to develop combinatorial optimisation models to tackle the problems of human capital investment and productivity in the informal sector, the optimisation factors are identified and programmed into the envisaged models. Such factors include but are not limited to the following: global workforce dynamics: migration, diasporas, demand/supply of human capital, recognition of prior learning: indigenous knowledge of local plants/technology, development of national vocational qualification frameworks, linkages with the formal education system, an adoption of modern production processes (including the use of information communication technology), productivity: attitude to work, pride, commitment, soft skills, political leadership in Sub-Saharan Africa, informal sector characteristics. Developing econometric models through combinatorial optimisation may sound like a tall order but there are super computers that have been modelling more subjective human behaviour. Certainly, if more efforts are put into modelling the informal sector in SSA there could be initial errors but steady efforts would yield sustainable solutions towards improved productivity.

Hardly does anyone doubt the remarkable efforts made by the United Nations' agencies in ensuring world peace, economic growth and justice. These agencies as well as non-governmental organisations have made inroads in the areas of health, education, trade, security, wealth creation and so on. It will yield considerable dividends if these agencies and organisations assist in providing the needed interventions to boost informal sector productivity. There have been solitary efforts by UNICEF, UNESCO and UNDP to encourage different forms of intervention. However, if these solitary efforts are synergised, they would have

---

[23] Hoffman, K., and M. Padberg. 2000. *Combinatorial and Integer Optimization.* http://iris.gmu.edu/~khoffman/papers/newcomb1.html (accessed August 5, 2010).
[24] Boorman, S. A. 1975. "A Combinatorial Optimization Model for Transmission of Job Information through Contact Networks," *The Bell Journal of Economics* 6, No. 1:216-249.

multiplier effects. By this token, they could set up regional centres of excellence in SSA to handle different aspects of the informal sector interventions. The resources invested by the Bill and Melinda Gates Foundation in tackling identified problems across formal and informal sectors in SSA are worthy of acknowledgement.

The other aspect of the combinatorial approach concerns the introduction of more modern production technologies and scientific techniques in improving the activities of the informal sector. Ogwo, Oranu and Oranu[25] reported the adoption of ICT in improving the delivery system in market/mechanic village schools designed to address educational needs of informal sector practitioners. Through these forms of intervention, the informal sector would be well prepared for closer linkage to the formal education system. Other factors like political leadership, work attitude and mindset on the urgency for catching up and significantly contributing to the global economy are also very essential optimisation issues. Not in the least is the issue of compensatory trade regimes for the SSA countries. In the present world trade order, raw materials are undervalued and finished products overpriced, thus undermining development initiatives of SSA countries. In the spirit of a "neighbour-my-friend" attitude towards globalisation, SSA countries should be aided to benefit the most from international transactions. It only takes systemic thinking to appreciate the importance of providing such assistance to SSA countries.

---

[25] Ogwo, B. A., G. C. Oranu, and R. N. Oranu. "Application of ICT-based Open Learning Principles for Market/Mechanic Village Schools in South Eastern Nigeria," Paper presented at the IST-Africa 2008 Conference, Windhoek, Namibia, 7-9 May 2008. http://www.ist-africa.org/Conference2008/default.asp?page=my-page.

Combinatorial Approaches to Informal Sector Human Capital
Investments and Youth Employment in Sub-Saharan Africa

Fig. 2-2. Re-engineering SSA's Informal Sector Human Capital Investments for Youth Employment

Conceptual Framework

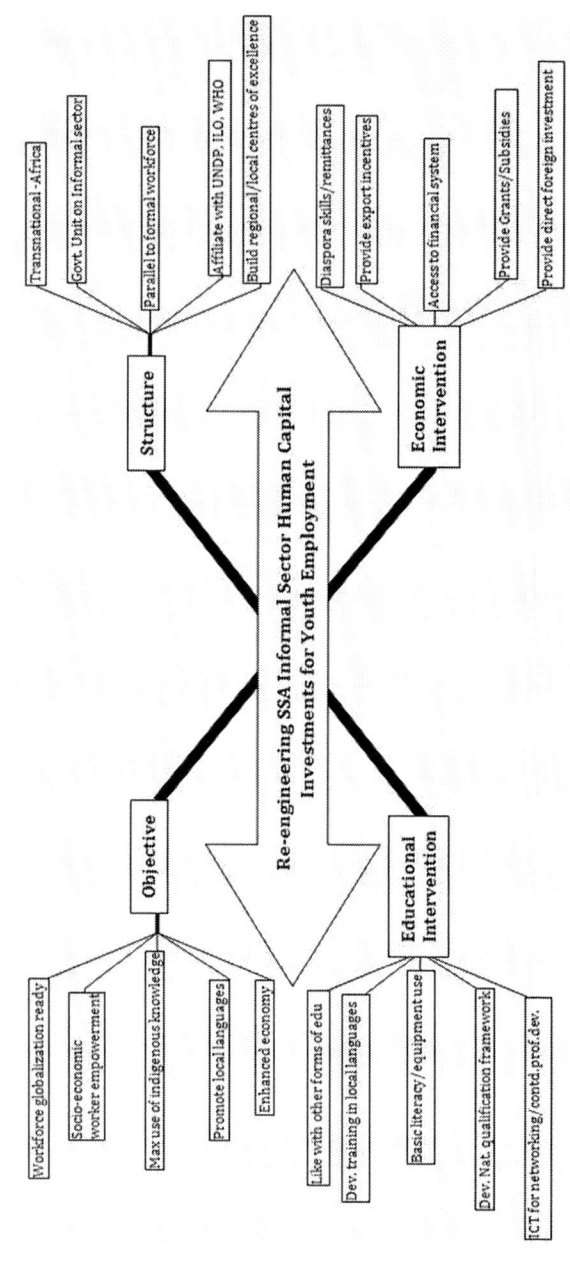

Globalisation continues to intriguingly highlight the uniqueness of human capital investments practices of the world's peoples. A number of historical antecedents, pride, world view, natural endowment and most of all attitudes inform the prevalent human capital utilization paradigms in different continents. The greatest focus on the re-engineering effort is the re-orientation of the attitude (mindset and inner transformation) of SSA youths on the relationship between effort and chance in attaining success in life. The world view of "what will be will be" does not work for productivity. Nnadi,[1] illustrated this aptly in the following equation:

$$\int_f \rightarrow f^n \frac{\sum E}{\sum C}$$

$$\int_f \rightarrow \frac{50}{50} = \frac{1}{1}$$

At all times $E + C = 100$ (boundary Condition)
Where $\int_f$ = Success index or success factor (Higher productivity)
$\qquad$ E = Effort (mental, intellectual, physical, technological)
$\qquad$ C = Chance (extraneous variable, luck, good fortune etc)
$\qquad$ f^n = function
$\qquad$ $\sum$ = Summation

Some erroneous religious and traditional practices have promoted the belief that chance factors are predestined, implying that human efforts cannot alter the course of events. Community perceptual re-engineering should start with the idea that most of life's circumstances can be altered by investing more efforts rather than depending on chance (benevolent spirit) and in this lie the prospects of stimulating sustainable development through which African economies can contribute uniquely to the global economy. If there is an area where SSA should emulate the western attitude, it is in the belief that humans can presumably play responsible roles in determining the course of earthly events.

With the increasing incidence of corruption amongst African governments coupled with poorly implemented western development paradigms, many interventionists now prefer to deal directly with community-based institutions. Even the African Diaspora prefer to remit

---

[1] Nnadi, I. I. 1998. "Modern management techniques, tool and skills for technology development and application," Paper presented at the Regional Programme For Technology Management REPTEM, Yaba, Lagos, Nigeria.

directly to the community and people with minimal formal sector involvement. The bulk of Diaspora remittances are transacted informally and sent to individuals[2] hence lending credence to the supposition that the Diasporas would be more comfortable in participating in informal sector initiatives. Thus, the valid alternative is to empower the domineering Africa's informal workforce in order to maximise its disposition for socio-economic empowerment as well as enhance globalisation readiness without significantly altering its characteristics.

The informal sector workforce in mining, manufacturing, agriculture and health occupations remains relevant in the 21st century. The "medicine men or women", for example, have been handling the continent's health care problems, providing traditional solutions to African diseases and midwifery. Even with its subsistence structure, agriculture in the informal sector has continued to provide food for the teeming African population with varying levels of success and producing those crops unique to Africa. If embraced, the African informal sector could provide the global economy with substances and materials only the continent can produce. In order to achieve this, the sector has to be re-engineered to perform at its peak.

The re-engineering should include the adoption of ICT to improve training within the informal sector. Rather than an attempt to formalise its structure, ICT training modules should be developed in local languages and there should be increased collaborations among formal and non-formal forms of education. Against this background, a national vocational framework should be developed by African countries akin to those developed in Europe and America that allow transferability of skills and credits among different educational systems. This approach will increase training opportunities within the sector and sustain its capacity to provide jobs for youth as well as bases for networking that could be enhanced by creating centres of excellence within the African region. A wealth of indigenous knowledge lies within the informal sector which the world is presently robbed of. Indigenous knowledge should be studied to determine materials and methods that the African workforce should exploit for more advantageous economic repositioning.

In economic terms the informal sector has remained the assured employment provider even for those who failed in the formal education system or who graduated with insufficient skills and cannot secure

---

[2] Ratha, D., and X. Zhimei. 2008. *Migration and Remittances Fact book 2008.* Migration and Remittances Team, Development Prospects Group, World Bank. http://siteresources.worldbank.org/INTPROSPECTS/Resources/334934-1199807908806/SSA.pdf (accessed April 17, 2010).

employment in trained occupations. The numerous grants and foreign direct investments in the formal sectors of African economies should be extended to the informal sector. Its people-oriented structure affords it the trust of the community which is necessary to sustain people's commitment to enduring development. Diasporas are longing to have alternative ways for investing in Africa. The boosting of the sector would afford the continent a parallel development niche other than that provided by the formal sector. The financial sector should continue to develop paradigms suited to the informal sector in order to be nationally inclusive. The more inclusive the financial sector becomes, the more it would provide employment and other resources to boost the African economy. Furthermore, agriculture in Africa still possesses rich flora and fauna that can be of good pricing when properly managed for exports. When the economic value of these materials is identified, their rarity would lend it high export values while increasing sustainability quotients.

5. Conclusion and Closing Argument

Globalisation is here for the long haul. The strength and effectiveness of the process can aptly be ascertained by the efficacy of the productive efforts of the weakest regions. The systemic nature of globalised relationships dictates that every sub-system should function effectively otherwise efforts of other seemingly effective sub-systems would be compromised by the malfunctioning of the defective sub-system. Imagine what could have happened to the United States of America if the acclaimed capitalist nation did not provide government assistance to the ailing banking sector. On the other hand, the bailout packages approved by many European economies were all in response to ameliorating ailing sub-systems without which their financial systems would have, by all accounts, collapsed. It is also easy to imagine an improved global security when African youths now involved in piracy, terrorism, illegal migration and other crimes will be gainfully employed. The argument is consistent with the suggestion of perceiving global human capital investment in a holistic international framework. Investment practices in the informal sector in SSA countries deserve international attention so that one bad apple will not spoil the whole bunch.

References

Adams, A. V. 2008. *Skills Development in the Informal Sector of Sub-Saharan Africa*. The World Bank.
http://info.worldbank.org/etools/docs/library/251006/day3SkillsfortheI nformalApril1Se2.pdf (accessed April 19, 2010).

Aluko-Olokun, I. 1997. "Institutional Building for Effective Capacity Development," in *Realizing National Vision by the Year 2010: The Human Resource Development Imperatives,* ed. ITF, (Jos: Industrial Training Fund), 69-76.

Boorman, S. A. 1975. "A Combinatorial Optimization Model for Transmission of Job Information through Contact Networks," *The Bell Journal of Economics* 6, No. 1:216-249.

Dabla-Norris, E., M. Gradstei, and G. Inchauste. 2005. *What Causes Firms to Hide Output? The determinants of informality.* IMF Institute.
https://www.imf.org/external/pubs/ft/wp/2005/wp05160.pdf (accessed August 23, 2010)

European Centre for the Development of Vocational Training (CEDEFOP). 2009. *European Guidelines for the Validation of Non-formal and Informal Learning.* CEDEFOP.
http://www.cedefop.europa.eu/EN/Files/4054_en.pdf
(accessed December 03, 2010).

Chen, M. A., R. Jhabrala, and F. Lund. 2002. "Supporting Workers in the Informal Economy: A Policy Framework," Working Paper on the Informal Sector, No. 2. Geneva: Employment Sector, International Labour Office.

De Soto, H. 1990. *The Other Path.* London: I.B.Tauris and Co.

Ekpenyong, D. B., and M. O. Nyong. 1992. *Small and Medium-scale Enterprises in Nigeria: Their Characteristics, Problems and Sources of Finance, RP16.* Nairobi: African Economic Research Consortium (AERC).

Hoffman, K., and M. Padberg. 2000. *Combinatorial and Integer Optimization.*   http://iris.gmu.edu/~khoffman/papers/newcomb1.html (accessed August 5, 2010).

International Labour Organization (ILO). 2000. *Employment and Social Protection in the Informal Sector.* Geneva: ILO.

—. 2008. *Skills for Improved Productivity, Employment Growth and Development.*   ILO.
http://www.ilo.org/public/libdoc/ilo/2008/108B09_54_engl.pdf
(accessed August 23, 2010).

—. 2010a. *Global Employment Trends.* ILO.

http://www.ilo.org/public/libdoc/ilo/P/09332/09332(2010-January).pdf
(accessed December 6, 2010).
—. 2010b. *Global Employment Trends for Youth.* ILO.
http://www.ilo.org/empelm/what/pubs/lang--en/docName--
WCMS_143349/index.htm (accessed August 16, 2010).
Kent, D. W., and P. S. D. Mushi. 1995. *The Education and Training of Artisans for the Informal Sector in Tanzania, Serial No. 18.* London: Overseas Development Administration.
Liimatainen, M. 2002. *Training and Skills Acquisition in the Informal Sector: A Literature Review.* Geneva: International Labour Office.
Nnadi, I. 2010. "Knowledge-Centred Capacity Building Imperative In the Context of Industrial Raw Material Development," (lecture, 13th Herbert Macaulay Memorial Lecture, Faculty of Engineering University of Nigeria, Nsukka, July 24, 2010).
Nnadi, I. I. 1998. "Modern management techniques, tool and skills for technology development and application," Paper presented at the Regional Programme For Technology Management REPTEM, Yaba, Lagos, Nigeria.
Odetola, T. 1993. "The Informal Sector and National Development: Contributions, Problems, Prospects and their Implications for Human Resources Development—An overview," in *12th National Training Conference proceedings,* ed. ITF, (Jos: ITF press), 1–30.
Ogwo, B. A., and E. O. Ede. 2009. "Training and Continuing Education Program in Nigeria's informal Sector Automobile Industry," *International Journal of Vocational Education and Training* 17, No. 1:60-73.
Ogwo, B. A., G. C. Oranu, and R. N. Oranu. "Application of ICT-based Open Learning Principles for Market/Mechanic Village Schools in South Eastern Nigeria," Paper presented at the IST-Africa 2008 Conference, Windhoek, Namibia,7-9 May 2008. http://www.ist-africa.org/Conference2008/default.asp?page=my-page.
Ogwo, B. A., V. C. Onweh, and S. C. Nwizu. 2010. "Globalized Workforce Development and Responsible Global Citizenship through E-literacy Capacity Building Programs for Low Income African Countries," in *E-agriculture and E-government for Global Policy Development: Implications for Future Directions*, eds. Maumbe, B. M., and V. T. Owei, (Hershey: IGI Global Publishers).
Ogwo, B. A. 1994. "Transactional Analysis on the Activities of the Nigerian Technicians on the Nation's Technological Growth," in *Vocational/Technical Education and Technological Growth,* eds.

Anyakoha, E. U., and E. C. Osuala, (Nsukka: Nigerian Vocational Association), 55-61.

Ratha, D., and X. Zhimei. 2008. *Migration and Remittances Fact book 2008.* Migration and Remittances Team, Development Prospects Group, World Bank. http://siteresources.worldbank.org/INTPROSPECTS/Resources/33493 4-1199807908806/SSA.pdf (accessed April 17, 2010).

Schneider, F., and D. Enste, 2002, "Shadow Economies: Size, Causes and Consequences,"*Journal of Economic Literature*, Vol. 38:77–114.

Soetan, R. O. 1996. *Technology and Female-owned Business in the Urban Informal Sector of South-west Nigeria.* Nairobi: ATPS.

YOUTH EMPLOYMENT: STUDENTS' PREFERENCES FOR MOBIFLEX WORK

FRANZ JOSEF GELLERT AND RENÉ SCHALK

1. Introduction

The traditional relationship between employers and employees is no longer appropriate to respond to the challenges posed by some recent developments in the world of work at a European level.[1]
As pointed out, for example, by Cohen,[2] Paridon and Hupke,[3] and also by the European Commission,[4] future employment relationships are expected to be characterised by high levels of mobility and flexibility, thus leading to an increase in the number of so-called "Mobiflex workers".[5]

Accordingly, job-related and firm-related preferences of young potential labour market entrants have been examined, to further develop the concept of Mobiflex work(ers).

[1] Eichhorst, W., A. Kuhn, E. Thode, and R. Zenker. 2009. *Traditionelle Beschäftigungsverhältnisse im Wandel. Benchmarking Deutschland: Normalarbeitsverhältnis auf dem Rückzug.* Programm Evidenzbasierte Politikstrategien, Bertelsmann Stiftung, 1-64. Cohen, R. L. 2010. "Rethinking 'Mobile Work': Boundaries of Space, Time and Social Relation in the Working Lives of Mobile Hairstylists," *Work, Employment & Society* 24, No. 1:65-84.

[2] Cohen, R. L. 2010. "Rethinking 'Mobile Work': Boundaries of Space, Time and Social Relation in the Working Lives of Mobile Hairstylists," *Work, Employment & Society* 24, No. 1:65-84.

[3] Paridon, H., and M. Hupke. 2009. "Psychosocial Impact of Mobile Telework: Results from an Online Survey," *Europe's Journal of Psychology*, No. 1.

[4] European Commission. 2007. *Communication from the Commission to the Spring European Council, Integrated Guidelines for Growth and Jobs (2008-2010)*, Brussels: European Commission.

[5] Avery, C., and D. Zabel. 2001. *The Flexible Workplace: A sourcebook of Information and research.* UK: Quorum Books.

The research focus has been on preferences[6] with respect to Mobiflex work and autonomy.

As for firms, the investigation included the expectations on the part of labour market entrants with regard to their future employers, who are supposed to provide opportunities for individual career development and promote work-life balance.

Against this background, the aim of this paper is to identify students' preferences for their future job and employer, and to provide a valuable contribution to further research in this field.

The study has been carried out considering students from two German universities which are located in northern Germany. Here, 175 respondents provided data about job-related and firm-related preferences that have been analysed on a case-by-case basis.

While the first section of the paper introduces a theoretical framework, and the second part presents research methodology and results, the final section provides conclusions, recommendations and a future research agenda.

2. Changing Employment Relationships

The changing nature of work results in major consequences in terms of employment relations. Firms are reviewing their strategy and perspective on employment, and employers increasingly negotiate flexible and fixed-term contracts with their employees, thus posing new challenges to workers in terms of flexibility and their ability to meet new employment requirements. More and more, workers and employers resort to Flexible Work Agreements (FWAs)[7] with relevant studies showing that positive effects can be observed not only for employers but also for employees, due to lower levels of work-family conflict, increased productivity, and higher rates of job satisfaction.[8] Drawing on the concept of mobility and

---

[6] Eurofound. 2006. *Fourth European Working Conditions Survey, FEWCS.* Eurofound Publication Office.

[7] Lambert, A. D., J. H. Marler, and H. G. Gueutal. 2008. "Individual Differences: Factors Affecting Employee Utilization of Flexible Work Arrangements," *Journal of Vocational Behavior* 73, No. 1:107-117.

[8] Lapierre, L. M., P. E. Spector, T. D. Allen, S. Peolmans, C. L. Cooper, M. P. O'Driscoll, J. I. Sanchez, P. Brough, and U. Kinnunen. 2008. "Family-supportive Organization Perceptions, Multiple Dimensions of Work-family Conflict, and Employee Satisfaction: A Test of Model across Five Samples," Journal of Vocational Behavior 73, No. 1:92-106.

flexibility, the main features of the new employment relations have been identified.

In this sense, autonomy is regarded as a job-related characteristic, and employer's provisions, career opportunities and work-life balance as firm-related features, with such aspects that have been the subject of earlier studies on employment trends.

2.1 Mobility and Flexibility

Traditionally, the relevant literature defines mobility as frequent changes within the workplace—i.e. workers operating at multiple work sites[9]—but such definition might also encompass workers who are involved in cooperative work groups (also by means of social networks), various types of buyer-supplier relationships, R&D collaborations, or those performing their task on a temporary basis as a part of certain employment exchanges.

According to Turner:[10]

> modern societies (organisations, unions, and political parties) in particular are characterised by a deep contradiction between the economic need for labour mobility and the state's political need to assert sovereignty.

Workers' mobility is promoted by the European Union as one of the objectives set out by the Lisbon Strategy and should increase their employment opportunities and productivity, also settling a balance between work and private life. Mobility provided to Mobiflex workers is closely associated with their levels of flexibility (in terms of market, employers, clients and job demand).

Flexibility is regarded as the ability to change working time or tasks, and can be seen as a multidimensional construct that consists of job, behaviour, and task flexibility.[11] Flexibility is of high importance to both

---

[9] Nas, S. O., A. Ekeland, C. Svanfeldt, and M. Åkerblom, M. 1998. *Summary Report of the Focus Group on Mobility of Human Resources in Nordic Countries. An Analysis Based on Register Data.* STEP Report R-06/98
http://www.sol.no/step/ (accessed June 3, 2010). Cohen, R. L. 2010. "Rethinking 'Mobile Work': Boundaries of Space, Time and Social Relation in the Working Lives of Mobile Hairstylists," *Work, Employment & Society* 24, No. 1:65-84.
[10] Turner, B. S. 2007. "The Enclave Society. Towards a Sociology of Immobility," *European Journal of Social Theory* 10, No. 02:287-304.
[11] European Commission. 2008. *European Employment Strategy (EES).* Brussels: European Commission. http://ec.europa.eu/employment_social (accessed August 10, 2010).

employers and employees, as it represents an instrument to simultaneously meet requirements in terms of markets, organisations and societies.[12] Mobiflex workers are flexible in relation to where and when their working activity is performed and to the number of hours exceeding the standard working day. Avery and Zabel[13] identified benefits arising from flexibility, *inter alia* including higher levels of customer satisfaction and productivity, reduced absenteeism and turnover, heightened employees morale, remuneration policies for survivors of downsizing, and flexibility as a recruitment tool. The main disadvantage of flexibility lies in the unwillingness to acknowledge the value of FWAs on the part of middle and top management, unions, and supervisors, as they find it difficult to manage flexible workers.

Further barriers are represented by the adoption of some restrictive policies on the part of the company, issues in terms of working task to be assigned, information and reporting systems, as well as cultural issues. Although it can be argued that FWAs have been intensively implemented by workers, further research is required in this connection, with studies carried out so far revealing that upper-level managers are more likely to resort to FWAs only when used by their peers.[14] However, flexibility and FWAs are essential tools for Mobiflex workers as allowing for better management of work and private life at an individual level.[15] In this connection, FWAs are regarded by Mobiflex workers as an effective instrument to reduce conflict between the work and family domains.

2.2 Autonomy

Job autonomy is defined as the extent to which employees are able to decide for themselves the way they perform their main tasks and the order they complete subtasks.[16] The traditional definition of autonomy is also

---

[12] Birindelli, L. and E. Rustichelli. 2007. *The Transformation of Work? Work Flexibility in Europe.* Work organisation and restructuring in the knowledge society—WORKS project, Project number: CIT3-CT-2005-006193.

[13] Avery, C., and D. Zabel. 2001. *The Flexible Workplace: A sourcebook of Information and research.* UK: Quorum Books.

[14] Lambert, A. D., J. H. Marler, and H. G. Gueutal. 2008. "Individual Differences: Factors Affecting Employee Utilization of Flexible Work Arrangements," *Journal of Vocational Behavior* 73, No. 1:107-117.

[15] Ibid.

[16] Van Mierlo, H., C. G. Rutte, J. K. Vermunt, M. A. J. Kompier, and J.A.M.C. Doorewaard. 2006. "Individual Autonomy in Work Teams: The Role of Team

related to increased employees' performance and job satisfaction at organisational, individual or team levels,[17] as well as to reduced psychological complaints and turnover.[18] Individual autonomy can be seen as somehow limiting interactions with others, even though group/team autonomy is often the result of individual outcomes and not just the work of a self-organised or self-managed group.[19] That said, employees are to some extent still dependent on their employers.

On the employer's side, dependency means obligations towards clients, markets, competitors, stakeholders and shareholders.

From where the worker stands, dependency is associated with the type of work performed either as a white-collar or a blue-collar worker. Mobiflex work is mainly found in service organisations or consultancy companies, where autonomy is generally valued more. Workers in this sector resort to their expertise over time, and are consequently less dependent on their employers for paid work.[20] In considering the distinction between white-collar and blue-collar workers, it has been found that managers are more used to Mobiflex work, as they need to be mobile and flexible to perform their jobs. Accordingly, they are already accustomed to operate independently. It is worth pointing out that blue-collar workers, e.g. in the automotive industry, perceive a lower degree of autonomy due to strictly organised processes and sets of tasks. Autonomy is therefore limited, especially when employees have obligations to their employers, as in the case of delivering services, when a delivery date has to be met.

Autonomy, Self-efficacy, and Social Support," *European Journal of Work and Organizational Psychology* 15, No. 3:281-299.

[17] Langfred, C.W. 2000. "The Paradox of Self-management: Individual and Group Autonomy in Work Groups," *Journal of Organizational Behavior* 21, No. 5:563-585.

[18] Van Mierlo, H., C. G. Rutte, J. K. Vermunt, M. A. J. Kompier, and J.A.M.C. Doorewaard. 2006. "Individual Autonomy in Work Teams: The Role of Team Autonomy, Self-efficacy, and Social Support," *European Journal of Work and Organizational Psychology* 15, No. 3:281-299.

[19] Langfred, C.W. 2000. "The Paradox of Self-management: Individual and Group Autonomy in Work Groups," *Journal of Organizational Behavior* 21, No. 5:563-585.

[20] Donelly, R. 2006. "How 'Free' is the Free Worker? An Investigation into the Working Arrangements Available to Knowledge Workers," *Personnel Review* 35, No. 1:78-97.

3. Organisational Issues

Expectations and needs on the part of graduates with regard to their future employer mainly include significant financial benefits (in terms of salary, fringe benefits and so on). However, "more than 95% of European employees have a regular, fixed salary",[21] with 50% of them being granted the opportunity to increase their monthly income. Despite that, findings revealed a rise in the number of "working poor", primarily the result of an increase in low-paid employment in the European Union.[22] Equally important are also less tangible organisational issues, e.g. work environment, open-minded communication and so on.

3.1 Opportunities for Career Development

Nowadays, organisations tend to outsource projects, assignments, or even entire departments, thus reducing workers' opportunities to plan a more predictable career path within the company. A reduction in the workforce results in higher levels of job insecurity, which may lead to severe discontinuity in career competences.[23]

The nature of personal development can be of subjective or objective nature. Subjective development is related to the employees' perception of their level of development,[24] whereas objective development means that a person can achieve higher positions, or moving to a new one, as a result of career advancement. Mobiflex workers' individual development—as well as career advancement—is to a certain extent limited by projects assigned within the organisation, which, at the same time, provide opportunities for them to pursue a career inside the company. Further, there are some factors that influence Mobiflex workers' personal development. First, the risk of losing social interaction could lead to isolation. This is particularly the case of Mobiflex workers, who are usually requested to interact with other people (colleagues, team mates and peers) on a constant basis.

---

[21] Eurofound. 2006. *Fourth European Working Conditions Survey, FEWCS.* Eurofound Publication Office.
[22] Eichhorst, W., W. Marx, and E. Thode. 2010. *Atypische Beschäftigung und Niedriglohnarbeit.* Research Report Series, Bertelsmann Stiftung.
[23] DeFillippi, R. J. and M. B. Arthur. 1994. "The Boundaryless Career: a Competency-based Perspective," *Journal of Organizational Behavior* 15, No. 4:307-324.
[24] Arthur, M. B., S. N. Khapova, and C. P. M. Wilderom. 2005. "Career Success in a Boundaryless Career World," *Journal of Organizational Behavior* 26, No. 2:177-202.

Secondly, the "psychological" relationship between an employer and Mobiflex workers is unlikely to include obligations in terms of career perspectives. Thirdly, job insecurity, or uncertainty associated with the task to be performed more generally, could be detrimental to Mobiflex workers who, due to their cultural background, work philosophy and strategy, are in need of employment stability.

It should also be considered that, in the event of a reduction in productivity, Mobiflex workers are more exposed to dismissal, and that in terms of monthly remuneration, they should be treated on the same footing as employees hired on a permanent basis.

Supporting Mobiflex workers and providing them with a suitable and smart working environment by properly resorting to telecommunication technologies does not necessarily lead to career development, but rather to new opportunities in terms of work-life balance.

3.2 Work-life Balance

Although 80% of workers in the European Union are satisfied with their relationship between working hours and time off (WLB), it is now worth considering the type of work and family responsibilities that need to be balanced. Work-Family Conflict (WFC) or Family-Work Conflict (FWC) takes place when demands from both work and family collide with each other, consequently affecting personal satisfaction and well-being.[25] In this respect, individual and family well-being can be positively influenced by employers by means of an effective organisational culture within the company that takes account of family needs.[26] There is no doubt that a family-supportive work environment is essential for Mobiflex workers, also because it might be the case that different companies assign them different projects. In this sense, they experience less work-family conflict if they perceive they are able to successfully combine expectations at both an individual and organisational level.

Further, whereas employees show their willingness to perform homework and telework—provided that these forms of employment are

---

[25] Rantanen, J., U. Kinnunen, T. Feldt, and L. Pulkkinen. 2008. "Work-family Conflict and Psychological Well-being: Stability and Cross-lagged Relations with One- and Six-year Follow-ups," *Journal of Vocational Behavior,* No. 73:37-51.

[26] Lapierre, L. M., P. E. Spector, T. D. Allen, S. Peolmans, C. L. Cooper, M. P. O'Driscoll, J. I. Sanchez, P. Brough, and U. Kinnunen. 2008. "Family-supportive Organization Perceptions, Multiple Dimensions of Work-family Conflict, and Employee Satisfaction: A Test of Model across Five Samples," *Journal of Vocational Behavior* 73, No. 1:92-106.

adequately supported and complemented by telecommunication technologies, such as wireless local area networks (LAN)—their presence at the office is no longer needed and they can operate from home.

4. Mobiflex Work(er): A Composition of Mobility and Flexibility

Mobility and flexibility of workers evolved to meet the needs of markets, employers, clients and jobs.[27] As we have seen, a form of employment that responds to the demands of both mobility and flexibility can be defined as Mobiflex work, and workers in these positions are Mobiflex workers. The concept comprises the willingness to travel and to be flexible around the clock, and a certain level of autonomy in terms of decision-making, which is important for workers and their job satisfaction. A research question arises as to whether Mobiflex work would match students' preferences. Fig. 2-3 summarises the variables (job- and firm-related preferences, and individual attributes) that have been examined.

Fig. 2-3. Conceptual Framework: Students' Job and Firm-related Preferences

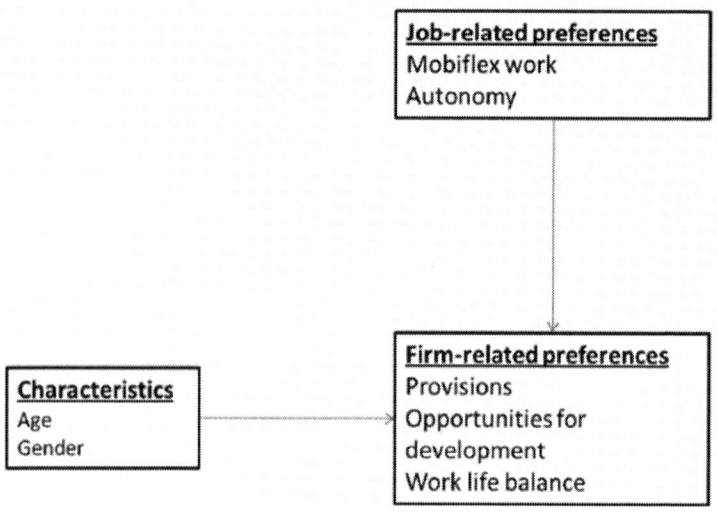

Source: authors' own elaboration.

---

[27] Portugali, J. 1989. "Nomad Labor: Theory and Practice in the Israeli-Palestinian Case," *Transactions of the Institute of British Geographers,* 14, No. 2:207-220.

5. Methodology

5.1 Procedure

Students were asked about their expectations, needs and wishes with respect to their job-related and firm-related preferences (15 and 18 questions, respectively). Respondents answered the questions according to a 4-point scale ranging from 1 (fully disagree) to 4 (fully agree). Questions were based on earlier studies on students' job- and firm-related preferences in Germany.[28]

A Principle Axis Factor Analysis (PAF) was first carried out in order to examine the number of factors with respect to student preferences related to the job and the firm. Two main students' job-related preferences have been identified:

- autonomy, including the following features (Cronbach's alpha = .70): work variety, challenging tasks, autonomy, independency, and leadership;

- mobiflex work (Cronbach's alpha = .65), including project work, contact with customers, team-working, and national and international travelling.

With respect to students' firm-related preferences, three factors have emerged: some employer-related aspects, opportunities for career development, and some instruments for work-life balance:

- employer-related aspects (Cronbach's alpha = .65) deal with the company reputation, financial benefits (e.g. a company car) and career prospects;

- opportunities for further development (Cronbach's alpha = .62) included five factors: the absence of hierarchy, the opportunity to be part of an international team, entrepreneurial climate, levels of attractiveness of products/services, and learning opportunities;

- opportunities offered in terms of work-life balance (Cronbach's alpha = .51) included: work climate, work-life balance, flexible working hours and working conditions.

---

[28] Kienbaum Consultants International GmbH. 2008. *Absolventenstudie und Arbeitgeberattraktivität 2007/2008,* Gummersbach: Kienbaum www.kienbaum.de (accessed August 10, 2009). Trendence Institute GmbH. 2008. *Das deutsche Absolventbarometer 2008*. IT-edition Auszüge aus den Ergebnissen, Berlin: Trendence Institute. http://www.trendence.de (accessed April 20, 2009). Universum Communications Sweden AB, 2007. *The Universum Graduate Survey 2007.* Stockholm, http://www.universumglobal.com (accessed April 20, 2009). McKinsey & Company. 2008. *Most wanted. Die Arbeitgeberstudie 2008.* McKinsey & Company.

We processed the answers of our research questions on a case-by-case basis by means of hierarchical multiple regression analyses, considering *in primis* gender and age and subsequently job-related preferences, in order to investigate the relationship with firm-related preferences.

5.2 Sample

For the purposes of this research, responses of students in two selected universities in northern Germany (175 students: 58% males and 42% females) were gathered. The average age of students was 25 and their educational level ranged from Bachelor's to Master's. Of note is also the fact that respondents were planning to take their first steps into the labour market as employees. The response rate was 98%.

5.3 Results

Table 2-8 shows a negative correlation between age and Mobiflex work which indicates that Mobiflex work is less considered with age while it is closely associated with employer-related aspects, and with those opportunities for career development mentioned above. Students prefer Mobiflex work as long as they receive tangible and intangible support from the employer. However, among young people, preference for autonomy is higher than the one for Mobiflex work, and work-life balance is perceived as less relevant than opportunities for career advancement.

Table 2-9 shows that students' preference for Mobiflex work is an important element to consider at the time they opt for employers who provide a certain amount of financial benefits (R square is .15), and opportunities for development (R square is .19). A preference for autonomy predicts a choice for employers that provide opportunities for work-life balance; however, the relationship is not deemed to be consistent (R square is .03).

With reference to the above mentioned question "Do students' job- and firm-related preferences match the characteristics of Mobiflex work?", the outcomes of the present study revealed that respondents have a higher preference for autonomy than for Mobiflex work. The preference for Mobiflex work predicts what type of employer young entrants will choose especially with regard to financial benefits and opportunities for career advancement. Moreover, the results of our research confirms that the opportunity for individual career development has a positive influence on students' mobility, flexibility, and the management of work-life balance.

Table 2-8. Means, SDs, and Correlations for the Student Sample (N=175)

Nr.	Variable	Mean	SD	1	2	3	4	5	6
1	Gender	1.42	.49	-					
2	Age	2.05	.22	.06	-				
3	Mobiflex work	2.75	.51	.10	-.19*	-			
4	Autonomy	3.21	.40	.00	-.08	.24**	-		
5	Employer provisions	2.96	.43	.02	-.02	.38**	.23**		
6	Opportunity development	3.03	.43	.17*	-.05	.42**	.34**	.20**	-
7	Opportunities for WLB	3.41	.37	.05	.03	.03	.17*	.05	.08

Significance at: **p<0.01; *p<0.05.

Table 2-9. Regression Analyses Student Sample (N=175)

Variable	Employment Provisions		Opportunities for development		Opportunities for WLB	
	R^2	β	R^2	B	R^2	B
Gender	.00	-.01	.03	.14*	.00	.05
Age	.00	.06	.03	.00	.00	.06
Mobiflex work	.15	.35**	.19	.34**	.00	-.00
Autonomy	.16	.14	.25	.25	.03	.18*

Significance at: **p<0.01; *p<0.05.

6. Discussion

The aim of this paper is to shed some light on current trends in the field of employment relationships considering the students' viewpoint. We took FWAs as a starting point to further develop the concept of Mobiflex workers, to whom organisations will give increasing importance in the years to come.

New tools and supportive activities are currently being developed to promote Mobiflex work, although they need to be further implemented. Mobiflex workers prefer to operate independently and appreciate self-managing tasks and job autonomy. They are able to deal with changing markets and clients' demands rapidly, thanks to their flexibility and to new contractual arrangements, teleworking, contingent or temporary work. In order to balance job and non-work-related activities, Mobiflex workers need to operate in a family- and individual-supportive work environment.

Further, as a member of different networks, Mobiflex workers can reduce their social isolation, improve their communication skills, further develop their knowledge and employability, and positively affect their relationship with employers, not to mention that such an approach might prove to be effective in reducing stress and conflicts. Generally speaking, a network is a set of employees or actors (e.g. mobiflex workers) who are loosely or strongly linked to each other,[29] and the relationship between such networks and the outside world has to be in line with established common processes and goals.[30]

It should be noted that, as mainly task-driven, it is more difficult for Mobiflex workers to pursue career advancement.

In this connection, a substantial body of research focusing on two apparently conflicting career theories has been carried out recently.

The first theory is based on the traditional idea of career, according to which an employee attains promotion from one position to the next.[31] The second theory, as pointed out by Arthur et al.,[32] is based on the concept of "boundaryless" career that can be distinguished into subjective and objective careers involving internal and external labour markets. This new concept is strongly related to what DeFillippi and Arthur argued in 1994, that fixed systems of job position and stable career paths have reduced significantly over the last few years.

Despite that this paper provides a useful contribution to this research strand by examining a wide sample of new entrants, there is still scope for improvement. For instance, when respondents were asked about their perception of some specific issues, we realised that questions might have been biased. Furthermore, we did not consider gender-specific differences in terms of perception; here variation patterns could be identified in specific areas, such as work-life balance.

---

[29] Bartol, K. M., and X. Zhang. 2007. "Networks and Leadership Development: Building Linkages for Capacity Acquisition and Capital Accrual," *Human Resource Management Review* 17, No. 4:388-401.

[30] Wenger, E. 2000. "Communities of Practice and Social Learning Systems," *Organization* 7, No. 2:225-246.

[31] Arthur, M. B., S. N. Khapova, and C. P. M. Wilderom. 2005. "Career Success in a Boundaryless Career World," *Journal of Organizational Behavior* 26, No. 2:177-202.

[32] Ibid.

As this cross-sectional study was conducted only at a national level, the perception of respondents might be affected by different economic and labour market situations.

Organisational research on Mobiflex work is still at an early stage and there are some areas that deserve further investigation.

First, the influence on the conceptualisation of Mobiflex work as presented here has yet to be demonstrated on the basis of productivity, cost development and performance. Secondly, the influence of Mobiflex work on changes in demand on the part of customers, stakeholders and shareholders could be of interest for researchers and practitioners. Further, in times of globalisation, research on the effects of Mobiflex work on intercultural business would increase knowledge in this area, contributing to further develop "boundaryless" businesses. At the individual level, research on psychological consequences of Mobiflex work is required since so far this area has not been sufficiently investigated. Finally, it would be of interest to evaluate the influence of psychological and physical stress factors on Mobiflex workers. The acknowledgement and value of their work is now well established, and so is their occupational status. Therefore, data are required to understand whether such workers might contribute to moderating or mediating the effects and outcomes of certain processes.

7. Relevance for Research and Practice

7.1 In Political Terms

Current European Commission policies provide that workers have to develop their own employability to maintain state-of-the-art skills, to increase their value and enhance career opportunities. In this connection, Mobiflex workers have to be able to deal with changes in work and workplace conditions rapidly, and to take part in training and personal development opportunities when available. In the same vein, Europe needs to adopt new strategies to increase work and workers' flexibility, and to increase employment security. Furthermore, policies must be implemented with the view to provide a fair and performance-based pay system, and to value the work of Mobiflex workers, for whom issues such as equal treatment for men and women, the recognition of differences in terms of cultural background among the workforce and the employment of health promotion schemes are of significant importance.

The founding principle to consider while analysing such categories of workers is the shift from *job security* to *employment* or, *employability security*, which also includes—to a certain extent—income security.[33]

7.2 At a Company Level

Companies need to design new recruitment policies and strategies to deal with Mobiflex workers, ensuring equal treatment for Mobiflex and permanent workers. Human resources managers should develop training programmes aimed at improving social, communication, network-building and motivation skills, also by the setting-up of *ad-hoc* workshops. In addition, family-supportive programmes are regarded as necessary to give Mobiflex workers the chance to balance work and private life. Equally important are career prospects which need to be properly and fairly developed. Of note is also the fact that aging workers tend to become Mobiflex workers, thus raising new questions in this connection.

Furthermore, Mobiflex workers usually handle their personal business on their days off, therefore reducing absenteeism. In comparison with traditional workers, Mobiflex workers can also work with minor illnesses or with sick children at home, whereas traditional workers would need to take leave without being able to work. In this sense, Mobiflex workers are more productive. In addition, having people working from home or from other mobile locations allows companies to save money, reducing the office space required and gas emission caused by daily commuting. Finally, Mobiflex work arrangements contribute to build loyalty in employees and reduce costly turnover.

---

[33] NIDI, Netherlands Interdisciplinary Demographic Institute. 2008. *Demographic Trends, Socio-Economic Impacts and Policy Implications in the European Union-2007*. Executive Summary of the Monitoring Report. Brussels: European Observatory on the Social Situation-Demography Network. European Commission. 2007. *Communication from the Commission to the Spring European Council, Integrated Guidelines for Growth and Jobs (2008-2010)*. Brussels: European Commission. Bekker, S., and T. Wilthagen. "Europe's Pathways to Flexicurity: Lessons Presented from and to the Netherlands," unpublished paper presented at IERA Conference, Nijmegen, Netherlands, June 2008. European Commission. 2008. *European Employment Strategy (EES)*. Brussels: European Commission. http://ec.europa.eu/employment_social (accessed August 10, 2010).

7.3 From the Workers' Viewpoint

Mobiflex work increases employability of circumstantially marginalised groups, such as mothers and fathers with small children, the disabled or people living in remote areas. Mobiflex work offers possibilities for increased service and international reach, since workers in different time zones can ensure that a company is virtually always open for business. Such approach results in higher levels of job security as improving customer satisfaction. Further, Mobiflex workers who are involved in international projects develop social skills—such as communication skills—and the ability to deal with people of different cultural backgrounds. Homework increases the balance between family and work and therefore can positively influence the relationship between parents and children. However, there are some disadvantages that need to be taken into account. Workers may be exposed to increased workloads, facing higher levels of stress. Distractions at home can have a similar effect, especially among home workers who need to take care of small children. Mobiflex workers may lack the sense of loyalty to the company that they would have if working in an office and they could lose space in their homes, also suffering some consequences of converting a room into an office. They can experience social isolation and must be able to deal with this issue by socialising outside the company, developing close ties with colleagues (e.g. via social media) and sharing common experiences within and outside the company.

Physical and psychological effects of Mobiflex work have so far not been thoroughly examined and further research is required. At present, it can be said that Mobiflex workers themselves have to take care of their workload in terms of working hours, as well as of their physical and mental condition. In particular, students who start their career as Mobiflex workers right after completing their education need to pay attention to their mental and physical state.

7.4 From the Students' Viewpoint

According to the survey, students are more interested in autonomy than in Mobiflex work. However, if they start working as Mobiflex workers, they should be trained to work in different teams. In this respect, diversity means to be able to cope with people of different cultural backgrounds, different attitudes of participants, and differences in beliefs, behaviour, education and professional background. Finally, students also need to be trained in project management, use of technical equipment and managerial tools, always paying attention to their mental and physical well-being.

References

Arthur, M. B., S. N. Khapova, and C. P. M. Wilderom. 2005. "Career Success in a Boundaryless Career World," *Journal of Organizational Behavior* 26, No. 2:177-202.

Avery, C., and D. Zabel. 2001. *The Flexible Workplace: A sourcebook of Information and research.* UK: Quorum Books.

Bartol, K. M., and X. Zhang. 2007. "Networks and Leadership Development: Building Linkages for Capacity Acquisition and Capital Accrual," *Human Resource Management Review* 17, No. 4:388-401.

Bekker, S., and T. Wilthagen. "Europe's Pathways to Flexicurity: Lessons Presented from and to the Netherlands," unpublished paper presented at IERA Conference, Nijmegen, Netherlands, June 2008.

Birindelli, L. and E. Rustichelli. 2007. *The Transformation of Work? Work Flexibility in Europe.* Work organisation and restructuring in the knowledge society—WORKS project, Project number: CIT3-CT-2005-006193.

Cohen, R. L. 2010. "Rethinking 'Mobile Work': Boundaries of Space, Time and Social Relation in the Working Lives of Mobile Hairstylists," *Work, Employment & Society* 24, no 1:65-84.

DeFillippi, R. J. and M. B. Arthur. 1994. "The Boundaryless Career: a Competency-based Perspective," *Journal of Organizational Behavior* 15, No. 4:307-324.

Donelly, R. 2006. "How 'Free' is the Free Worker? An Investigation into the Working Arrangements Available to Knowledge Workers," *Personnel Review* 35, No. 1:78-97.

Eichhorst, W., A. Kuhn, E. Thode, and R. Zenker. 2009. *Traditionelle Beschäftigungsverhältnisse im Wandel. Benchmarking Deutschland: Normalarbeitsverhältnis auf dem Rückzug.* Programm Evidenzbasierte Politikstrategien, Bertelsmann Stiftung, 1-64.

Eichhorst, W., W. Marx, and E. Thode. 2010. *Atypische Beschäftigung und Niedriglohnarbeit.* Research Report Series, Bertelsmann Stiftung.

Eurofound. 2006. *Fourth European Working Conditions Survey, FEWCS.* Eurofound Publication Office.

—. 2010. *Flexible Forms of Work: "Very Atypical" Contractual Arrangements.* European Foundation for the Improvement of Living and Working Conditions.

European Commission. 2007. *Communication from the Commission to the Spring European Council, Integrated Guidelines for Growth and Jobs (2008-2010)*. Brussels: European Commission.

—. 2008. *European Employment Strategy (EES)*. Brussels: European Commission. http://ec.europa.eu/employment_social (accessed August 10, 2010).

Kienbaum Consultants International GmbH. 2008. *Absolventenstudie und Arbeitgeberattraktivität 2007/2008*. Gummersbach: Kienbaum www.kienbaum.de (accessed August 10, 2009).

Lambert, A. D., J. H. Marler, and H. G. Gueutal. 2008. "Individual Differences: Factors Affecting Employee Utilization of Flexible Work Arrangements," *Journal of Vocational Behavior* 73, No. 1:107-117.

Langfred, C.W. 2000. "The Paradox of Self-management: Individual and Group Autonomy in Work Groups," *Journal of Organizational Behavior* 21, No. 5:563-585.

Lapierre, L. M., P. E. Spector, T. D. Allen, S. Peolmans, C. L. Cooper, M. P. O'Driscoll, J. I. Sanchez, P. Brough, and U. Kinnunen. 2008. "Family-supportive Organization Perceptions, Multiple Dimensions of Work-family Conflict, and Employee Satisfaction: A Test of Model across Five Samples," *Journal of Vocational Behavior* 73, No. 1:92-106.

McKinsey & Company. 2008. *Most wanted. Die Arbeitgeberstudie 2008*. McKinsey & Company.

Nas, S. O., A. Ekeland, C. Svanfeldt, and M. Åkerblom, M. 1998. *Summary Report of the Focus Group on Mobility of Human Resources in Nordic Countries. An Analysis Based on Register Data*. STEP Report R-06/98 http://www.sol.no/step/ (accessed June 3, 2010).

NIDI, Netherlands Interdisciplinary Demographic Institute. 2008. *Demographic Trends, Socio-Economic Impacts and Policy Implications in the European Union-2007*. Executive Summary of the Monitoring Report. Brussels: European Observatory on the Social Situation-Demography Network.

Parent-Thirion, A., E. Fernández Macías, J. Hurley, G. Vermeylen. 2006. *Fourth European Work Conditions Survey*. European Foundation for the Improvement of Living and Working Conditions. Eurofound Publications Office, http://www.eurofound.europa.eu/pubdocs/2006/98/en/2/ef0698en.pdf (accessed June 15, 2010).

Paridon, H., and M. Hupke. 2009. "Psychosocial Impact of Mobile Telework: Results from an Online Survey," *Europe's Journal of Psychology*, No. 1.

Portugali, J. 1989. "Nomad Labor: Theory and Practice in the Israeli-Palestinian Case," *Transactions of the Institute of British Geographers,* 14, No. 2:207-220.

Rantanen, J., U. Kinnunen, T. Feldt, and L. Pulkkinen. 2008. "Work-family Conflict and Psychological Well-being: Stability and Cross-lagged Relations with One- and Six-year Follow-ups," *Journal of Vocational Behavior*, No. 73:37-51.

Trendence Institute GmbH. 2008. *Das deutsche Absolventbarometer 2008.* IT-edition Auszüge aus den Ergebnissen, Berlin: Trendence Institute. http://www.trendence.de (accessed April 20, 2009).

Turner, B. S. 2007. "The Enclave Society. Towards a Sociology of Immobility," *European Journal of Social Theory* 10 No. 02:287-304.

Universum Communications Sweden AB, 2007. The Universum Graduate Survey 2007, Stockholm, http://www.universumglobal.com (accessed April 20, 2009).

Van Mierlo, H., C. G. Rutte, J. K. Vermunt, M. A. J. Kompier, and J.A.M.C. Doorewaard. 2006. "Individual Autonomy in Work Teams: The Role of Team Autonomy, Self-efficacy, and Social Support," *European Journal of Work and Organizational Psychology* 15, No. 3:281-299.

Wenger, E. 2000. "Communities of Practice and Social Learning Systems," *Organization* 7, No. 2:225-246.

Training and Temporary Agency Work: A Comparative Analysis of National Regulatory Patterns

Lilli Casano

1. Introduction

Nowadays, vocational training—particularly the one undergone on a continuous and permanent basis—is regarded as a key tool to take on new employment challenges which affect contemporary society. Training programmes carry out a fundamental function in that they ensure the alignment between labour supply and demand, further enhancing individuals' employability and adaptability to an ever-changing world of work. Measures of this kind can also be implemented to bring together different levels of protection within the labour market, so as to constitute a set of "portable social rights"[1] provided to workers over their career, whether they are employed on a permanent or temporary basis.

Therefore, there is a need to promote training opportunities and safeguards in the form of stability of employment in some sectors, and to operate for the benefit of both employers and employees. This is particularly the case of temporary agency work, that, because of its nature, exposes workers to high levels of precariousness. At the same time, this form of employment can prove useful as allowing unemployed workers to re-enter the labour market. It seems worth pointing out that agency work is regarded by the youth as a stepping stone to more secure positions, even though in some cases it represents the only alternative to unemployment. In this respect, workers resorting to agency work often consider it as temporary, a tool to enter the labour market and to increase their chances to gain access to long-term employment. However, the transition from temporary to permanent employment is often dependent on the workers' ability not to "become trapped" in contractual arrangements of a temporary

---

[1] Gautié, J. 2003. "Lavoro: dai mercati interni ai mercati di transizione Implicazioni sulla solidarietà, le tutele, la formazione," *Assistenza sociale,* No. 1-2.

nature. Therefore, by regularly updating and certifying their skills, and adapting them to the needs of the labour market, workers can further increase their employability.

The importance of this issue has been acknowledged also by the European Union through the issuing of Directive No. 104/2008/CE, pursuant to which temporary agency workers should be provided with training opportunities (Art. 6). To this end, a number of measures previously intended to standard workers have been also extended to those in non-permanent employment; in other cases, *ad-hoc* provisions have been laid down, with bilateral bodies which should ensure their implementation.

Over the last decades, agency work has been increasingly used, even though a decrease in the recourse to this form of employment has been reported lately, as a consequence of the financial downturn. It seems useful to highlight that agency workers in Europe are primarily young people: in Finland they are mostly students looking for a part-time job, while in France and Germany, agency work represents a tool to help young workers with low qualifications access the labour market. The same can be said of Italy, where school leavers resort to agency work to take their first steps in the world of work.

This paper carries out a comparative analysis of provisions regulating training for temporary agency workers in Europe, focusing on regulatory schemes adopted in Italy and France. Here, the specificity of the national legislative framework and the peculiarities of the domestic labour market will be discussed, with major issues related to unemployment models, continuing vocational training, and the profile of agency workers which will be studied in detail.

Of note is the fact that both the significance and the impact of the foregoing measures depend on several factors (e.g. work environment, cultural background and profile of those involved), and on whether priority is given to company performance or workers' employability.

Furthermore, in comparing different training national systems, the focus is on those country-specific factors of legal nature, viz.: the nature of the employment relationship, workers' mobility, the average duration of the assignment and the transition rate to permanent employment. In this respect, it is also useful to analyse aspects characterising vocational training, as well as relevant aspects at a micro-level, such as: workers' educational and professional background, their employment status when entering the training programme, and their motivation to perform in the temporary agency work sector, as they are significant variables in the evaluation of the effectiveness of the measures adopted. In the context of this paper, it has not been possible to provide an in-depth investigation of these aspects; however, reference has been made to studies in sociology carried out in Italy and France, aimed to point out the profile of temporary agency workers, as well as their expectations and career prospects.[2]

2. Training Regulatory Patterns for Temporary Agency Workers in Europe

The comparison between different training regulatory patterns dealing with temporary agency work is problematic because of some significant differences in their national legislative framework and labour market, especially when the continuing vocational training system at large is considered.

With reference to the legislative framework regulating temporary agency work, there are differences concerning both the use of this form of work in several sectors, as well as aspects associated with contractual arrangements and working activity (duration of the contract, worker's rights and so on).

In this connection, and with respect to regulatory standards, a distinction can be made between countries with high regulatory standards (Belgium, Italy, France, Spain); reasonable regulatory standards (Germany, Luxembourg, Portugal, the Netherlands); low regulatory standards (Greece, Finland, Ireland, the United Kingdom). Special reference should be made to those countries where the intervention of social partners somehow mitigated the impact of relevant provisions (Austria, Denmark, and Sweden).

As we will see, training programmes dealing with temporary agency work have been institutionalised in countries falling within the first category, as here priority has been given to the social consequences resulting from the recourse to this form of employment and to the contribution to employment protection on the part of social partners, primarily in legal terms.

---

[2] Fullin, G. 2006. *Vivere l'instabilità del lavoro.* Bologna: Il Mulino. Altieri G., F. Dota, and M. Piersanti. 2009. *Percorsi nel lavoro atipico: il caso dei lavoratori interinali.* Milano: Franco Angeli. Jourdain, C. 2002. "Intérimaires, le monde de l'intérim," *Travail et Emploi* No. 89. Lacroux, A. 2009. *Peut on faire carriére dans l'intérim?,* IUT Université de Toulon. Belkacem, R. 2009. *Les logiques de la formation dans l'intérim.* Nancy: Groupe de Recherche sur l'Education et l'Emploi (GREE), Université de Nancy et de Metz.

The main characteristics of the labour market are also of importance at the time of assessing the implications and significance of training for temporary agency workers, as well as the legislative instruments adopted to ensure its effectiveness. In this respect, it should be recalled that in many European countries the promotion of temporary agency work has been based on the assumption that it would result in positive effects on employment trends. In this sense, relevant studies[3] have highlighted significant differences in unemployment models nationwide, especially if a number of factors are examined (age, gender, and employment status). However, notwithstanding the variables at a national level, both academics and decision-makers have deemed viable to identify shared solutions in order to narrow the mismatch between labour demand and supply in different countries, for instance by providing the labour market with higher levels of flexibility.[4] Originally forbidden in a number of countries, such as Italy, the recourse to temporary agency work, which is one of the most controversial forms of atypical employment, is part of this logic and produced different consequences in Europe. In countries such as Italy, characterised by high unemployment rates among entry-level workers (especially the young and women), the spread of this contractual arrangement caused already-existing social inequalities to become more pronounced, which resulted in the creation of a dual labour market, with some categories that are now more exposed than others to risks arising from atypical work.

These trends are also confirmed by national statistics, which reveal that most of those engaged in atypical employment are individuals under 30 with average and high levels of education. More specifically, the fact that temporary work is mainly regarded as a tool provided by the labour market to allow qualified workers to have access to stable employment should induce a reflection on the effectiveness of the measures adopted to enhance training programmes. Such effectiveness might produce different results also considering a number of factors related to the labour market. A case in point is Germany. Here, most low-qualified workers resort to agency work, with the duration of the contracts which is the longest in Europe (6 to 12 months). Further—and particularly in East Germany— more than 60% of agency workers are employed by the agency on a permanent basis.[5]

---

[3] Reyneri, E. 2005. *Sociologia del mercato del lavoro*. Bologna: Il Mulino.
[4] Regini, M. 2000. *Modelli di capitalismo*. Bari: Laterza.
[5] IdeaConsult. 2009. *Report on Temporary Work Agencies' Contribution to Transitions in the Labour Market: the Example of Vocational Training*. IdeaConsult.

Finally, the provision of training to agency workers should be analysed against the background of the overall continuing vocational training system. In this connection, notwithstanding a growing engagement by social partners in the governance of training systems, which paves the way for a shared scheme of an associative nature,[6] there is general consensus that existing training schemes at a European level are highly diversified. The comparison between the Italian and the French case will be useful to point out the extent to which, despite similarities at a formal level, continuing training systems can differ in terms of outcomes. In all European countries, however, irrespective of the effectiveness and the financial support granted to such programmes, access to continuing vocational training proved more difficult for temporary workers, and atypical workers, more generally. As a result, the setting up of *ad-hoc* legislative measures would help fill the gap with other workers, however failing to clarify most controversial aspects contained in the relevant European Directive.

In Europe, the provision of training for agency workers is regulated by national legislation and collective agreements—in some cases, it is up to social partners to ensure their enforcement by means of internal regulations—although in those countries where a reference legal framework is not adopted (e.g. the UK), agencies cooperate on a voluntary basis with the public employment services or local institutions. In six countries (Austria, Belgium, France, Italy, Spain and the Netherlands), national governments have designed specific training schemes for agency workers, to be put in place by bilateral bodies and funded by contributions paid by the agency.

As a result, two models of training systems (a *voluntaristic* and a *regulated* model) can be classified considering two elements: 1) the existence of a specific set of rules issued through national provisions or collective agreements, 2) the existence of a funding scheme—either voluntary and mandatory—to be provided by the agency.

In the case of a *voluntaristic* model, there is no a specific set of rules and agencies invest in training only on a voluntary basis. It might happen that companies, mainly medium and large enterprises, set up training schemes despite the absence of obligations in this regard. Notwithstanding this aspect, differences in terms of training provisions might arise if one considers qualified and unqualified workers, or the amount of funds

---

[6] Winterton, J. 2007. "Training, development and competence," in *The Oxford Handbook of Human Resource Management*, Oxford: Oxford University Press: 324-343.

allocated to training programmes, especially if the implementation of these provisions is in practice left to the discretion of the agency. Moreover, the fact that agencies are equipped with adequate facilities and competence to fulfil this task is far from being obvious, especially if one takes into account that training opportunities are often the result of the needs of the user enterprise.

With regard to the *regulated* model, a number of countries (Italy, France and Spain) have adopted a set of measures at a national level aimed to promote access to training among agency workers. In other cases, it is down to collective agreements to provide a regulatory framework in this connection. However in those countries where a specific training system for such workers has been set up, the management and the allocation of financial resources, as well as the planning of further interventions are usually assigned to bodies overseen by social partners. The advantages in implementing such systems lie in the fact that they are the result of social dialogue and that they represent an instrument to collect and (re-)allocate funds, while serving several other functions (e.g. the setting-up of training programmes, cooperation with relevant bodies and so on).

3. The French Case: Educational Disadvantages and the Role of Training for Young Temporary Agency Workers

A first question arises as to whether provisions regulating the training system for agency workers are sufficient, not only to live up to the agency expectations, but also to meet workers' needs in terms of job opportunities. In the context of this paper, the aim is to provide a comparative analysis of the Italian and the French cases (the former being characterised by a new training system, the latter by a well-established training development programme, in force since 1983) in order to shed light on both general and specific factors affecting the smooth running of those systems, which are similar only at a formal level. In this connection, these two cases will be analysed, by focusing on domestic labour markets, as well as on general continuing training systems.

In considering the French case, reference should be made to the fact that the national employment rate is close to the European average, with a considerable difference in terms of gender (the employment rate for males is 10% higher than the corresponding rate for females).

Unemployment is a major issue particularly among young people, and it is generally associated with the individual's educational background, as it is higher among those who completed vocational/technical education

(*Certificat d'aptitude professionnelle, CAP,* and *Brevet d'études professionnelles BEP*), and high school.

In addition, of young workers usually engaged in non-permanent jobs, 26% of them are aged under 24 and are employed under temporary contracts. Significantly, 7% of them are agency workers.[7] Also due to the sharp increase reported over the last 20 years, there has been a widespread use of agency work nationwide, to the extent that France is the fourth largest agency work market in the world, after the United States, Japan, and the UK (PRISME 2009). France has almost 500,000 agency workers—the highest rate in Europe among those countries with more stringent legislation—that is four times the number of those in Italy. Against this background, the regulation of agency work always aimed at providing employees with high levels of employment protection.[8]

It is also worth pointing out that agency workers are predominantly male (71%) with low levels of education (52%), and that people in these positions were previously unemployed.[9]

In assessing the level of the continuing vocational training system, France has always been regarded as an outstanding country in terms of best practices, particularly because of the *virtuous circle* involving lawmakers at a national level, employers and representatives of the social partners, who operate side by side to provide workers with higher levels of qualifications.

A crucial role is therefore played by both social partners at a decisional and management level in the implementation of collective agreements, and by the national government through a more and more stringent set of rules governing the provision of training. In this sense, lawmakers attempted to safeguard employees' right to continuing vocational training over the past 40 years (as set forth by Law No. 391 of May 2004), also extending this right to all workers, particularly to the most vulnerable ones (the unemployed, low-qualified and atypical workers).

An analysis of the employment trends reveals that statistics are encouraging: 35% of adults in France (36.4% in Europe) are engaged in continuing training, and participation rates are even higher for people

---

[7] Blasco S., and P. Givord. 2010. "Les trajectoires professionnelles en début de vie active. Quel impact des contrats temporarires?" *Economie et Statistiques-Travail Emploi* No. 431-432.

[8] Auvergnon, P. 2004. "A proposito del lavoro temporaneo in Francia," *Lavoro e Diritto, estate-autunno* No. 3-4:671-694.

[9] IdeaConsult. 2009. *Report on Temporary Work Agencies' Contribution to Transitions in the Labour Market: the Example of Vocational Training.* IdeaConsult.

already employed (46% against 33% in Europe). A closer reading of such data highlights that a significant difference arises among workers in considering the levels of vulnerability. This is particularly the case of atypical workers, as being characterised by low levels of engagement in further training programmes.

In this connection, the *non-participation rate* in France comprises: those on training contracts (*Stage et Contract Aidés*) (51%); those employed on non-permanent contracts (72%); agency workers (66%).

As a result, the planning of an *ad-hoc* training system for agency workers can be seen as a way to respond to a number of social needs. Further, the provision of training programmes is also regarded as a matter of urgency following the rise in temporary employment and the predominance of low-qualified workers, so as to give them the opportunity to compete for semi-skilled jobs.

Also in the case of temporary workers, the provision of training is ensured by a bilateral fund, that is FAF.TT (Training Insurance Fund for Temporary Work—*Fond Assurance Formation pour les Travailleurs Temporaires*), which is managed by both representatives from the agencies (PRISME) and sectoral unions (CFDT, CFE-CGC-FNECS, CFTC, USI-CGT, CGT-FO). The fund is financially supported by the temporary agency and by the company, on the basis of its size (e.g. 2% of the employees' salary in the event of large companies). Starting from 1996, another bilateral fund has been set up, that is FPE.TT (*Fonds Professionnel pour l'Emploi du Travail Temporaire*), the aim of which is to reduce unemployment rates among more disadvantaged people by resorting to temporary contracts. Like FAF.TT, FPE.TT is partly funded by the employees' salary (0.15%).

In 2009, thanks to the support of a number of institutions (apart from FPE.TT, the government, the regional councils, the European Social Fund, and other training funds), the yearly FAF.TT budget was maintained despite the financial crisis, making it possible to provide training for different categories of workers.

With regard to FAF.TT training measures, there are a number of points that need to be further clarified: agency workers have access to both general and specific training measures; a certain amount of money has been allocated to the planning of the agency HR strategies (*le Plan de Formation*); on the other hand, there has been a need to develop *ad-hoc* training programmes on the basis of the task the employee is assigned under both *fixed-term training* and *access-to-work* contracts (*Contrat de Professionnalisation Intérimaire; Contrat d'Insértion Professionnelle Intérimaire; Contrat de Development Professionnelle intérimaire*) and the safeguarding of workers' right to *individual training leave* (*Congé Individuel de Formation*).

On the basis of these considerations, the present study will primarily examine a number of contractual schemes, notably *fixed-term training contracts* (*CPI—Conrat de Professionnalisation Intérimaire*), *access-to-work contracts* (*CIPI—Contrat d'insertion professionnelle intérimaire*) and *individual training leave* (*CIF—Congé individuel de formation*).

In the first two cases, training is usually provided in accordance with the tasks to be performed. In 2009, 53% and 51% of workers employed under either fixed-term training and access-to-work contracts respectively, were aged under 24. Furthermore, those hired on a fixed-term training contract were young workers with higher levels of education, with only 37% of them holding a high-school diploma (FAF.TT 2008). As for access-to-work contracts, they are intended to facilitate the entry or the return of those workers who are at a disadvantage in terms of age, disability, and personal issues. Accordingly, individuals resorting to this contractual scheme are usually characterised by lower levels of education.

Finally, agency workers can also take temporary paid leave to take part in training (CIF), so as to improve their chances to gain access to more secure jobs. In 2009, 15% of workers on training leave were aged less than 24 years old, and 56% of them were under 34.[10] This is mainly due to some eligibility criteria, as only agency workers who have worked for at least 1,600 hours (600 hours for the same agency) can ask for training leave. If eligible, the worker will be entitled to a period of leave, with the training and wage costs to be covered by FAF.TT. Notably, according to a survey carried out by trade unions (IdeaConsult 2009),[11] the request for training to be provided on an individual basis might be ascribed to the worker's will only at a formal level, as in practice it often represents the result of the agency willingness. The relevance of such measures will be discussed in detail, particularly focusing on the impact that vocational training has on young agency workers in terms of job opportunities.

Significantly, as conducting and publishing studies on the employment effects on trainees, and pointing out the extent to which these programmes improve their entry-level qualifications, FAF.TT is the only source of information on this issue. An analysis of the Italian case will follow, as being of interest in that it might help to clarify the conditions under which regulated and agreed-upon continuing training schemes can benefit the

---

[10] FAF.TT. 2009a. *Intérim et Formation en France.* FAF.TT .
[11] IdeaConsult. 2009. *Report on Temporary Work Agencies' Contribution to Transitions in the Labour Market: the Example of Vocational Training.* IdeaConsult.

employment situation of temporary agency workers, now and in the years to come. This is the starting point of the present investigation, as employability training systems resulting from a process of consultation and regulation proved more effective than those overseen by the agency on an exclusive basis.

Drawing on the outcomes of a sociological survey[12] carried out in France about the profile of agency workers—mostly poorly educated young people—it emerges that the youngs regarded such forms of employment as a way to enter the labour market (*intérim tramplin professionnel*) or to gain experience while waiting for better job opportunities (*intérim en attendant de mieux*). In both cases, training can be crucial, as providing newly hired workers with more practical skills—in accordance with the employers' needs—and further developing competences of people looking for more secure jobs.

With reference to fixed-term training contracts, 53% of contract holders are young people in the 16-24 age group, with 84% of them aged under 30. They are mainly male (83%) who have completed secondary education (30% of them hold a high school diploma).

Generally speaking, before being hired: 61.5% of workers were already employed—mostly as an agency worker; 25% were unemployed; 13% were inactive. Once the employment relationship with the agency is terminated, 73% of workers found a job and 35% were hired on a permanent basis. Further, the percentage of agency work among workers under fixed-term training contracts reported a significant decrease (-17%) compared to those people who maintained their position, meaning that fixed-term training contracts are a more effective instrument in the transition from agency to permanent work. According to a survey conducted by FAF.TT, some 75% of people perform tasks in accordance with qualifications obtained during vocational training, and 60% of them are highly satisfied with their current position, especially because it provided more opportunities in occupational terms.[13]

The profile of those hired under access-to-work contracts is rather different from the previous one, primarily in terms of age (51% of those entering into these agreements are young workers), as this contractual scheme is mainly intended to support job-seekers. Notwithstanding this aspect, 2,725 out of 3,449 access-to-work contracts were concluded with individuals aged less than 30 years old in 2008. In addition, young

---

[12] Jourdain, C. 2002. "Intérimaires, le monde de l'intérim," *Travail et Emploi* No. 89.

[13] FAF.TT. 2008. *La formation des jeunes intérimaires dans le travail temporaire.* FAF.TT.

workers employed under access-to-work contracts also have lower levels of education, especially if compared with those hired under training contracts (28% of them have no qualifications, 21% of them hold a high school diploma, and 43% of them completed technical education).

At the end of the employment relationship, 35% of workers remained unemployed, 12% had a permanent job, 11% worked on a temporary basis, and 34% of them were hired as agency workers, with only 37% who were satisfied with their current position.

With reference to individual training leave, it usually involves a small percentage of young people (12.5%) as access to such training opportunities is dependent on the length of service (at least a 10-month period working as an agency worker, 4 months with the same agency). Further, training leave is usually the prerogative of young people who have completed vocational education. Generally speaking, training programmes have a considerable impact in terms of both skills development and employment opportunities. In this sense, after being on training leave, 30% of trainees are employed permanently, 12% remain unemployed, and 42% are hired as agency workers. The high percentage of those taking training leave who are subsequently engaged in temporary agency work is due to the fact that such a period of leave is usually granted to workers who have an employment relationship of continuing collaboration with the agency. Accordingly, these figures do reflect the effectiveness of agency work as an instrument which supports career transition and enhances job stability.

Surprisingly, there has been a significant increase in the number of high-qualified professionals, with the percentage of white-collar workers rising from 8% to 26%, and that of specialised and non-specialised blue-collar workers decreasing from 21% to 41%, and from 67.5% to 28% respectively. In addition, 83% of those who took part in training are now satisfied with the skills they had acquired and 74% of them believe they have improved their employment status.[14]

In considering the effects of training measures, of note is the fact that in contractual terms, both access-to-work and training contracts can be regarded as work-training contracts, as the worker is hired by the agency and might be able to put in practice what he/she has learnt in the course of previous assignments, therefore combining training and working activity. The nature of these employment relationships also favour young workers in that the agency will provide them with certain benefits, such as the chance to access to further training. The impact of the measures mentioned

---

[14] Ibid.

above should be assessed considering those engaged in this form of work. For individuals who have completed technical education and for those with a high-school diploma (very few, indeed), an *ad-hoc* training programme, to be designed in accordance with job contents and expectations, might prove effective. However, access-to-work contracts are concluded primarily with low-qualified young workers, thus leading to unsatisfactory results in terms of employment stability. With regard to individual training leave (CFI), the effects are not dissimilar from traditional training schemes provided on an individual basis. The overall improvement in workers' qualifications demonstrates the effectiveness of the above mentioned measures particularly in relation to the needs of those who take part in such programmes.

4. The Italian Case: Training for Young Temporary Agency Workers between Company Strategy and Work Socialization in a Dualistic Labour Market

With reference to the Italian case, agency workers represent only a small percentage of the total workforce (around 1%), notwithstanding their relevance in certain sectors and regions. However, although a low incidence of agency workers has been reported among the working population, the agency workers aged under 24 account for 4% of the total labour force in the same age group.[15] In order to gain full awareness of the spread of agency work among young workers and to understand the significance of this form of employment in both the South and the North of Italy, further details will be given about the Italian labour market.

In Italy, young people entering the labour market are at a particular disadvantage, mainly because of a two-tier labour market. In fact, the unemployment rate in the North is in line with the one of the most developed European countries, and the same can be said of employment trends for people in the 20-24 age group. Conversely, unemployment rate in the southern regions is very high (30% for those aged under 24, against 18% in the North), especially among young women: 41% of women in the South are unemployed, compared to 20% in the North.

Unlike the northern regions, the decrease in what has been termed "intellectual unemployment" reported in the South of Italy at the beginning of the 1990s was not associated with the development of more qualified employment opportunities—especially in the new service sectors—but to the need on the part of more educated workers to compete

---

[15] Forma.Temp. 2005-2008. *Vademecum.* Forma.Temp.

for unqualified positions.[16] In this context, agency work might give them the opportunity to gain first-time work experience, to apply for other positions, and to enhance mobility from less developed regions to more developed ones.

Bearing this in mind, the legislator has made provision aimed at further developing this form of employment, such as Law No. 196/97, which for the first time allows for—although with certain limitations—the recourse to temporary agency work, thus widening its scope of application, by means of Legislative Decree No. 276/2003.

In Italy—particularly in the North West and, since 2006, also in the North East and in the centre—agency workers are mostly employed in the industrial and the tertiary sector. Starting from 2010, a widespread use of this form of employment has been reported also in other sectors, such as IT, education, health, and so on.[17] Whereas in the northern regions agency work is used mainly in the manufacturing and construction industries and in the private service sector, agency workers in the South are usually employed in public services. As for their profile, they are generally high-qualified young people (20% of them are aged under 24, and 54% are under 34, even though an increase in the use of agency work has been reported in the 40-49 age group).

Equally in this case, there is a significant difference between the North and the South. Generally speaking, agency workers living in the South are mainly qualified individuals who have completed secondary education and are employed in the service sector. In the North, they are both well-educated people employed in the service sector, or low-qualified workers operating as blue-collars in the manufacturing and construction sectors.[18]

In addition to the figures just discussed, it is important to consider all those aspects associated with the national continuing vocational training system, characterised by high levels of segmentation, lack of public and private funding, inequalities in terms of job opportunities, shortcomings in the development of career paths, a mismatch between educational programmes, training and the expectations within the labour market.

In this connection, bilateral bodies are becoming increasingly important, as they manage training funds (e.g. Intrasectoral Funds for Continuing Vocational Training—*Fondi Interprofessionali per la Formazione*

---

[16] Cortese, A. 2005. "Lavori poveri per giovani istruiti. La costruzione microsociale del mercato fluido," *Inchiesta* No. 149:62-95.

[17] Ebitemp. 2010. *Il lavoro interinale nel 2010 attraverso i dati INAIL.* Osservatorio Nazionale Ebitemp.

[18] Altieri G., F. Dota, and M. Piersanti. 2009. *Percorsi nel lavoro atipico: il caso dei lavoratori interinali.* Milano: Franco Angeli.

Continua) and plan active policies to promote employment. However, the implementation of a bilateral system faced a number of difficulties, also becoming the subject of heated debate among several trade unions representatives.[19] Strong reservations have been expressed about the effectiveness of the continuing vocational training bilateral system in Italy, which also result from a misuse of the funds, especially if one considers that there is no reallocation of resources—unlike the French case—as this is closely connected to contributions paid by every single company on the basis of its size.

Therefore, notwithstanding the spread of good practices at a local level, the continuing training system has so far produced unfavourable results. The rate of participation of adults in training is one of the lowest in Europe, and the implementation of the bilateral system is still under way and far from being homogeneous at a national level. Participation in training is higher among well-educated (70%) than low-educated young people (28%). Furthermore, white-collars (70%) are engaged in training programmes more than blue-collars (29%), especially in large companies (36%).[20]

The situation is even worse for atypical workers, to the extent that a number of actions have been taken in terms of equal treatment and access to training. The provision of training to agency workers, which is regulated by Art. 12 of Legislative Decree No. 276/2003 (recently amended by Law No. 183/2010), seems to provide best practices. First, it promotes cooperation among social partners, especially when it comes to issues arising from the recourse to this form of employment, also due a certain level of engagement of bilateral bodies. Secondly, it proved effective in translating the main principles of flexibility into practical actions, by means of major investments and important measures.

More specifically, Legislative Decree No. 276/2003 sets forth that money collected from the agency should be paid to a bilateral fund that has been set up to train temporary workers, as a way to further develop their skills and "promote continuity in terms of job opportunities". As pointed out by Caruso,[21] training, together with additional measures (e.g. an *ad-hoc* welfare system set up by another bilateral body, Ebitemp), was intended to provide agency workers with high levels of job security. In this

---

[19] Leonardi, S. 2004. "Gli enti bilaterali tra autonomia e sostegno normativo," *Giornale di diritto del lavoro e di relazioni industriali* No. 103.
[20] Isfol 2008-2009. *Rapporto sulla formazione continua.* ISFOL.
[21] Caruso, B. 2007. "Occupabilità, formazione e capability nei modelli giuridici di regolazione dei mercati del lavoro," *Giornale di diritto del lavoro e relazioni industriali* No. 113.

sense, Law No. 183/2010 introduced a number of provisions, from which it emerges little commitment towards the promotion of people's employability, as the legislator seems to neglect the duty to foster a certain degree of continuity. This is not a trivial issue, especially if one considers that further training is regarded as useful to enable workers to carry out specific tasks and, in the long run, to help them to compete for more qualified and stable positions.[22]

With regard to Forma.Temp, this fund performs the same functions as French FAF.TT, as being a bilateral body managed by social partners representing the agency sector (ASSOLAVORO, FelSA-CISL, NIDIL-CGIL, CPO-UIL). Forma.Temp provides funding for a number of programmes: vocational training, general training, on-the-job training, continuing training, and vocational guidance. With the exception of individual training, it is usually the agency which submits the request for further training on behalf of the workers, often prompted by the user company. In 2008, some 160 million Euros have been allocated to the planning of 36,000 training projects, with this investment reporting a 33.5% decrease over 2009 due to the financial downturn. According to Forma.Temp,[23] the financial resources have been allocated as follows: 81.4% in vocational training; 7.5% in general training; 7.1% in on-the-job training; 2.7% in continuing training; 13% in vocational guidance.

In the context of this paper, it is useful to point out that 60% of those engaged in training programmes set up by Forma.temp were young people aged under 30, holding both a high school diploma (54%), or a university degree (17%). In terms of gender, women usually take part in training courses more than men, and they are also more educated than their male counterparts (21% of them hold a university degree).
The majority of the initiatives aimed at promoting training took place in the North of Italy (67% in the North and in the North East). The focus of this work is on different types of training, particularly vocational training, to which a considerable amount of funds have been allocated, and continuing training provided through a voucher system. In both cases, young people are the majority (55% of them undergo vocational training and 33% continuing training, provided that they comply with requirements in terms of length of service, such as in the French case).

In reference to vocational training and its impact on young workers, there are two aspects that are worth mentioning. First, there is a close

---

[22] Caruso, B. 2002. "Formazione e lavoro temporaneo. Disciplina del Fondo di formazione e prassi applicativa," *I quaderni di Metis* No. 4.
[23] Forma.Temp. 2005-2008. *Vademecum.* Forma.Temp.

connection between the training provided and the tasks to be performed. Secondly, the engagement in training courses does not necessarily result in a work experience, as the internal regulation of the Fund sets forth that the percentage of those who are assigned a real working task should not exceed 35% of the overall number of trainees, with such a percentage which is calculated on the total number of the projects funded to the agency in one year. Due to such a state of affairs, it is not possible to assess the real impact of training in terms of job opportunities, in that we are not aware of the number of trainees who find a job after completing the training period.

On the other hand, it is crucial for those involved that skills developed over training might be used in the labour market in the short and the long run. From where the agency and the user company stand, it is important to employ a certain number of qualified (and trained) workers to fulfil specific tasks. As for workers, it is basic that training—often comprising intensive programmes requiring full commitment—is intended as a means to gain access to job opportunities.

Equally important is to recall the significance of the profile of those who take part in training, for instance in vocational training, as 70% of trainees hold a high school diploma and 30% are low-qualified.[24] Eighty-four per cent of highly-qualified young workers attend training programmes in order to have access to job opportunities in the service sector. Training courses mainly provide transversal skills for jobs in IT and managerial positions, although trainees are generally white collar workers applying for low-qualified positions (e.g. secretarial staff).

Poorly educated young workers also engage in training courses in the tertiary sector, but they are more focused on those preparing them for job opportunities in tourism, catering, health and education. In the North, 27% of the poorly educated young also attend courses to work in the manufacturing and construction sectors (blue collars in metalworking and food industry, particularly).[25]

Accordingly, among TAWs, individuals engaged in training are mainly highly qualified young people usually trained to operate in the service sector. Further considerations about their profile can be made if differences between northern and southern Italy are examined. In the South, they are mainly high-school leavers trained to perform in the service sector, while in the North they are both graduates working in the service sector and unskilled workers operating in the manufacturing

---

[24] Ibid.
[25] Ibid.

sector. If we consider that in the southern regions temporary agency work is mainly used in the Public Sector (where, by definition, there are few opportunities to have access to stable employment) and that generally agency workers in the service sector—unlike the manufacturing sector, where fixed-term contracts are offered to probationers before being hired—are employed to face peaks in production, such state of affairs induces to reflect on the effectiveness of such training programmes as an instrument to develop further skills for future and more secure jobs.

Measures of this kind might positively affect the employment situation of low-qualified young workers trained for the manufacturing sector in the North of Italy, as they allow for the development of practical competences and offer the chance to maintain the contact with—and presumably be hired by—the company. However, without an empirical analysis, it is hard to confirm this theoretical assumption. At present, it can be stated that the limited impact of training on young people is due to a mismatch between their characteristics and the training contents, usually unfit to semi- and highly-qualified workers as designed to meet the needs of the user companies, which look for low-qualified personnel.

In analysing continuing training provided on an individual basis, it becomes plain that programmes funded through these initiatives are of considerable importance to temporary agency workers, who can potentially benefit from measures of this kind. Courses have a duration ranging from 50 to 250 hours, with their cost varying from 200 to 6,000 Euros. As intended to help develop careers in the service sector (38% of trainees are employed as financial experts, accountants, bank clerks, software analysts, and web designers), training programmes are provided by means of a voucher scheme, with a part of it (30%) which is usually meant to assess transversal skills, e.g. basic English, computer literacy, communicative skills. In a number of cases (3%), Forma.Temp also funds master's degrees, by resorting to the voucher scheme mentioned above.

Despite its effectiveness, the provision of this form of training only concerns a few young workers aged under 24 (10%), as those in the 25-34 age group represent the majority (48%).[26] They are mainly people who have completed secondary education and who are already engaged in a temporary agency contract and are willing to take part in more specific courses outside working hours. Participation on the part of those aged over 25 is by no means obvious, especially considering that eligibility criteria are not as strict as those adopted in France. In this connection, according to Forma.Temp, in order to apply for a training voucher, it is sufficient to be

---

[26] Ibid.

unemployed and have worked for an agency for at least 30 days in the previous 12 months.

Therefore, although continuing training mainly promotes training opportunities among adults who are already in employment, it should also represent an opportunity for young agency workers to re-enter the labour market after being engaged on a temporary basis.

However, investments in continuing training (3 million Euros) have so far not been sufficient to meet the demand for training on the part of agency workers. For this reason, representatives from the relevant bilateral fund have stressed the need to both provide local bodies with higher levels of decision-making in terms of vocational guidance (at the moment implemented only at a theoretical level), and limit the power of certified training centres, which are often interested in self-promotion—and, in some cases, self-supporting.

In conclusion, it would be interesting to evaluate the extent to which bilateral funds, e.g. Forma.Temp contribute to vocational guidance (for both students and the unemployed), along with schools, students, and employment services. Originally, vocational guidance was used as a way to promote those activities carried out by the agencies;[27] at the time, the Fund required the agencies to cooperate more actively with actors involved in the planning of vocation guidance, especially at a local level. Such interplay between agencies, public employment services, local authorities and training providers can make an essential contribution to the functioning of the training courses.

5. Conclusions

This paper has investigated whether—and under which conditions— the setting up of a training scheme for temporary agency workers characterised by a specific regulation (overseen by bilateral bodies which are also in charge of reallocating the funds collected through contributions paid by employees) can harmonise the needs of both the worker and the agency in terms of training.

In this connection, the agency and the user company are interested in a training programme which helps workers to fulfil the requirements of the assignment. From the viewpoint of the agency workers, training is regarded as a tool to promote job security, and to further develop their

---

[27] Cucchi and Querci, eds. 2009. *Analisi dell'andamento della formazione realizzata da Forma.Temp su iniziativa delle Agenzie per il lavoro Formazione di base: l'orientamento, il caso ITINERA Verona*, Enfap.

skills in order to have access to more qualified positions. This is particularly the case of young people entering the labour market, as training programmes can ease the transition from precarious employment to more secure jobs, with temporary agency work no longer considered an "endless trap" but a "springboard to permanent employment".[28] As for France, training contracts (CPI) and access-to-work contracts (CIPI), as well as individual training leave (CIF) have demonstrated that, training can enhance the transition to permanent employment as well, also raising entry-level qualifications of workers, provided the existence of certain conditions. Unfortunately, FAF.TT fund is the only one that gives out data about the impact of training programmes in terms of job opportunities and skills development. As a result, the French training system represents a reference point in terms of best practices within the European context,[29] although its effectiveness mainly depends on the national institutional framework.

In this sense, mention should be made of those elements that positively affected the French system: its national legislation, which traditionally promotes the individual right to continuing vocational training, extending through recent reforms such a right also to low-qualified and atypical workers; a well-established training system provided by bilateral bodies, whose running has been possible under some very strict provisions, as a way to avoid the mere exercise of self-interest; a strong cooperation among different institutions, and the recognition of the role played by the agency, which supported the measures adopted by public authorities as regards strategy to be taken at a qualitative level; the profile characterising agency workers, mainly young workers with technical/vocational education (CAP-BEP), which really increases the chance for them to be hired as there is a significant use of agency workers in the industrial sector; work-training contracts usually combine educational and working activities, as being characterised by an interplay between learning, on-the-job initiatives, income and protection measures.

In Italy, a question arises as to whether the drawing up of a number of provisions aimed at regulating the training system for temporary agency workers can be sufficient to meet the needs of the agency and the workers themselves. In order to answer this question, it is important to consider

---

[28] Ichino, A., F. Mealli, and T. Nannincini. 2005. "Temporary Agencies in Italy: a springboard toward permanent employment?" *Giornale degli economisti e Annali di economia*, 64, No. 1.

[29] IdeaConsult. 2009. Report on Temporary Work Agencies' Contribution to Transitions in the Labour Market: the Example of Vocational Training. IdeaConsult.

certain aspects: the individual right to continuing training is not yet part of the cultural background of both employers and employees; the general continuing training system is far from being widely established; there are divergent views about the role of the bilateral system among stakeholders (agencies, social partners, user company and local authorities); the training fund is often exposed to "institutional isolation", as poorly supported by public entities at a local level, and often regarded as promoting a positive image of agency workers (in this sense, it is difficult to deal with such a prejudicial stance towards this form of employment, even though it carries out a pivotal role in promoting youth employment); and the profile of those engaged in agency work—young people holding a high school diploma or even a university degree—for whom the effectiveness of training in terms of job creation and employability is controversial, considering the spread of this form of work in the service sector to face peaks in production (mainly among low-qualified workers).

Finally, mention should be made also of the legal perspective, with the legislator expressing strong reservations about the capability of these training measures to provide continuity of employment, as shown by recent amendments to relevant provisions (Art. 48 of Law No. 183/2010). The risk in this case is to undermine the efforts made to harmonise the interests of both the agency and the workers, also belittling the role of bilateral bodies, and suggesting that they somehow disregard the issue of trainees' long-term employability.

On the basis of these considerations—and despite the French case—the statement that the effectiveness of a measure relies on the existence of some prerequisites would be misleading. The setting up of a bilateral fund (Forma.Temp) increased awareness of the fact that agency workers are in need of special protection, especially in terms of skills development as a "promotional tool".[30] For this purpose, the role of both trade unions and training providers operating at a local level is also significant, especially if they provide adequate information and support. On the other hand, the investigation of vocational training and lifelong learning on an individual basis reveals that the agency plays a predominant role in terms of training planning and guidance, affecting to some extent the choice on the part of workers.

---

[30] Caruso, B. 2007. "Occupabilità, formazione e capability nei modelli giuridici di regolazione dei mercati del lavoro," *Giornale di diritto del lavoro e relazioni industriali*, No. 113. Caruso, B. 2002. "Formazione e lavoro temporaneo. Disciplina del Fondo di formazione e prassi applicativa," *I quaderni di Metis*, No. 4.

With special reference to vocational training, the analysis shows a certain degree of "structural" difficulty, above all the mismatch between young people's level of education and demand-based training programmes. On the other hand, the analysis has highlighted the importance of continuing training, even for young workers, who usually are less engaged in initiatives of this kind. The focus is once again on promotion and guidance, the effectiveness of which depends on the agency, but also on trade unions and local institutions. Training is crucial, particularly for young people, but the awareness of a number of alternatives to unemployment should be a responsibility to be shared among all those involved. Mention must be made also of the fact that, unlike other training programmes, continuing training on an individual basis has been poorly supported in financial terms. In order to cope with this issue, the allocation of financial resources should be reviewed—as in the case of France, where a number of courses have been co-financed by external partners in 2008—with new institutional partners that should be allowed to fund such programmes, especially considering recent cuts in training funding.

References

Addabbo, T. 2005. "Chi è fuori è fuori? Alcune riflessioni sul lavoro interinale in Italia," *Sociologia del lavoro,* No. 97.

Altieri G., F. Dota, and M. Piersanti. 2009. *Percorsi nel lavoro atipico: il caso dei lavoratori interinali.* Milano: Franco Angeli.

Arrowsmith, J. 2006. *Temporary Agency Work in an Enlarged European Union.* Eurofound.

—. 2009. *Temporary Agency Work and Collective Bargaining in the EU.* Eurofound.

Auvergnon, P. 2004. "A proposito del lavoro temporaneo in Francia," *Lavoro e Diritto, estate-autunno*, No. 3-4:671-694.

Avola, M. 2005. "Flessibilità e precarizzazione del rapporto d'impiego: giovani meridionali tra rischio e nuove opportunità," *Inchiesta* No. 149:46-61.

Belkacem, R. 2009. *Les logiques de la formation dans l'intérim.* Nancy: Groupe de Recherche sur l'Education et l'Emploi (GREE), Université de Nancy et de Metz.

Blasco S., and P. Givord. 2010. "Les trajectoires professionnelles en début de vie active. Quel impact des contrats temporarires?" *Economie et Statistiques-Travail Emploi*, No. 431-432.

Caruso, B. 2002. "Formazione e lavoro temporaneo. Disciplina del Fondo di formazione e prassi applicativa," *I quaderni di Metis*, No. 4.

—. 2007. "Occupabilità, formazione e capability nei modelli giuridici di regolazione dei mercati del lavoro," *Giornale di diritto del lavoro e relazioni industriali*, No. 113.

Cester, C. 2003. "Il futuro degli enti bilaterali: collaborazione e antagonismo alla prova della riforma del mercato del lavoro," *Lavoro e Diritto, anno XVII*, No. 2:211-218.

CNEL. 2008-2009. *Rapporto sul mercato del lavoro*. CNEL. http://www.governo.it/backoffice/allegati/48588-5509.pdf   (accessed April 20, 2010)

Cortellazzi, S., ed. 2009. *La formazione continua. Culture, norme, organizzazione*. Milano: Franco Angeli.

Cortese, A. 2002. "Lavoro e rischi sociali nella transizione all'età adulta. Percorsi lavorativi di giovani svantaggiati nel Mezzogiorno," in *Politiche del lavoro*, ed. Luciano, A., (Milano: Franco Angeli).

—. 2005. "Lavori poveri per giovani istruiti. La costruzione microsociale del mercato fluido," *Inchiesta*, No. 149:62-95.

—. 2008. "Carriere mobili di giovani istruiti nel Mezzogiorno," in *Mobilità e transizioni nei mercati del lavoro locali*, eds. Colasanto, M., and E. Zucchetti, (Milano: Franco Angeli).

Corti, M. 2007."L'edificazione del sistema italiano di formazione continua dei lavoratori," *Rivista giuridica del lavoro* 58, No. 1:163-244.

Cucchi and Querci, eds. 2009. *Analisi dell'andamento della formazione realizzata da Forma.Temp su iniziativa delle Agenzie per il lavoro Formazione di base: l'orientamento, il caso ITINERA Verona*. Enfap.

De Rita, G. 2009. *Rapporto sul futuro della formazione in Italia*. Commissione di studio e di indirizzo sul futuro della formazione in Italia.

Del Punta, R. 2003. "Enti bilaterali e modelli di regolazione sindacale," *Lavoro e Diritto, anno XVII*, No. 3: 219-22.

Dufour, C. 2008. "La protezione sociale e il metodo paritetico in Francia," *La Rivista delle Politiche Sociali*, No. 4.

Ebitemp. 2009. *Il lavoro interinale nel 2008 e nel primo trimestre 2009*. Osservatorio Nazionale Ebitemp.

—. 2010. *Il lavoro interinale nel 2010 attraverso i dati INAIL*. Osservatorio Nazionale Ebitemp.

FAF.TT. 2008. *La formation des jeunes intérimaires dans le travail temporaire*. FAF.TT.

—. 2009a. *Intérim et Formation en France*. FAF.TT .

—. 2009b. *Rapport d'activité*. FAF.TT.

Fondimpresa, ed. 2007. *Formazione e contrattazione nei fondi paritetici interprofessionali*.

Forma.Temp. 2005-2008. *Vademecum.* Forma.Temp.

Fullin, G. 2006. *Vivere l'instabilità del lavoro.* Bologna: Il Mulino.

Gautié, J. 2003. "Lavoro: dai mercati interni ai mercati di transizione Implicazioni sulla solidarietà, le tutele, la formazione," *Assistenza sociale,* No. 1-2.

Gazier, B. 2003. "Au fundament d'une réforme du marché du travail: les marches transitionnels du travail et la gestion contemporaine de la rareté," *L'Année Sociologique* 53, No. 2.

Givord, P. 2005. "Forms particuliéres d'emploi et insertion des jeunes," *Economie et Statistique-Emploi*, No. 255-256.

Ichino, A., F. Mealli, and T. Nannincini. 2005. "Temporary Agencies in Italy: a springboard toward permanent employment?" *Giornale degli economisti e Annali di economia* 64, No.1.

IdeaConsult. 2009. *Report on Temporary Work Agencies' Contribution to Transitions in the Labour Market: the Example of Vocational Training.* IdeaConsult.

Isfol 2008-2009. *Rapporto sulla formazione continua.* ISFOL.

Jourdain, C. 2002. "Intérimaires, le monde de l'intérim," *Travail et Emploi,* No. 89.

Lacroux, A. 2009. *Peut on faire carriére dans l'intérim?* IUT Université de Toulon.

Leonardi, S. 2004. "Gli enti bilaterali tra autonomia e sostegno normativo," *Giornale di diritto del lavoro e di relazioni industriali*, No. 103.

—. 2005. *Bilateralità e servizi: quale ruolo per il sindacato.* Roma: Ediesse.

Marion-Vernoux, I., M. Théry, C. Gauthier. 2008. "Le DIF, un outil pour reduire les inégalitées d'accèss à la formation continue," *Bref*, No. 255.

Martinengo, G. 2006. "Gli Enti bilaterali dopo il decreto legislativo 276/2003," *Lavoro e Diritto*, No. 2.

Méda, D. 2006. "Fair la choix d'une politique d'éducation et de formation mieux adaptée," *La révue de la CFDT*, No. 78.

Ministero del Lavoro e delle Politiche Sociali. 2004. *Lavoro interinale e formazione.* Ministero del Lavoro e delle Politiche Sociali. http://db.formez.it/fontinor.nsf/9a613ee7a97aaf54c1256aee003aeb6b/AC350EC19A77E835C1256FF600309DA3/$file/RapportoLavoroInterinaleaprile2005.pdf (accessed April 20, 2010).

OME (Observatoire Métiers Empoli). 2009. *Les jeunes, le premier emploi et l'intérim.* OME.

—. 2010. *Regards croisées sur l'intérim.* OME.

PRISME. 2009. *Rapport économique et social.* PRISME.

Regini, M. 2000. *Modelli di capitalismo*. Bari: Laterza.

Reyneri, E. 2005. *Sociologia del mercato del lavoro*. Bologna: Il Mulino.

Ruda, A., ed. 2004/2006-2007-2008-2009. *Rapporto di attività Forma.Temp.* Forma.Temp.

Timellini, C. 2004. "Il sistema di finanziamento delle iniziative formative a sostegno dei lavoratori assunti in regime di somministrazione: i fondi per la formazione e l'integrazione del reddito," *Il Diritto del Mercato del Lavoro*, No. 1-2.

Tiraboschi, M. 2005. "Esternalizzazione del lavoro e valorizzazione del capitale umano: due modelli inconciliabili?" *I Working Papers, Centro studi diritto del lavoro europeo "Massimo D'Antona"*, No. 29/IT.

Trigilia, C. 1998. *Sociologia economica*. Bologna: Il Mulino.

Vaccaro, S., and P. Richini. 2006. "I sistemi di sviluppo delle competenze dei lavoratori in Francia, Spagna ed Inghilterra: un confronto con il sistema italiano di formazione continua," *Osservatorio Isfol*, No. 1-2.

Verdier, E. 2006. "Les paradoxes du système éducatif francais," *La révue del la CFDT*, No. 78.

Weiler, A. 2007. *Impact of Training on People Employability*. Eurofound.

Winterton, J. 2007. "Training, development and competence," in *The Oxford Handbook of Human Resource Management*, Oxford: Oxford University Press:324-343.

Zappalà, L. 2004. "Verso un nuovo assetto dei rapporti interpositori. Prime riflessioni sulla tipizzazione del contratto di somministrazione di lavoro," *I Working Papers, Centro studi diritto del lavoro europeo "Massimo D'Antona"*, No. 2/IT.

CHAPTER THREE:

FROM SCHOOL-TO-WORK TRANSITION TO THE CHALLENGE OF YOUTH EMPLOYMENT: DIFFERENT APPROACHES IN DIFFERENT REALITIES

Quality Criteria for Establishing Work- Based Learning: An Evaluation of In-Company Learning Arrangements

Ludger Deitmer

1. Introduction

An important initiative in terms of human resource development is represented by in-company training, for it allows for the maximisation of employees' productivity and the innovation potential of the organisation, also assisting in achieving higher levels of efficiency and flexibility in production.

Employees could be seen as a key resource to improve the levels and the quality of production, and they also play a fundamental role in enhancing the quality of customer-oriented service.

Apart from those human potential issues, another factor which is of great significance is a balanced and successful work-based learning environment within the enterprise. In this sense, skills are further developed by allowing emerging professionals—e.g. apprentices or trainees—to be engaged in working and learning activities.

This paper provides a contribution to the debate of work-based learning and its quality factors by presenting an evaluation tool for cost-effectiveness and quality of in-company vocational training. The Quality, Returns, and Costs Tool (QRC Tool) makes it possible for companies to assess their costs and returns as well as the quality of training provided. It was tested and implemented in a pilot study in the Bremen region and more than one hundred companies have made use of this diagnosis instrument so far.[1] A case of good practice from the German manufacturing industry will be therefore discussed in the final section of

---

[1] Rauner, F., and B. Haasler. 2010. *Lernen im Betrieb. Eine Handreichung für Ausbilder und Personalentwickler*. Kostanz: Christiani.

this paper, along with some recommendations on how young people can learn best in enterprises.[2]

2. The Principle of Apprenticeship: Working and Learning

Apprenticeship training provided by means of a "dual" VET system represents a long-standing tradition which is common to Germany and some other Western European countries (e.g. Austria, Denmark, Switzerland and the Netherlands).

The "dual system" consists of two structural elements:

• working and learning activity carried out at workplaces and within different departments (sales, assembly line, and so on) in companies regarded as qualified to provide training[3] on the basis of a collectively agreed-upon framework;

• systematic, subject-based learning activities that should take place in classroom-like environment at local vocational schools. The dual system is mainly based on vocational education provided by public (educational bodies) and private institutions (mostly business-oriented enterprises), and on the engagement of apprentices in a systematically organised working activity.[4]

Unlike other VET systems in Europe, which are characterised by either state-based (like in France), or company-based systems including modular training elements,[5] a "mixed structure" approach of this kind requires the

---

[2] Deitmer, L. 2011. "Building Up of Innovative Capabilities of Workers," in *Fostering Enterprise: the Innovation and Skills Nexus—Research Readings,* ed. Curtin, P., (Adelaide: NCVER).

[3] Companies have to meet certain standards to be officially recognised as training centres and be able to hire apprentices. Compliance with such standards is certified by the regional Chambers of Commerce, Trade and Industry.

[4] Greinert, W. D. 1994. *The German System of Vocational Training. History, Organization, Prospects.* Baden-Baden: Nomos. Deissinger, T. 1996. "Germany's Vocational Training Act: its Function as an Instrument of Quality Control within a Tradition-based Vocational Training System," *Oxford Review of Education* 22, No. 3:317-336.

[5] Like in England, see Ryan, P. 2001. "Apprenticeship in Britain: Tradition and Innovation," in *Berufliche Bildung als Orientierungs- und Anpassungsproblem. Analysen zur Berufsbildungsreform und zur Vorbildfunktion internationaler berufsbildungspolitischer Entwicklungsperspektiven,* ed. Deissinger, T., (Baden-Baden: Nomos).

involvement of both private and public actors. It should be considered that VET students mainly operate within the company (from 50% up to 75% of their working and learning time) over their 2 (in lower qualified occupations) to 3.5 years of training, with a major impact on the development of their vocational and organisational skills. In effect, educational institutions (e.g. schools) play a secondary role in that they offer technical or more general education (e.g. language learning). The provision of on-the-job training and education calls for adequate levels of interaction between the company and the school with regard to the planning of learning activities. Over the years, how to foster such cooperation between education providers and the world of work has been the subject of a lively debate.

At present, divergent views exist on apprenticeship models, especially considering the following points.

1. Lack of cooperation among training and educational institutions

In general terms, critics argue that actors involved in the provision of training co-exist, without however cooperating with respect to the planning of learning programmes, meaning that there is no active cooperation between trainers and teachers, also considering a lack of communication among their apprentices. Accordingly, learning at school is not properly integrated with what apprentices learn on-the-job. In this sense, it would be reasonable to combine learning processes at school with practical experience gained within the company, be it in the industrial, the craft or the service sector. A systematic and theory-based investigation could help to further understand the practical dimension of on-the-job learning, also in terms of résumé-building, which is considered a priority to achieve a better interaction between enterprises and schools.

2. Poor quality learning provided at a company level

In Germany, there have been initiatives promoting educational programmes at the workplace by the setting up of *ad-hoc* training workshops. After a decade, however, the reintegration of vocational learning within the production process seems to be a more viable solution. This requires continuous evaluation of the learning process—both on-the-job and off-the-job—in order to indentify strengths and weaknesses of this cooperation. Therefore, the active involvement of the apprentice within the company processes is also strongly advisable.[6]

---

[6] Deitmer, L., and L. Heinemann. 2009. "Evaluation Approaches for Workplace Learning Partnerships in VET: How to Investigate the Learning Dimension?" in

3. Little support on the part of company personnel and other organisational issues

It often happens that training companies develop inadequate learning plans for their VET students in terms of tasks to be fulfilled, so that they are not offered necessary information relating to business flow or order processing. This is a remarkable aspect, as apprentices end up with poor performance in their examination. A possible response to this problem is a combination of vocational training with mentoring or coaching activities.[7]

4. Heading for multi-skilled workers

A work environment in which workers plan, control and validate their own tasks is said to provide higher levels of competitiveness.[8] Equipped with multiple skills, including quality assurance, skilled workers are able to discuss necessary adjustments, therefore also developing communication and team building skills in order to respond to job requirements, and to increase the "manufacturability" of products by resorting to a *design-to-assembly* approach. Accordingly, it can be stated that workers needs to develop "holistic problem solving skills".[9]

However, a number of questions remain:

How can we access and identify examples of good practices in production firms, industrial enterprises and companies? How can we differentiate between good (and bad) practices in order to single out necessary conditions for an innovative learning environment, also taking account of attitudes and roles played by different actors within a future scenario?

New features of training development instruments for trainers and trainees can be helpful in this connection. To demonstrate so, a tool which

Towards Integration Of Work and Learning, Strategies for Connectivity and Transformation, eds. Stenström, M.-L., and P. Tynjälä, (Dordrecht: Springer International).

[7] Reinhold, M., B. Haasler, F. Howe, M. Kleiner, and F. Rauner. 2002. *Curriculum Design II: Entwickeln von Lernfeldern. Von beruflichen Arbeitsaufgaben zum Berufsbildungsplan* [Curriculum Design II: Development of Learning Arenas. From Occupational Work Task towards a Vocational Education Plan]. Konstanz: Christiani.

[8] Ruth, K., and L. Deitmer. 2010. "Role of TVET and Innovation," in *International Encyclopaedia of Education*, eds. McGaw, B., E. Baker, and P. Petersen, (Oxford: Elsevier).

[9] Rauner, F. 2007. "Competence Development in Vocational Curricula and Work Situations," *European Journal of Vocational Training* 1, No. 40.

helps to analyse the quality of in-company training will be presented in the following.

3. A Tool to Evaluate the Quality of In-company Training: the Quality, Returns and Costs (QRC)Tool

The QRC Tool enables companies to self-assess the cost-effectiveness as well as the quality of their apprenticeship training. The QRC Tool, which can also be used in VET research, consists of practical questions to both trainers and co-trainers. The first set of questions is about the exact cost of training, and relevant information, such as apprentices and trainers' individual gross wage (also including social benefits).

Further, additional operational costs are considered, which include those borne to buy teaching and learning materials, and training equipment used at the company, as well as fees to be paid to industrial bodies, and costs for work clothes and for extra-courses at special training centres.

To assess benefits, a few adjustments to the already existing cost-benefit model have been made. In this sense, benefits are measured comparing apprentices' levels of productivity—over the period they spent at the company carrying out their task—with those of more skilled workers.

The quality of apprenticeship is evaluated by the QRC Tool on the basis of six main quality dimensions, designed considering vocational pedagogy, and subsequent indicators:

- *Learning in the workplace through experience-based learning*: this criterion considers the number of tasks fulfilled by the apprentice and, in assessing his/her potentials, it aims at verifying the probability—as expressed in percentage—to become a skilled worker over the three-year apprenticeship programme (see Fig. 3-1).

- *Level of work-related tasks*: this factor takes into account both the average score of the final examination testing practical skills and knowledge and the time required to become acquainted with main activities within the field at the end of an apprenticeship programme.

- *Degree of "self-regulated" learning*: this criterion investigates the relationship between detailed assignments and the degree of a student's job autonomy in fulfilling his/her tasks.

- *Learning while involved in work and business processes*: the willingness of apprentices to fulfil assignments which are part of operational business processes is evaluated.

- *Occupational competence*: this criterion is measured by considering the levels of expertise developed through in-company training.

- *Vocational commitment*: such criterion assesses the apprentices' commitment to work, to pursue quality in accomplishing work-related tasks and orders, also evaluating whether they complete their task responsibly.

While the first four indicators describe the training process, the last two criteria are more output-related, that is associated with the impact that it has on apprentices, their commitment, as well as on their occupational competence, with the latter regarded as an outcome of the whole training process.

Once an answer has been provided to each of these questions, a number of visualisations are generated by the tool (e.g. spider-web diagrams, bar and line charts) that allow for the examination of the quality of training as well as the costs and returns, and to assess the level of the apprenticeship programme. Further, the tool also provides a comparison between data from different companies and their apprenticeship schemes, so that it can be stated that the function of such instrument is twofold: to assess and to investigate.

In the following pages, a case will be analysed for illustrative purposes in order to learn how to deal with innovative training programmes for young workers.

By resorting to the QRC Tool, the quality of the apprenticeship scheme, as well as the levels of innovation and effectiveness, have been further investigated.

Fig. 3-1. Apprentices' Increase in Productivity over the Three Years of Training

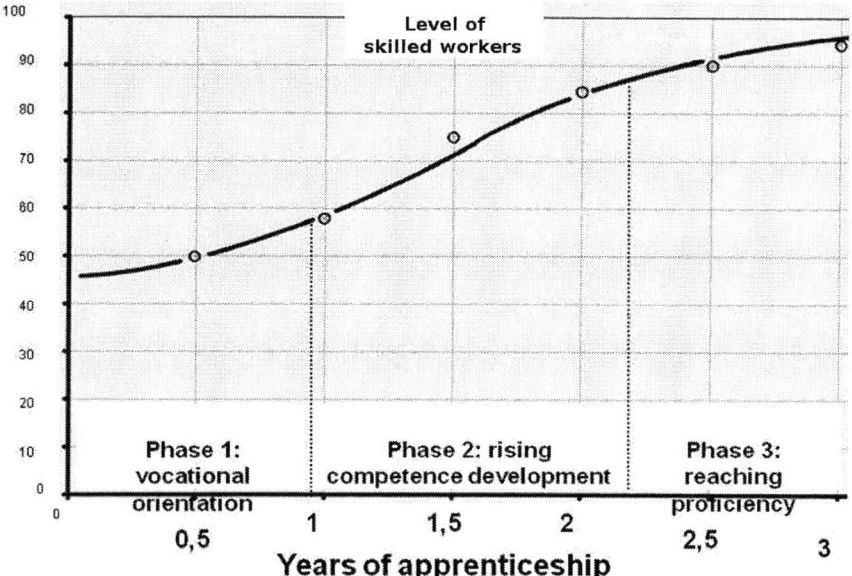

Source: Rauner and Heinemann 2009.

4. A Case of Good Practice

The German manufacturing company in question was founded 40 years ago by an innovative mechanical engineer. Drawing on his previous experience as a designer in the food processing industry, he developed packaging machines for usage also in fields other than traditional ones. The idea was to widen the scope of application of steering and control technologies to the packaging of some consumer goods, like computer disks, textiles or pharmaceuticals. In an official statement issued by the company, it was argued that the use of such cutting-edge technology would make it possible to meet customers' special needs in terms of design. Products could be tailored to meet different requirements, by making use of state-of-the-art tools that provided satisfactory results in terms of performance.

Timeliness of delivery and machinery reliability were also important aspects that were highly considered by customers. Accordingly, apart from the creativity of the engineer, the company could also count on increased levels of manufacturing and customer care skills of their workers, who had attended a three-year apprenticeship in certain sectors (mechanical, electricity supply and manufacturing).

Over the years, higher turnover rates and increased sales figures led this manufacturing company to become a medium-sized company, with the number of its employees which rose up to 300 workers. Fifty per cent of them were engaged in manufacturing and production activities, while design, sales and business administration involved 21% of the workforce. In many cases, engineers started their careers as apprentices, studying at the university and returning to work as engineers. The overall number of apprentices within this company stands at the level of 6% of the total workforce. Such figures are similar to the average figures of the proportional numbers of the apprentices in typical medium-sized companies in Germany, which range between 4 to 6% depending upon the sector and the financial situation of the company.

Apprenticeship schemes for positions in the technical and commercial field were adopted in the company from the very beginning either for well-established forms of employment (such as industrial mechanics and clerks) or new jobs (mechatronic experts or process mechanics for plastics and rubber technology, in 1999 and 2006, respectively).

Apprenticeship programmes provided in this company—which has a duration of three and a half years—usually involved a number of visits at the local technical and vocational schools, with an exam (both written and oral) to be taken before a commission of company representatives and technical/vocational school teachers at the local Chamber of Commerce and Trade.

Now, what makes apprenticeship schemes here so different from those implemented in other German establishments? Why can they be regarded as innovative, especially in terms of good practices?

Drawing on some related principles, a number of answers to these questions will be provided in the following three points.

1. Apprentices are regarded as "core workers" within the company

In the company mentioned above, apprentices have a first-hand experience of production and manufacturing issues, as taking part in highly complex production and/or assembly processes within the workshop departments. As a result, trainees play an active role within the company also interacting with colleagues, and internal and external customers. The activity of the apprentices is overseen by the company trainers, who are also in charge of adjusting their workload on the basis of a "learning map"—which includes the working tasks to be carried out within each production units. Before being involved in the production process, which takes up 80% of their working time, apprentices take part in intensive basic training (mainly dealing with tasks such as cutting, filing and drilling) and in a number of related projects, supported by a *Meister*, that is a master craftsman.

2. Involving apprentices in the production process should take place as early as possible

Apprentices are encouraged to gain practical experience with orders and product management from the very beginning of their programmes, in order to help them to develop full awareness of issues involving production quality, finished products, components and so on. In this connection, they learn to recognise all actors involved in such processes as well as the role they play over the different manufacturing stages, in order to increase their levels of qualifications also with regard to product management. Further, as a highly export-oriented company, workers usually travel and work abroad, so that apprentices are expected to have a sufficient command of English as a working language.

3. Production, manufacturing and design: Knowledge-sharing as a key issue

Employees within the company are fully aware of the importance of establishing a close relationship between engineers and workers, meaning that dialogue between those involved in several production processes is a key issue, also in consideration of the fact that they take on different responsibilities. For this reason, constructive dialogue has to be established between skilled workers, engineers and apprentices over their vocational training so that they can learn more about several steps in production. This goal might be achieved, for instance, by involving them in the design process or allowing them to work within the construction departments for a number of months. Equally important in this respect are the so-called company action projects, which are team projects—to be carried out within the first year of the apprenticeship programmes—where team members gain some practical experience on their own, and learn to communicate and provide feedback to engineers.

5. Relevant QRC Results and Regional Studies

Company Trainers are in charge of assessing the quality of the training programmes also in relation to the cost-benefit ratio. In order to do so, the QRC Tool has been used, as it provides important insights into their main characteristics. Findings revealed that rates of return were significant (13%), with this percentage that could even increase if learning tasks are included within the working activities. One of the key features was the strong emphasis placed on self-organised learning and its incorporation into the production process. This is true if one considers that both trainers and apprentices have the same perception of the quality of training. In this respect, a self-evaluation analysis showed that major differences arise between those enrolled in the first and in the second year of the apprenticeship programme. For example, those in their first year had difficulty in achieving high levels of productivity in their tasks, although high quality standards result from apprentices' increased levels of job autonomy—especially in case of demanding tasks—for which such an innovative apprenticeship provides a significant contribution. Therefore, apprentices quickly develop competitive skills and become more committed to work, as they are provided with higher levels of qualification. However, productivity might also be increased in the event of more adequate "production-based" training, so that it is important for trainees to be more involved in related activities (on the production line, with machinery and so on). Conversely, a number of studies pointed out that companies taking part in self-assessment at a regional level have considerable room for improvement in terms of training programmes.

In this respect, the results from a survey carried out on more than 170 companies in the industrial region of Bremen, which reported an increase in net returns for apprentices, have been analysed.[10]

For instance, some 55% of companies that took part in this self-evaluation programme generated net income; even though with considerable differences (yearly investments/profit per apprentice for some companies amounted to more than 12,000 Euros).

---

[10] Rauner, F., L. Heinemann, and D. Piening. 2008. "Costs, Benefits and Quality of Apprenticeships—a Regional Case Study," Conference proceedings of the second international INAP Conference. Vienna: INAP Innovative Apprenticeship Research Network, 170–5. http://www.inap.uni-bremen.de (accessed January 6, 2011). Heinemann, L., and F. Rauner. 2009. *Qualität und Rentabilität der beruflichen Bildung: Ergebnisse der QEK Studie im Lande Bremen* [Quality and Return of Investment of Vocational Training and Education: Results of the QRC Study in the Laender of Bremen]. IBB Forschungsbericht. http://www.inap.uni-bremen.de/dl/inap%20conference%20proceedings%202009.pdf (accessed March 16, 2011).

Fig. 3-2. Quality of Training over the Three Years of Apprenticeship[11]

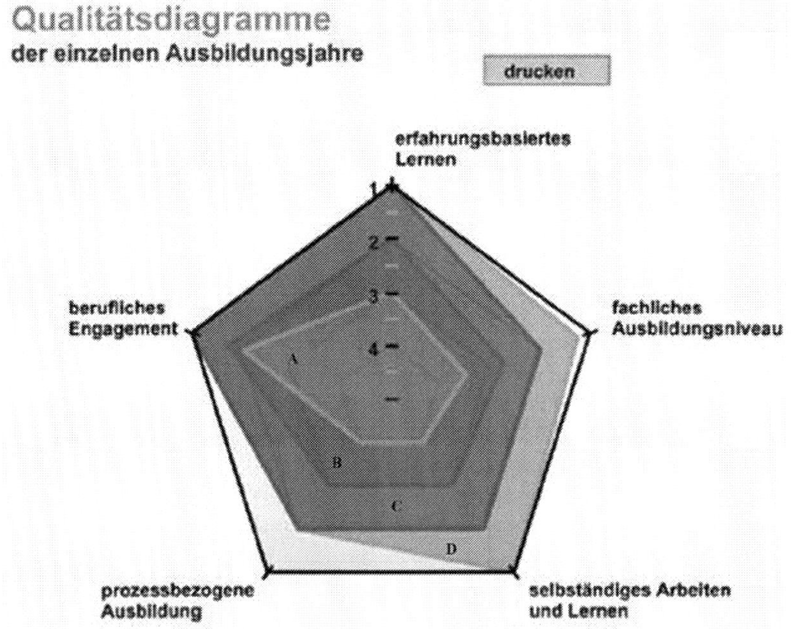

Qualitätsdiagramme
der einzelnen Ausbildungsjahre

drucken

erfahrungsbasiertes
Lernen

berufliches
Engagement

fachliches
Ausbildungsniveau

prozessbezogene
Ausbildung

selbständiges Arbeiten
und Lernen

Another aspect which is worth mentioning is that high-quality apprenticeship programmes within the company increased the cost-effectiveness of apprentices, confirming that the company itself can influence the levels of efficiency by adjusting the way apprenticeships are

[11] Translations of fig.3-2: Heading: Quality diagramme of the single apprenticeship years; Ausbildungsjahr = apprenticeship year
- Erfahrungsbasiertes Lernen: *Experience-based learning in real work situations;*
- Fachliches Ausbildungsniveau: *Level of proficiency in the occupational field;*
- Selbständiges Arbeiten und Lernen: *Capability for self-organised working and learning;*
- Prozessbezogene Ausbildung: *Training for company-specific work processes;*
- Berufliches Engagement: *Occupational Commitment.*
Letters: A: Development of apprentice in the first training year; B: development of the apprentices after the second training year; C: development of the apprentice after the third training year; D: development of the student after the fourth training year (which has a duration of 6 months as students undergo examination to be issued a certificate of training in this year).

structured, although a number of differences can be highlighted in this connection, even between similar establishments. Therefore, in mere economic terms, it can be stated that high-quality apprenticeships might be of benefit to both the apprentice and the company.

6. Concluding Remarks

Concluding remarks provide recommendations for the development of the learning process of apprentices within the enterprise.

1. Job assignments within the company: Maximising learning outcomes
From where the workers stand, the development of more innovative ideas is basic to generate learning experiences from the working activity, so that the apprentice should deal with work and learning tasks (WLTs), which are a fundamental aspect of the company's business processes. The cases of good practices discussed earlier demonstrated that work and learning tasks aimed at maximising "on-the-job" learning, rather than gaining expertise in workshops or training centres, proved very effective on the assumption that learning is an integral part of the job assignment. Therefore, it is also important to set up a "learning map" which gives them the opportunity to play an active role in the production process, with those in charge of providing training who should oversee their progress.

2. From beginners to young experts: levels to be considered while assigning a work and learning task
Work and learning tasks should be organised and assigned considering some criteria such the apprentice's working experience (beginner, advanced beginners, advanced and young experts). In this sense, apprentices with higher levels of expertise should be in charge of carrying out the most difficult tasks, on the basis of their prior knowledge and progress made. For this reason, the training plan should provide for assignments whose complexity should increase gradually.[12]

3. Once completed, "comprehensive" work tasks should be properly assessed
Tasks included in the training package should be verified to ensure that they are "comprehensive" in the sense that they comprise the main aspects

---

[12] Rauner, F., and B. Haasler. 2009. *Lernen im Betrieb—eine handreichung für ausbilder und personalentwickler* [Learning in the company—guideline for trainers and personal managers]. Konstanz: Christiani Verlag.

of the production process, so that the apprentice is provided with an overview of all activities within the company. Equally important is the issuing of documentation certifying the training that has been undertaken, which should include feedback on the part of engineers and organisers on the working activity.

4. WLTs: common quality standards within company's business process

Work and learning tasks must be arranged in a systematic order, and not on an arbitrary basis.

It is therefore important for the trainer to consider the suitability of such tasks in relation to the apprentices' current level of expertise. In some cases, a more detailed examination of the company on the part of the trainer might be advisable, in order to assess the quality of the workplace, with an investigation grid that can be of use. Equally useful might be to interview other workers to verify the type of work tasks to be assigned to the apprentice. It is up to the trainer to coordinate this investigation with company management, also to obtain financial support.

5. WLTs as an instrument to encourage apprentices and colleagues to cooperate

The idea behind WLT is to develop complete units of working and learning that match practical skill needs of work-specific tasks and which, although covering a complete task, build upon each other, and cover the entire business process.[13]

Apart from including the objectives of the working activities, methodology, instruments and other aspects, WLTs should promote cooperation with other workers, so that the working environment is given considerable importance. As a result, the apprentice might be encouraged to work with other apprentices and more qualified colleagues, and to learn to discuss design and manufacturing issues from the first stage of the programme. This can help to develop innovative skills and to deal with more complex questions relating to the finished product.

6. The setting-up of a training logbook: A learning process itself

A training logbook helps to gain organisational skills while supporting self-directed learning, as what has been learned and what could be learned in the future becomes more clear.

---

[13] For further details on the development of such WLT see Howe, F., R. Heermeyer, H. Heuermann, H. Höpfner, and F. Rauner. 2001. *Lern- und Arbeitsaufgaben für eine gestaltungsorientierte Berufsbildung*. Konstanz: Christiani Verlag.

Apart from keeping records of the main tasks carried out by the apprentice, the training logbook also allows for a reflection on the training experience at large and forces one to ask self reflexive questions like: What were the challenges of the work task? What have I learned best so far? Are there still problems and difficulties? How do others regard my work and results?

As we can see, such documents cannot be regarded as a diary but rather as a self-assessment tool. They pave the way for further cooperation with company trainers, and lay the foundations for dialogue between those involved in the shift from self-assessment towards external assessment.[14]

7. Self-assessment of individual learning makes external assessment by others necessary

Self-assessment of the apprentice in relation to individual learning progress makes external assessment by others also necessary.

Those in charge of overseeing activities of the learner apprentice within the company—trainers or colleagues—should provide feedback and advice. An important element in this connection is the *competence assessment sheet*, which clarifies the goals to be achieved.[15] Accordingly, the apprentice becomes aware of his/her own competences also giving rise to relevant processes of both reflection and self-reflection. This requires extensive knowledge of domain-specific and domain-independent competences on the trainers' side, as an additional indicator of the need for in-company trainers with strong knowledge of the work processes and the subject fields. The challenge to be dealt with is how to match and balance between individual wishes and the needs of the company, to the benefit of all actors involved, also in terms of career advancement.

---

[14] Rauner, F., and B. Haasler. 2009. *Lernen im Betrieb—eine handreichung für ausbilder und personalentwickler* [Learning in the company—guideline for trainers and personal managers]. Konstanz: Christiani Verlag.

[15] Deitmer, L., and K. Ruth. 2007. *Cornerstones of Mentoring Processes: How to Implement, Conduct and Evaluate Mentoring Projects?* ITB Forschungsberichte 29. Bremen: University of Bremen.

8. The use of tools (QRC) to support and analyse the training programme

The QRC Tool[16] is primarily an instrument for companies and responsible trainers or part-time trainers to (self-) assess the quality and cost-effectiveness of their company's apprenticeship training. In terms of costs, significant factors for workplace training, such as allowances and benefits for apprentices (the amount of which is externally negotiated), need to be measured according to their productivity. The QRC Tool is an applied research tool that allows the examination of workplace training within industrial companies, also making it possible to analyse most innovative practices and to discuss their effectiveness among companies and VET researchers.

References

Deissinger, T. 1996. "Germany's Vocational Training Act: its Function as an Instrument of Quality Control within a Tradition-based Vocational Training System," *Oxford Review of Education* 22, No. 3:317-336.

Deitmer, L. 2011. "Building Up of Innovative Capabilities of Workers," in *Fostering Enterprise: the Innovation and Skills Nexus—Research Readings,* ed. Curtin, P., (Adelaide: NCVER).

Deitmer, L., and L. Heinemann. 2009. "Evaluation Approaches for Workplace Learning Partnerships in VET: How to Investigate the Learning Dimension?" in *Towards Integration Of Work and Learning, Strategies for Connectivity and Transformation*, eds. Stenström, M.-L., and P. Tynjälä, (Dordrecht: Springer International).

—. "Innovation through Evaluation and Quality Development of In-company Training and Workplace Learning," in Second International Online Conference on Innovation in Training Practice, 9-10 November 2009.

---

[16] Rauner, F., L. Heinemann, and D. Piening. 2008. "Costs, Benefits and Quality of Apprenticeships—a Regional Case Study," Conference proceedings of the second international INAP conference. Vienna: INAP Innovative Apprenticeship Research Network, 170–5. http://www.inap.uni-bremen.de (accessed January 6, 2011). Heinemann, L., and F. Rauner. 2009. *Qualität und Rentabilität der beruflichen Bildung: Ergebnisse der QEK Studie im Lande Bremen* [Quality and Return of Investment of Vocational Training and Education: Results of the QRC Study in the Laender of Bremen]. IBB Forschungsbericht.
http://www.inap.uni-bremen.de/dl/inap%20conference%20proceedings%202009.pdf (accessed March 16, 2011).

http://www.trainersineurope.org/activities/conference09/proceedings-and-recordings/ (accessed March 16, 2011).

Deitmer, L., and K. Ruth. 2007. *Cornerstones of Mentoring Processes: How to Implement, Conduct and Evaluate Mentoring Projects?* ITB Forschungsberichte 29. Bremen: University of Bremen.

Greinert, W. D. 1994. *The German System of Vocational Training. History, Organization, Prospects.* Baden-Baden: Nomos.

Heinemann, L., and F. Rauner. 2009. *Qualität und Rentabilität der beruflichen Bildung: Ergebnisse der QEK Studie im Lande Bremen* [Quality and Return of Investment of Vocational Training and Education: Results of the QRC Study in the Laender of Bremen]. IBB Forschungsbericht.   http://www.inap.uni-bremen.de/dl/inap%20conf erence%20proceedings%202009.pdf (accessed March 16, 2011).

Howe, F., R. Heermeyer, H. Heuermann, H. Höpfner, and F. Rauner. 2001. *Lern- und Arbeitsaufgaben für eine gestaltungsorientierte Berufsbildung.* Konstanz: Christiani Verlag.

Rauner, F., and B. Haasler. 2009. *Lernen im Betrieb—eine handreichung für ausbilder und personalentwickler* [Learning in the company—guideline for trainers and personal managers]. Konstanz: Christiani Verlag.

Rauner, F. 2007. "Competence Development in Vocational Curricula and Work Situations," *European Journal of Vocational Training* 1 No. 40.

Rauner, F., L. Heinemann, and D. Piening. 2008. "Costs, Benefits and Quality of Apprenticeships—a Regional Case Study," Conference proceedings of the second international INAP conference. Vienna: INAP Innovative Apprenticeship Research Network, 170–5. http://www.inap.uni-bremen.de (accessed January 6, 2011).

Rauner, F., and B. Haasler. 2010. *Lernen im Betrieb. Eine Handreichung für Ausbilder und Personalentwickler.* Kostanz: Christiani.

Reinhold, M., B. Haasler, F. Howe, M. Kleiner, and F. Rauner. 2002. *Curriculum Design II: Entwickeln von Lernfeldern. Von beruflichen Arbeitsaufgaben zum Berufsbildungsplan* [Curriculum Design II: Development of Learning Arenas. From Occupational Work Task towards a Vocational Education Plan]. Konstanz: Christiani.

Ruth, K., and L. Deitmer. 2010. "Role of TVET and Innovation," in *International Encyclopaedia of Education*, eds. McGaw, B., E. Baker, and P. Petersen, (Oxford: Elsevier).

Ryan, P. 2001. "Apprenticeship in Britain: Tradition and Innovation," in *Berufliche Bildung als Orientierungs- und Anpassungsproblem. Analysen zur Berufsbildungsreform und zur Vorbildfunktion internationaler berufsbildungspolitischer Entwicklungsperspektiven,* ed. Deissinger, T., (Baden-Baden: Nomos).

THE IMPACT OF INTERNATIONAL MOBILITY ON YOUTH EMPLOYABILITY IN VET

LÉNA KRICHEWSKY

1. Introduction

An analysis of the debate at a European level on the international student mobility carried out by Kristensen[1] identified four claims commonly put forward to justify the importance of the issue. Mobility is therefore regarded as a means for:

- promoting the movement of workers within an integrated European labour market;
- further developing technology transfer between the countries;
- raising awareness and understanding among people living in Europe;
- fostering skills, particularly intercultural and personal ones.

The key concept of this debate is "employability", which is referred to in the opening sentence of the Green Paper "Promoting the learning mobility of young people":[2] "Learning mobility, i.e. transnational mobility for the purpose of acquiring new skills is one of the fundamental ways in which individuals, particularly young people, can strengthen their future employability as well as their personal development."

This sentence refers to a presumed causal link between learning mobility on the one hand, and enhanced employability on the other hand. To what extent are those phenomena related? Is there any evidence in support of such a peculiar statement?

---

[1] Kristensen, S. 2001. "Learning by Leaving—Towards a Pedagogy for Transnational Mobility in the Context of Vocational Education and Training (VET)," *European Journal of Education* 36, No. 4:42-30.
[2] European Commission. 2009. *Grünbuch: Die Mobilität junger Menschen zu Lernzwecken fördern* KOM(2009) 329. http://ec.europa.eu/education/lifelong-learning-policy/doc/mobility/com329_de.pdf (accessed November 12, 2010), 2.

The aim of this paper is to provide an answer to these questions by reviewing existing literature on the impact of international mobility on employability, with a special focus on vocational education and training (VET).

2. Methodology

The methodology used to carry out this review draws on a research design proposed by Ogawa and Malen[3] to investigate what has been termed "multivocal" literature. Multivocal literature includes published materials from different sources, e.g. policy documents, academic journals and books, and evaluation reports. This exploratory method usually proves effective to address contemporary issues, especially when little research has been carried out on the topic, as is the case of international mobility in VET. Selection criteria for the review have been formulated to include a broad corpus of publications, subsequently categorised and rated in accordance with the type, the validity and the reliability of the evidence they provided. The content analysis has been conducted through a set of categories reflecting the main dimensions of the research questions.

As suggested by Ogawa and Malen,[4] in order to enhance the objectivity of the review, the final part of the study will provide an analysis of rival interpretations in the body of texts. This is deemed to be necessary particularly in the current case, because of the interest-driven nature of the relevant literature (e.g. policy documents), which usually favours the spread of mobility.

3. Theoretical Background and Research Questions

3.1 Definitions of the Key Concepts

The definition of the key terms adopted within this paper—e.g. mobility and employability—determined the criteria used to select publications to be included in the literature review and to define the research questions and categories for the content analysis.

The term mobility was specified following three criteria:

---

[3] Ogawa, R. T., and B. Malen. 1991. "Towards Rigor in Reviews of Multivocal Literatures: Applying the Exploratory Case Study Method," *Review of Educational Research* 61, No. 3:265-286.
[4] Ibid.

- Geography: only cross-border mobility was examined. The focus was on mobility within the European Union, with special attention paid to outgoing mobility in Germany.
- Duration: only mobility taking place within the framework of a learning programme leading to a qualification in the home country was examined, leaving aside the case of learners staying in one foreign country for the whole study programme.
- Purpose: only mobility with an explicit learning purpose was taken into account. Formal and informal learning (e.g. during an internship) were considered, however excluding voluntary services or *au-pair* programmes.

In the EU documents, employability is defined as "the combination of factors which enables individuals to progress towards or get into employment, to stay in employment and advance in their career".[5] Following Hillage,[6] employability depends on four factors related to individuals, as comprising:

- their assets in terms of knowledge, skills and attitudes;
- the way they use and deploy these assets;
- the way they introduce themselves to employers;
- the context (personal circumstances and labour market environment) within which they seek employment.

To simplify the picture, the employability of a person results from the matching between personal abilities (the assets and the way they are used and presented) and labour market requirements.[7]

In order to assess the impact of international mobility on employability, two approaches can be distinguished. The first approach focuses on the output of the matching process, measuring for instance the employment rate, the time needed for finding the first job, or the type of employment and the entry salary of learners with an international experience in

---

[5] Cedefop. 2008. *Terminology of European Education and Training Policy: A Selection of 100 Key Terms.* Luxembourg: Office for Official Publications of the European Communities, 70.

[6] Hillage, J. 1998. *Employability: Developing a Framework for Policy Analysis.* Department for Education and Employment research report No. 85. London: Department for Education and Employment (DfEE).

[7] Forrier, A., and L. Sels. 2003. "The Concept of Employability: A Complex Mosaic," *International Journal of Human Resources Development and Management* 3, No. 2:102-24.

comparison with similar groups of learners who have never studied abroad. The other approach sets the focus on the input of the process by analysing and comparing the specific competences developed through an international mobility experience on the one hand and the requirements of the labour market in terms of skills needed on the other hand. Both types of approaches are represented in this literature review.

3.2 Scope of the Study

The research focus of this paper is on vocational education and training, but research on mobility in higher education has been also considered, upon the condition that it provided empirical data on the output of the matching process underpinning the concept of employability. These publications were used for comparative purposes, to shed some light on the findings in VET. Research on international mobility in higher education is much more developed than in VET, so that it was assumed that VET research could benefit from its findings to develop new research questions and methodological tools.

The study considered texts published after 1995, the year the Leonardo da Vinci programme was launched by the European Union to boost mobility in VET.

3.3 Research Questions

According to the existing literature, what is the impact of international mobility on employability in VET? The overarching question of this paper is addressed by answering three related questions based on the definition of employability:

- what specific competences and skills are enhanced through international mobility?
- What are the needs of the labour market in terms of competences and skills which can be developed through international mobility (e.g. language skills, intercultural competence, occupational skills and knowledge related to a foreign country)?
- What is the impact of international mobility on learners' transition to the labour market and further career?

This review has an explorative character. It is not possible to answer these questions with a reasonable degree of certainty on the basis of existing literature, but these questions should help to identify research gaps and to develop new strands of research for further enquiries.

4. Overview of Existing Literature

Systematic literature research was conducted considering a number of general and specialised databases, also including websites of French, German and British National Agencies coordinating the EU Lifelong Learning Programmes, as well as databases of several research institutions (e.g. Bundesinstitut für Berufsbildung, Cedefop, Deutsches Institut für Internationale Pädagogische Forschung). As a result, 30 publications were selected as they meet the requirements for further analysis. This corpus of publications can be described on the basis of different criteria.

Firstly, it appeared that very little academic literature is available on the subject. Most empirical studies take the form of evaluations and reports commissioned by various stakeholders.

Table 3-1. Publications

Type of publication	Number of publications found*
Academic journals, books	15 (5)
Evaluation studies	11 (9)
Policy documents	2
Others	4 (4)

* The numbers in brackets () represent the empirical studies.

Turning to methodological aspects, Stronkhorst[8] pointed out that depending on their focus, publications assessing the effects of international mobility can be classified into four categories:

- Effect Level 1: participants' perception (e.g. in terms of satisfaction, impact, and so on);
- Effect Level 2: participants' learning in terms of:
o foreign language competency;
o occupational and academic competences, for example, international and intercultural competences;

[8] Stronkhorst, R. 2005. "Learning Outcomes of International Mobility at Two Dutch Institutions of Higher Education," *Journal of Studies in International Education* 9, No. 4:294.

o   personality characteristics, for example, multicultural personality characteristics;
- Effect Level 3: career-related outcomes;
- Effect Level 4: organisation, company, or society-related outcomes.

Most of publications based on empirical research which were examined for this review have a focus on effect Level 1, with a few addressing also Level 3. Some studies also include a survey among employers, project coordinators or other experts involved in mobility, such as teachers and trainers, who have been asked to give their opinion about the impact of mobility. Only a small percentage of the studies resorted to control group—before and after comparisons—or controlled the variables.

Table 3-2. Research Method

Research method	With control group / controlled variables*	Without control group*
Participants' survey or interview	4 (3)	3 (2)
Expert interview	2 (2)	4 (3)
Output indicators	2 (0)	2 (0)

* The numbers in brackets represent studies focused on VET only.
NB: a total of 13 studies were examined, but some studies may appear twice in this table if they combine several research methods.

A classification of publications resulting from the type of mobility addressed (e.g. formal vs. informal learning, duration, age of participants and so on) is not feasible, because most studies do not operate any differentiation or do not make the data available for secondary analysis. This is a major limitation to our research, as it can be expected that significant factors influencing employability are left out of the scope of inquiry.

5. Findings from the Literature Review

5.1 The Benefits of Mobility: International Skills and Competences

In German-speaking literature, there is general consensus on the benefits of international mobility in terms of skills and competences in

VET. Here, National literature is based on a series of studies initially carried forward by the Bundesinstitut für Berufsbildung (BIBB), which progressively led to the concept of "international action competence" (*internationale Handlungskompetenz*).[9] International competence has four dimensions:

- international occupational skills: these are branch- or occupation-related skills, knowledge and competences associated with an international context, such as an awareness of international norms, foreign markets and so on;
- foreign language skills;
- intercultural competence;
- networking skills: these include IT competences as well as social competences for working in (international / virtual) networks.

Although the concept of international action competence has not yet drawn the attention of the French- or English-speaking scientific community, it accounts to a large extent for the various types of skills and competences regarded as an outcome of international mobility elsewhere. A fifth category could however be added to include the "personal development" dimension of international mobility, which is also addressed by almost all the studies. It covers more or less what has been termed "personal competence" (or self-competence) in German VET:

> Personal competence describes the willingness and ability, as an individual personality, to understand, analyse and judge the development chances, requirements and limitations in the family, job and public life, to develop one's own skills as well as to decide on and develop life plans. It includes personal characteristics like independence, critical abilities, self-

---

[9] Borch, H., A. Diettrich, D. Frommberger, H. Reinisch, and P. Wordelmann. 2003. *Internationalisierung der Berufsbildung.* Bielefeld: Bertelsmann. Busse, G., and K. Fahle. 1998. *Lernen durch Mobilität: Untersuchung zu längerfristigen Auslandsaufenthalten von Auszubildenden und jungen Berufstätigen im Auftrag des CEDEFOP.* Köln: Carl Duisberg Gesellschaft. Wordelmann, P. 1995. *Internationale Qualifikationen: Inhalte, Bedarf und Vermittlung.* Bielefeld: Bertelsmann. http://www.gbv.de/dms/hbz/toc/ht006693817.PDF. Wordelmann, P. 2010. "Internationale Kompetenzen in der Berufsbildung - Stand der Wissenschaft und praktische Anforderungen: Einleitung," in *Internationale Kompetenzen in der Berufsbildung: Stand der Wissenschaft und praktische Anforderungen*, ed. Wordelmann, P., (Bielefeld: Bertelsmann), 7-31.

confidence, reliability, responsibility and awareness of duty, as well as professional and ethical values.[10]

Although personal competence is not specifically international, it represents one of the main learning outcomes of mobility and, therefore, it cannot be ignored.

In the context of this question, looking for contrary evidence or rival interpretations, as suggested by Ogawa/Malen,[11] implies to ask first: does international mobility really foster the above mentioned skills and competences? And secondly: in terms of mobility, what is perceived as being beneficial in the eyes of employers?

As discussed earlier, most empirical studies reviewed here are based on self-assessment of participants, except for foreign language skills, which are more often assessed through tests.

Concordant results show that international mobility in VET fosters personal competence: for instance, the ability to adapt to new situations, self-confidence,[12] team-working skills and autonomy.[13] Gains in intercultural competence and language skills are also significant, although on negative effects Stronkhorst[14] reports that:

> In short, there were reasonable overall effects for the Case 1 students [i.e. BA students in horticulture and agriculture who made an internship abroad], especially as far as cultural empathy and open-mindedness are concerned, and rather limited overall results for the Case 2 students [BA students in communication and public administration, who participated to a

---

[10] Delamare-Le Deist, F., and J. Winterton. 2005. "What Is Competence?" *Human Resource Development International* 8, No. 1:38.

[11] Ogawa, R. T., and B. Malen. 1991. "Towards Rigor in Reviews of Multivocal Literatures: Applying the Exploratory Case Study Method," *Review of Educational Research* 61, No. 3:265-286.

[12] WSF Wirtschafts- und Sozialforschung. 2007. *Analyse der Wirkungen von LEONARDO DA VINCI Mobilitätsmaßnahmen auf junge Auszubildende, Arbeitnehmerinnen und Arbeitnehmer sowie der Einfluss sozioökonomischer Faktoren: Untersuchung im Auftrag der Europäischen Kommission Generaldirektion Bildung und Kultur.* Kerpen: WSF. http://ec.europa.eu/education/pdf/doc218_de.pdf (accessed March 3, 2010).

[13] Barthold, B. 2010. "Betriebliche Mobilitätsmaßnahmen - Nutzen und inhaltliche Ausgestaltung," in *Internationale Kompetenzen in der Berufsbildung: Stand der Wissenschaft und praktische Anforderungen*, ed. Wordelmann, P., (Bielefeld: Bertelsmann), 125.

[14] Stronkhorst, R. 2005. "Learning Outcomes of International Mobility at Two Dutch Institutions of Higher Education," *Journal of Studies in International Education* 9, No. 4:292-315.

study exchange programme]. Yet, it should be stressed that a considerable number of students in both institutions hardly made any progress at all and, even worse, the period abroad had a negative impact on the MP [multicultural personality, i.e. cultural empathy, open-mindedness, social initiative, emotional stability, and flexibility] of quite a few students.[15]

In general terms, learning outcomes of international mobility seem to depend to a great extent on features associated with the stay and on learners' characteristics. In those studies, which distinguish between the effects of such variables, as the duration and the setting (i.e. structured programme, internship, study abroad), different results can be observed. Differences mainly refer to the extent to which mobile learners enhance their occupational skills: the longer is the stay, the stronger the effect on occupational skills and competences.[16] An evaluation of the effects of the Leonardo da Vinci programme came to the conclusion that only 52% of the participants of mobility projects considered that their occupational skills had been enhanced through mobility, but the proportion was higher for those who had spent at least 6 months abroad.[17] The proportion is slightly higher (55%) in Busse and Fahle,[18] but this can be explained by the longer average duration of the stay (37% of participants stayed abroad for more than 6 months, against 7% in the sample of WSF 2007).

---

[15] Ibid. 302.

[16] Wordelmann, P. 2010. "Internationale Kompetenzen in der Berufsbildung—Stand der Wissenschaft und praktische Anforderungen: Einleitung," in *Internationale Kompetenzen in der Berufsbildung: Stand der Wissenschaft und praktische Anforderungen*, ed. Wordelmann, P., (Bielefeld: Bertelsmann), 7-31. Busse, G., and K. Fahle. 1998. *Lernen durch Mobilität: Untersuchung zu längerfristigen Auslandsaufenthalten von Auszubildenden und jungen Berufstätigen im Auftrag des CEDEFOP*. Köln: Carl Duisberg Gesellschaft.

[17] WSF Wirtschafts- und Sozialforschung. 2007. *Analyse der Wirkungen von LEONARDO DA VINCI Mobilitätsmaßnahmen auf junge Auszubildende, Arbeitnehmerinnen und Arbeitnehmer sowie der Einfluss sozioökonomischer Faktoren: Untersuchung im Auftrag der Europäischen Kommission Generaldirektion Bildung und Kultur*. Kerpen: WSF. http://ec.europa.eu/education/pdf/doc218_de.pdf (accessed March 3, 2010), 49-50.

[18] Busse, G., and K. Fahle. 1998. *Lernen durch Mobilität: Untersuchung zu längerfristigen Auslandsaufenthalten von Auszubildenden und jungen Berufstätigen im Auftrag des CEDEFOP*. Köln: Carl Duisberg Gesellschaft.

Fig. 3-4. The Benefits of International Mobility in the Eyes of Participants

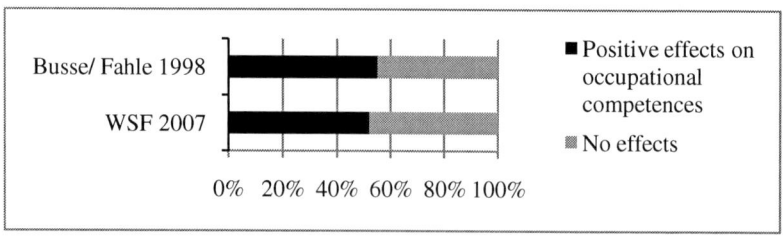

These results might not be surprising, but they call for further research on the benefits of international mobility, especially in terms of occupational skills and competences, with factors affecting the learning outcomes of mobility that should also be examined. Recent developments in EU cooperation, especially the introduction of a European Credit System for VET (ECVET), is expected to increase attention paid by providers and funding institutions to the objectives and outcomes of international mobility. By generalising the assessment of learning outcomes obtained abroad, ECVET might also prove helpful for further developing tools for empirical research in the field.

Apparently, the lack of benefits arising from international mobility in terms of occupational skills is not taken into serious consideration by evaluators:

> From the viewpoint of the evaluators, these results [i.e. only 52% of participants considering their stay abroad to be positive for occupational skills] do not represent a weakness of Leonardo mobility projects; these projects are generally too short and they primarily target the learning of languages and social competences. These goals, as demonstrated, are reached to a large extent.[19]

Employers tend to share the view that international mobility primarily affects intercultural and personal competences as well as language skills,

---

[19] WSF Wirtschafts- und Sozialforschung. 2007. *Analyse der Wirkungen von LEONARDO DA VINCI Mobilitätsmaßnahmen auf junge Auszubildende, Arbeitnehmerinnen und Arbeitnehmer sowie der Einfluss sozioökonomischer Faktoren: Untersuchung im Auftrag der Europäischen Kommission Generaldirektion Bildung und Kultur.* Kerpen: WSF.
http://ec.europa.eu/education/pdf/doc218_de.pdf (accessed March 3, 2010), 49.

whereas occupational skills are not considered to increase significantly abroad.[20] This raises the question as to how these skills are deemed by employers, especially in comparison with occupational skills.

5.2 The Demand Side: Labour Market Requirements in Terms of International Skills and Competences

Following Diettrich and Reinisch,[21] there is broad consensus among all stakeholders in VET and in the labour market that the need for international skills and competences is increasing. Various trends and rationales are mentioned to support this claim: globalisation, which implies growing transnational interaction between economic actors, including SMEs;[22] new forms of work organisation, characterised by flat hierarchies, which provide employees with higher levels of responsibilities when it comes to communicate to (foreign) clients and partners;[23] a growing cultural diversity even within companies, which requires better intercultural communication skills.[24]

---

[20] Berner, K. 2004. *Qualifizierung durch Auslandspraktika: Eine Studie des Forschungsinstituts für Berufsbildung im Handwerk an der Universität zu Köln in Kooperation mit dem Niedersächsischen Kultusministerium.* Köln: FBH, 19. Klimmer, S. 2010. "Was bringen Auslandspraktika von Lehrlingen den Unternehmen? Ergebnisse einer Befragung von österreichischen Unternehmen," in *Internationale Kompetenzen in der Berufsbildung: Stand der Wissenschaft und praktische Anforderungen,* ed. Wordelmann, P., (Bielefeld: Bertelsmann), 217-25. BIBB. 2002. "Grenzüberschreitender Austausch von Auszubildenden und jungen Fachkräften," *RBS-Information,* No. 21. In the case of higher education: Bundesministerium für Bildung und Forschung. 2009. *Der berufliche Ertrag der ERASMUS-Mobilität: Die Auswirkungen internationaler Erfahrung auf die Berufswege von ehemals mobilen Studierenden und Lehrenden.* Berlin: BMBF.
[21] Diettrich, A., and H. Reinisch. 2010. "Internationale und interkulturelle berufliche Handlungskompetenz als Zielkomponent beruflicher Bildung," in *Internationale Kompetenzen in der Berufsbildung: Stand der Wissenschaft und praktische Anforderungen,* ed. Wordelmann, P., (Bielefeld: Bertelsmann), 34.
[22] Hering, E., W. A. Pförtsch, and P. Wordelmann, eds. 2001. *Internationalisierung des Mittelstandes: Strategien zur internationalen Qualifizierung in kleinen und mittleren Unternehmen; mit Checkliste zu Qualifikationen für die Internationalisierung.* Bielefeld: Bertelsmann.
[23] Borch, H., A. Diettrich, D. Frommberger, H. Reinisch, and P. Wordelmann. 2003. *Internationalisierung der Berufsbildung.* Bielefeld: Bertelsmann.
[24] Wordelmann, P. 2010. "Internationale Kompetenzen in der Berufsbildung - Stand der Wissenschaft und praktische Anforderungen: Einleitung," in *Internationale Kompetenzen in der Berufsbildung: Stand der Wissenschaft und praktische Anforderungen,* ed. Wordelmann, P., (Bielefeld: Bertelsmann), 8.

These general statements are usually found in policy documents and academic literature, and are supported by empirical research. According to a survey carried out in Germany in 1999 and 2006 among employees, the proportion of employees with VET qualifications in need of at least basic knowledge of English at the workplace increased from 10% to 22%.[25] A survey conducted among 2,017 Austrian companies in 2005 revealed an even higher demand for language skills: 86% of companies were in need of workers with foreign language command, with 64% who believe that requirements for foreign language skills will continue to increase in the future. The same survey pointed out that foreign language skills always— or nearly always—played a pivotal role in recruitment processes in 22% of the company, whereas less than 20% ignored this criterion for recruitment purposes. Some 19% of the companies would like young people to have better language skills and intercultural competences.[26] A study carried out at a European level identified those fields with the highest levels of commuting (i.e. construction industry, gastronomy and manufacturing) coming to the conclusion that, although the secondary sector still dominates, fields in the tertiary sector are increasingly subject to transnational commuting in border regions.[27] This indicates an increasing need for international competence from workers in these regions. At a supra-regional level, requirements in terms of language skills may be even higher in other branches. In Germany, Hall[28] identified a number of occupations where English skills are in high demand, for instance positions in ICT sector, or jobs in electrical engineering, security and sales. Requirements for English language skills in Germany are higher in large companies (23% of companies with more than 500 employees

---

[25] Wordelmann, P. 2010. "Internationale Kompetenzen in der Berufsbildung— Stand der Wissenschaft und praktische Anforderungen: Einleitung," in *Internationale Kompetenzen in der Berufsbildung: Stand der Wissenschaft und praktische Anforderungen*, ed. Wordelmann, P., (Bielefeld: Bertelsmann), 11.
[26] Tritscher-Archan, S. 2008. "Fremdsprachenbedarf und -kompetenzen in Österreichs Unternehmen," in *Fremdsprachen für die Wirtschaft: Analysen, Zahlen, Fakten*, ed. Tritscher-Archan, S., IBW-Forschungsbericht 143 (Wien: Inst. für Bildungsforschung der Wirtschaft), 181-182.
[27] MKW Wirtschaftsforschung GmbH and Empirica. 2009. *Scientific Report on the Mobility of Cross-Border Workers within the EU-27/EEA/EFTA Countries: Final report, commissioned by European Commission DG Employment and Social Affairs.* Munich: MKW GmbH, 8.
[28] Hall, A. 2008. "Fremdsprachen im Beruf—Wer benötigt Fremdsprachenkenntnisse und auf welchem Niveau?" in *Fremdsprachen für die Wirtschaft: Analysen, Zahlen, Fakten*, ed. Tritscher-Archan, S., IBW-Forschungsbericht 143 (Wien: Inst. für Bildungsforschung der Wirtschaft), 224.

express this need), than in medium-sized companies (16%), decreasing to 6% for small companies.[29]

Some studies on requirements in terms of international competences suggest that companies are often unmindful of their needs, or may not value international competence as they should in the light of globalisation. Some branches, such as the chemical industry[30] or logistics and transports,[31] have acknowledged the potential benefits of mobility, not only in terms of language skills but also in terms of key competences. In other cases, the potential need for international competence is estimated to be higher than companies expect.[32] This is particularly the case of SMEs. Based on the assumption that international mobility does "only" affect soft skills, an evaluation of the mobility programme PIU (*Praktik I Udlandet*) in Denmark showed that many SMEs consider international mobility to be superfluous.[33] Such findings raise the question as to whether or not companies take international mobility as a selection criterion in recruitment processes. Should some further research confirm the fact that a significant percentage of employers are not aware of the benefits of mobility for their own business, this would also question the impact of mobility on employability.

---

[29] Ibid. 221.

[30] Storz, P., and W. Hübel, eds. 2010. *Berufsbildung im europäischen Verbund: Erfahrungen aus der Chemiebranche.* Bielefeld: Bertelsmann.

[31] Dybowski, G., and U. Wiegand. 2001. "Qualifizieren für den Globalisierungsprozess. Das Beispiel der Deutschen Bahn AG," *BWP*, No. 4:11-16.

[32] Paul, K. D., and P. Wordelmann. 2010. *Ermittlung transnationaler Qualifizierungsbedarfe in der Region Berlin: Studie im Auftrag der Senatsverwaltung für Wirtschaft, Technologie und Frauen Berlin.* Berlin: u.bus GmbH. http://www.berlin.de/imperia/md/content/sen-strukturfonds/esf/studieesfinternational30032010final.pdf?start&ts=1277127706&file=studieesfinternational30032010final.pdf (accessed December 5, 2010).

[33] Kristensen, S., and P. Wordelmann. 2010. "Transnationale Mobilität in kleinen und mittleren Unternehmen," in *Internationale Kompetenzen in der Berufsbildung: Stand der Wissenschaft und praktische Anforderungen,* ed. Wordelmann, P., (Bielefeld: Bertelsmann), 180.

5.3 Measuring Employability: Research Results on the Impact of International Mobility

Policy documents often assume a direct link between international mobility and employability.[34] The Green Paper on Learning Mobility offers a good example in this connection:

> Studies confirm that learning mobility adds to human capital, as students access new knowledge and develop new linguistic skills and intercultural competences. Furthermore, employers recognise and value these benefits.[35]

However, studies measuring direct effects of international mobility on employability in VET are still rare. The statement above refers to a footnote to two evaluation studies of the EU programmes Leonardo[36] and Erasmus,[37] which, as demonstrated below, actually provide only a weak basis for such thesis.

As regards the studies, the most recent is the Final Evaluation of the Leonardo-da-Vinci II programme, published in 2008,[38] which is based on an online survey among 38,780 project coordinators and partners from all the participating European countries, resulting in almost 6,000 questionnaires (response rate: 27%). The second evaluation, referred to in the Green Paper on Learning Mobility, was published in 2007. It is based

---

[34] Diettrich, A., and H. Reinisch. 2010. "Internationale und interkulturelle berufliche Handlungskompetenz als Zielkomponent beruflicher Bildung," in *Internationale Kompetenzen in der Berufsbildung: Stand der Wissenschaft und praktische Anforderungen*, ed. Wordelmann, P., (Bielefeld: Bertelsmann), 35.

[35] European Commission. 2009. *Grünbuch: Die Mobilität junger Menschen zu Lernzwecken fördern* KOM(2009) 329. http://ec.europa.eu/education/lifelong-learning-policy/doc/mobility/com329_de.pdf (accessed November 12, 2010), 2.

[36] WSF Wirtschafts- und Sozialforschung. 2007. *Analyse der Wirkungen von LEONARDO DA VINCI Mobilitätsmaßnahmen auf junge Auszubildende, Arbeitnehmerinnen und Arbeitnehmer sowie der Einfluss sozioökonomischer Faktoren: Untersuchung im Auftrag der Europäischen Kommission Generaldirektion Bildung und Kultur.* Kerpen: WSF. http://ec.europa.eu/education/pdf/doc218_de.pdf (accessed March 3, 2010).

[37] Maiworm F., and U. Teichler. 2004. *Study Abroad and Early Career: Experiences of Former Erasmus Students.* Jessica Kingsley Publishers.

[38] ECORYS. 2008. *Final Evaluation of the Leonardo da Vinci II Programme: Final Report.* Rotterdam: ECORYS.

on over 8,000 questionnaires completed by former participants from all over the EU.[39]

The survey carried out in 2008 among coordinators and partners of Leonardo mobility projects indicated that 73% of 3,702 respondents thought their project had "improved the employability/adaptability of participants", with this rate decreasing to 39% in the case of participants facing disadvantages.[40] The study conducted by WSF[41] asked participants to compare their job situation before and after mobility. Among those who were unemployed before taking part to a mobility project, 58% were employed at the time the survey was conducted (approximately one year after their coming back). Some 60% of them said that the international experience had positively influenced their employability.[42] These results have been interpreted by the authors and cited by the Commission as an indicator for enhanced employability directly resulting from transnational mobility.[43]

A few other studies in the field of VET confirm these findings on the basis of similar research methods. The study conducted by Busse and Fahle on behalf of Cedefop in 1998 surveyed 403 German participants in European and bilateral mobility programmes. Seventy-five per cent of the respondents believed that mobility had a (very) positive influence on their prospects on the labour market, whereas only 9% fully disagreed with this

---

[39] WSF Wirtschafts- und Sozialforschung. 2007. *Analyse der Wirkungen von LEONARDO DA VINCI Mobilitätsmaßnahmen auf junge Auszubildende, Arbeitnehmerinnen und Arbeitnehmer sowie der Einfluss sozioökonomischer Faktoren: Untersuchung im Auftrag der Europäischen Kommission Generaldirektion Bildung und Kultur.* Kerpen: WSF.
http://ec.europa.eu/education/pdf/doc218_de.pdf (accessed March 3, 2010).
[40] ECORYS. 2008. *Final Evaluation of the Leonardo da Vinci II Programme: Final Report.* Rotterdam: ECORYS, 95.
[41] WSF Wirtschafts- und Sozialforschung. 2007. *Analyse der Wirkungen von LEONARDO DA VINCI Mobilitätsmaßnahmen auf junge Auszubildende, Arbeitnehmerinnen und Arbeitnehmer sowie der Einfluss sozioökonomischer Faktoren: Untersuchung im Auftrag der Europäischen Kommission Generaldirektion Bildung und Kultur.* Kerpen: WSF.
http://ec.europa.eu/education/pdf/doc218_de.pdf (accessed March 3, 2010).
[42] Ibid., 63.
[43] Ibid., 46. The exact quote: "*Hervorzuheben ist insbesondere der Beschäftigungseffekt bei den zuvor Arbeitslosen*" ("the employment effects are significant particularly for those who were previously unemployed")

statement.[44] Participants to bilateral exchange programmes in the study carried out by Neugebauer (2005) among 204 young Germans in the dual system expressed similar views: 59% of them think that their job perspectives were improved through mobility.[45] Trainers in companies involved in mobility are more cautious regarding the direct effects of mobility: only 33% of them think that it will improve the chances for young people to be employed in the company which trained them at the end of their training.[46]

Fig. 3-5. Participants' View on the Effects of Mobility on Employability

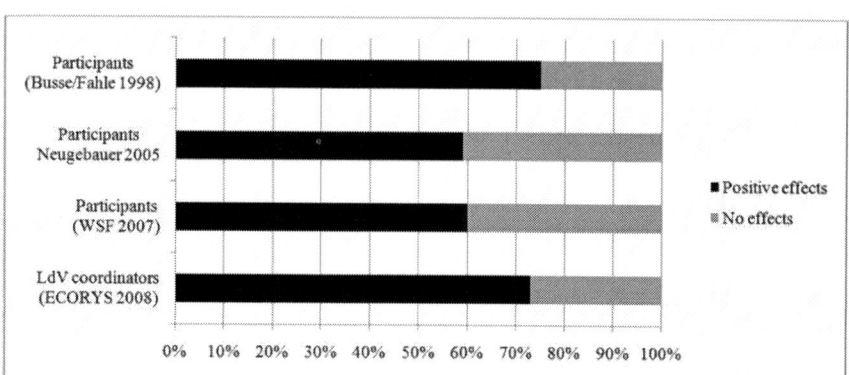

Summarising the findings in the field of VET, mobility seems to make a difference on the labour market, according to both participants and trainers. However, empirical evidence is weak with regard to methodology; some studies tried to compare the subjective perception of mobile learners with the perception of other actors, such as project coordinators or trainers and companies, but there is a lack of "objective" indicator-based research to examine the link between mobility and employability.

In the field of higher education, even the most cited study, which is based on the VALERA (VALue of ERAsmus mobility) survey from

---

[44] Busse, G., and K. Fahle. 1998. *Lernen durch Mobilität: Untersuchung zu längerfristigen Auslandsaufenthalten von Auszubildenden und jungen Berufstätigen im Auftrag des CEDEFOP.* Köln: Carl Duisberg Gesellschaft, 16.
[45] Ibid., 11.
[46] Ibid., 12.

2005[47] among mobile students, employers and higher education experts, is limited to subjective perceptions of employability.[48] "Hard facts" presented by this study concerning the transition from university to work, such as the duration of unemployment periods and the number of applications, cannot be adequately interpreted because of a lack of any comparable data for non-mobile students. A methodologically interesting study was conducted among students in the French region of Rhône-Alpes between 1998 and 2001.[49] The transition to the labour market of mobile students was compared to the transition of a non-mobile group of students displaying the same socio-economic characteristics and study profile identified earlier, as regarded as good predictors of employability. Differences between the two groups could therefore be attributed to a large extent to the mobility experience. The authors came to the conclusion that mobile students experience a slightly smoother transition to the labour market than non-mobile students. In terms of career prospects and job satisfaction, benefits are not significant or do not exist at all, except for young women, who rate their satisfaction and prospects a little better than average.

---

[47] Bundesministerium für Bildung und Forschung. 2009. *Der berufliche Ertrag der ERASMUS-Mobilität: Die Auswirkungen internationaler Erfahrung auf die Berufswege von ehemals mobilen Studierenden und Lehrenden.* Berlin: BMBF.

[48] According to the VALERA survey, there is a high degree of consensus among participants in the Erasmus programme, employers and experts (for instance teachers and heads of universities) concerning the positive impact of international mobility on employability. For instance, 53% of former Erasmus students think that international experience was decisive for their employer to hire them (BMBF 2009, p. 34).

[49] Di Vito, P., and L-A. Pichon. 2003. *Séjour d'études à l'étranger et Insertion professionnelle: Étude n° 2003-01.* Observatoire Universitaire Régional de l'Insertion Professionnelle (OURIP).

Fig. 3-6. Time Needed to Find First Job

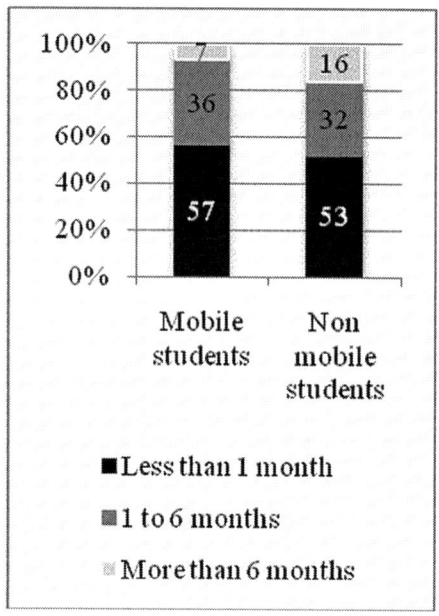

Fig. 3-7. Unemployment Rate after Graduation

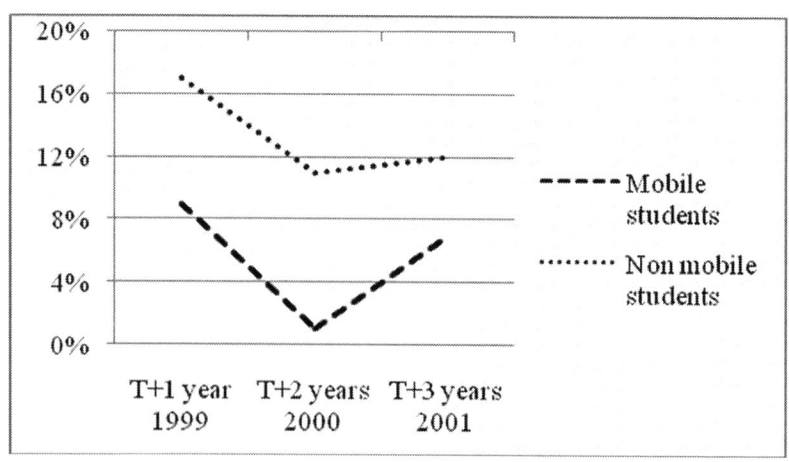

Taking a sceptical attitude towards the existing literature, as suggested by Ogawa and Malen,[50] it is striking how little evidence has been provided to assess the link between international mobility and employability in the field of VET. In higher education, empirical data collected are more significant, even though in a recent literature review Ahrens et al. pointed out that:

> When we look at the published literature on this topic, evidence on the true added value of a study experience abroad remains extremely scarce, to be replaced by generalised statements such as the following: "Study-abroad programmes enjoy prestige mainly because they enhance one's academic credentials, offer better-paid employment opportunities and provide entry to influential professional networks".[51]

The authors go on to imply that "Erasmus discourse" is over-enthusiastic and, at best, a self-fulfilling prophecy.

A second remark concerns the biases characterising many studies, because participants' background (e.g. qualification profile, socio-economic background) is not taken into account. Selection processes determine who will benefit from institutionalised mobility programmes, resulting in an under-representation of disadvantaged groups. This has already been pointed out by an investigation carried out within the Leonardo Da Vinci Programme on the socio-economic background of participants[52] and can be confirmed also by research dealing with higher education.[53]

---

[50] Ogawa, R. T., and B. Malen. 1991. "Towards Rigor in Reviews of Multivocal Literatures: Applying the Exploratory Case Study Method," *Review of Educational Research* 61, No. 3:265-286.

[51] Ahrens, J., A. Findlay, and R. King. 2010. *International Student Mobility Literature Review: Report to HEFCE, and co-funded by the British Council, UK National Agency for Erasmus*. HEFCE.
http://www.hefce.ac.uk/pubs/rdreports/2010/rd20_10/rd20_10.pdf
(accessed December 3, 2010), 34-35.

[52] WSF Wirtschafts- und Sozialforschung. 2007. *Analyse der Wirkungen von LEONARDO DA VINCI Mobilitätsmaßnahmen auf junge Auszubildende, Arbeitnehmerinnen und Arbeitnehmer sowie der Einfluss sozioökonomischer Faktoren: Untersuchung im Auftrag der Europäischen Kommission Generaldirektion Bildung und Kultur*. Kerpen: WSF.
http://ec.europa.eu/education/pdf/doc218_de.pdf (accessed March 3, 2010).

[53] Di Vito, P., and L-A. Pichon. 2003. *Séjour d'études à l'étranger et Insertion professionnelle: Étude n° 2003-01*. Observatoire Universitaire Régional de l'Insertion Professionnelle (OURIP).

6. Conclusion

With a view to sum up the results of this literature review, there seems to be a significant lack of independent high-quality empirical research on the benefits and impact of international mobility in VET. This might be partly explained by the difficulty to obtain reliable data, especially for cross-country comparisons, given the diversity of national VET systems in Europe. Large scale surveys and datasets as those available for higher education, like the datasets from Eurostat and OECD or the surveys VALERA and Careers after Higher Education European Research Study (CHEERS), do not yet exist in VET.

Equally important is the potential for more qualitative-oriented research. An aspect of employability which has not been further developed in this review pertains to the use of international experience in job-seeking strategies. Two studies were found which analysed for instance the mentioning of international experience on CVs (including online CVs in the social networking platforms Linked-In and Viadeo).[54]

Current research does not confirm the existence of a simple and direct relationship between international mobility and employability. On the contrary, the relationship could be more complex and paradoxical than it seems at first glance. This should not lead to denying international mobility any value and usefulness—as the positive view participants have of their experience abroad is a good argument in favour of expanding mobility programmes. However, this should invite us to further reflect on a number of questions and provide empirical evidence regarding the following issues:

-   Who takes part in mobility, and why? What kinds of selection processes take place especially in institutionalised mobility programmes?

Messer, D., and S. C. Wolter. 2007. "Are Student Exchange Programs worth it?" *Higher Education* 54, No. 5:647-63.

[54] Conseil régional de Franche-Comté et CEDRE. 2005. *Etude relative à l'évaluation de la mobilité internationale des étudiants, des jeunes diplômés et des jeunes demandeurs d'emploi aidés par la région Franche-Comté en 2001/2002.* AMNYOS. Escourrou, N. 2010. *Effets d'un programme double diplôme européen et des stages Léonardo: Enquête de trajectoires 7 à 10 ans après le diplôme: Colloque "L'européanisation et la professionnalisation de l'enseignement supérieur, quelles convergences?"* Paris : Médiatèque Université Paris Descartes. http://mediatheque.parisdescartes.fr/article.php3?id_article=4699 (accessed December 8, 2010).

- How do the forms and duration of mobility influence the benefits in terms of competences and satisfaction of participants? More specifically, this aspect raises the question about the quality of mobility projects and the way mobility is integrated into national curricula.
- How do employers react to the international experience of young people: How do they value the benefits of mobility? What are the determining factors enhancing or diminishing the value of mobility in the eyes of employers? What role does mobility play as a relevant factor in recruitment processes?

These questions need to be examined above all in relation to new developments concerning the recognition and certification of learning outcomes gained abroad (i.e. ECVET, EQF).

References

Ahrens, J., A. Findlay, and R. King. 2010. *International Student Mobility Literature Review: Report to HEFCE, and co-funded by the British Council, UK National Agency for Erasmus.* HEFCE. http://www.hefce.ac.uk/pubs/rdreports/2010/rd20_10/rd20_10.pdf (accessed December 3, 2010).
Barthold, B. 2010. "Betriebliche Mobilitätsmaßnahmen—Nutzen und inhaltliche Ausgestaltung," in *Internationale Kompetenzen in der Berufsbildung: Stand der Wissenschaft und praktische Anforderungen*, ed. Wordelmann, P., (Bielefeld: Bertelsmann), 123-361.
Berner, K. 2004. *Qualifizierung durch Auslandspraktika: Eine Studie des Forschungsinstituts für Berufsbildung im Handwerk an der Universität zu Köln in Kooperation mit dem Niedersächsischen Kultusministerium.* Köln: FBH.
—. 2005. *Fremdsprachen im Handwerk: Eine Konzeption des Forschungsinstituts für Berufsbildung im Handwerk an der Universität zu Köln.* Köln: FBH.
BIBB. 2002. "Grenzüberschreitender Austausch von Auszubildenden und jungen Fachkräften," *RBS-Information*, No. 21.
Borch, H., A. Diettrich, D. Frommberger, H. Reinisch, and P. Wordelmann. 2003. *Internationalisierung der Berufsbildung.* Bielefeld: Bertelsmann.
Bundesministerium für Bildung und Forschung. 2009. *Der berufliche Ertrag der ERASMUS-Mobilität: Die Auswirkungen internationaler*

Erfahrung auf die Berufswege von ehemals mobilen Studierenden und Lehrenden. Berlin: BMBF.

Busse, G., and K. Fahle. 1998. *Lernen durch Mobilität: Untersuchung zu längerfristigen Auslandsaufenthalten von Auszubildenden und jungen Berufstätigen im Auftrag des CEDEFOP.* Köln: Carl Duisberg Gesellschaft.

Cedefop. 2008. *Terminology of European Education and Training Policy: A Selection of 100 Key Terms.* Luxembourg: Office for Official Publications of the European Communities.

Conseil régional de Franche-Comté et CEDRE. 2005. *Etude relative à l'évaluation de la mobilité internationale des étudiants, des jeunes diplômés et des jeunes demandeurs d'emploi aidés par la région Franche-Comté en 2001/2002.* AMNYOS. http://www.efigip.org/index.php?action=ListPublication&idp=133&op=theme&publ_page=3&ido=155 (accessed December 3, 2010).

Delamare-Le Deist, F., and J. Winterton. 2005. "What Is Competence?" *Human Resource Development International* 8, No. 1:27-46.

Di Vito, P., and L-A. Pichon. 2003. *Séjour d'études à l'étranger et Insertion professionnelle: Étude n° 2003-01.* Observatoire Universitaire Régional de l'Insertion Professionnelle (OURIP).

Diettrich, A., and H. Reinisch. 2010. "Internationale und interkulturelle berufliche Handlungskompetenz als Zielkomponent beruflicher Bildung," in *Internationale Kompetenzen in der Berufsbildung: Stand der Wissenschaft und praktische Anforderungen*, ed. Wordelmann, P., (Bielefeld: Bertelsmann), 33-43.

Dybowski, G., and U. Wiegand. 2001. "Qualifizieren für den Globalisierungsprozess. Das Beispiel der Deutschen Bahn AG," *BWP*, No. 4:11-16.

ECORYS. 2008. *Final Evaluation of the Leonardo da Vinci II Programme: Final Report.* Rotterdam: ECORYS.

Escourrou, N. 2010. *Effets d'un programme double diplôme européen et des stages Léonardo: Enquête de trajectoires 7 à 10 ans après le diplôme: Colloque "L'européanisation et la professionnalisation de l'enseignement supérieur, quelles convergences?"* Paris: Médiatèque Université Paris Descartes. http://mediatheque.parisdescartes.fr/article.php3?id_article=4699 (accessed December 8, 2010).

European Commission. 2009. *Grünbuch: Die Mobilität junger Menschen zu Lernzwecken fördern* KOM(2009) 329. http://ec.europa.eu/education/lifelong-learning-policy/doc/mobility/com329_de.pdf (accessed November 12, 2010).

Forrier, A., and L. Sels. 2003. "The Concept of Employability: A Complex Mosaic," *International Journal of Human Resources Development and Management* 3, No. 2:102-24.

Görgmaier, D., ed. 2003. *Lernort Europa im Zeichen der EU-Erweiterung: Durch Auslandsorientierung der Ausbildung - Aufbau einer europäischen Unternehmenskultur.* Reihe Tagungsberichte / Europäisches Informations-Zentrum Thüringen 49. Erfurt: Thüringer Staatskanzlei.

Hall, A. 2008. "Fremdsprachen im Beruf—Wer benötigt Fremdsprachenkenntnisse und auf welchem Niveau?" in *Fremdsprachen für die Wirtschaft: Analysen, Zahlen, Fakten*, ed. Tritscher-Archan, S., IBW-Forschungsbericht 143 (Wien: Inst. für Bildungsforschung der Wirtschaft), 217-34.

Hering, E., W. A. Pförtsch, and P. Wordelmann, eds. 2001. *Internationalisierung des Mittelstandes: Strategien zur internationalen Qualifizierung in kleinen und mittleren Unternehmen; mit Checkliste zu Qualifikationen für die Internationalisierung.* Bielefeld: Bertelsmann.

Hillage, J. 1998. *Employability: Developing a Framework for Policy Analysis.* Department for Education and Employment research report, No. 85. London: Department for Education and Employment (DfEE).

Klimmer, S. 2010. "Was bringen Auslandspraktika von Lehrlingen den Unternehmen? Ergebnisse einer Befragung von österreichischen Unternehmen," in *Internationale Kompetenzen in der Berufsbildung: Stand der Wissenschaft und praktische Anforderungen*, ed. Wordelmann, P., (Bielefeld: Bertelsmann), 217-25.

Kristensen, S. 2001. "Learning by Leaving—Towards a Pedagogy for Transnational Mobility in the Context of Vocational Education and Training (VET)," *European Journal of Education* 36, No. 4:42-30.

Kristensen, S., and P. Wordelmann. 2010. "Transnationale Mobilität in kleinen und mittleren Unternehmen," in *Internationale Kompetenzen in der Berufsbildung: Stand der Wissenschaft und praktische Anforderungen*, ed. Wordelmann, P., (Bielefeld: Bertelsmann), 177-89.

Lindberg, M. E. 2007. "At the Frontier of Graduate Surveys. Assessing Participation and Employability of Graduates with Master's Degree in nine European Countries," *Higher Education* 53, No. 5:623-44.

Maiworm F., and U. Teichler. 2004. Study Abroad and Early Career: Experiences of Former Erasmus Students. Jessica Kingsley Publishers.

Messer, D., and S. C. Wolter. 2007. "Are Student Exchange Programs worth it?" *Higher Education* 54, No. 5:647-63.

MKW Wirtschaftsforschung GmbH and Empirica. 2009. *Scientific Report on the Mobility of Cross-Border Workers within the EU-27/EEA/EFTA Countries: Final report, commissioned by European Commission DG Employment and Social Affairs.* Munich: MKW GmbH.

Neugebauer, U. 2005. *Evaluation der bilateralen Austauschprogramme in der beruflichen Bildung zwischen Deutschland und Frankreich, den Niederlanden und Großbritannien: Kurzfassung der Studie im Auftrag des Bundesministeriums für Bildung und Forschung.* Köln: Univation.

Ogawa, R. T. and B. Malen. 1991. "Towards Rigor in Reviews of Multivocal Literatures: Applying the Exploratory Case Study Method," *Review of Educational Research* 61, No. 3:265-286.

Paul, K. D., and P. Wordelmann. 2010. *Ermittlung transnationaler Qualifizierungsbedarfe in der Region Berlin: Studie im Auftrag der Senatsverwaltung für Wirtschaft, Technologie und Frauen Berlin.* Berlin: u.bus GmbH. http://www.berlin.de/imperia/md/content/sen-strukturfonds/esf/studieesfinternational30032010final.pdf?start&ts=12 77127706&file=studieesfinternational30032010final.pdf   (accessed December 5, 2010).

Storz, P., and W. Hübel, eds. 2010. *Berufsbildung im europäischen Verbund: Erfahrungen aus der Chemiebranche.* Bielefeld: Bertelsmann.

Stronkhorst, R. 2005. "Learning Outcomes of International Mobility at Two Dutch Institutions of Higher Education," *Journal of Studies in International Education* 9, No. 4:292-315.

Tritscher-Archan, S. 2008. "Fremdsprachenbedarf und -kompetenzen in Österreichs Unternehmen," in *Fremdsprachen für die Wirtschaft: Analysen, Zahlen, Fakten,* ed. Tritscher-Archan, S., IBW-Forschungsbericht 143 (Wien: Inst. für Bildungsforschung der Wirtschaft), 171-90.

Wordelmann, P. 1995. *Internationale Qualifikationen: Inhalte, Bedarf und Vermittlung.* Bielefeld: Bertelsmann. http://www.gbv.de/dms/hbz/toc/ht006693817.PDF.

—. 2010. "Internationale Kompetenzen in der Berufsbildung - Stand der Wissenschaft und praktische Anforderungen: Einleitung," in *Internationale Kompetenzen in der Berufsbildung: Stand der Wissenschaft und praktische Anforderungen,* ed. Wordelmann, P., (Bielefeld: Bertelsmann), 7-31.

WSF Wirtschafts- und Sozialforschung. 2007. *Analyse der Wirkungen von LEONARDO DA VINCI Mobilitätsmaßnahmen auf junge Auszubildende, Arbeitnehmerinnen und Arbeitnehmer sowie der Einfluss sozioökonomischer Faktoren: Untersuchung im Auftrag der*

Europäischen Kommission Generaldirektion Bildung und Kultur. Kerpen: WSF. http://ec.europa.eu/education/pdf/doc218_de.pdf (accessed March 3, 2010).

Zedler, R. 2006. "Förderung von Mobilität und Freizügigkeit in der Europäischen Union," *Wirtschaft und Berufserziehung* 58, No. 7:16-2.

Youth Employment and Relevant Labour Market Programmes in Hungary

Attila Kun and Balázs Rossu

1. Introduction

The aim of this paper is to provide an overview of the current state of unemployment with particular consideration of youth unemployment in Hungary. The labour market system here is rather complex, and may be considered difficult to understand. Certain features of the labour market function well and should be maintained, while others should be improved and customised to suit the needs of the future. Possibly, the most significant problem is the lack of information about labour market opportunities, or rather employers' unwillingness to provide, and the inability of future employees to acquire labour market information. With the use of numeric data describing the labour market, and by examining laws and legislation pertinent to unemployment, our goal is to highlight areas in the labour market system that are unsuitable for fulfilling the roles they were once assigned. In order to achieve this, a number of seemingly unrelated regulations and data were reviewed and compared, including demographic structures, economic and social effects of the current global crisis, and a wide variety of initiatives to reduce unemployment amongst graduates entering the labour market.

In Hungary, and similarly to the majority of Central and Eastern European (CEE) post-socialist countries, the economic transition period of the early 1990s brought about a serious worsening of the labour market position of young people. Although the labour market situation of young people in Hungary improved to some extent after the second half of the 1990s, their unemployment rate is still relatively high and the overall issue of youth employment/unemployment is still crucial.[1]

---

[1] The situation of young people in the labour market was especially precarious during the transition period. Youth unemployment exploded at the beginning of the transition and grew far beyond standard unemployment. During the transition, the

It is evident that young people experience special difficulties in finding a stable position in the labour market. Among the numerous factors hindering the employment of the youth, perhaps one of the most significant is that employers have no incentive to hire school leavers. Young people lack work experience, and there is often a disparity between their knowledge and the skills required in the labour market. Furthermore, common charges (taxes and contributions) are considerably high in Hungary. For these reasons, and in order to improve the labour market situation of young people, there is a need for targeted support, that may create incentives for employers to hire school leavers. Due to the complexity of the situation, this paper will provide an understanding of the avenues available via various structures to support the transition of young people from education to work. It will also highlight the flaws within the system, and recommend a multidisciplinary approach towards solutions.

2. Young People and the Labour Market in Hungary

The most important characteristic of the Hungarian labour market is its low labour force participation rate, coupled with relatively low unemployment and high inactivity. This is especially the case amongst the youth. Until now, the labour market situation of the 15-24 years age group is marked by the tendency of decreasing employment and increasing unemployment.

Almost 80% of those aged between 15-24 years are inactive, this is in part a consequence of increasing enrolment rates in higher education.[2] High inactivity rates amongst young women can also be explained partly by the extensive Hungarian parental leave / family benefit schemes.

Hungary experienced a sharp rise in the youth unemployment rate during the period between 2000 and 2006, however, this is still not considerably far from the EU average (in 2007, it was slightly decreasing,

---

strong decline in employment made entering the very tight labour market extremely difficult for young people, worsening their situation in comparison with the rest of the labour force. Demographic developments have further aggravated this situation as the number of young entrants in the labour market increased in the first half of the 1990s, due to the post-war baby-boom. The number of entrants declined in the second half of the 90s. Keune, M. 1995. *Youth Unemployment in Hungary and Poland, ILO, Action Programme on Youth Unemployment.* http://www.ilo.org/public/english/employment/strat/publ/etp20.htm   (accessed February 21, 2009).

[2] Gerzsényi, Á., and L. Neumann. 2007. *Contribution to EIRO Thematic Feature on Youth and Work—Case of Hungary.* EIROnline.

but in 2008, it was quite high again at 19.9%). On the other hand, the situation is more problematic if we consider youth employment rates. Compared to the year 2000, employment rates among youth (15-24) decreased in most EU Member States. Amongst the EU27, the most significant decrease was reported in Hungary, where the overall youth employment rate dropped by almost 12 percentage points from 33.5% to 21.7% between 2000 and 2006 (2008: 20%). As for those Not in Education, Employment or Training (NEET), amongst the EU27 only a few (6) countries (France, Italy, Poland, Romania, Slovakia and Bulgaria) have NEET rates amongst 20-24 years olds' in excess of 20%. Hungary is the seventh underperforming country in this regard with a NEET rate of only slightly below 20%.[3]

Unemployed new entrants to the labour market can be classified by educational level. In 2007, 40% of unemployed new entrants were low-educated (primary school or less), 18% had vocational education, one-third had secondary school certificate and 8.3% had a university diploma. It follows that the general assumption that young university graduates face a lower risk of being jobless is still valid. In other words, young people with lower education are more affected by unemployment than those with higher education. However, the share of jobseekers with a university diploma is considerably higher amongst unemployed young people (8.3%) than among all the unemployed (4.6%). On the other hand, the share of people with vocational education is considerably lower among unemployed young people (18%) than among all unemployed people (31.5%). These facts reveal the changing needs of the Hungarian labour market: there is a growing need for well-trained skilled "blue-collar" labourers, but the labour market is less and less able to absorb the growing number of young people with a university diploma. Although the proportion of graduated unemployed young people among all young unemployed has been shrinking in the last couple of years (2005: 11.2%, 2006:10%, 2007: 8.3%), according to many experts this may easily change in the years to come.[4]

As the above mentioned data show, the youth unemployment problem is not a new phenomenon. Unemployment has been a serious issue in Hungary for more than two decades now. The number of people registered as unemployed was 509,907 in January 2009 and, it increased to 546,094

---

[3] European Commission. 2007b. *Employment in Europe 2007*. Brussels: European Commission. See also European Commission. 2009. *Employment in Europe 2009*. Brussels: European Commission.
[4] ÁFSZ. 2008. *MUNKAERŐPIACI HELYZETKÉP, 2007. évi összefoglaló,* Budapest: ÁFSZ.

by August 2010, although it was not a continuous increase, as the number reached and even exceeded 650,000 in January 2010. This means that the unemployment rate underwent a steady decrease, however, the problem should not be ignored, but rather the necessary steps to reduce it must be taken.[5]

The fact that during the past 20 years (after the regime was overthrown) some major economic changes have occurred makes the situation even harder to handle, since there is no solid background model to go back to and "start from scratch" from. Along with changes in the structure of the economy, changes in patterns of learning and work have occurred as well. In 1989, 5.2015 million people were employed in Hungary, this decreased to 3.9916 million by 2004. At the same time, during the academic year of 1989-90, there were altogether 100,868 students engaged in higher education. By the 2004-2005 academic year this number increased to 378,466 students. That is, while the number of employed people had decreased by almost three quarters, the number of students engaged in higher education multiplied by more than 3.75 times. The graph below (Fig. 3-8) shows the trend during 1990 and 2004 with regards to graduates registered as unemployed. The graph shows young, graduate jobseekers who would like to enter the labour market for the first time, and graduates who have been in the labour market for some time.[6]

Despite differences in the last five years, the trend has undergone slight changes. The reasons for this are many. This paper deals with the period above (1991-2004) in order to show that the unemployment problem is not a new one. In fact, it may be the result of a failure to recognise the problem and act accordingly to improve the situation.

---

[5] Data provided by the Szeged Branch Office and Service Centre of the Southern Great Plain Regional Employment Centre.

[6] Berde, É. 2005. *Work Conceptions of Young People Before Graduation and Labour Statistics Based on the Facts of the Expected Short-Term Trends* [in Hungarian]. Budapest: OFA.
http://www.google.hu/url?sa=t&source=web&cd=1&ved=0CBcQFjAA&url=http%3A%2F%2Fwww.ofa.hu%2Findex.php%3FWG_NODE%3DWebIntRedirect%26WG_OID%3DDSDf66b686134d06d53e&ei=J2FlTevpDo_pOdT2jJcE&usg=AFQjCNHpIZgd8I4L6CkKFxCWxPoSuFZnrw pg 1-14 (accessed October 28, 2010).

Fig. 3-8

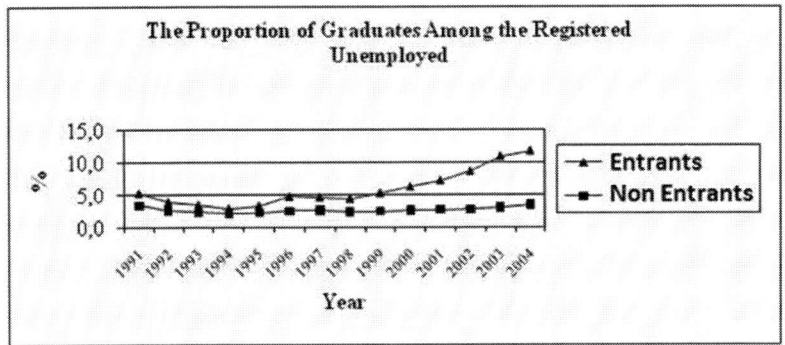

Data and graph elaborated by Éva Berde, for OFA Budapest, October 2005.

As mentioned above, the situation regarding youth employment is an issue of concern, particularly because data point to the propensity for recent graduates and other youth leaving education and training towards unemployment. In January 2009, the number of unemployed entrants was 41,659 and it increased to 56,289 by August 2010, which accounted for 10.3% of the total registered unemployed. Just as unemployment as a whole had an outstanding peak, the number of unemployed entrants was exceptionally high, but in this case it was around September 2009, when it went above 58,000 (for exact data about the Southern Great Plain Region of Hungary, please see Fig. 3-9 and for more details, please see Fig. 3-10 below).

Fig. 3-9

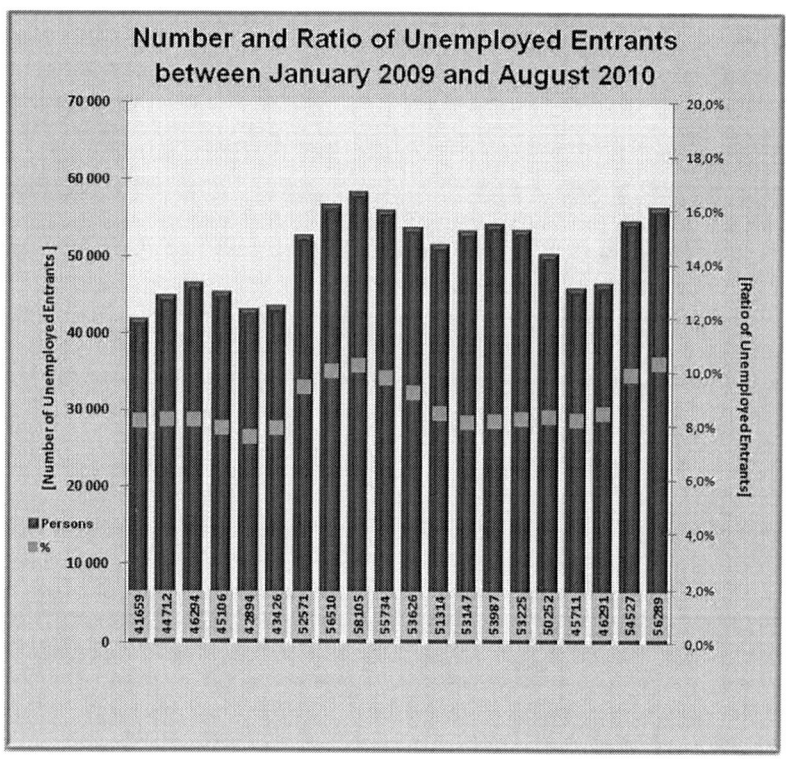

Data provided by the Szeged Branch Office and Service Centre of the Southern Great Plain Regional Employment Centre.

Fig. 3-10

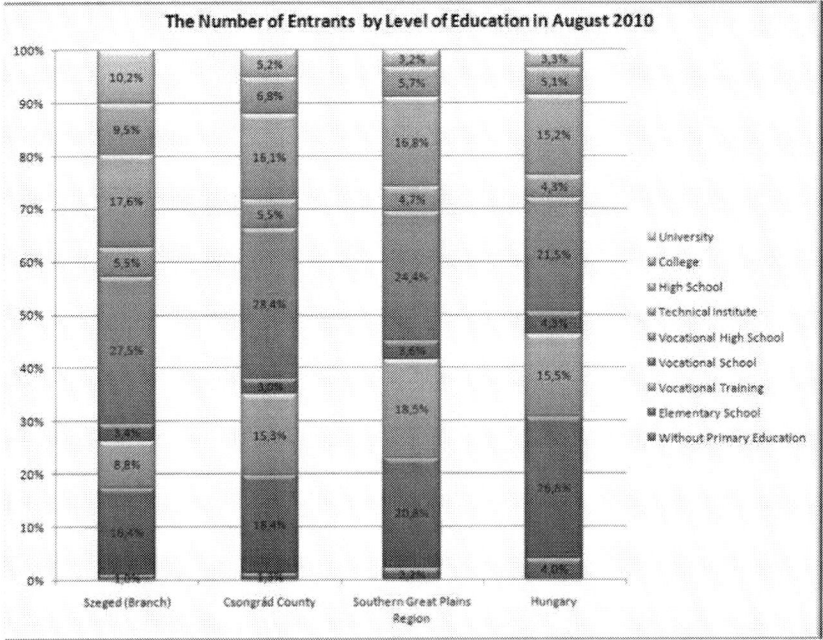

3. Threats Posed by Youth Unemployment

3.1. Philosophical Background

Youth unemployment in particular poses perhaps the most serious threat compared to unemployment in other age groups. Unlike the second most precarious sector, the unemployment of the elderly, in instances where the elderly are pushed out of the labour market at a certain age, never entering the labour market has more serious consequences at a national level. For an individual who has never worked before, it is extremely difficult to enter the labour market the longer he/she remains unemployed. In addition to this, in a family where parents experience a long period of unemployment, or worse yet, have never been employed, their children are more likely to have no incentives to pursue employment. A closer analysis of youth unemployment will reveal that differences occur amongst unemployed youth based on their education level. In general, society's response to unskilled or semi-skilled unemployed people is that their unemployment status is their own fault, and that they cannot enter the labour market without the completion of a university degree. As inaccurate as this is, in certain cases this is enough to turn some people towards furthering their education. The real problem occurs when recent graduates are unable to find work. This in itself may lead to the false assumption that it is pointless to pursue education, as even with a degree it is almost impossible to enter the labour market. A review of academic literature reveals that graduate unemployment is a complex problem, with its origin challenging to locate. Furthermore, solutions to this problem are difficult to come up with. Experts tend to be divided into two streams. The first group takes a more positive stance seeing the growth in the number of students in higher education as clearly useful for the individual and society at large, and as such we should not be concerned about the possible "over qualification" of youth. The second group seems to acknowledge that participation in higher education, regardless of the field of study, would contribute largely to the improvement of the relative positions of the individual and to society as a whole, but that "over-qualification" is a serious risk, or threat.[7]

An interesting find shows that the higher the number of students (engaged in higher education) per capita in a country, the greater the proportion of unemployed graduates and labour market entrants. In other words, the situation of young graduates becomes relatively worse with the increase in their numbers. Another interesting fact about this data is that due to a fascinating characteristic, this "phenomenon" cannot be detected immediately, but only after a three-year delay. According to calculations by experts, if the number of university (or college) students increases by a 0.1 percentage points compared to the total population of a country, in three years time, the proportion of graduates among the registered unemployed entrants will increase by 0.7 percentage points.[8]

3.2. Demand, Supply and Oversupply

The basis of the problem seems to be a kind of saturation in the graduate workforce, although a similar statement regarding the Hungarian labour market as a whole would be out of proportion, whereas in some fields of work this may very likely seem to be the case. The increased amount of working capital implies that a higher level of development has

---

[7] Ibid.
[8] Ibid., 4.

been achieved, and as such, there seems to be an increasing need for lower-skilled workers.

The complexity of the problem can be found in the difference in supply and demand. For example, some popular sectors are extremely over supplied, whereas other sectors are almost completely abandoned. Further complicating this problem is the time (approximately three to five years depending on the nature of the qualification) that it takes to become highly-skilled. As time passes, due to constant change, the needs and demands of the labour market may not be the same. An efficient method of synchronising the needs of the labour market and the number of appropriately qualified people is yet to be found. Until then, our attention should be focused on providing work for qualified entrants currently unemployed.

We can expect that in the coming years, during the process of an economic "recovery", marked by GDP growth, the needs of the labour market will be for less qualified workers, making the situation worse for graduate entrants.

The following section will concentrate on the examination of the occupational structure of the unemployed graduate entrants from an alternative viewpoint, aiming to uncover yet another flaw of the current system that greatly hinders youth trying to enter the labour market. In order to do so and uncover professions and fields of work where there seems to be an oversupply of (actual and potential) employees, two data sets are compared. These two sets are the career distribution of registered unemployed entrants and the graduate occupational distribution of professional staff. In other words, we compare the fields where youth aim to be employed once they enter the labour market and the numbers of youth already employed in those fields. Unfortunately, there is no guarantee that the numbers used here represent reality, as the willingness to register may vary (thus making a perfect calculation impossible). We may assume though, that youth intending to be employed in the public sector would most likely register, unlike the ones in the private sector. Even though these are only assumptions, the following five findings, without a doubt, will be instructive:[9]

-   The number of young, registered and unemployed entrants hoping to become teachers or tutors who have obtained the appropriate degrees in 2004 was the same as the number of educators employed at that time. It may seem that in 2004, the

---

[9] Ibid., 5-9.

sector of the labour market in question was not exposed to a level of oversupply that exceeded the average. Since then, the situation has slightly changed. Mostly because a significant number of schools were closed or merged with other schools in the past few years, and although the changes in numbers are not vast, the lack of opportunities for educators appears in some cities or towns. Since the willingness for mobility is almost extremely low in Hungary, the problem is yet to be solved.

- When it comes to comparing statistical data, the situation seems to be similar for those engaged in computer studies, however there is one major difference. Due to the legal system in Hungary, most educators will most likely seek occupation in the public sector, even though this is not the case for computer experts. They tend to enter the private sector where competition for work is greater, and where available data are not as accurate.

- There are hardly any entrants registered in the field of health occupations. Even though it is most unlikely to be true that there are no unemployed entrants aiming to work in the field of health care, according to the numbers we cannot say if there is an oversupply of workers in this sector.

- Considering the engineering professions, there were 2.5 times more registered entrants aiming to work in this field than the ones in the field at that time. Although there is no data on the specific separate disciplines of engineering.

- In most cases, the levels of graduates already employed and those hoping to enter the labour market differ significantly, meaning that the labour market seems to be experiencing a situation of unbalance.

3.3 "First Person View"—Statistics from the Entrants' Perspective[10]

After having identified the basic flaws and problems and taken a glimpse at some statistical data to confirm the situation, another perspective should be taken into account, with reference to how young people themselves see their own situation and possibilities in their final year of tertiary education, right before acquiring their university or college degrees. This section concentrates on revealing the complexity of this issue, focusing on two key factors respectively, income expectations and the amount of time passed before recruitment. Since asserting oneself in the labour market is more difficult than obtaining the necessary education, other factors must be considered even if the connection is not obvious at first sight.

Some responses lead to the expected conclusions, but others revealed a few intriguing finds:

-   On average, the better the results of the student, the lower the net income they expect and accept for work. Of course, the answers to such questions may be expressively influenced by psychological factors, but the majority of the students are able to see what their exact possibilities are (or will be) in the labour market, especially if they have already tried to find a job.
-   The results of female students' expectations are significantly higher on average than those of male students. In addition, even though the students paying tuition fees performed weaker, their income expectations have still exceeded those of the ones participating in publicly funded training programmes. It appears that there is no connection between payment expectations and study results, as data did not show any examples of positive

---

[10] Based on a research conducted by Hungarian National Employment Foundation (OFA), analysing some 1,500 questionnaires filled out by university and college students from various regions of Hungary. Berde, É. 2005. *Work Conceptions of Young People Before Graduation and Labour Statistics Based on the Facts of the Expected Short-Term Trends* [in Hungarian.] Budapest: OFA.
http://www.google.hu/url?sa=t&source=web&cd=1&ved=0CBcQFjAA&url=http%3A%2F%2Fwww.ofa.hu%2Findex.php%3FWG_NODE%3DWebIntRedirect%26WG_OID%3DDDSDf66b686134d06d53e&ei=J2FITevpDo_pOdT2jJcE&usg=AFQjCNHpIZgd8I4L6CkKFxCWxPoSuFZnrw, 1-14 (accessed October 28, 2010).

connections that would prove that stronger performance would result in higher expectations of financial remuneration.

- Although the result of studies seems not to have an influence on income expectancies, language skills do. Good knowledge of a certain language clearly coupled with the associated expectations of a higher income. The English language appears to be prestigious among all languages, as results show that speaking English on a high level would be enough to boost the expected payment.

- The widespread opinion is that acquiring work experience substantially improves one's income opportunities. However, according to data this was also proven wrong, or at least it has not been strengthened.

- The institution (or faculty), on the other hand as well as the profession itself seems to have an influence on the amount of income expected.

  o The future representatives of the following professions expect a higher initial income (in descending order): computer engineers, bio-engineers, mechanical engineers, economists, employees of internal affairs, dental practitioners, artists, programmers, and lawyers in Budapest.

  o The following declared claim for a payment lower than average (in descending order of the absolute value of the difference in expected payment): pastors, musicians, elementary school teachers, health school attendants, psychologists, linguists, gardeners, doctors and lawyers (aiming to work outside of Budapest).

In general, students of the same profession had a higher demand for income if they were from Budapest.

- The expected income is also influenced by the level of education of the parents. The children of mothers and fathers with lower education are more willing to accept less than the daughters and sons of higher educated parents.

- Curiously it seems that youth coming from families where the parental house had internet connection and so could access the World Wide Web, picture higher income rates for themselves.

- Students who are interested in working abroad immediately after receiving their degrees (CA. 8%), understandably expect significantly higher income than the individuals left at home. It was found that in almost every institution there were one or two students who pictured their first workplace abroad. The following professions are those where the number of students eager to leave their home country for better working standards was significantly high: art (music and art) apprentices, tourism, trade and catering, and physiotherapy.

The other important element (mentioned above) is the period that recent graduates expect to wait before being granted the opportunity to work in their favoured sector (or to work at all for that matter).

- Similar to the case of payment expectations, there does not seem to be any connection between study results and the waiting period before employment. Men might be a bit more confident about this than women are. There seems to be slightly more men who expect to be able to get a job instantly. Data show that the connection between payment expectations and the desired speed of being employed is directly proportional, meaning someone with higher payment expectancy than average also trusts that he/she will be employed (slightly) faster than the others.
- Regarding the expected duration of the time before being employed, gaining experience during the school years of higher education does mean (at least some) advantage.
- The chosen institution (or faculty) also has a hastening effect on the time it takes to be employed.
- The factor of the education of parents' appears to have a reversed effect compared to the one it has on the level of expected income. Employment right after completion of tertiary education is envisioned marginally more common by children of lower educated parents.
- A similar trend might be discovered in respect of languages. Speakers of foreign languages anticipate that waiting for a longer period of time will be essential before they will be able to find a job.

An interesting fact after taking the trends in young entrants opinions of their own possibilities into account is that an increasing group of young people consider staying away from the labour market for the time being (or in some cases even permanently) to be the solution. This of course leads to an array of problems, starting with financial difficulties (for the parents supporting them or for the students themselves being self-supporting) for staying in education, going all the way to future demographic problems by further delaying the time of having children.

A decisive majority of the youth entrants (who are willing to enter the labour market) plan to find a job at the lower end of the business hierarchy and most women do not even aim to get much higher any time soon (if ever). Although the phenomenon known as "glass ceiling" is present in many sectors of Hungarian labour market, the situation is far from being this serious.

3.4 Conclusions—"Making Ends Meet"

Upon a review of the situation of young people entering the labour market (those in their last year in tertiary education), it would seem that the decision to continue education for an undetermined amount of time (saving themselves from possible rejection) is rarely made. According to available data,[11] the intention to keep on learning, (with the exception of languages) is relatively low. Comparing this find with the above mentioned phenomenon of using further training as a "safeguard option" or "plan B" we seem to have come across a contradiction. The truth is that most of the time youngsters leaving school after finishing education try to find a job, but due to their lack of knowledge in the practical field of how to "sell yourself" they get rejected and discouraged after a few attempts. The employment situation has not been too bright in the last two decades in Hungary, which means one has to give more to be chosen. Possessing the required education alone is hardly ever satisfactory, and after a series of job rejections young entrants tend to head back to school. Their primary goal is to obtain more knowledge in the hopes of being able to meet the constantly changing needs of the technical-economic environment, but in a considerable number of cases a kind of "defence mechanism" activates, and this keeps the student in school driving them further, and deeper into different training courses (most likely achieving "over-qualification") and having them drift further and further away from the labour market. Psychologically, this is a normal reaction, but in the long run it has serious consequences in many areas of life, economy itself is an example. It is easy to misunderstand the situation discussed above and overlook the difference between Lifelong Learning, and constantly updating our knowledge (which is a necessity) and piling up different diplomas and qualifications we may never need in our life.

---

[11] Ibid., 84.

4. Possible Solutions—Effective Support Programmes and State Initiatives

4.1 Legal Background

In order to solve this issue and assist in the employment of young people, there is a variety of support programmes and allowances granted to employers who would hire recent graduates. These are meant to somewhat compensate employers for the lack of direct work experience of recently employed graduates.

It must be emphasised though, that currently there are no specifically targeted passive (financial) benefit entitlements for young unemployed people in Hungary.[12] At the moment, if young school leavers register as unemployed (jobseekers), first, they receive guided job search (without any passive benefits) assistance. Secondly, they are typically placed on training courses where they receive an allowance. If they complete the course but remain unemployed they can be eligible for general jobseekers' benefits. It should be mentioned that the original version of the Employment Act (1991) still established a special "passive" unemployment benefit for young people/school-leavers.[13] However, in 1996 the school-leavers unemployment benefit was abolished completely, partly due to financial motives and partly to put more emphasis on active measures. Indeed, the youth need labour market activating services (active measures) rather than welfare provisions.[14] Thus, we shall concentrate on related active labour market programmes (ALMPs).

---

[12] Similarly, there are no individual social security benefit entitlements for young (unemployed) persons (apart from general family benefits).

[13] It applied initially to graduates from day-time secondary school or higher education graduates having finished school within the last two years, and included a waiting period of three months. The benefit had a duration of 6 months and amounted to 75% of the minimum wage. The criteria for disqualifying for the benefit were the same as those for general unemployment benefits: starting a job, entering training, non-co-operation with the labour offices or refusing a suitable job or training. In 1992 some minor changes were made in the eligibility criteria for school-leavers' benefits and in the disqualification criteria, see Keune, M. 1995. *Youth Unemployment in Hungary and Poland. ILO, Action Programme on Youth   Unemployment* http://www.ilo.org/public/english/employment/strat/publ/etp20.htm   (accessed February 21, 2009).

[14] Ministry of Employment and Labour of Hungary. 2005. *Youth on the Labour Market.* Budapest: Ministry of Employment and Labour of Hungary, 1.

Due to the complexity of the Hungarian system, before going into details about the possible programmes and initiatives, there is firstly a need to explain the definition of unemployed entrants, so that the criteria used to have access to particular benefits and support options are clarified. One of the most important acts in this respect is Act IV of 1991 on Job Assistance and Unemployment Benefits, which contains the following:

> An entrant aiming to be employed should: be no more than 25 years of age, —30 for graduate persons—, possess conditions required for employment, and be registered at the Public Employment Service, provided that he/she is not entitled to unemployment allowances upon completion of his/her studies.

This seems to be a clear set of conditions, but due to the aforementioned complexity of Hungarian legislation, among the other important Acts regarding youth employment, a similar but yet alternate definition should be reviewed. Act CXXIII of 2004 on Job Assistance Provided to Unemployed Entrants to the Labour Market, Unemployed Workers Over Fifty, and to Persons Seeking Employment After Caring for a Child or Nursing a Family Member, and on Employment Under Scholarship Agreement provides the following definition:

> A person should be considered a young entrant, if he/she is no more than 25 years of age—30 for graduate persons— and possesses conditions required for employment and also a valid START-card.

The START-card is probably the most efficient and broadly used option among the available active measures aiming to help entrants to be employed. Its popularity lies in the allowances it provides, as an employer hiring an entrant with a START-card will have to pay less contributions for them for a given period of time (for further details regarding the START-card, please see section 4.3 The Start Programme and its "Achievements").

4.2 Labour Market Policies for Young People – the Past and the Present

Until 1993, there were hardly any active labour market measures exclusively designed for young people. Nevertheless, young people participated in general labour market programmes, as they were considered a priority target group at the time. Particularly in labour market training, the share of young people has constantly been high in the period between 1992 and 1995 (around 30%). However, training policies were mainly for persons with secondary or higher education or with a vocational certificate, while those with the most disadvantaged positions in the labour market and most in need of training, typically the unskilled or semi-skilled, made only quite a small share of trainees. Labour market training for young people served as a substitute for insufficient quality or quantity of education, underlining the emerging need for educational reforms. Many young persons benefited from the various types of wage subsidies (around 6,600 in 1994 and 1995) and from participation in public works (close to 4,000 in 1994 and close to 3,000 in 1995). Naturally, employers preferred to hire skilled and/or higher educated people (in the case of wage subsidies) and the programmes often demanded the General Certificate of Secondary Education. Wage subsidies were generally granted to employers providing for additional jobs for the long-term unemployed, defined as three months of registered unemployment for school leavers, and six months for the others.[15]

Right from the start, school leavers have been one of the target groups of the National Employment Foundation (OFA), established in 1992 by the Ministry of Labour with the original aim to address issues falling outside the Employment Act, in particular experimental or innovative labour market programmes.[16]

Since 1993, when the youth unemployment problem became more pressing, numerous targeted initiatives were introduced to tackle this problem. For instance, in 1993 the government introduced a special youth unemployment action programme named "Give a Chance". One of the programme's main aims was the improvement of the information supply on labour market conditions and opportunities, on labour legislation and on the services of the labour centres. In 1993, 82% of school leavers were covered by the programme. In general, local labour offices started to pay more attention to the involvement of school leavers in the various labour market programmes and started to give priority to searching for employment opportunities for young people. They intensified their contacts with local enterprises on this issue and also provided them with information on the conditions for receiving financial support for employing school leavers. Within the framework of the programme, new

---

[15] Keune, M. 1995. *Youth Unemployment in Hungary and Poland, ILO, Action Programme on Youth Unemployment.*
http://www.ilo.org/public/english/employment/strat/publ/etp20.htm
(accessed February 21, 2009).
[16] Ibid.

apprentice schemes for school leavers were developed in co-operation with various ministries, mainly for skilled young people.[17]

Without doubt, the most important paradigm shift in policies for unemployed young people took place in 1996 when the "passive" unemployment benefit for school leavers was abolished and was replaced by the School Leavers' Employment Programme in a move to provide more direct assistance to the unemployed youth. To provide better assistance for young people the government also introduced special targeted measures in 1996 [68/1996 (V. 15.), Government Decree on Promoting the Labour Market Integration of Young People]. The regulation defined the main target group of these measures as follows: registered unemployed career starters (young unemployed people with secondary education under the age of 25 or with tertiary education under the age of 30). For a long time (till 2007), there were two young entrants' specific ALMP-schemes:

- the Work Experience Scheme[18]
- the Employment Subsidy Scheme[19]

Of the two schemes, the first one clearly seemed to be more successful: its uptake was quite good and generally, two thirds of young entrants were still in the job three months after the end of the required employment period. The employment subsidy scheme had a very low uptake because its amount was not proportionate to the requirements and administrative burden. Furthermore, the number of businesses that could afford to employ their apprentices was very low and not many businesses were willing to provide apprentice contracts to their apprentices.[20]

After the hiatus between 2007 and 2009, the Work Experience Scheme has been reintroduced on 4 April 2009 [70/2009. (IV. 2.) Government Decree].

---

[17] Ibid.

[18] Support for acquiring work experience for job starters was available to those employers who employed skilled or unskilled young persons—for at least four hours a day—in a position where they are able to get experience beneficial in the labour market. The support could be 50 to 100% of the wages payable for the job starter and was available for the maximum term of one year. Positions eligible for support were defined by the employment councils.

[19] Employment support for job starters: this grant was intended to promote continuous employment of skilled young people at the place of training.

[20] Frey, M. 2008. "Evaluation of Active Labour Market Programmes between 2001-2006 and the Main Changes in 2007," in *The Hungarian labour market—Review and analysis 2008.* (Budapest: Institute of Economics, HAS; Hungarian Employment Foundation).

In 2007,[21] an across-the-board reform has been introduced in the system of employment promotion. The organisational structure of Public Employment Service (PES) has also changed: the tasks of Budapest and county job centres have been transferred to new regional job centres. Also the above mentioned targeted measures for young people have been re-regulated. Prior to 1 January 2007, employers could receive different discount rates on wage and contributions for a variety of target groups (e.g. young entrants). This fragmented system underwent fundamental changes, previous subsidies were either merged into the new scheme, or abolished. For instance, the above mentioned schemes for young entrants were partly abolished (the work experience scheme) and partly integrated (subsidy scheme) into the new systems of support for the employment of disadvantaged persons (a new overall definition has been created for the category of "disadvantaged" persons). The reform was mainly justified by the availability of other schemes, such as the new general system of wage subsidies[22] and the universal eligibility for a discount contributions within the Start Programme introduced in 2005 which are promoting the recruitment of young entrants in an effective manner. The former universal training scheme for young job seekers was integrated with the new general training scheme.

---

[21] The Parliament adopted Act CXIII of 2006 on the amendment of Act IV of 1991 on the Promotion of Employment and Provision for Unemployment on December 11, 2006. The new act entered into force on 1 January 2007.

[22] As "disadvantaged" persons [uniformly defined by Section 11 of Decree No. 6/1996 (VII. 16.) MüM on aid for promoting employment and on the aid that can be provided from the Labour Market Fund for the management of employment crises], young jobseekers are one specific target group of this wage subsidy. Relevant groups of disadvantaged persons: person with only primary education at maximum; young jobseekers up to the age of 25; unemployed persons who did not perform any gainful activity over 6 months prior to registering as unemployed See: Section 11 of Decree No. 6/1996 (VII. 16.) MüM.
The wage subsidy ('Assistance to Employers for the Creation of New Jobs') is regulated by Section 16. of Act IV of 1991 on Job Assistance and Unemployment Benefits: Employers may be granted subsidies up to 50% of the employee's wages (60% in case of disabled persons), for a maximum period of 1 year (2 years for those who have been unemployed for at least 24 months), if a) they undertake to employ such disadvantaged person while receiving such subsidies; b) they did not terminate, by regular dismissal, the employment of an employee working in the same position within the 12-month period preceding the hiring of an employee in subsidised employment for reasons in connection with its operations, and c) they undertake the obligation that the employment relationship described in Paragraph b) shall not be terminated during the employment of the unemployed person.

The renewal, merger, simplification and "flexibilisation" of different schemes have been an important step towards modernisation: the creation of a simpler and more transparent system of employment promotion. The previous system had already become excessively complicated as a result of a series of amendments. Furthermore, it is increasingly difficult to solve employment problems by over-standardised and rigid measures in an era of escalating de-standardisation of life and employment patterns. The overall concept of a "disadvantaged person" (including young jobseekers) was given a precise definition,[23] in line with the previous practice. As a consequence of these reforms, nowadays the most important labour market policy measure for young entrants is—without doubt—the Start Programme.

4.3 The Start Programme and its "Achievements"

The Start Programme was introduced on 1 October 2005 and, implemented on a significantly large scale, it could by all means be named success. In Hungary, The Start Programme is an innovative and by far unmatched way to help career starters not only promoting their access to the labour market as workforce, but by also granting notable allowances to the employers (willing to employ these young entrants), thus effectively promoting youth employment.

The main purpose of this programme is to achieve a general change of mind in the labour market. It is common for employers to be reluctant to employ an entrant with no work experience. Usually, they argue that doing so would result in vast expenses that could be easily evaded by simply hiring someone who possesses both the theoretical and practical knowledge needed for the job. This reasoning is hard to argue within the short term, but in the long run, its flaws are easy to identify. If a new entrant is not allowed to work without experience, they will never get actual work experience, then this will result in a never-ending spiral that leads to the lack of replacements in particular sectors once the generation currently employed reaches the age of retirement or decides to change career. Of course this is exaggerating the problem, but there is no doubt that the issue mentioned above is serious and could have consequences in the future if not properly dealt with. The Start Programme takes on a fair approach as it offers financial allowances to the employer in exchange for

---

[23] Section 11 of Decree No. 6/1996 (VII. 16.) MüM on aid for promoting employment and on the aid that can be provided from the Labour Market Fund for the management of employment crises.

the lack of field experience of the entrants, i.e. as a kind of compensation. An increase in the employment of the target group (the young entrants in our case) can therefore be achieved, and young people are also able to enter the labour market lawfully. Since there seems to be a trend for young entrants to seek solutions in the black (or grey) economy, either because that way contributions do not have to be paid for them and they are employed and at least get to earn a living, or because they are so in need of practical knowledge and field experience that they accept to be exploited. Some firms "employ" young employees full-time (in some cases making them work overtime) with no salary at all and convince them that if they do a good job for a given period of time and gather enough experience they will be employed by the firm in the future. These are all serious problems, which initiatives such as the Start Programme aim to solve.

Naturally, the success of the Start Programme is the result of many years of experience gained through previous state initiatives, such as the one that directly preceded the Start Programme; through a new support scheme—which entered into force on 1 January 2005—the government aimed to promote the employment of school leavers and the unemployed young who had been facing increasing difficulties in the labour market.[24] The subsidy aimed at assisting school leavers to gain work experience. The policy brief of the legislative proposal argued as follows:

> It is justified to introduce measures that create more favourable conditions to employers than the general rules on social security contributions. The opportunities of the disadvantaged groups to gain work experience should be further enhanced.

In this scheme, employers were eligible for the subsidy if they employed a person from the target group. The subsidy was paid for 9 months, after which the worker should have remained in employment for at least an additional 3 months. Working time could be full-time as well as part-time, however part-time employment could not be less than 4 hours per day. The subsidy was 50% of the social security contributions payable by the employer, and was reimbursed retrospectively. In 2005 the wage eligible for the subsidy was capped at a monthly gross HUF 90,000.

---

[24] Act CXXIII of 2004 on the Promotion of the Employment of School Leavers, Unemployed Aged 50 Years and over, People Returning to Work after Child Care or Nursing and the introduction of the Paid Internship Programme was adopted by Parliament on 13 December 2004 and entered into force on 1 January 2005.

School leavers were eligible if they were under the age of 25 and had not held a job previously.[25]

In reality, the above discussed scheme (introduced as of January 2005) to promote the employment of school leavers was not successful. Employers did not consider the level of support high enough and they also found the whole procedure overly bureaucratic (including the fact that the subsidy was reimbursed at the end of the 9-month period and that there was a requirement to maintain the employment relationship after that point) As a consequence, this subsidy was replaced by the Start Programme valid from 1 October 2005.[26]

The Start Programme is intended to promote the employment of career starters. The main aims are as:

- helping young persons to enter the labour market,
- increasing employment in the target group,
- making it easier to hire young people and encouraging employers to recruit young workers,
- creating incentives for employers to follow employment regulations and employ workers lawfully (since it is a characteristic feature of young employees that they are attracted to the grey or black economy).

All in all, the programme aims at helping young people entering the labour market by providing essential work experience. The Programme's personal coverage is quite wide. It covers:

- all young entrants of the labour market (career starters with secondary education under the age of 25 or with tertiary education under the age of 30),
- young people who finished (or interrupted) their studies and,
- young people who take up regular employment for the very first time.

---

[25] Frey, M. 2006. "Changes in the Legal and Institutional Environment of the Labour Market," in *The Hungarian Labour Market: Review and Analysis*, eds. Fazekas, K., and J. Koltay, (Budapest: Institute of Economics, HAS; Hungarian Employment Foundation).

[26] Act LXXIII of 2005 on Incentives to Promote the Employment of Young Entrants, Unemployed People Aged 50 Years and over and People Returning to Work after Child Care or Nursing, and on the Amendment of Act CXXIII of 2004. The act was adopted on 27 June 2005 and entered into force on 1 October 2005.

All these youngsters are entitled to apply for a so-called "START-card". It is not at all obligatory to enter into the scheme: the young person might decide not to obtain the card and use the discount. Jobseekers themselves can apply for the card which they present to employers when applying for jobs. The card certifies that its holder is eligible for the discount. The Hungarian Tax Authority is responsible for administering the Programme. The card itself is basically free of charge. The card is valid for 2 years from the date of issue (as of 1 January 2010, the card is valid for only 1 year in the case of university graduates). The card can be applied only once (except in the case of loss or physical damage of the card). It may be used by several employers consecutively or by the same employer. In other words: the subsidy is directly linked to the young worker (but it can only be "activated" and used by the employer). In practice it is very easy to obtain the card; registration as unemployed is not a prerequisite. During the employment period employers keep the card. In the event that the young person works (part-time) for more than one employer (for at least 4 hours/day) the subsidy can be used by the employer to whom the card is submitted.

Employers who hire young entrants with a "START-card" are eligible for a specific subsidy. There is no obligation to maintain the employment relationship after the termination of the subsidy. Employers hiring young people with the START-card will be granted a considerable universal reduction on social security contributions for a 2-year period, but only up to a certain wage limit. The reduction is available on wages equalling 150% of the minimum wage, except for employees with a degree in higher education, where the upper limit equals up to 200% of the minimum wage. This does not mean, however, that the actual wage cannot be higher than this amount: only the amount of the subsidy is capped at these levels. Till December 2009, the reduction in contributions was as follows:

- in the first year: the preferential total social security contribution paid by the employer was 15% of the gross wage—instead of the general 32% (29% social insurance contribution and 3% employers' contribution).
- In the second year: the preferential total social security contribution paid by the employer was 25% of the gross wage—instead of the general 32% (29% social insurance contribution and 3% employers' contribution).
- Additionally, employers are exempt from the monthly fixed-sum health care contribution for the whole period of 2 years.

As of 1 January, 2010, the reductions are even more preferential:

- in the case of career starters with secondary education: in the first year, the total social security contribution paid by the employer is only 10% of the gross wage; in the second year: the total social security contribution paid by the employer is only 20% of the gross wage (instead of the general 27%).
- In the case of career starters with tertiary education (in this case, the card is valid for only 1 year now, instead of the previous 2 years validity): in the first 9 months, the total social security contribution paid by the employer is only 10% of the gross wage; in the second part of the card's validity (additional 3 months): the total social security contribution paid by the employer is only 20% of the gross wage (instead of the general 27%).

We can illustrate the accessible savings of employers with the following examples:

Table 3-3. Employers' Savings with the Start card, 2007 (HUF/person/year)

	Employer savings on the wages of workers with secondary education or lower with a monthly wage equal to 150% of the minimum wage (2007)	Employer savings on the wages of graduate workers with a monthly salary equal to 200% of the minimum wage (2007)
Contributions without Discount	400,680	526,440
Contributions with Discount	1st year: 176,850 2nd year: 294,750	1st year: 235,800 2nd year: 393,000
Saving	1st year: 223,830 2nd year: 105,930	1st year: 290,640 2nd year: 133,400
Total saving	329,760	424,040

Source: Frey 2008, 163.

Between October 2005 and February 2009, the National Tax Authority issued altogether more than one hundred thousand (116,033) START cards (from which 32,223 were issued for young people with tertiary education).[27] Nearly 41,000 young people found jobs with the support of the programme between 1 October 2005 and 1 August 2007.[28] However, no information is available yet to determine to what extent these job seekers were employed additionally or replaced other jobs and how many stayed in these jobs after the running out of the subsidy.[29] According to a report, at the national economy level, 15% of firms avail themselves of the possibility to employ school leavers with a START-card. This form of employment involving school leavers is most widespread in tourism. The highest number of START-card employees is in the industrial, building industry, driver, machine operator and assembly jobs and it is also widespread in graduate employment, like in commerce and engineering.[30]

Although it is not strictly related to the topic of the present paper, it can be mentioned that—as the original Start Programme for young entrants is quite promising and successful—from 1 July 2007 new schemes were added to the Start family (Start Plus, Start Extra).

From the perspective of regulatory theories, the Start Programme can be interpreted as a symbolical example of innovative regulatory models in the realm of CSR (Corporate Social Responsibility)-related public policies. Although in Hungary CSR-related public policy is not well developed in general and the Start Programme is also rarely considered in this context, there are some initial signs of this kind of inventive contextualisation. For instance, in the Hungarian chapter of the official European compilation called "Corporate Social Responsibility—National public policies in the European Union", the Start Programme is mentioned as a good example for CSR-supportive social policies.[31] Indeed, if CSR-related public policy is fundamentally about "providing incentives for

---

[27] National Tax Authority. 22. 02. 2009.

[28] National Development Agency. 2007. *Report on the Implementation of the Revised National Lisbon Action Programme*. National Development Agency, 38.

[29] Council of Europe International Review Team. 2008. *Youth Policy in Hungary*. Report of the Council of Europe international review team, 48.

[30] Magyar Kereskedelmi és Iparkamara, Gazdaság- és Vállalkozáselemző Intézet. 2007. *Hungarian Labour Market Outlook 2007*. Budapest: HCCI Research Institute of Economics and Enterprises.

[31] European Commission. 2007a. *Corporate Social Responsibility—National public policies in the European Union*. European Commission, 54.

businesses to produce positive externalities",[32] the Start Programme genuinely fits into this framework. Such CSR-related public policies are typically designed to enable "voluntary" (or semi-voluntary) CSR initiatives that are not feasible without (at least some) public support. In this sense businesses are producing collective goods (e.g.: employment) on a voluntary (semi-voluntary) basis, but the burdens are borne by society through publicly organised incentive schemes and subsidies. In the case of the Start Programme, the publicly supported positive externality is the social inclusion of young people in the labour market. Such programmes are based on a so-called partnership approach and on the envisaged "win-win" situation. Both society and businesses make a "profit" in a sense. This kind of public political thinking is still very dispersed, hidden and informal in Hungary. That is why the Start Programme can be depicted as a really successful measure—both in practical and theoretical terms.

4.4 Paid Internship Employment

The Paid Internship Employment is yet another successful programme launched to combat (and hopefully solve) the problem mentioned above. This initiative was created for the sole purpose of making it possible for young graduates of higher education to gain work experience.

The Paid Internship Employment[33] is in fact a specific stipend or stagier programme, which helps young graduates of tertiary education gain work experience under regular employment-like conditions. The Programme was originally introduced in 2004. The duration of the programme ranges from 9 to 12 months, and it can be concluded only once, for a definite period. The application of a probation period is prohibited. The minimum amount of the grant equals the minimum wage per month, and it is backed by tax-incentives. From the point of view of social security, young people participating in the scheme are considered insured (this is one of the main advantages of the scheme). The programme can be combined with the above described START-card and is supported by reductions in tax and contribution burdens. It is advantageous for the employers as well because of the subsidies and the possibility to recruit and train talented young people.

---

[32] Jørgensen, A. L. 2004. *The Rule of CSR and the Role of Law—Re-defining the Role of Policy in CSR*. Think Piece, The Copenhagen Centre.

[33] Waldmann, G. 2006. "Az ösztöndíjas foglalkoztatás," *Munkaügyi Szemle,* No. 2:48-50.

The system is designed to help young people (up to the age of 30) with college and university degrees (obtained in the preceding 2 years) to start their careers, to gain work experience, acquire skills and knowledge absolutely necessary in the world of work, and to shorten the transition between education and working life. During the Programme, the participant is supervised by a designated vocational "mentor" (according to a pre-defined individual work experience-plan, which is an essential part of the underlying specific employment contract). The mentor gives individual career guidance, regular feedback and evaluation. The intern cannot fill a position independently; nevertheless, the paid internship is a form of employment. At the end of the internship the employer provides the intern with a recommendation letter that certifies the work experience.

Although this programme is also extended to the private sphere, it is much more popular in public administration. Indeed, in the public sector, the Programme is partly state-funded: pursuant to Government Decree No 20/2005 (II. 11.), 50% of the amount of the stipend can be reimbursed directly from the state budget (not from the own budget of the relevant administrative agency). The government saw this new scheme as a tool to improve the labour market prospects of graduate school leavers and to allow central administration bodies to recruit new civil servants from a wider pool of talented young people.

4.5 Other Possibilities

Beyond all the different programmes available, there are support schemes that are set up to suit basic needs, for example reimbursement of travelling expenses to support mobility and widen the range of possibilities for the individual.

Prevention is also becoming even more important among the services offered by the PES. The local Employment Centres and other institutions (both private and state-funded) regularly provide counselling and commonly organise job fairs and open days, set up and operate informational services and consultation offices for example in schools and work closely together with educational facilities to further the cause of assisting, aiding and preparing the youth to make the choice that suits them the most both in terms of higher education or training and career.

There is a general assumption that more attention could be paid to the subjective motivation of young job seekers. It is important, because statistics are alarming in this sense: the monitoring process of the European Employment Strategy—since 2003—includes indicators of how many young unemployed people have not benefited from preventative services (intensive counselling, job search assistance) or a new start (training, retraining, work experience, job, employability measure). For Hungary both indicators are at a rather high level and have increased since 2003.[34]

5. Closing Remarks

After reviewing a number of problems, issues, possible solutions, programmes and initiatives, analysing and studying them from a considerable number of viewpoints, we should return to the fundamental statement that has been mentioned throughout the paper: almost all the problems Hungary has to face originate from the thoughts and beliefs that should have been changed together with the socialist regime more than 20 years ago. No matter what opportunities will be made available by the State, NGOs, or even private investors; as long as most people are reluctant to search for information and take these opportunities, there is no real chance of improvement.

What still proves the system worthy to be upheld is that its implementation made it possible to moderate the number of unemployed young people even during the recent economic crisis. To keep this up, employers and (future or current) employees should be working closely together with the state and take their part in helping and forming the work of legislative bodies to achieve better conditions for more personalised options to be more efficient in the long run.

Thus, the most important conclusion is that—in the field of youth employment—the key to success is to implement complex and cross-sectoral solutions that cover and harmonise the economic, educational and social system. Moreover, related policy measures cannot be successful without harmonising the interests of all related stakeholders (society / public policy; businesses, young workers). The Start Programme may serve as a good example for such complex, multi-stakeholder oriented measures. However, it is by no means a panacea in itself. Labour market policies alone can only have a limited impact. Initiatives aimed at improving the position of young people should be embedded in the broader context of general socio-economic policy.[35] All in all, it is a

---

[34] Council of Europe International Review Team. 2008. *Youth Policy in Hungary.* Report of the Council of Europe international review team, 43.

[35] As regards overall "Youth Policy in Hungary", the Council of Europe's international review team has recently articulated the following policy recommendations for education and employment (February 2008):

commonplace that the successful integration of youth into the labour
market depends, for a big part, on the countries' overall labour market
performance.[36] Taking into account this perspective, even if we have some
notable targeted measures in favour of youth employment in Hungary
(such as the Start Programme), the overall labour market performance of
the country does not allow us to be optimistic since developments on the
youth labour market are mostly following general labour market
tendencies.

References

ÁFSZ. 2008. *MUNKAERŐPIACI HELYZETKÉP, 2007. évi összefoglaló,*
    Budapest: ÁFSZ.
Berde, É. 2005. *Work Conceptions of Young People Before Graduation
    and Labour Statistics Based on the Facts of the Expected Short-Term
    Trends* [in Hungarian]. Budapest: OFA.
    http://www.google.hu/url?sa=t&source=web&cd=1&ved=0CBcQFjA
    A&url=http%3A%2F%2Fwww.ofa.hu%2Findex.php%3FWG_NODE
    %3DWebIntRedirect%26WG_OID%3DDSDf66b686134d06d53e&ei

- counteract the impact of social inequality and poverty by widening access to
scholarships;
- strengthen policies against school segregation, possibly restrict free school
choice;
- integrate formal and non-formal learning both inside school and vocational
training and through cooperation with youth work; this includes ways of
recognising non-formal learning;
- in active labour market policies for young people counselling in terms of life
planning rather than control, possibilities of choice among measures and flexible
regulations of access are needed; measures might extend to providing work
experience or voluntary work in youth work; include outreach approaches of
professional orientation, counselling and support in rural areas;
- improve the analysis of youth unemployment and the evaluation of education,
training and active labour market policies by including longitudinal and qualitative
methods;
- integrate labour market policies and regional economic development; balance
supply side and demand side measures;
- increasing funding to secure wider access to education and choice and quality
in active labour market policies, partly by improving use of EU funds and partly
rebalancing priorities (Council of Europe International Review Team 2008, 5).

[36] European Commission. 2008. *Employment in Europe 2008*. Brussels: European
Commission, 50.

=J2FITevpDo_pOdT2jJcE&usg=AFQjCNHpIZgd8I4L6CkKFxCWxP
osuFZnrw pg 1-14 (accessed October 28, 2010).
Council of Europe International Review Team. 2008. *Youth Policy in Hungary.* Report of the Council of Europe international review team.
European Commission. 2007a. *Corporate Social Responsibility— National public policies in the European Union.* Brussels: European Commission.
European Commission. 2007b. *Employment in Europe 2007.* Brussels: European Commission.
—. 2008. *Employment in Europe 2008.* Brussels: European Commission.
—. 2009. *Employment in Europe 2009.* Brussels: European Commission.
Frey, M. 2006. "Changes in the Legal and Institutional Environment of the Labour Market," in *The Hungarian Labour Market: Review and Analysis*, eds. Fazekas, K., and J. Koltay, (Budapest: Institute of Economics, HAS; Hungarian Employment Foundation).
—. 2008. "Evaluation of Active Labour Market Programmes between 2001-2006 and the Main Changes in 2007," in *The Hungarian labour market—Review and analysis 2008*, (Budapest: Institute of Economics, HAS; Hungarian Employment Foundation).
Gerzsényi, Á., and L. Neumann. 2007. *Contribution to EIRO Thematic Feature on Youth and Work—Case of Hungary.* EIROnline.
Jørgensen, A. L. 2004. *The Rule of CSR and the Role of Law—Redefining the Role of Policy in CSR.* Think Piece, The Copenhagen Centre.
Keune, M. 1995. *Youth Unemployment in Hungary and Poland, ILO, Action Programme on Youth Unemployment.* http://www.ilo.org/public/english/employment/strat/publ/etp20.htm (accessed February 21, 2009).
Magyar Kereskedelmi és Iparkamara, Gazdaság- és Vállalkozáselemző Intézet. 2007. *Hungarian Labour Market Outlook 2007.* Budapest: HCCI Research Institute of Economics and Enterprises.
Ministry of Employment and Labour of Hungary. 2005. *Youth on the Labour Market.* Budapest: Ministry of Employment and Labour of Hungary.
National Development Agency. 2007. *Report on the Implementation of the Revised National Lisbon Action Programme.* National Development Agency.
Waldmann, G. 2006. "Az ösztöndíjas foglalkoztatás," *Munkaügyi Szemle*, No. 2:48-50.

Issues of the Learning through Work Experience Programme for Junior High School Students: "The 14-Year-Old's Challenge" in Toyama Prefecture

Satomi Terasaki

1. Introduction[1]

In this paper, we examine the effects and challenges of learning through work experience programme as a part of school education by looking at a five-day programme introduced for all junior high schools in Toyama Prefecture as an example. Given that more than 98% of junior high school students advance to schools beyond junior high, it is difficult to evaluate career education and learning through work experience programmes that are implemented by junior high schools within the same framework as those implemented by senior high schools and universities, whose students are likely to enter the labour market soon after graduation. Therefore, before moving on to our analysis, let us first organise the perspectives for evaluating career education and learning through work experience programmes at junior high schools, and then describe the emphasis on the learning through work experience in junior high school students' career education.

1.1 Two Perspectives on Career Education

Around 10 years have passed since the Central Council for Education, in a report entitled "Improvements in Articulation between Elementary and Secondary Schools, and Higher Education Institutions" (referred to as the "Report on Articulation," below) and issued in 1999, argued for the

---

[1] Terasaki, S. 2011. "Issues of the learning through work experience program for junior high school students: 'The 14-year-old's challenge' in Toyama prefecture," *Japan Labor Review* 8, No. 1:48-66.

need to provide career education from elementary school upwards in accordance with the students' stages of development. "Career education," a phrase which was used in a public document for the first time in the Report on Articulation,[2] has since then attracted attention as one of the effective measures against the deterioration of young workers' employment situation and an increase youth unemployment. There are two perspectives of evaluating the promotion of career education over this period: one is perspective of measures against the problem of the transition from school to work and the other is as reflecting a change in how school education—career guidance in particular—should be carried out.

Taking the viewpoint of people who had called for measures against an increase of youth unemployment and early stage turnover under the deterioration of economical situation and changes in the labour market in the 1990s, the Report on Articulation prompted the implementation of various measures for the purpose of career education. Among those measures are the promotion of career education by the Ministry of Education, Culture, Sports, Science and Technology and programmes implemented by other ministries, including the "Youth Independence and Challenge Plan" (2003) and the "Youth Independence and Challenge Action Plan" (2004), both of which featured career education as the pillar.

On the other hand, taking the viewpoint of people who saw the promotion of career education as reflecting a change in how school education should be carried out, it is considered that the career guidance was back on form to aim at a lifelong career development by the Report on Articulation. Career guidance, which aimed at finding employment or going on to school after graduation based on academic achievements, had already started to change around 1990 into guidance that valued individual students' interests and concerns. The following events can be considered as an event that shows this shift: a decision of not using class curve at career guidance in 1992 (Saitama Prefecture), and an enhancement of way of life guidance in each school stage such as elementary, junior and senior high schools in course of study in 1998.

We give this explanation because these two viewpoints differ not only on the way of assessing the Report on Articulation and the references to career education in it, but also on what kind of people should be the subjects of career education and what measures should be taken to promote career education. From the former viewpoint, the subjects of career education should be people who have exactly faced the vocational

---

[2] Mimura, T. 2004. *Kyaria kyoiku nyumon: Sono riron to jissen no tameni* [The basics of career education: Theories and practices]. Tokyo: Jitsugyo no Nnihonsha.

choice and the labour market entry, such as high school students, university students and unemployed youth. Meanwhile, the latter viewpoint focuses mainly on career education for junior high school students. In Japan, where high school advancement rate exceeds 98% of high-school aged youths, junior high school students are regarded as still having some time to spare before choosing a specific job or doing any practical life planning.

Interest in finding the effects of career education—learning through work experience programmes and internships in particular—to the vocational selection is observed mainly among people who take the former viewpoint. Past research papers have studied which people took advantage of school career guidance on the transition to work and which failed to do so, and what traits are seen in those who failed to do so as well as what kind of career guidance would be effective.[3]

On the other hand, many research papers that have studied career education and learning through work experience programmes for junior high school students from the latter viewpoint have focused on very practical matters, such as how career education and activities under these programmes should be positioned within annual plans for school career guidance, and how to evaluate the results of such activities and use them for future career guidance.[4] Most of the cases cited in those research papers are highly practical activities conducted by individual teachers who

[3] Kariya, T., K. Tsuburai, M. Nagasu, and M. Inada. 1997. "Shinro mikettei no kozo: Kosotsu shinro miketteisha no sekishutsu mekanizumu ni kansuru jisshoteki kenkyu" [The rise of uncertain future plans among Japanese high school students], *Bulletin of the Graduate School of Education, the University of Tokyo*, No. 37:45-76. Hiroaki, M., M. Omichi, M. Nagasu, Y. Morota, K. Tuburai, Y. Hori, and R. Kosugi. 2000. *Kosotsu mugyosha no kyoiku shakaigakuteki kenkyu* [Study on unemployed high school graduates from the perspectives of education and sociology], a report funded by the Fiscal 1999-2000 Science Research Subsidy (Basic Research) (c) (2). Honda, Y. 2005. *Wakamono to shigoto: "Gakko keiyu no shushoku" wo koet*e [Youth and work: Beyond "employment via school"]. Tokyo: University of Tokyo Press. Kosugi, R. 2003. *Furita to iu ikikata* [The freeter's way of living]. Tokyo: Sokei Shobo. Kosugi, R. 2005. *Frita to nito* [Freeters and NEETs]. Tokyo: Sokei Shobo. Kosugi, R, ed. 2002. *Jiyu no daisho: Furita— Gendai wakamono no shugo ishiki to kodo* [The price of freedom: Freeters— Modern youth's perception of employment and behaviour]. Tokyo: The Japan Institute for Labour Policy and Training.
[4] Mimura, T. 2004. *Kyaria kyoiku nyumon: Sono riron to jissen no tameni* [The basics of career education: Theories and practices]. Tokyo: Jitsugyo no Nnihonsha. National Institute for Educational Policy Research, ed. 2007. *Kyaria kyoiku e no shotai* [Invitation to career education]. Tokyo: Toyokan Shuppansha.

actually educate students at their schools. There are two reasons why this trend is seen among research papers concerning junior high school students.

First, it is widely recognised that the career education being promoted now, unlike career guidance on post-graduation careers aimed merely at enabling the choice of a school, is intended to enable students to think in their own way about life based on an individual's interests and concerns. However, in the current situation in Japan that almost all junior high school students go on to higher levels of education, if the effects of career education are to be measured in terms of concrete results, the concern might concentrate only on the school choice, and is likely to turn back to the old career guidance that was able to abandon at last. Therefore, it is difficult for the effect measurement at the time of graduation of the junior high school to find the effect of the career education as the way of life guidance.

Second, it is also recognised that the scope of career education as part of school education extends beyond career guidance, and that it should be provided in a comprehensive, systematic, and organised way through all of a school's educational activities. For example, learning through work experience programmes, which are carried out to meet social needs related to human resource development, are also treated as part of moral education intended to develop sound minds and bodies in young people (under the Basic Plan for Promoting Education). In other words, career education and learning through work experience programmes at elementary and junior high schools may be provided for various purposes and through various methods. It has been thought that any debate on the effects of such activities should give consideration to their desirability from the perspective of education, and that it is inappropriate to attempt to evaluate their effects from any single perspective. Because of this, there has been no attempt to find the effects of career education from the perspective of career guidance alone.

1.2 Emphasis on Learning through Work Experience

The above explanations should also help understand why career education places an emphasis on the learning through work experience. Under the course of study in 1998, the year before the Report on Articulation was written, career guidance (way of life guidance) was enhanced at elementary, junior, and senior high schools. In elementary school, career guidance is not treated as a separate field of education in the curriculum. However, general provision 5 of the course of study, "matters to which consideration should be given in designing the syllabus" stipulated that "in providing instructions concerning each of the subjects, schools should use specific measures, such as providing children with the opportunity to find learning tasks and activities on their own and think about their own futures".

Under the general provisions of the course of study, junior high schools are required to provide "systematic and organised career guidance through all educational activities so that students can think in their own way about life and choose their career proactively". The cultivation (establishment) of a view of career and work is regarded as an important link between an understanding of the significance of learning, the cultivation (establishment) of an attitude toward learning, and the examination (understanding) of career aptitudes so as to "enrich school life and enable appropriate choice of a way of life and a career (decision)". Although the phrase "career education" was not used in the 1998 course of study, the emphasis on proactive career choice based on individual's interests and concerns can be viewed as the first step toward the implementation of career education.

However, it should be kept in mind that the proactive career choice emphasised in the 1998 course of study was interpreted as a policy change in relation to the existing career guidance, but not as a policy shift toward promoting a smooth transition from school to work. There occurred a significant policy change in career guidance, from a meritocratic approach based on academic achievements to counselling focusing on students' own personalities, interests and concerns. From the former viewpoint that places emphasis on "work", this shift may be regarded as a step toward incorporating career education into all curriculum subjects. However, from the latter viewpoint that emphasises "education", it was invariably seen as a change in school education in relation to career choice.

And yet at the same time, it is worth noting that following this policy shift, learning based on first-hand experience came to be regarded as important for cultivating students' view of career and work, making it necessary to secure opportunities for enlightened experience related to jobs and career. This is because the importance of learning based on first-hand experience was emphasised again in the Report on Articulation. Behind the argument for the need to provide systematic career education from elementary school upwards was the recognition that appropriate view of career and work had not been cultivated in accordance with children's development. The Report on Articulation placed particular emphasis on learning through work experience, acknowledging it as a problem that children lack life experience and social experience in highly urbanised local communities and in families with fewer children, where they can only experience limited human relationships and limited roles. The National Institute for Educational Policy Research[5] pointed out that even more than the need for children to develop view of career and work, which is the purpose of career education, children lacked experience with the reality of society and experience in building an extensive relationships with different generations, both of which are essential to their growth, and that they are faced with a situation in which it is difficult for them to find models for the ways they want to live their lives.

There are now strong expectations that learning through work experience programmes in elementary and junior high schools will have effects for young people's future vocational selection from the viewpoint of placing an emphasis on "work". However, when they were introduced at such schools, experiential activities were expected to help secure the opportunity for the life and social experiences that had been lost. Rather than providing the opportunity for children to feel the difficulties and joys of working and to learn about its significance, learning through work experience programmes were expected to have a broad range of effects, including enabling children to have the experience of forming human relationships while recognising their own positions and roles in a group and giving them the motivation to learn based on their first-hand experience.[6] In this respect, the programmes run in elementary and junior high schools are different from the learning through work experience programmes and internships in high schools and universities, which are strongly linked with the vocational selection.

1.3 Implementation of Experiential Activities and Toyama Prefecture's Programme, "the 14-Year-Old's Challenge"

According to the "Survey on the Implementation of Experiential Activities in Schools" (fiscal 2006)[7] conducted by the Ministry of

---

[5] National Institute for Educational Policy Research, ed. 2007. *Kyaria kyoiku e no shotai* [Invitation to career education]. Tokyo: Toyokan Shuppansha.
[6] Ibid., and Guidance and Counselling Research Centre, National Institute for Educational Policy Research. 2002. *Jido seito no shokugyokan, rodokan wo hagukumu kyoiku no suishin ni tsuite* [Promotion of education fostering school children's view of career and work]. Tokyo: Guidance and Counselling Research Centre, NIER. http://www.nier.go.jp/shido/centerhp/sinro/sinro.htm (accessed November 25, 2010).
[7] Survey subject schools: A total of 564 schools—188 each of elementary schools and junior and senior high schools

Education, Culture, Sports, Science and Technology, the total annual credit hours for experiential activities related to production, workplaces, jobs, and employment[8] totalled 12.6 hours at elementary schools and 20.1 hours at junior high schools (See Table 3-4). Given that in fiscal 2003, the total credit hours for such activities totalled 10.3 hours at elementary schools and 13.8 hours at junior high schools, the time allocated for experience-based learning increased significantly over a short period of time, indicating that measures to secure opportunities for such learning had been taken promptly.[9]

Table 3-4. Implementation of Experiential Activities at Schools

	Elementary schools		Junior high schools	
	Fiscal 2003	Fiscal 2006	Fiscal 2003	Fiscal 2006
Experiential activities related to community service	**4.3**	**3.1**	**2.9**	**2.5**
Experiential activities to foster familiarity with nature	**13.1**	**13.3**	**5.4**	**5.0**
Experiential activities related to production, workplace, jobs and employment	**10.3**	**12.6**	**13.8**	**20.1**
Primary industries	9.2	10.6	1.9	2.4
Secondary industries	0.4	0.8	1.9	4.9
Tertiary industries	0.7	1.2	10.0	12.8
Experiential activities to foster familiarity with culture and the arts	**5.5**	**3.6**	**3.2**	**3.7**
Experiential activities related to exchanges	**5.3**	**5.0**	**2.7**	**2.3**
Other experiential activities	**3.4**	**3.3**	**3.2**	**2.3**
Total	**41.9**	**41.0**	**31.2**	**35.9**

1. Compiled from "Collection of Data Related to the Current Circumstances Surrounding Child Development" by Ministry of Education, Culture, Sports, Science and Technology.

[8] Average of the total annual credit hours for fifth graders at elementary schools and for junior high and high school students in their second years.

[9] Excluding experiential activities related to community service such as volunteer visits to social welfare facilities. The total credit hours for this activity stood at 3.1 hours at elementary schools and 2.5 hours at junior high schools.

2. Details of the above activities are as follows:
- Experiential activities related to community service: Cleanup activity on the streets and beaches, improvement and beautification of local environment, visits to social welfare facilities and other volunteer work.
- Experiential activities to foster familiarity with nature: Field excursions, field camping, observation of wild birds and other wild life, nature school, and so on
- Experiential activities related to production, workplace, jobs and employment.
- Primary industries: Experience activities related to agriculture, forestry and fishery such as rice planting, cutting grass, beach seine, and so on;
- Secondary industries: Workplace experiential activities at factories, internships, and so on;
- Tertiary industries: Workplace experiential activities and internships at local business offices, stores, and so on;
- Experiential activities to foster familiarity with culture and arts: Wall painting, Experiential activities related to Japanese and foreign cultures and the arts, and so on. Activities to maintain local traditional events, performing arts and industrial arts.
- Experiential activities related to exchanges: Exchanges with young children, elderly people, people with disabilities, foreign nationals and people in other regions.

The increase in the time allocated for experience-based activities at junior high schools was due in large part to an increase in the hours spent on learning through work experience programmes. Of the 10,089 public junior high schools, 9,667, or 95.8%, implemented such activities in fiscal 2007, according to the Survey on the Implementation of Learning through Work Experience Programmes and Internships in Fiscal 2007 (Outline), which was conducted in March 2008 by the Guidance and Counselling Research Centre of the National Institute for Educational Policy Research. The implementation ratio came to 100% in seven prefectures, Ibaraki, Toyama, Ishikawa, Fukui, Nagano, Gifu, and Shiga, and in two of them— Toyama and Shiga—all schools implemented five days or more of activities under the programmes. Irrespective of the initial purpose of their introduction, almost all junior high schools implement some kind of learning through work experience programme as a part of the educational activities.

In Toyama Prefecture's programme, "The Learning through Work Experience Programme: The 14-Year-Old's Challenge", 14-year-old second-year junior high school students do work experiences or welfare activities and volunteer works for five days, mainly in the local community of the school district. Such activities, which have been implemented in the name of "The Learning through Work Experience Programme: The 14-Year-Old's Challenge", since 1999, are implemented by municipalities supported by subsidies from the Toyama prefectural government. According to the implementation guidelines, the purpose of this programme is to "enable junior high school students in their second year, whose activities broaden in scope and increase in intensity, to become tough enough to overcome the challenges typical of that period of growth for young people, such as developing a consciousness of social norms and becoming more social, as well as thinking about their own futures, by participating in activities that allow them to gain experience of the world of work and social services and volunteer activities outside their schools for one week" (Fiscal 1999 Implementation Guidelines for the 14-Year-Old's Challenge Programme).

In recent years, this programme has come to be taken up as a part of a career education initiative that is effective in developing students' job consciousness. However, as indicated in the implementation guidelines, initially, the main purpose of this programme was not to develop students' view of career and work. Around 1995, as school bullying emerged as a social problem, each municipality launched and implemented a Community-Wide Programme to Prevent School Bullying (in fiscal 1996 through 1998). The purpose of the programme was to deal with an increase in school bullying and school truancy through community-wide efforts, by encouraging the recognition that the local community should be responsible for children's upbringing. This programme continued as it evolved first into the "Activities for a Mental Education Network in Junior High School Districts" (in fiscal 1999 through 2002) and then into the "Implementation Programme for Heartfelt Activities" (in fiscal 2003 through 2005). The 14-Year-Old's Challenge Programme started in 1999 as part of these activities.

Therefore, if the situation in Toyama Prefecture is to be understood within the framework of "work" and "education", it can be said that the 14-Year-Old's Challenge Programme, which was initially introduced for the purpose of providing education to junior high school students through community-wide efforts, is being forced to change into a work-oriented activity. In this respect, the situation in Toyama Prefecture is different from that in other regions that have started learning through work experience programmes in recent years.[10] The current challenge for the 14-Year-Old's Challenge Programme is how to adapt to the shift in its purpose from education to work.

Shown below are the results of a survey of students on the effects to be gained if learning through work experience programme are treated as activities to facilitate the vocational selection. We will also explain the problems related to experiential activities as identified through interviews with local business establishments.

2. Data Used for Analysis

This research uses data collected through the Survey of Junior High School Students' Outlooks on the Future and Job Consciousness, which was conducted as part of the "Communication System Development Programme," a project implemented by Ochanomizu University with special educational research funds.

2.1 Student Survey

The survey of students was conducted in two areas—Area X and Area Y—in Toyama Prefecture in September and October 2006, with the questionnaires distributed to students through their schools[11] Questionnaire A asked the students about their school lives and learning environments and about their job consciousness and the career choice they had for their futures. Questionnaire B asked the students about the details of their activities under the learning through work experience programme, how they felt about them, and their consciousness of family and workplace norms. These questionnaires were distributed and collected twice, both before and after the students surveyed had participated in the activities. The same questions were asked with regard to norm consciousness before and after the experience so as to make a comparison. The results of

---

[10] This provides a contrast to "Work, Work Week Tokyo," a workplace experience activity for junior high school students in Tokyo that started in 2005, whose purpose was, from the beginning, to encourage students to develop appropriate perceptions of jobs and work (Implementation Guideline for "Work, Work Week Tokyo").

[11] Terasaki, S., and M. Hiroaki. 2007. *Chugakusei no shorai tenbo to shokugyo ishiki ni kansuru chosha: gaiyo* [Survey on junior high school students' outlooks on the future and job consciousness (outline)]. Tokyo: Ochanomizu University, Faculty of Letters and Education, communication system development programme office.

Questionnaires A and B were matched by student number. The collection rate and the matching conditions for Questionnaires A and B are as shown in Table 3-5. In this paper, we treat the survey results in Area X and Area Y[12] as a unit, with no distinction made between them.

Table 3-5. Collection Rate and Matching

	A	B (before the activities)	B (after the activities)	Matching
Number of students	556	556	556	556
Number of collected replies	522	523	517	500
Collection rate (%)	93.9	94.1	93.0	89.9

2.2 Local Business Survey

Until now, few surveys have been conducted on the local business establishments that accept students from workplace experience programmes and internship trainees. The "Survey of Business Establishments about Learning through Work Experience Programmes and Internships", conducted in 2005 by the Guidance and Counselling Research Centre of the National Institute for Educational Policy Research, did not ask

---

[12] The system of implementing the "The 14-Year-Old's Challenge" program in each area is as follows:

Area X (four schools): Implemented jointly by neighboring junior high schools.

• Organisation: Prefectural education board → City education boards and promotion committees → Groups of implementing organisations → Schools and steering committees

• Businesses that accept students: Schools dispatch teachers to local businesses in their school districts to ask for their cooperation. After the number of students to be accepted has been finalised, each junior high school determines the number of students to be allocated to each. Accordingly, under the program, some students may take part in activities outside their own school district, but within the districts of either one of the other three partner schools in Area X. Area Y (one school): Implemented independently by the school.

• Organisation: Prefectural education board → Town education board and promotion committee → School and steering committee

• Businesses that accept students: Teachers visit local businesses to ask for their cooperation. After the number of students to be accepted has been finalized, the school determines the number of students to be allocated to each. As the number of business establishments and type of businesses available in the school district are limited, businesses outside the school district are also asked for cooperation.

business establishments whether or not they had accepted students for learning through work experience programme. Although cooperation from local businesses is essential to the implementation of these programmes, there had not been any survey, other than simple questionnaires prepared by the schools that asked them their frank opinions on the programme. In this research, we asked local businesses that accepted students to cooperate with our survey via the schools, and we accordingly conducted semi-structured, 60 to 90-minute interviews with nine local businesses within one month from the end of the 14-Year-Old's Challenge Programme. The data used for the research is based on the records of the interviews as compiled from tape recordings and written notes. The attributes of the interviewees and establishments are as shown in Table 3-6.

3. Analysis

3.1. The Learning through Work Experience Programme in Student Survey

When implementing learning through work experience programmes, schools ask their students about what kind of works they wish to do, and allocate them to local businesses in accordance with the number of students the businesses can accommodate, in a way that reflects the students' wishes as much as possible.

Table 3-6. Outline of Interviewees and Business Establishments Surveyed

Interviewees				Business establishments	
	Gender	Position	Age	Business type	Years of cooperation
A	Female	Instructor	30s	Sales	4 years
B	Female	Manager	60s	Social services	3 years
C	Male	Instructor	50s	Construction	Approx. 10 years
D	Male	Manager	50s	Manufacturing	Since the start of the programme
E	Female	Part-time worker	50s	Food service	3 years
F	Male Male	Association chief Instructor	60s 30s	Agriculture, forestry and fishery	5 years
G	Female	Manager	50s	Social services	Since the start of the programme
H	Male	Manager	30s	Manufacturing & sales	1st time
I	Female	Instructor	50s	Agriculture, forestry, and fishery	Since the start of the programme

Table 3-7. Contents of Activities

(%)

	Overall	Male	Female
Production, engineering & construction	15.8	28.2	3.2
Services, sales & food service	28.4	30.2	26.6
Child care	30.0	19.2	40.9
Medical & health service	5.1	3.1	7.1
Social services	4.9	1.6	8.3
Cultural experience	2.2	2.4	2.0
Public service	10.8	12.9	8.7
None of the above	2.6	2.4	2.8
No reply	0.2	0.0	0.4
Total	100.0	100.0	100.0
N	507	255	252

Excluding the respondents who did not reveal their gender.

Table 3-7 shows the distribution of students by type of business. The largest percentage of students, 30.0%, participated in childcare, followed by 28.4% for services, sales, and food service, and 15.8% for manufacturing, engineering, and construction. It should be noted that there was a gender disparity by type of business in that more female students participated in childcare and a greater number of male students participated in manufacturing, engineering, and construction.[13]

How, specifically, did the difference in the contents of their activities under the programme affect the students' overall impressions? We examined the effects of these activities by focusing on the three most popular business categories: childcare; services, sales, and food service; and manufacturing, engineering, and construction.

Fig. 3-11 indicates the results of a question that asked students about what was required of them in their activities. Most of the students who took part in childcare replied that they had been required to think of how to do the job for themselves and be creative (80.7%) and that they had

---

[13] The percentage of students who replied that the contents of the activities had not satisfied their wishes was 17.9%. This number did not differ significantly according to the contents of activities.

been required to give due consideration to other people's feelings (96.0%). Meanwhile, of the students who participated in manufacturing, engineering, and construction, 91.1% replied that they had been required to exercise their physical strength. This shows that what was required of them differed depending on the type of business they experienced.

Fig. 3-12 indicates the results of a question that asked students about their findings from their activities. After participating in the experience, many junior high school students found that long-term training would be necessary to make it possible to do the job properly. This suggests that these experiences have potential as an opportunity that motivates students to pursue further learning. However, the ratio of students who felt that way varied somewhat according to the type of business; the ratio was slightly lower for services, sales, and food service compared with the other two business categories.[14]

3.2 Problems Related to the Learning through Work Experience Programme in the Local Business Survey

(1)   Significance of the Experience: "Heart" Is More Important Than "Skills": here, we examine whether the learning through work experience programmes are recognised as being geared toward the students' future employment or are seen as a part of the students' educations. The results of the interviews show that all business establishments regard it as important that students put themselves in the workplace and have a first-hand experience doing a job. Some business establishments pointed out that the roles that children have in their families are too limited, as did the Report on Articulation.

---

[14] The impact on the perception of a student's future career or the motivation for learning did not differ significantly according to the contents of the activities.

Fig. 3-11 What was Required in the Experiential Activities
("Yes" + "Yes, to a degree" [%])

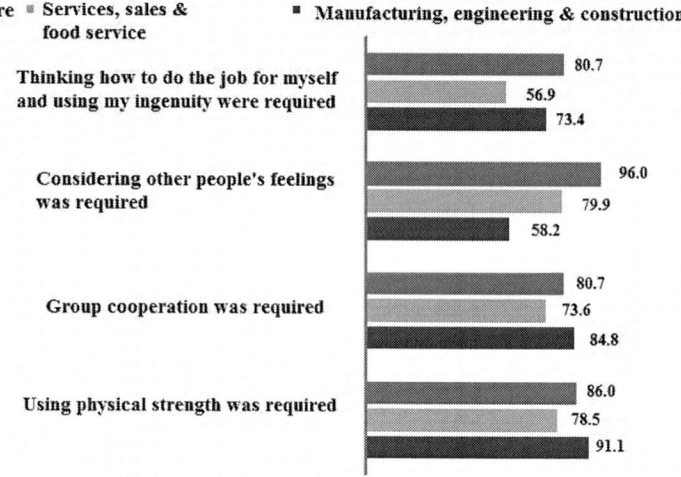

Fig. 3-12 Students' Findings from the Experiential Activities
("Yes" + "Yes, to a degree" [%])

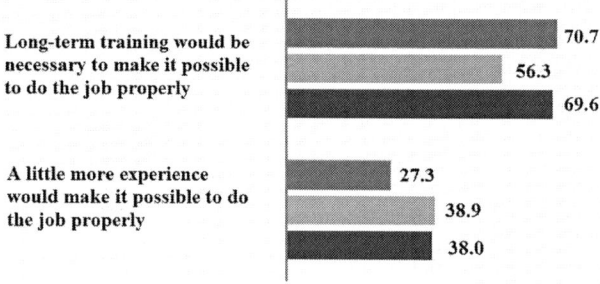

Interviewee A: It's important to provide an opportunity for the kids to work, and more than that, it's also important for them to learn how to act in society—to learn about social norms. It doesn't seem like most kids really know how to act anymore. Parents don't do anything about it, and more and more kids expect their parents to do everything for them and don't think about trying to learn that kind of thing by themselves. We have to encourage them to want to try.

In our interviews, it was only once that we heard the view that the activities that the students participate in under the learning through work experience programme help to provide information about a job. Rather, these activities are expected to promote communications between parents and their children by providing young people with opportunity to get a feel for the real world and gain first-hand experience in society. Having the children gain experience on what a given job is like is not seen as the top priority.

Interviewer: The 14-Year-Old's Challenge Programme has two purposes. The first is to provide the opportunity for young people to gain the experience of working and the second is to provide them with the opportunity to have contact with adults other than their parents and teachers through work. Which of the two do you think is more important?

Interviewee I: Well, I would say the second, if I had to pick. If we're talking about engaging in a job… I think probably the schools' education policy places more emphasis on the second one. Having the kids be engaged in society, so to speak… It seems like the schools' policy is to broaden the kids' perspectives, of course to show them the right ways to behave in school and in their classes, but also to show them what the real world is like. That's what it seems like, anyway. Also—and I think a lot of the local businesses want this too—I really want to do something to keep an eye on them and help them grow, you know, to develop as people.

Interviewee C: Giving 14-year-olds their first opportunity to have contact with working people… I'm not real sure, but I guess that's one of the purposes. It seems like the goal is to get the students not just to talk with other students and teachers but to communicate with working people, not so much to get them to learn how to do a job. What's important is giving them that experience.

(2) Problem 1: Insufficient Labour: the problems related to the implementation of activities, which were identified on the basis of frank opinions expressed by local businesses, can be divided into two categories: problems that are inevitable for activities undertaken by 14-year-old junior high school students and problems that could be improved upon if some measures are taken.

A decrease in business efficiency is a problem that cannot be avoided when junior high school students are accepted into the workplace under the supervision of an instructor.[15] In Toyama Prefecture, many of the local businesses that accept students under the programme are small and medium-size companies with relatively small workforces, and the activities presumably impose a significant burden on such companies. However, in most cases, this problem was overcome because of the goodwill of local businesses that believed in the importance of the effects of learning through work experience.

Interviewee D: Teachers will ask us if their students are doing it right. But, frankly speaking, there's no way that they can be doing it right. We wouldn't be able to accept students if we didn't allow for the fact that this is learning through work experience. It's been 14 or 15 years since this programme started, but it wasn't until a few years ago that our employees started to be willing to really accept the students. No matter how you look at it, it's just faster for us to do the work ourselves.

Another inevitable problem is that although the business establishments would like to have students engage in jobs useful as experiential activities, it is difficult to do so because they cannot afford to allow product quality to deteriorate from the perspective of their commercial interests. Consequently, students tend to be assigned to do peripheral jobs—which are not directly related to business—such as cleaning and dish washing, and this tendency is particularly notable in the manufacturing industry.

Interviewee H: First of all, we took care to ensure—if I may say so— that the quality of our products would not change. We were also careful to prevent the kids from sustaining any injuries.

Interviewee C: To tell the truth, I know that the kids want to work with a hammer and nails while the carpenters supervise them. But if we let them do that and our customers see it, it would turn into a big thing about "How could you be letting kids do that!" I guess they used to let the kids do it, wearing a helmet and all. So we at least let them wear the helmets this time, too. I couldn't believe how happy it made them to put on those helmets. So they wore their helmets and we had them clean up a bit, and this and that. But I don't think that letting them work with a hammer and nails would be a very good idea. We're talking about products that customers are going to buy, so that's asking a little too much.

---

[15] Toyama Prefecture requires the local businesses to appoint an instructor to supervise junior high school students accepted into the workplace. One person we interviewed stated that compensation ranging from several hundred yen to 1,000 yen is paid to the supervisor. The precise amount of compensation was not revealed.

(3) Problem 2: Poor Communications: the problem cited most frequently in interviews with business establishments was poor communication with the students' parents. In both Areas X and Y, junior high schools prepare notebooks for the students to use specifically for the activities under the programme. These notebooks list matters related to directions to be provided to students before and after the programme. It also contains a section for students to write down what they did each day and a section for comments by the instructors and the parents. However, in the worst cases of neglect, the notebooks were crumpled, with nothing written in them. When the students and parents take this attitude, it discourages the receiving businesses.

Interviewee C: I want them to make sure that the students understand what it means for them to participate in the 14-Year-Old's Challenge Programme and what they need to do as a part of it. And I want the students to communicate with their parents. The kids bring the notebook to record their activities every day and the instructors go to all the trouble of writing down an explanation of the activities on that day, but the section for the parents' comments often comes back blank. I just can't understand it.

It has also been pointed out that since surveys of the business establishments conducted by the schools after the activities are completed have become a nothing more than a formality, the problems pointed out by the local businesses are not reflected in future activities. From this, we may presume that state of communications between the local businesses, families, and schools is poor. The poor state of communications was indicated by the comment that the 14-Year-Old's Challenge Programme has become a matter of formality and by the doubt expressed about the significance of the activities under the programme.

Interviewee D: Every year, I'm more and more at a loss about how the kids really feel. There are things that I can't tell, like whether they appreciate the experience of doing a job or whether they understand how difficult it is. I know it's partially because there's a bigger age gap between me and them every year, but they seem to be apathetic about these things, whereas every year I become more aware of these changes in the kids. So I wonder whether the fact that they become quicker at doing a job or better at selling products is really an effect of the 14-Year-Old's Challenge Programme.

4. Conclusion

The 14-Year-Old's Challenge Programme in Toyama Prefecture started as part of community-wide efforts to help children's development, as importance was placed on giving children the opportunity to get the feel of society and to gain first-hand experience in it through learning through work experience programme. Implementation of out-of-school activities is regarded as a change in how educational activities should be conducted and as a positive development. This is evidenced by what we have heard through interviews with local businesses, such as that children should grow through community-wide efforts and that it is good for students to form relationships with people with whom they usually do not have contact. Local businesses expected not that these activities would lead directly to future career choice or career plans, but that it would help to facilitate smooth communications between parents and their children by providing the opportunity for students to get the feel of society and gain first-hand experience in the real world—even though the results may sometimes be disappointing for them because of poor communications between schools, business establishments, and parents. The 14-Year-Old's Challenge Programme in Toyama Prefecture is an activity that has been conducted as part of efforts to study how school education should be carried out from the viewpoint of "emphasising education".

Fundamentally, businesses operate based on a rationale that is different from that on which school activities are based, such as the realities of economic rationality and profitability. Nonetheless, local businesses have cooperated with the 14-Year-Old's Challenge Programme, because they see educational value in schools' efforts to improve the state of education. As schools and businesses have shared the idea that the purpose of activities under the programme is to raise children through community-wide efforts, no questions have been raised about the difference between the rationales of businesses and those of schools, nor about specific effects—such as acquisition of skills and improvement of the quality of labour. The efforts to reconfigure the 14-Year-Old's Challenge Programme from an educational activity implemented by the schools into a career education activity with a view to helping students' smooth transition to the labour market is directing attention to these issues, about which questions had not previously been raised.

In interviews with the local businesses, some of them pointed out that the role of this programme is limited to providing an opportunity for students to gain new experiences that they cannot have at school, rather than providing vocational training and increasing familiarity with jobs, because of the practical constraint that the programme is aimed at 14-year-old junior high school students. A decrease in work process efficiency caused by the acceptance of junior high school students into the workplace imposes a significant burden on the local businesses. In addition, although these businesses would like to have junior high school students engage in jobs that provide them with a useful experience if possible, the range of jobs that can be assigned to them are limited when considering their commercial interests. If the 14-Year-Old's Challenge Programme is to be positioned as an activity related to the vocational selection from the viewpoint of "work", it will be necessary to review how to evaluate the insufficient aspects of the programme, because of which the students are unable to be involved in a full share of the work. Through our survey, we identified a case in which a student who took part in activities at a construction company under the programme only engaged in cleanup of the site every day, and a case in which a student who participated in activities at a university did nothing more than keeping parked bicycles in order all day long. Of course, for some types of business, students cannot be allowed to do jobs that require special training, jobs that would bring them into contact with private information or those that may involve company secrets. As a result, their activities are limited to simple jobs, making it difficult for students to gain a variety of experiences and professional knowledge. This situation, which has been accepted from the viewpoint of placing an emphasis on education, that is, from the viewpoint of placing importance on having the students form relationships with people outside school, can no longer be easily tolerated from the viewpoint of placing an emphasis on "work", namely, from the viewpoint of stressing the effects of the activity on vocational selection. From now on, it will be necessary to consider how to enhance the contents of experiential activities.

Gaining the cooperation of business establishments with the programme is also an important task. Junior high school students have learned many things through these experiences, such as thinking about how to do a job for themselves, giving consideration to other people's feelings, and exercising their physical power, and found out that they would need education and training to do the job properly. It is evident that the programme has increased their interest in jobs and given them the motivation to learn. However, these results depended heavily on the goodwill of local businesses and their expectations about the educational effects of the experience as allowing children to feel and experience the real world and facilitating smooth communications between them and their parents. As a problem related to the programme, some local businesses have already pointed out the poor communication with parents and with schools. If the schools continue to rely on the local businesses' generosity, they may soon lose the community's support. In fact, some companies have refused to accept students due to the increased burden of the recession in recent years. While 95% of schools nationwide are now implementing some sort of experiential activities, business establishments that accept students have come to feel an increasing burden. Finding out how to reward cooperative businesses and how to secure the cooperation of the parents through appropriate communications will be the key to the success of learning through work experience activities.

In conclusion, the question bears raising: Is it possible to set specific benchmarks and goals for junior high school students in terms of their view of career and work? In Japan, where almost all students who complete junior high school continue their educations, to answer this question, it will be necessary to overcome the difference between the perspective of placing an emphasis on "education" and that of placing an emphasis on "work," and to discuss in detail what kind of activities junior high school students should engage in under this programme and for what purpose.

References

Guidance and Counselling Research Centre, National Institute for Educational Policy Research. 2002. *Jido seito no shokugyokan, rodokan wo hagukumu kyoiku no suishin ni tsuite* [Promotion of education fostering school children's view of career and work]. Tokyo: Guidance and Counselling Research Centre, NIER. http://www.nier.go.jp/shido/centerhp/sinro/sinro.htm (accessed November 25, 2010).

—. 2005. *Shokuba taiken, intanshippu ni kansuru jigyosho chosa, chosa gaiyo (sokuho-ban)* [Outline of the survey of business establishments about learning through work experience programmes and internships (preliminary version)]. Tokyo: Guidance and Counselling Research Centre, NIER. http://www.nier.go.jp/shido/centerhp/intern/jigyosyo.pdf (accessed November 25, 2010).

—. 2008. *Heisei 19 nendo shokuba taiken, intanshippu jisshi jokyoto chosa kekka (gaiyo)* [Survey on the implementation of learning through work experience programmes and internships in fiscal 2007 (Outline)]. Tokyo: Guidance and Counselling Research Centre, NIER. http://www.nier.go.jp/shido/centerhp/ i-ship/h19i-ship.pdf (accessed November 25, 2010).

Hiroaki, M., M. Omichi, M. Nagasu, Y. Morota, K. Tuburai, Y. Hori, and R. Kosugi. 2000. *Kosotsu mugyosha no kyoiku shakaigakuteki kenkyu* [Study on unemployed high school graduates from the perspectives of education and sociology]. a report funded by the Fiscal 1999-2000 Science Research Subsidy (Basic Research) (c) (2).

Honda, Y. 2005. *Wakamono to shigoto: "Gakko keiyu no shushoku" wo koete* [Youth and work: Beyond "employment via school"]. Tokyo: University of Tokyo Press.

Kariya T., K. Tsuburai, M. Nagasu, and M. Inada. 1997. "Shinro mikettei no kozo: Kosotsu shinro miketteisha no sekishutsu mekanizumu ni kansuru jisshoteki kenkyu" [The rise of uncertain future plans among Japanese high school students], *Bulletin of the Graduate School of Education, the University of Tokyo,* No. 37:45-76.

Kosugi, R. 2003. *Furita to iu ikikata* [The freeter's way of living]. Tokyo: Sokei Shobo.

—. 2005. *Frita to nito* [Freeters and NEETs]. Tokyo: Sokei Shobo.

—. ed. 2002. *Jiyu no daisho: Furita—Gendai wakamono no shugo ishiki to kodo* [The price of freedom: Freeters—Modern youth's perception of employment and behaviour]. Tokyo: The Japan Institute for Labour Policy and Training.

Mimura, T. 2004. *Kyaria kyoiku nyumon: Sono riron to jissen no tameni* [The basics of career education: Theories and practices]. Tokyo: Jitsugyo no Nnihonsha.

Ministry of Education, Culture, Sports, Science and Technology. (2008). "Kodomo no sodachi wo meguru genjoto ni kansuru detashu" [Collection of data related to the current circumstances surrounding childrearing]. Ministry of Education, Culture, Sports, Science and Technology. http://www.mext.go.jp/b_menu/shingi/chousa/shotou/053/shiryo/__icsFiles/afieldfile/2009/03/09/1236114_3.pdf 2009/05/01 (accessed November 26, 2010).

National Institute for Educational Policy Research, ed. 2007. *Kyaria kyoiku e no shotai* [Invitation to career education]. Tokyo: Toyokan Shuppansha.

Terasaki, S, and M. Hiroaki. 2007. *Chugakusei no shorai tenbo to shokugyo ishiki ni kansuru chosha: gaiyo* [Survey on junior high school students' outlooks on the future and job consciousness (outline)]. Tokyo: Ochanomizu University, Faculty of Letters and Education, communication system development programme office.

CHILD LABOUR IN TUNISIA: LAW AND REALITY

SALMA KHALED SLAMA

1. Introduction

With a view to boosting the national economy and attracting foreign investments, lawmakers in Tunisia have designed a set of provisions to support international commerce and encourage investors from other countries to operate in different sectors—particularly in the industrial sector[1]—at a domestic level. Therefore, legislative measures regulating foreign investment provided a significant contribution to tackling unemployment in that they helped to create job opportunities. To this end, and as a way to fight poverty, social exclusion, and joblessness, the legislator introduced fiscal incentives in the form of tax exemptions to promote investment primarily into rural and poorer regions of the country.

It should be noted, however, that unemployment is above all a social issue affecting the community at large.

The employment situation worsened following the international financial crisis, which aggravated economic difficulties of some companies, to such an extent that they had no alternative but to dismiss their employees, causing national unemployment rates to rise. However, such a state of affairs cannot explain the fact that another major issue, namely child labour, is given scant consideration.

Child labour, which is regarded as an international matter, led national governments to implement more stringent rules on the employment of minors. In spite of this, children are increasingly exposed to poor conditions arising from the social, economic, and political situation in their countries.

According to the International Labour Organization (ILO) one child out of four is engaged in various forms of work, and ten million are exploited,

---

[1] Promulgation of the Investment Incentives code by Law No. 1993 (120) of 27 December 1993.

the victims of practices such as: slavery, debt bondage, prostitution, pornography, forced recruitment for armed conflict, drug trafficking, and other illicit and hazardous activities, which are also demeaning to minors.

More specifically, the ILO Global Report *Accelerating Action Against Child Labour*,[2] reported that 215 million children are still engaged in child labour worldwide. The ILO is one of the leading organisations committed to fight child labour (in this context the challenge is to eliminate child work by 2016), and the report argued that the persistence of child labour is an indicator of the ineffectiveness of measures in terms of development efforts.[3]

At an international level, in order to regulate child labour, several provisions have been set forth,[4] particularly after the ILO follow-up. In this sense, the most important are Convention No. 138 concerning the Minimum Age for Admission to Employment (1973),[5] and Convention No. 182 regarding the Worst Forms of Work (1999).[6]

Traditionally, children in Tunisia work during their summer vacation to help their families, to earn extra pocket money, or to buy school equipment in order to attend school, with some others who are engaged in family-owned farm businesses, mainly in rural areas.

On the contrary, some children are forced to work at a very early age— notwithstanding that education is compulsory between the ages of 6 and 16—in order to help their families to meet their basic needs.[7]

---

[2] ILO. 2010a. *Accelerating Action against Child Labour.* ILO Report, International Labour Conference 99th session. Geneva: ILO. www.ilo.org/wcmsp5/groups/public/@dgreports/@dcomm/documents/publication/ wcms_126752.pdf (accessed November 5, 2010).

[3] Ibid.

[4] Convention No. 6 regarding night work of children in the industry field (1919), Convention No. 16 regarding medical control of children and youth working on boats (1921), Convention No. 58 regarding minimum age of work in the maritime sector (1936), Convention No. 59 regarding the minimum age in industry (1937), Convention No. 77 regarding the medical control of children and youth working in industry (1946), Convention No. 90 regarding night work of children in industry as amended in 1948, and Convention No. 112 dealing with minimum age for fishermen (1959),

[5] Ratified on 10 July 1995, Law No. 62/1995, Official Journal of the Tunisian Republic, No. 13 of 13 February 1996.

[6] Ratified on 24 January 2000, Law No. 1/2000, Official Journal of the Tunisian Republic, No. 8 of 28 January 2000.

[7] Guidance Law No. 80/2002 on school education issued on 23 July 2002, Official Journal of the Tunisian Republic, No. 62, issued on 30 July 2002.

In this connection, child labour is the result of poor living conditions[8] and not a deliberate choice, with children who are obliged to work by their parents and against their will.

Money is the only aspect that matters and children are subject to conditions of forced labour. In many cases, girls are required to move from rural areas to work as housekeepers—or are trafficked for such work—while boys are usually employed in the industry sector, or are sent out to the streets to beg.[9]

At a national level, and in an awareness of the need to provide children with *ad-hoc* protection, as regarded as a resource in both social and economic terms, the legislator has adopted and ratified the conventions mentioned above regarding child labour, in order to transpose into national legislation measures advocated by international institutions and bring them into line with standards of other developing countries. This is necessary to provide children with higher levels of protection—particularly when engaging in work—and to tackle their economic and sexual exploitation. The harmonisation of national and international legislation represents the starting point of an emerging country in this connection.

The increased focus on human rights on the part of the government is evident also if one considers that Tunisia has implemented the Convention on the Rights of the Child,[10] recognising the right of children to education, which is compulsory until a certain age and free for all citizens, also forbidding their economic exploitation as compromising their physical, mental and social development.

In the same vein, Tunisia was the first Arab country to promulgate a Code of Child Protection[11] which safeguards children and ensure the apt development over their life.

A definition of *child* is adopted in Art. 3 of the Code, which makes provision also against economic and sexual exploitation (Art. 25 and Art.

---

[8] Note that, according to the National Institute of Statistics, indicators of poverty in Tunisia have increased from 33% in 1967 to 33.8% in 2007.

[9] Hindman, D. H., ed. 2009. *The World of Child Labor: an Historical and Regional Survey*. New York: M. E. Sharpe, Inc.

[10] Convention on the Rights of the Child signed on 20 November 1989, ratified on 29 November 1991. Law No. 1991-92 issued on Official Journal of the Tunisian Republic, No. 82 issued on 3 December 1991.

[11] Worldwide, Tunisia is the 5th country adopting the Child Protection Code, after Canada, Belgium, Norway and Sweden.

26 of the Code of Child Protection),[12] according to which a child is "any person aged under 18 who has not yet reached the age of majority and protected by special provisions".[13]

With reference to the Labour Code, the definition of child is not provided, even though special legal protection is ensured particularly to children classified as workers.

Following this line of reasoning, children engaged in work are covered with legal protection especially considering their immaturity and lack of expertise.[14]

Child labour is a major issue worldwide, the seriousness of which differs from one country to another, also depending on relevant legislation—civil, labour, penal and human rights law and rules currently in force at a national level.

In Tunisia, the main problem is concerned with being aware of main instruments to deal with such an issue.

In view of the above, the way child labour is regulated at a national level will be further discussed in the first part of this paper, with the second part which will deal with child labour infringements.

1. Child Labour: An Issue Regulated by Law

The ratification of Convention No.138 concerning minimum age for admission to employment required the national government to conform domestic legislation to international provisions. In this connection, Art. 1 of Convention specifies that:

> Each Member for which this Convention is in force undertakes to pursue a national policy designed to ensure the effective abolition of child labour and to raise progressively the minimum age for admission to employment or work to a level consistent with the fullest physical and mental development of young persons.

With a view to fulfil such international commitment, and also by adopting a number of codes, Tunisian lawmakers tried to tighten up child

---

[12] Bardel, E. 2010. *L'exploitation sexuelle et commerciale des enfants: un fléau mondial*. Paris: L'Harmattan.

[13] It should be noted that the age of majority under Tunisian law was 20 years. After the passing of Law No. 2010 (39) issued on 26 July 2010, it has been reduced to 18 years.

[14] Mzid, N. 1996. "La protection de l'enfant en droit du travail Tunisien," *Etudes Juridiques*, No. 4:65.

labour laws. In addition, they also laid down a series of legislative measures in order to comply with objectives set out in the Convention in terms of education and employability. Both these points will be investigated in detail.

1.1 The Regulation of Child Labour through the Labour Code: Child Protection Code and Penal Provisions

The regulation of child labour involves different branches of law, even though most aspects are governed by provisions laid down in the Labour Code, with the Child Protection Code that makes provision for children as regarded as "human being".

In addition, both the Penal and the Labour Code laid down penal sanctions in the event of failing to comply with such rules.

1.1.1 Protection of Child Labour through the Labour Code

The regulation of child labour under the Labour Code provides protection at various levels and is based on legal principles applied at an international level. The law usually protects minors either at the time of recruitment and while performing their working activity, primarily to safeguard their moral and physical development.

Protection over the Recruitment Process

Minimum working age is set up by law, with the employer who has to fulfil certain obligations at the time of hiring individuals under the age of 16.

-Minimum age for employment

In order to comply with international standards, and pursuant to Convention No. 138, according to which minimum working age should not be below 15 years old, lawmakers in Tunisia have introduced minimum age for admission to employment at a national level, that is 16 years old.[15] This age requirement is higher than the one proposed by the ILO, as taking into consideration the end of compulsory education.

However, in developing countries, due to the fact that employers are in some cases under the obligation to employ children, the convention allows for the reduction or the raising of the minimum working age under certain

---

[15] Art. 2 (4) ILO Convention on the minimum age for employment.

circumstances. In this light, the law provides a number of exceptions at national level, especially considering that minimum age for employment is often dependent on the field of employment. For instance, with a view to protect children in health, physical and moral terms, the legislator has raised minimum working age for underground work (Art. 77 LC).

The legislator has also reduced such age to 13 years old in the event of "light work", provided that it does not endanger children's health, nor affect their performance at school.

In this connection, Art. 56 of the Labour Code provides more stringent measures for the protection of their working conditions, allowing the child to perform light work-related tasks for two hours a day, and setting forth that for those aged between 13 and 16 years, working time should not exceed 7 hours a day, including school hours. In addition, pursuant to this article, children are not allowed to work on public holidays and during weekly rest times.[16]

The legislator also regulates activities carried out by children at school or within an educational institution, also taking account of their ability to fulfil such tasks as a part of vocational training. In this case, children aged under 16 are authorised to work. More generally, as discussed earlier, Art. 53 (2) provides some exceptions in terms of minimum working age.

In reference to family firms, children under the age of 16 can be employed provided that they are operating under the supervision of their parents/legal tutors. In the event that, due to its characteristics, the task to be performed by the child might jeopardise his/her health and moral integrity, the working activity should be carried out only at the age of 18 (Article 54 No. LC), even though the law does not specify the activity in question.

In the agriculture sector, children aged 13 can be engaged in light work only if it is not dangerous in terms of health and morals, and if it does not interfere with their education (Art. 55 LC). Derogations to light work are the result of the national social context, as child labour is widespread in rural areas, and, as we have seen, mainly in the agricultural sector.

Bearing this in mind, it is important to note that the legislator in Tunisia made an attempt to conform to international standards, with employers who need to strictly comply with the law at the time of hiring a minor or a child.

---

[16] Art. 57 provides that the inspection body can authorise the child to participate in public events and take part in shows, for cultural, scientific and educational purposes.

-Recruitment procedures
Such procedures include: medical examination, an authorisation released by an inspection body and the collection and storing of personal data.

-Medical examination
International Convention No. 77—concerning Medical Examination for Fitness for Employment in Industry of Children and Young Persons— and Convention No. 78—Medical Examination of Children and Young Persons for Fitness for Employment in Non-Industrial Occupations— require children to undergo medical check-ups in order to assess their fitness to perform the assigned working activity.

In an awareness of the fact that children are at a considerable disadvantage and more exposed to health risks due to their lack of physical strength, the national government envisaged similar provisions on compulsory medical examination in an *ad-hoc* section of the Labour Code (Art. 61 to 63 (2) LC).

Art. 61 specifies that employers are under the obligation to attest to the health status of individuals aged under 18 years old by means of a full check-up, the results of which need to be included in a medical certificate.

In this sense, Art. 60 sets forth that an inspection can be carried out by authorised bodies on their own initiative in order to assess children's ability to work, and they might even ban them from working if deemed to be unfit for work. As for the medical certificate, it should provide relevant information regarding specific working conditions if a specific task needs to be fulfilled on a temporary basis.[17]

-Authorisation
In some sectors, a statement issued by the inspection authority certifying the medical condition of children is required. This is, for instance, the case of those employed in the film industry or performing in public shows, as laid down by Art. 57 of LC. In this sense, Art. 58 also provides that such authorisation is mandatory for individuals aged under 16, regardless of the sector of industry they are engaged in.

-Registration
In compliance with provisions on child labour laid down by the Labour Code, employers are required to maintain a register indicating the name

---

[17] Art. 61 (3), par. 4 of LC provides that the employer must keep track of information about employees' medical conditions (e.g. the medical certificate) and make it available to labour inspections.

and the date of birth of employees under 18, specifying information about the nature of their work, the number of working hours and rest periods.

This also applies to employees engaged in non-agricultural work (Art. 73 LC). This register is helpful to competent authorities in that it allows them to monitor children and their working conditions, and to safeguard their physical and mental development. In other fields, such protection is also ensured by medical examination carried out on a regular basis, or by more stringent regulation regarding night work.

Children and Health Protection

With a view to focus on health and safety of children and provide them with higher levels of protection, the law specifies that children cannot be engaged in work regarded as hazardous (Art. 54-55-58 of LC). Order issued on 15 January 2000 by the Ministry of Social Affairs includes a list of jobs classified as dangerous for children, such as underground work in mines and quarries, or work involving the handling of explosive materials and exposure to pesticides.[18]

The order also makes provision for medical examination to be carried out frequently. The check-up is usually conducted until the age of 18 (Art. 62 of LC) or even 21, depending on the case (Art. 63 of LC).

As regards children, Tunisian Labour Code also regulates working hours (Art. 56 of LC) and night work. In this sense, International Convention No. 79 concerning the Restriction of Night Work of Children and Young Persons in Non-Industrial Occupations, sets forth that children are banned from working at night time. Since Tunisia has not ratified the convention, the legislator has imposed a maximum number of working hours for those aged under 14, who should not be employed at night for a period exceeding fourteen consecutive hours. This also applies to those aged between 14 and 18, for whom night work is forbidden. In both cases, rest periods are provided on annual basis.

Safeguarding Young Workers' Morals

With reference to their moral rights, the law provides substantial safeguards for children while working, particularly for those aged under 16.

In the same vein, employers are required to comply with some moral standards if employing an apprentice. Art. 347 and Art. 348 of LC specify that they are not allowed to hire children if they are divorced or unmarried,

---

[18] Khemekhem, R. 2009. *L'enfant et le droit pénal.* Tunis, 201.

and some of them should not employ an apprentice, particularly if they have been imposed penal sanctions for a violation of moral duties.

Order issued on 15 January 2000 provides *inter alia* a list of working activities which might jeopardise the morals of young workers, notably those performed in pubs or night clubs, or where alcoholic liquors are distilled and manufactured. The seriousness of this issue is also confirmed by International Convention No.182 regarding the Worst Forms of Work of 1999, according to which such forms of employment are those whose nature might harm the morals of children.

Labour inspectors are in charge of verifying the implementation of provisions laid down by the Labour Code, and of carrying out investigations so as to prevent abuse and discriminatory practices against children at work, with the Ministry of Social Affairs, Solidarity and Tunisians Abroad that conducted some 3,000 labour inspections in 2008.[19] It seems worth pointing out that, apart from *ad-hoc* protection measures for children involved in working activities laid down by the Labour Code, substantial safeguards are ensured to all children by the Child Protection Code.

1.1.2 Protection of Child Labour: the Child Protection Code

Provisions laid down in the Child Protection Code[20] are mainly concerned with the protection of human rights, therefore also applying to children engaged in employment. In this sense, Art. 20 of the Code sets out a list of "work situations" regarded as hazardous for such category of workers (abuse, sexual exploitation, engagement in organised crime, begging and so on), as well as a relevant sanctioning mechanism.

Children can be exposed to risks of this kind while performing their activity or be forced by intimidation to carry out some activities (e.g. begging). For this reason, Article 25 specifies that the following practices are to be considered illegal:
- sexual exploitation of children, be it free or remunerated;
- economic exploitation of children, such as organised begging.

Once recruited, the child runs the risk of being exposed to these dangerous situations, and to abuses on the part of the employer with a serious impact on his/her health and morals.

---

[19] US Embassy of the United States. 2009. *The Trafficking in Persons Report.* http://tunisia.usembassy.gov/dos_reports2/trafficking-in-persons-report--tunisia-2010.html, (accessed November 28, 2010).

[20] The Code includes an *ad-hoc* chapter regarding the "protection of the child in danger".

Further, many criminal organisations recruit children illegally as street vendors, or to take part in immoral activities such as pornography. However, a consolidated set of measures, as well as the work of competent authorities provide a significant contribution to stem child labour.

The so-called delegates, who are mandated to safeguard children in difficult conditions, perform the same functions as the judiciary police[21] in terms of law enforcement, in that they might take necessary measures if an infringement has been reported (Art. 30-31-32 of Child Protection Code). Furthermore, Art. 31 of the same Code obliges all persons—including those who are bound to professional secrecy—to report cases of violence which involve children and which might jeopardise their health, safety and moral integrity.[22] Notwithstanding such legal provisions, the importance placed in the role of family (Art. 95 to 106 of Child Protection Code), as well as in the sense of responsibility on the part of children, is still significant. On the basis of these considerations, a number of penal sanctions are laid down by both the Penal and the Labour Code with a view to ensure the implementation of such measures and provide children with effective protection.

1.1.3 The Protection of Child Labour: Penal Provisions

Both the Labour and Penal Code lay down provisions in the event of child labour violations, in order to protect child workers also from a legal point of view.

As regards the Labour Code, it sets forth that penal sanctions should be applied in the case of non-compliance with recruitment procedures relating to children, primarily in terms of medical records, the maintenance of the register, and the issuing of the authorisation by the competent authority. Art. 234 of the Labour Code provides for penalties, ranging from fines to imprisonment, for those violating these rules.

Art. 171 of the Penal Code also lays down penal sanctions for anyone recruiting a child as a beggar,[23] while Art. 132 introduces a sanction mechanism against organised crime. If child abuse or maltreatment is reported, the employer might be punished with imprisonment as follows:

---

[21] Decrees No. 96 to 1134 issued on 7 July 1996 regarding the status of the delegate of child protection.

[22] Medani, K. 1999. "Le devoir de signalement comme instrument de protection de L'Enfant," *Revue de Jurisprudence et de Législation*, No. 1:235-250.

[23] In this case, Art. 171 (3) of the Penal Code envisages imprisonment of up to 6 months.

- up to 10 years of imprisonment in the event of child detaining and abduction;
- up to 2 years of imprisonment for forced child begging;
- up to 5 years of imprisonment for forced prostitution of women and children (Art. 220 to 250 of the Penal Code).

Apart from the foregoing legislative measures, a number of policies have been put in place to combat child labour dealing with education and employability.

1.2 The Regulation of Child Labour: Actions Enhancing Education and Employability

Both the Tunisian Constitution and the Child Protection Code recognise the right of all children to education. In this sense, the national government puts forward a set of legal provisions aimed at reforming the educational system and fostering youth employability, regarded as key factors to reduce child labour.

Improvements, mainly in terms of facilities, have been envisaged in Tunisia, to facilitate access to education, which is compulsory from the age of 6 to 16.

According to a 2009 report released by the Tunisian Observatory for Information, Training and Documentation on the Rights of the Child, schooling rates for children aged 6 have risen since 1997, reaching more than 97.2% in 2009, as well as for those aged 6 to 11 (97.7%).[24]

In order to create a knowledge-sharing culture, the government set up clubs, integrated, and computer training centres for young people and children, with the number of those attending such clubs amounting to 178,000 in 2009, according to the report mentioned earlier.

In addition to the setting up of facilities of this kind, the legislator also took action in terms of social protection. To this end, a number of recreation centres (so-called *cells of social actions*) and educational bodies have been created which cooperate with public schools and colleges to provide assistance to children who face difficulty of any kind (e.g. child workers who are exploited by their employer). In 2009, there were 2,371 cells located all over the country.

---

[24] Decree No. 2002 (327) issued on 14 February 2002, regarding the setting-up of the Tunisian Observatory for Information, Training and Documentation on the Rights of the Child, amended by Decree No. 2003 (1359) issued on 16 June 2003. For further reference on the Observatory activities, see www.observatoire-enfance.nat.tn.

In the same vein, several counselling centres have been created within schools in order to help children and young students to deal with certain matters, particularly sexual abuse and drug addiction. Those cells carry out a pivotal role in preventing early school leaving and juvenile delinquency.

In order to promote a better interplay between family, students and educational bodies, and reduce and analyse the phenomenon of dropping out, a number of meetings are convened by the union of women teachers. Over the meetings, members of the union discuss the issue with early school leavers and their families in order to reintegrate them into school.[25]

Another remarkable initiative is the setting-up of so-called *Centres for the Defence and Social Integration* (CDSI), the aim of which is to support children involved in difficult situations, particularly early school leavers, and help them to enter specialised schools. Such centres also investigate reasons behind delinquency and social maladjustment of young people, and here children are provided with psychological support and vocational training.

There are, however, other institutions that provide a similar service— e.g. *The Social Counselling Centre*—which take care of street children usually in the 6 to 12 age group, who have been deprived of family support and protection,[26] offering them education and training opportunity.

The Integrated Centre for youth and children[27] helps those aged between 6 and 18 already engaged in educational and training programmes, while *The Centre for Child Social Protection*[28] provides support to those involved in dangerous situations, pursuant to Art. 20 of the Child Protection Code.[29]

A number of bodies overseeing the activities of education providers have been also set up, such as the Superior Council of Childhood,[30] the National Institute of Child Protection, and the Observatory for Information, Training and Documentation on the Rights of the Child.

Regardless of specific functions carried out by these centres, the legislator made an attempt to regulate training and the entry of young

---

[25] These measures proved successful, as statistics show that 22 out of 54 students go back to school.

[26] Located in the delegation of Douar Hicher, Tunis, this centre was set up in 1999.

[27] Decree No. 99 (2796), issued on 13 December 1999.

[28] Decree No. 2007 (2875) of 12 November 2007.

[29] Gueldich, H. 2009. "Le traitement des mineurs victimes en Tunisie," *Revue de Jurisprudence et de Législation,* No. 12:97-126. Lahmar, I. 2009. "La protection de l'enfant en droit Tunisien," [in Arabic] *Revue de Jurisprudence et de Législation,* No. 12:27-51.

[30] Decree No. 2002 (574) of 12 March 2002.

workers into the workforce in order to safeguard their rights. Accordingly, the Labour Code sets forth that apprenticeship contracts should apply to children over the age of 15 (Art. 346 of LC). With a view to facilitating young entrants, Law issued on 1981[31] and subsequently amended also promotes their recruitment as trainees, with employers who are entitled to certain exemptions—in terms of social security contributions—and are also awarded grants to help cover the costs of the training period.[32]

Generally speaking, the importance of vocational and education training centres, as well as of private education providers—as pointed out also in relevant national guidelines—is significant in that 50% of early school leavers enrol in such institutions, thus reducing the number of child workers.

Equally remarkable is the role of public authorities—especially among female students living in rural areas—as they raise awareness of gaining adequate education as an instrument to promote individual rights.

The issue of child labour is closely connected to young workers' integration in the labour market in that they should be properly trained in order to have the right to fair remuneration[33] and provide higher levels of productivity.

2. Infringements of Child Labour Law

Despite the binding nature of legislation relating to the employment of children—which imposes various restrictions on employers with the aim to protect young workers—a considerable number of violations—also of children's rights—have been reported, due to socio-economic reasons and to the fact that such provisions are poorly enforced.

2.1 Socio-Economic Context and Child Labour: The Informal Labour Market

As discussed earlier, countries characterised by widespread child labour, Tunisia's case, are usually low-income economies plagued with unemployment and poverty.

---

[31] Law No. 81-75 issued on 9 August 1981 regarding the promotion of youth employment, as subsequently amended by Law No. 93 (17) issued on 22 February 1993.

[32] Art. 1 of Law No. 81-75 issued on 9 August 1981 mentioned above.

[33] For further details, please refer to the inter-agencies report from the ILO World Conference on Child Labor 2010.

At a national level, notwithstanding considerable efforts made to reduce unemployment and promote education and vocational training—which led to a decrease in the poverty rate—child work remains a major social issue that can be solved with a change of mentality and a rise in overall levels of education.

Such form of employment is usually under-qualified, low paid and with no prospects in terms of career advancement, as the aim of the employers is to maximise profits and minimise costs.

They tend to hire children fully aware of violating provisions on minimum working age and working conditions, with young workers who are often in danger of being economically and sexually exploited.

In this connection, in a survey carried out in 2002, *Compulsory versus Voluntary Remittances: Evidence from Tunisia* (Dostie and Vencatachellum 2002), it was argued that

> more than half of the domestic workers are younger than 18 years of age, and most migrated from the poorest region of the country. Most young domestic workers live with their employer and have their full wages remitted directly to their parents by their employer.

This is a form of compulsory remittance, which, as discussed above, is strictly connected with poverty and child labour. The study also demonstrated that 75% of girls employed as domestic workers entered the labour market before reaching 16 years old, thus clearly infringing the relevant law, particularly provisions laid down by the Labour Code and ILO Convention No. 138 on minimum age for employment. This holds true if one considers that 40% of domestic workers were 12 years old at the time of their recruitment. In addition, compulsory remittances also demonstrate that the spread of child labour is associated with a family's poor economic conditions.

According to the *Trafficking in persons Report 2009* elaborated by the US Embassy in Tunisia, a number of girls have been trafficked for domestic servitude. In addition, another survey carried out in 2008 on 130 domestic workers in Tunis stated that 52% of them were under the age of 16, while 23% reported to be victim of physical violence, and 11% of sexual violence. Some 99% also declared that they were hired illegally and that they were underpaid.

The recruitment of domestic workers, which violates children rights, is one of the most traditional practices in Tunisia.

Since such practice is regarded as illegal, with the hiring of youth workers not complying with relevant provisions[34] children are not included in the register of employees, and employers are often reluctant to provide information and answer questions about them. Furthermore, people are usually unwilling to report illegal child labour practices and relevant cases heard by the judge are not made public. The Ministry of Social Affairs pointed out that no cases of exploitation or forced child labour were reported in Tunisian courts in 2008. In the following year, a woman was sentenced to three years of imprisonment after being found guilty of physically abusing a seven year-old girl[35] and forcing her to domestic servitude. This was the only case of exploitative child labour reported in 2009. These are the reasons why, to the best of our knowledge, no national statistics have been collected about child labour, with the report presented by the Observatory for Information, Training, Documentation and Studies on the Rights of the Child which is significant in this connection, as providing reliable data on children who are at risk of being exploited.

Figures were released on the most serious forms of abuse, such as: sexual abuse, economic exploitation, forced begging, involvement in criminal matters, and so on.

In order to give an idea of the seriousness of such problem, it should be worth mentioning the number of children abuses reported in 2009, which were distributed as follows: 78 in Tunis, the capital; 95 in Bizert (a city in the North of Tunis), and 79 in Sfax (a city located in the South of the country, and regarded as the economic capital of Tunisia). Tunis also reported the highest number of children sexual exploitation (32), with the number of child beggars and economically exploited children which was also significant (87 cases), especially in Jendouba (12 cases).[36]

Since 2005, the number of cases of children regarded as being at risk, reported by child protection delegates, increased from 3,821 to 7,938 cases (notifications for the year 2009 were 8,272) with a rise also in the number of relevant judicial cases, amounting to 2,277 in 2008/2009.

In considering the factors mentioned above, it can be stated that child labour is a real issue to deal with at a national level. Solutions put forward tackle this question should be aimed at strengthening current legislation and designing adequate training facilities for young people.

---

[34] This takes place despite Law No. 2002(32), setting forth that the employer is under the obligation to register domestic workers for social security.

[35] Art. 218 of the Penal Code: Violence with Premeditation.

[36] To the best of our knowledge, no information has been provided on whether children involved in such dangerous situations were workers or not.

2.2 Child Protection: The Weakness of Legal Provisions

In Tunisia, employers take advantage of weaknesses and shortcomings affecting child labour laws. This holds true if one examines data on compliance with such provisions, the application of criminal penalties, the legal vacuum sometimes people operate in, and the lack of awareness of the issue on the part of the population.

- Penal Sanctions
Both the Labour and the Penal Code lay down criminal penalties, which are applied for violations of child labour rules, even though they are not sufficiently stringent.

Art. 234 of the Labour Code provides for a fine ranging from 12.60 to 31.50 Euro, in cases of non-compliance with rules on the employment of children in terms of minimum working age and medical examinations, as well as economic exploitation and begging.

Apart from not being in line with principles on child labour laid down at an international level and ratified by the Tunisian Government—in particular the optional Protocol to the Convention on the Rights of the Child regarding trafficking and exploitation of children in pornography and paedophilic matters[37] —the sum of money to be paid, however, is derisory, especially considering the seriousness of the offence. The same can be said of sanctions laid down by the Child Protection Code. Accordingly, the sanctioning mechanism should be reviewed, in order to ensure the effective implementation and enforcement of provisions relating to child labour.

---

[37] Tunisia has ratified this Protocol in 2002 by issuing Law No. 2002(42) on 7 May 2002 authorising the accession of the Republic of Tunisia to the two Optional Protocols annexed to the Convention on the Rights of the Child on the involvement of children in armed conflict and on the Sale of Children and Pornography depicting children, Official Journal of the Tunisian Republic, No. 37 issued on 5 May 2002.

- Compliance with Child Labour Rules

Compliance with child labour provisions is ensured, by both labour inspectors and child protection delegates, whose activity is overseen by the Ministry of Employment and the Ministry of Women's Affairs, Family, Children, and Elderly Persons, respectively.

Although facing considerable difficulty in terms of coordination, they also have to deal with problems associated with their presence across the country. There is a child protection delegate in each of the 24 districts, who are often supported by an assistant. However, the need to recruit additional staff members to cope with increased workload is becoming a matter of urgency. There are also complexities resulting from the limited number of labour inspectors, especially taking account of a rise in the percentage of companies which employ children and which are therefore more likely to escape inspections.

-The legal vacuum

The legislator set out significant legislative measures to tackle child labour and deal with this issue mainly in social terms. However, low legal protection is provided to children engaged in certain illegal activities (e.g. drug trafficking) as there is no *ad-hoc* legislation dealing with the employment of children in such activities.

For instance, law prohibiting drugs trade[38] issued in 1992 envisages penal sanctions for drug smugglings, and medical and psychological support for children engaged in this practice, only specifying that their involvement represents an aggravating circumstance (Art. 11).[39] However, sanctions in this connection are applied under the Labour and the Penal Code, which also prohibit the employment of minors in activities that could be detrimental for their morals and health.

- Issues in terms of attitudes:

In some regions of the country, negative attitudes and ignorance compromise the fight against child labour. There seems to be a lack of awareness of risks young workers are exposed to if engaged in illegal activities, which is associated with an unwillingness to report cases of sexual and economic exploitation involving children.

---

[38] Law No. 1992 (52) on Drugs issued on 18 May 2002, Official Journal of The Tunisian Republic, No. 33 dated 26 May 2002, as amended by the Law No.1998-(104) issued on 30 November, 1998.

[39] Khemekhem, R. 2009. *L'enfant et le droit pénal*. Tunis.

Despite the provision of penal sanctions as laid down by Art. 118 and Art. 119 of the Child Protection Code, the obligation to notify delegates of situations putting children at risk is widely disregarded.

3. Conclusions and Recommendations

The present study attempted to demonstrate that child labour is a reality in all developing countries. The legislator tried to deal with it by improving and amending relevant legislation, promoting education and vocational training for early school leavers, and helping children to gain access to primary education in *ad-hoc* educational centres. As regarded as a middle income country by the World Bank, Tunisia also faces challenges in terms of high unemployment rates, particularly among young people and women.

Despite a more stringent set of rules, a number of infringements of both international and national provisions have been reported.

The government, although succeeding in safeguarding children's rights, still encounters significant difficulty in combating child labour. In effect, the promotion and the compulsory nature of education seem insufficient to discourage families from sending their children to work. For this reason, and despite the continuous effort on the part of the government, there is a need for a major overhaul of the protection mechanisms at various levels.

In Tunisia, the reduction and the monitoring of such a social issue are not merely a matter of law enforcement, also depending on actions taken to ameliorate the situation.

In this respect, public awareness campaigns should be conducted, in order also to attract media coverage on the issue. Further, more resources should be devoted to labour inspectors and delegates—also in terms of training—with the number of officers in charge of child labour monitoring that should be increased.

It is also advisable that institutions at both international and national level cooperate in order to ensure the implementation of universally recognised principles and the detection of main causes of children exploitation. The provision of more effective penal sanctions to be applied in cases of violations of child labour laws is also regarded as a matter of urgency.

It should be worth recalling in this connection that Tunisia did not sign the Memorandum of Understanding—unlike Morocco, Egypt, Togo, Nigeria and South Africa—to join the International Program on the Elimination of Child Labour.

Child labour is a wide-ranging issue affecting many countries, not only Tunisia. In general, the situation at a national level is not as critical as in Asia, where 153 million child workers have been estimated. In any case, children should be provided with high levels of protection, because, as is recalled in the Declaration of the Rights of the Child:
Mankind owes the child the best it has to give (Declaration of the Rights of the Child 1924).

References

Bardel, E. 2010. *L'exploitation sexuelle et commerciale des enfants: un fléau mondial*. Paris: L'Harmattan.

Dostie, B., and D. Vencatachellum. 2002. *Compulsory Versus Voluntary Remittances : Evidence From Tunisia*. Montreal: Institute of Applied Economies HEC-Montreal — Montréal University. www.aed.auf.org/IMG/pdf/B.Dositie1-D.V._pdf (accessed November 15 2010).

Embassy of the United States. 2009. *The Trafficking in Persons Report*. Embassy of the United States. http://tunisia.usembassy.gov/dos_reports2/trafficking-in-persons-report--tunisia-2010.html, (accessed November 28, 2010).

Gueldich, H. 2009. "Le traitement des mineurs victimes en Tunisie," *Revue de Jurisprudence et de Législation,* No. 12:97-126.

Hindman, D. H., ed. 2009. *The World of Child Labor: an Historical and Regional Survey*. New York: M. E. Sharpe, Inc.

ILO. 2010a. *Accelerating Action against Child Labour*. ILO Report, International Labour Conference 99th session. Geneva: ILO. www.ilo.org/wcmsp5/groups/public/@dgreports/@dcomm/documents/publication/wcms_126752.pdf (accessed November 5, 2010).

—. 2010b. *Joining Forces against Child Labour. Inter-agencies for The Hague Global Child Labour Conference of 2010.* The Hague-Geneva: ILO. www.ilo.org/ipecinfo/product/download.do?type=document&id=13333 (accessed November 6, 2010).

Khemekhem, R. 2009. *L'enfant et le droit pénal*. Tunis.

Lahmar, I. 2009. "La protection de l'enfant en droit Tunisien," [in Arabic] *Revue de Jurisprudence et de Législation*, No. 12:27-51.

Medani, K., 1999. "Le devoir de signalement comme instrument de protection de L'Enfant," *Revue de Jurisprudence et de Législation*, No. 1: 235-250.

Mzid, N. 1996. "La protection de l'enfant en droit du travail Tunisien," *Etudes Juridiques*, No. 4:65.

FROM SCHOOL TO WORK:
A COMPARATIVE STUDY OF LABOUR
CAPACITY DEVELOPMENT
BETWEEN THAILAND AND VIETNAM

PHASINA TANGCHUANG

1. Introduction[1]

Previous research carried out on the transition from school to work[2] in Thailand has further confirmed that education is the most important determinant of career success in industrialised countries.[3]

Fredriksen and Tan[4] provide evidence of an increasing awareness of the pivotal role of technical and vocational education in the dynamic economies of South East Asia (SEA) over the last two decades. In this light, employers primarily consider educational credentials in the recruitment process for specific tasks, with individuals investing in education in order to gain competitive advantage in the labour market. However, Muller and Shavit[5] and Raggatt and Williams[6] pointed out that

---

[1] I am very grateful to Dr Xavier Oudin, my best co-researcher, for his great contribution. My sincere thanks also go to the Royal Thai Embassy in Hanoi for proposing the need of the study and facilitating my trips, and to the TRF for providing financial support.
[2] Mounier, A., and P. Tangchuang. 2010a. "From Education to Work," in *Education and Knowledge in Thailand: The Quality Controversy*, (Chiang Mai: Silkworm Books).
[3] Muller, W., and Y. Shavit. 2003. "The Institutional Embeddedness of the Stratification Process," in *From School to Work: A Comparative Study of Educational Qualifications and Occupational Destinations,* (Oxford: Clarendon Press), 1.
[4] Fredriksen B., and T. J. Peng. 2008. *An African Exploration of the East Asian Education Experience (Development practice in education).* Washington: The World Bank.
[5] Muller, W., and Y. Shavit. 2003. "The Institutional Embeddedness of the Stratification Process," in *From School to Work: A Comparative Study of*

the role of education in occupational attainment varies if some aspects, such as when time series and societal factors are considered. In Europe, for instance, Finland is a developed country where students perform best in the Program for the International Student Assessment (PISA), and where the aim of education is to increase the percentage of people holding vocational or post-secondary qualifications among younger age groups (25-to-34 year-olds) from current 73% to 88% by 2020. This would mean that those with vocational and tertiary qualifications should account for 46% and 42% of the relevant age group respectively.[7] On the other hand, in Vietnam, a developing country in South East Asia (SEA) with the best students' performance at the Academic Olympic awards, the objectives in terms of educational attainment are:

- by the year 2020, to provide at least 60% of students aged 11 to 15 over the country with the opportunity to enter secondary school;

- to increase the levels of education in polytechnic institutes and vocationally-oriented schools, as well as further develop foreign language teaching and learning and computer literacy in secondary school;

- to raise to one million the number of people enrolled in training programmes per year, amounting to 25% of the trained labour force (which amounts to a 3% increase);

- to enhance by one-and-a-half times the levels of higher education produced in 1995, also in conformity with the main characteristics of the national labour force and economy.

The purpose of the present study is to provide a comparative analysis of the education systems in both Thailand and Vietnam with a view to *inter alia* investigate the instruments the two countries resorted to during the crisis to provide their labour force with effective skills, in order to deal with increasing competition and socio-economic growth at a global level. As located in the same community (Association of Southeast Asian Nations—ASEAN) Thailand and Vietnam labour force participation and

---

Educational Qualifications and Occupational Destinations, (Oxford: Clarendon Press), 1.
[6] Raggatt, P., and S. Williams. 2009. *Government, Markets and Vocational Qualifications: An Anatomy of Policy.* London: Falmer Press.
[7] RefastNet Finland. 2009. *VET in Europe – Country Report.* Cedefop, 15.

growth will also be examined especially in terms of differences related to political issues, education, and facilities.

2. The Concept of Labour Force Development

2.1 Definition

In the context of this paper, I make use of the expression *labour force development* to refer to any kind of education that is provided by educational bodies.

On the basis of the literature reviewed, conclusions can be drawn according to which there are at least two educational pathways where workforce development takes place:

- educational institutions, that is places where the "finished product" is manufactured;
- educational institutions where cognitive skills are gained.

By "finished product", I mean that a school prepares graduates so that they can comply with market requirements, providing them with cognitive, technical and behavioural skills. The second point deals with the fact that educational providers have a major responsibility in that they help students develop cognitive skills on an exclusive basis, with behavioural and technical skills that are further strengthened on-the-job.[8]

2.2 Labour Force Development: Theoretical Background

In conceptual terms, the interplay between education and employment is considerably different among countries. In this connection, Maurice, Sellier and Silvestre[9] carried out an extremely useful analysis which distinguishes the concept of "qualificational space" from what has been termed "organisational space". While qualificational space is characterised by mostly providing specific vocational education, organisational space is mainly academic, or usually comprises occupational skills which are learnt on-the-job or during the courses taken once out of the school.

[8] Mounier, A., and P. Tangchuang. 2010c. *Education and Knowledge in Thailand: The Quality Controversy.* Chiang Mai: Silkworm Books, 148.

[9] In Muller, W., and Y. Shavit. 2003. "The Institutional Embeddedness of the Stratification Process," in *From School to Work: A Comparative Study of Educational Qualifications and Occupational Destinations,* (Oxford: Clarendon Press), 9.

The pros and cons of these two distinct principles of education—organisational and qualificational space—have been widely debated.[10]

However, the analysis provided by Muller and Shavit[11] considered three types of institutional contexts where the school-to-work transition might take place: qualificational space (Germany, Switzerland and the Netherlands), organisational space (Australia, Britain, Ireland, Japan, and the US) and mixed (France, Israel, Italy, Sweden and Taiwan).

There is common consensus that Vocational Education and Training (VET) is crucial in preparing individuals for work.[12] Due to the fact that most of VET's learners are increasingly characterised by different educational backgrounds—including marginalised people and those classified as being "at risk"—it is necessary for the VET workforce to be flexible, innovative and responsive, also as a way to meet the specific needs of learners.

Following the notion of Wood[13] that there have been tremendous transformations in the working world over the late twentieth century due to a number of factors such as the oil shock and economic recession—which have impacted employment patterns—job flexibility, multi-skilling, workload, production methods and so on—a question can be raised about the way school-to-work patterns should adapt to such a change effectively.

3. Labour Force Development

This paper presents the cases of Thailand and Vietnam, as these two countries are regarded as developing countries in SEA, although their education system and relevant policies are significantly different. Vietnam

---

[10] For further details see Muller and Shavit. 2003. "The Institutional Embeddedness of the Stratification Process," in *From School to Work: A Comparative Study of Educational Qualifications and Occupational Destinations,* (Oxford: Clarendon Press).

[11] Ibid., 11-35.

[12] Raggatt, P., and S. Williams. 2009. *Government, Markets and Vocational Qualifications: An Anatomy of Policy.* London: Falmer Press. Muller, W., and Y. Shavit. 2003. "The Institutional Embeddedness of the Stratification Process," in *From School to Work: A Comparative Study of Educational Qualifications and Occupational Destinations,* (Oxford: Clarendon Press), 2. Guthrie, H. 2010. "Professional Development in the Vocational Education and Training Workforce," National Centre for Vocational Education Research. http://www.ncver.edu.au/publications/2279.html (accessed November 10, 2010), 6.

[13] Wood, S. 1992. "The Transformation of Work?" in *The Transformation of Work?: Skill, Flexibility and the Labour Process.* (London: Routledge).

has a very selective education system and from the very beginning of the educational path children who do not meet the level of knowledge required must repeat the school year. From 199, this does not happen in Thailand anymore.[14]

According to quality indicators in education, such as average cost per student or number of students per teacher, Thailand is far ahead of Vietnam as the Thai government allocates more financial resources to education. In this sense, Thailand has allocated around 20% of its national budget—or 4.2% of GDP per annum—to educational programmes over the last decade.[15]

The Vietnamese government has also increased the educational budget since 2001 by 600%.[16] Investment in vocational training increased from 523 billion in 1997 to 1760 billion VND (Vietnamese dongs) in 2005 and 2200 billion VND in 2007. In 2002, the budget for vocational training programmes amounted to 110 billion VND, while 500 and 700 billion VND were allocated in 2006 and 2007, respectively.[17]

Those two countries are different also in the implementation of policies regarding Vocational and Technical Education (VTE), which comprise the development of labour capacity. For example, around one third of students drop out of school after 9th grade in Thailand, which is still regarded as a level of compulsory education. Among those who continue beyond grade 9, 45% of them opt for vocational schools, and the remaining 55% enrol in general education courses[18] with most of them who will continue up to higher education. Those who complete vocational education usually enrol in an associate's degree programme—lasting two years—and then in a degree programme. However, those who choose to enter the labour market will be employed in low-skilled and low-paid jobs. On the contrary in Vietnam, out of the same proportion of students who leave school after

---

[14] Oudin, X. 2009. "Education Systems in Thailand and in Vietnam: A comparison," *Faculty of Education Journal* 36, No. 1-2.

[15] Supachai, S. "Economist Criticized Thai Education Get a Lot of Financial Support but Poor Quality," Bangkokbiznews.com, (accessed June 24, 2010).

[16] Doanh nhan. 2009. "Education budget grows 600% from 2001 but quality gains hard to see," VietNamNet. http://www.lookatvietnam.com/2009/10/education-budget-grows-600-from-2001-but-quality-gains-hard-to-see.html   (accessed November 11, 2010).

[17] Mac Van Tien. 2008. "The Role of TVET Providers in Training for Employees in Vietnam," Paper presented at the APEC Forum on Human Resources Development, Chiba, Japan, November 2008, 9-10.

[18] Areeya R. "The Role of TVET Providers in Training for Employees," Paper presented at the APEC Forum on Human Resources Development, Chiba, Japan, November 2008, 8.

completing lower secondary education and among those who continue, only 10% of them opt for vocational education, as a two-to-four-year training period for manual jobs after graduation is required. Furthermore, many of them have to seek employment because they cannot attend higher education programmes.

Since advanced technical education and vocational education are different in terms of curriculum, college students who undertake technical studies usually have a "general" educational background and they have to pass a test allowing them to take certain classes. The same happens in Thailand if students want to enrol in both public and private colleges offering technical majors, even though some of them might already have a vocational and technical background.

Considering the same age cohort, the overall enrolment rate for students in non-technical higher education in Thailand is 40% and only 10% in Vietnam. Thus, Thailand produces a higher number of bachelor's, master's and doctoral degrees than Vietnam, apparently too many for the labour market.[19] Many graduates, especially from private universities and those with a degree in Social Sciences, are underemployed, that is, employed under their capacities and with lower wages than expected. In Vietnam, unemployment of graduates is a threat that may hamper the government from making provision for higher education in a consistent manner. However, there is increasing demand for individuals with higher levels of education. Private universities are cooperating with a number of foreign institutions in the setting up of bachelor's or master's programmes in Vietnam, and there is a proposal to review the selection process, in order to abolish the entrance examination. This is a major issue in both countries because the entry exam is a prerequisite for admitting highly-skilled students also considering that there will be higher levels of competition in terms of skills provision in the years to come.

More specifically, one of the main principles in terms of labour capacity development in Vietnam is *doi moi,* which means *renovation* and it has been referred to since 1986. This particular principle was recalled during the 9th Congress of the Vietnam Communist Party when the overall goals of the socio-economic strategic plan for 2001-2010 were set forth. In this connection, the purpose is:

---

[19] Tangchuang, P. 2010b. "Credentialism and the Diploma Disease in Higher Education," in *Education and Knowledge in Thailand: The Quality Controversy,* (Chiang Mai: Silkworm Books).

to bring our country out of an underdeveloped situation, to increase significantly the level of material, cultural and spiritual life of people, and to lay the foundations for our country to basically become an industrialised, modernised nation by 2020.

In order to achieve these goals, the role of education, science and technology has become decisive and requirements to comply with in terms of educational development are a matter of urgency. In the case of Thailand, current educational practices were regarded as successful during the 7th National Economic and Social Development Plan (NESDP 1992-1996). This success has been sustained, also because the growth of GDP has remained steady at 8-10% since the beginning of the 1990s. As a result, Thailand is expected to become one of the Newly Industrial Countries (NICs) of Asia. Also through the implementation of the 8th Plan (NESDP 1997-2001), the Thai government intended to improve the quality of life of the labour force. However, since the very beginning of the implementation of the programme, the country faced a financial crisis and many companies in the banking, construction, and the service industry, collapsed.

After 15 years of restruction, the national education system has achieved important results although still facing weaknesses and shortcomings. As for the achievements, the Vietnamese education system has improved considerably especially in terms of enrolment trends, diversification of delivery modes, school facilities, and the overall level of mass education. On the other hand, Vietnamese education is still weak in quality, unbalanced in structure and ineffective. This is due to several reasons: the educational path is too theoretical, training is not harmonised with employment; teaching staff are not prepared adequately; facilities are insufficient and, finally, a long time is required to update curricula, teaching manuals, methods of delivery and management.

3.1 Vocational and Technical Education (VTE)

In Vietnam, VTE encompasses vocational secondary education, which is administered by the Department of Vocational Education within the Ministry of Education and Training (MOET), whereas the General Department of Vocational Training (GDVT) of the Ministry of Labour, Invalids and Social Affairs (MOLISA) is in charge of providing vocational training. Recently, the Ministry of Industry and Trade (MIT) has overseen the main activities of a joint university, the Vietnam-Hungary Industry University. In Thailand, while the Ministry of Education (MOE) is in charge of several programmes including VTE and post-secondary education, the Ministry of Labour and Social Welfare administers the training and re-training process for the out-of-school labour force. It is up to relevant ministries to provide special training to professionals within the police, army, air force, and in some cases, nursing staff.

With reference to VTE, Oudin[20] argued that both countries suffer from shortcomings: facilities within VTE institutions are obsolete, and teaching methods—including topics to be covered—are not updated. In addition, students in the technical fields rarely have access to modern equipment, as most technical schools cannot afford to buy it, which is regarded as a major issue in small vocational schools—especially those located in rural areas. As a result, employers often complain about the fact that the workforce graduating from technical schools has inadequate skills or training, also in behavioural terms.[21]

3.2 Higher Education

Among the objectives of higher education institutions, mention should be made of the following: to provide learners with political and moral attributes, to support the educational attainment of people, to acquire occupational knowledge and practical skills in accordance with training requirements, to develop physical well-being and a strong feeling of national identity.

As mentioned earlier, the education systems of these two countries are quite different. In Vietnam, bodies providing higher education are under the strict control of the government with regard to the number of students and academic programmes, regardless of whether the college is public or private.

The same can be said of open universities, that is those schools admitting anyone—including workers—who passes the entrance examination. Institutions of this kind are allowed to hold evening classes and to provide distance learning opportunities as well as on-site lessons within satellite academic centres in order to meet the different needs of learners and facilitate job enrichment in human resource management at a

---

[20] Oudin, X. 2009. "Education Systems in Thailand and in Vietnam: A comparison," *Faculty of Education Journal* 36, No. 1-2.
[21] Doanh nhan. 2009. "Education budget grows 600% from 2001 but quality gains hard to see," VietNamNet.
http://www.lookatvietnam.com/2009/10/education-budget-grows-600-from-2001-but-quality-gains-hard-to-see.html (accessed November 11, 2010).
Supachai, S. "Economist Criticized Thai Education Get a Lot of Financial Support but Poor Quality," Bangkokbiznews.com, (accessed June 24, 2010).

national level. However, and unlike Thailand and the rest of the world, a maximum number of new students is allowed to attend certain degree programmes every year.

In Vietnam, higher education institutions are government-run, e.g. the Economics and Business schools would be under the management of the Ministry of Industry and Trade, Hanoi Medical College would be administered by the Ministry of Health, while the Ministry of Culture and Information will run the College of Culture and the Hanoi Conservatory.[22]

Apparently, Vietnam is in a better position than Thailand in terms of quality control, particularly if one considers the ratios between the number of instructors and students, as well as the number of higher education institutions. Despite this, Vietnamese students are far behind those in Thailand, as here there is an oversupply of people holding a university, bachelor's, master's and doctoral degrees and many of them have to accept jobs requiring lower levels of education. However, as a part of the government policy, students from neighbouring countries have free access to national schools, so that Thai higher education institutes could absorb thousands of students from Vietnam, Laos, Cambodia and the south of China.

3.3 Continuing Education

Both countries share the same objectives in terms of continuing education in that the aim is to help people to learn while working on a continuous basis, in order to further refine their personality, and broaden their understanding. To this purpose, lifelong learning should enhance educational, and operational aspects, thus improving workers' quality of life, employability and adaptability to society.

However, differences between the two countries arise in both theoretical and practical terms. In Vietnam, the way continuing education can be provided is twofold, that is by means of open universities (as discussed earlier), and by private institutions. Mention should be made of the fact that most popular classes in Vietnam are those where foreign languages— English, Japanese, and Korean are taught with such courses usually held in the evening. On the contrary, in Thailand, continuing education is mostly addressed to those holding postgraduate qualifications, i.e. bachelor's, master's and doctoral degrees, which represent the majority within the workforce. Also in this case, classes are organised in the

---

[22] IIE Vietnam. 2004. "Higher Education in Vietnam Update—May 2004," Institute of International Education.

evenings and during the weekend nationwide, according to the university system, the *Rajabhat*.

4. Analysis

4.1 Literacy

Although education can pursue many objectives, providing the population with reading and writing skills is considered a priority. In countries where a new education system has recently been adopted, and/or where the setting up of a universally acknowledged education system is somehow affected by budgetary constraints and negative population growth, the best indicator to assess progress within levels of education is the illiteracy rate.

This rate usually includes the adult population on an exclusive basis (aged 15 years and over), and it is more significant for the female population if one takes into account that universal education implies that women also should benefit from progress in education.

Starting from the 1970s, it can be said that both countries have achieved universal education, but obstacles remained to its effective implementation, especially in most remote areas. In 1970, the rate of illiteracy among adult women in Thailand was higher than that in Vietnam, although declining more steeply in the former. Once young educated cohorts came to the age of 15, and replaced old uneducated cohorts, illiteracy rates declined progressively. In the case of Thailand, younger generations were relatively better educated than those in Vietnam, and older generations were relatively less educated (it means they reported higher rates of illiteracy) than in Vietnam. As a result, progress is more rapid in Thailand. Around 6% of the adult female population is now illiterate, against 9% in Vietnam. In both countries, most illiterate people are elderly, but there are a few who are young among ethnic minorities.

Such an indicator shows the legacy of the education system in the past, since most illiterate people belong to old generations. Illiteracy among younger generations provides another picture, that can be seen as an indicator of the universality of the school system. However, a question remains: to what extent can young cohorts have access to school?

This indicator is rather discouraging for Vietnam, where nearly one young adult out of 20 is still illiterate. As for Thailand, the illiteracy rate among young adults has fallen dramatically and is now negligible. This means that the Thai education system is really universal (all children can have access to primary school), which is not yet the case of Vietnam.

4.2 Enrolment

By the 1980s, both countries had nearly achieved universal education or had at least set up an education system to welcome children in schools from all over the country: this means that primary schools, teachers and basic equipment have been provided in every village, and that access to school is free of charge.

In reference to secondary education, both countries reported low enrolment rates over the same period. In Thailand, the regulation of compulsory education up to the end of lower secondary resulted in higher enrolment rates, in both lower secondary and upper secondary levels, also including vocational education. In a ten-year span (from 1987 to 1997), enrolment doubled from two to four million pupils. In Vietnam, the spread of secondary education was even more evident, although it has been even more hectic decades before. At the end of the 1980s, there had been a sudden drop in secondary school enrolment due to the introduction of school fees. Starting from the 1990s, enrolment in secondary schools exploded—from a likely 3 million pupils in 1990, enrolment reached 10 million by 2005—amounting to 12% of the total population, as compared to 6% in Thailand. The burden of secondary education is particularly high for Vietnamese families.

Fig. 3-13. Secondary School Enrolment (thousand), 1975-2006

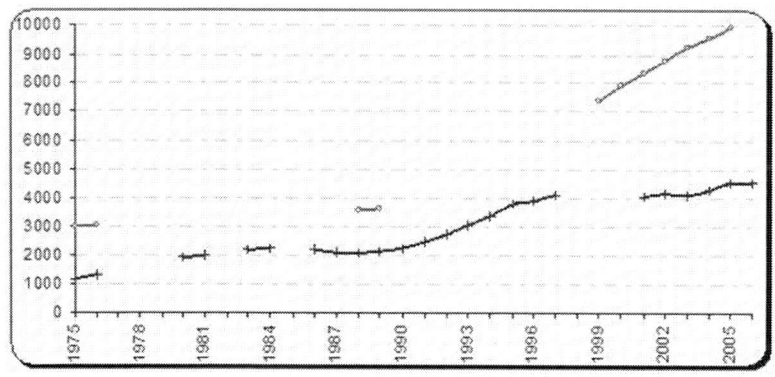

Source: UNESCO.

Measuring tertiary enrolment is difficult, and one has to be particularly cautious with international comparisons. First of all, the age of those enrolling at the university is not the same in all countries. Secondly, higher education may be accessed by individuals who have not completed formal secondary education. In Thailand for instance, open universities have enrolled thousands of students, mostly with a non-formal educational background. Thirdly, private institutions in Vietnam as well as in Thailand offer programmes designed for adults who are not necessarily classified as having "higher" education. Finally, many people within the labour force are also enrolled in institutions providing tertiary education and are therefore regarded as students. It is therefore difficult to distinguish between initial higher education and adult training.

Fig. 3-14. Tertiary Level Enrolment (thousand), 1975-2006

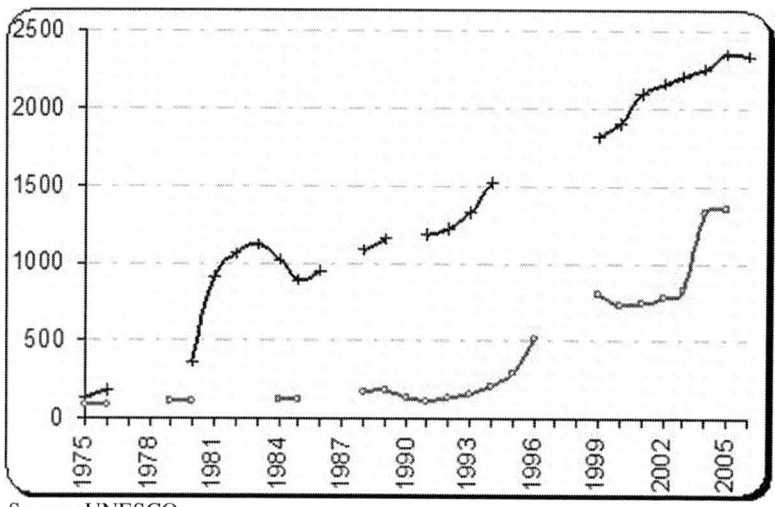

Source: UNESCO.

4.3 Enrolment Ratios

Fig. 3-15. Gross Enrolment Ratio, All Levels, 1970-2006

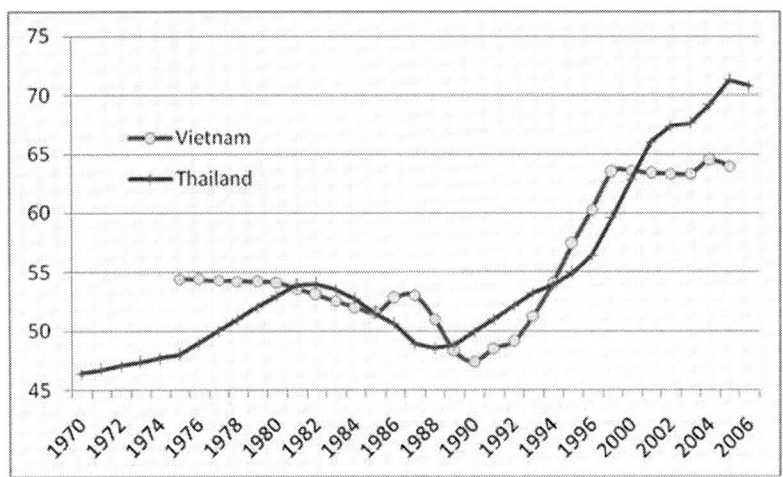

Source: Oudin, 2010.

Fig. 3-16. Secondary School Gross Enrolment Ratio, 1975-2006

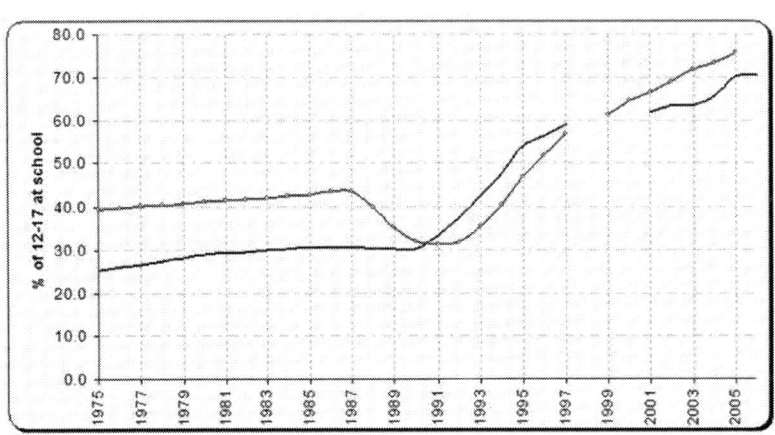

Source: UNESCO, varied data (incomplete and not homogenised data).

Fig. 3-17. Tertiary Gross Enrolment Ratio, 1975-2005[23]

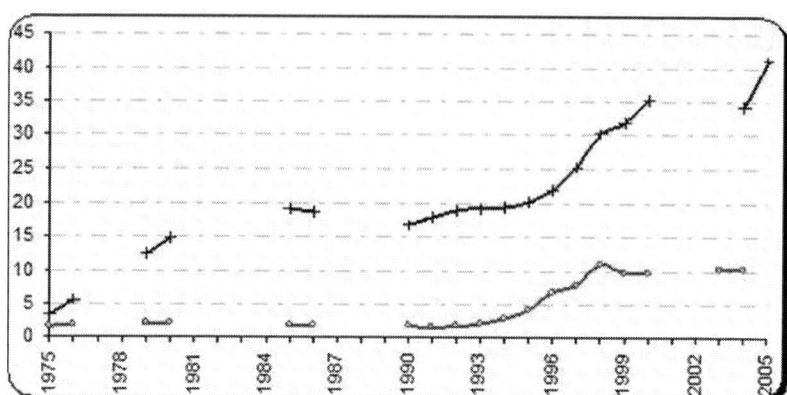

Source: World Bank, World Bank Indicators of Development.

4.4 Graduation

The total number of graduates at tertiary level is similar for both countries: 180,000 graduates/year. With reference to Thailand, this figure includes graduates from open universities (31% from Ramkhamhaeng and Sukhotai Thammathirat University) and 28% from private universities (of whom the distribution by field is not provided). Thus, 41% of school-leavers graduated from public universities, even though this proportion has probably declined since.

More general information is provided in reference to Vietnam. In particular, there are no data on different levels of graduation or the type of university or institution in which graduation is achieved.

---

[23] Survival rates (indicators of efficiency): survival rate at grade 5,7,9,12 (best fit to be chosen depending on education system); survival rates 1st year of secondary vs. last year of primary, first year of upper secondary vs. last year of lower secondary. Survival rates in vocational education, higher education vs. secondary general or vocational education.

Fig. 3-18 Graduates per Field

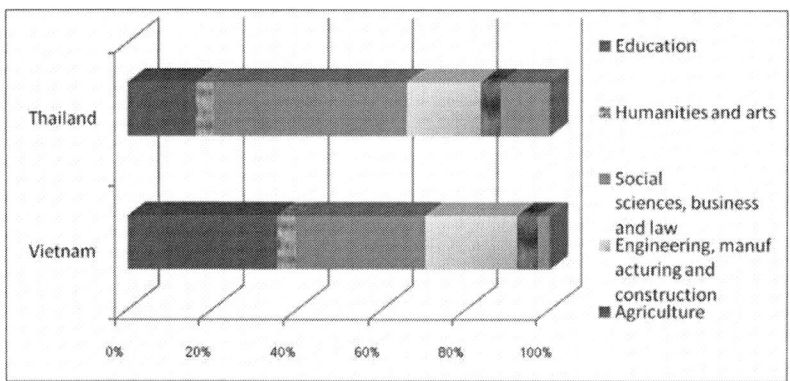

Source: Vietnam, UNESCO, year 2005; Thailand: Statistical Year Book 2004, year 2001.

One third of graduates in Vietnam are from educational sciences and teacher training. More generally, the reviewing of national education system in Vietnam is still under way and there is a high demand for teachers. On the contrary, in Thailand, the demographic trends and the rapid development of the education system in previous decades make the demand for teachers less relevant. However, this issue should be examined considering the field or discipline.

In Thailand, social sciences, law and business are the fields with the highest percentage of graduates: 46% of all graduates (not including private institutions) are in these fields, compared to 31% in Vietnam. This is partly due to the preference for social sciences on the part of female students. In Thailand, 58% of all female students are enrolled in social sciences (not including law) compared with 43% of their male counterparts. In contrast, the number of graduates in sciences and engineering is higher in Vietnam, even though, for instance, the number of graduates in medical sciences is surprisingly low in Vietnam compared with Thailand. This aspect might be due to differences in classification, and therefore deserve further investigation.

In Thailand, 57% of all graduates are female (mostly holding a bachelor degree) with such percentage corresponding to 42% in Vietnam.

5. Conclusion

5.1 Policies Regarding the Education System

In the last 15 years, the Thai education system has developed extremely rapidly, succeeding in accommodating many generations of youth. However, such improvement has proved detrimental to education, in both quantitative and qualitative terms. This can be seen in the study of the outlet of education. Employers often complain that the "cognitive content" of qualifications is not ascertained and this is a major issue particularly in small universities, as degrees issued by such institutions are poorly regarded in the labour market.

The comparison with Vietnam pointed out some shortcomings in the Thai school system and gives some hints to improve the quality of education. In short, policy measures that need to be adopted in this connection should aim to:

1) re-introduce the selection process between different levels of education, also envisaging the repetition of classes whereas deemed to be necessary;
2) stress the need to reduce household expenditure for education and relevant costs;
3) disseminate scientific education at universities, also by means of mid-level technologies;
4) campaign in favour of technical and scientific education through different media;
5) put an emphasis on research in academic curricula and careers;
6) differentiate between high-tech training for middle managers and vocational training for manual workers;
7) provide a stronger cooperation with enterprises.

References

ADB. 2008. *Viet Nam: Vocational and Technical Education Project.* Completion Report. ABD.

Ainley, J., S. Holden, and S. Rothman. 2010. "Apprenticeships and Traineeships: Participation, Progress and Completion," LSAY Briefing Paper, No. 19.

Areeya, R. "The Role of TVET Providers in Training for Employees," Paper presented at the APEC Forum on Human Resources Development, Chiba, Japan, November 2008.

Arenas, A. 2005. "Technical and Vocational Education and Training for Sustainable Development: The Challenges of Implementation," *Supplement to UNESCO-UNEVOC Bulletin,* No. 10.

Beddie, F., and P. Curtin. 2010. "The Future of VET: A Medley of Views National Centre for Vocational Education Research," NCVER. http://www.ncver.edu.au/publications/2284.html (accessed November 10, 2010).

Choi, Y. R. 2005. "Case Study—Korea. Vocational Education and Training, VET, for the Youth—Sustainable Economic Growth and Youth Employment: Prospect in Korea," Symposium Resources, APEC Human Resource Development Working Group.

Cummings, S. I. W. "Vocational Education and Training (VET) for Youth Employability and Training: Skilling Youth for Employability for the Knowledge Society: Roles and responsibilities," Symposium Resources, APEC Human Resource Development Working Group.

Doanh nhan. 2009. "Education budget grows 600% from 2001 but quality gains hard to see," VietNamNet. http://www.lookatvietnam.com/2009/10/education-budget-grows-600-from-2001-but-quality-gains-hard-to-see.html (accessed November 11, 2010).

Fredriksen B., and T. J. Peng. 2008. *An African Exploration of the East Asian Education Experience (Development practice in education).* Washington: The World Bank.

Gilley, J. W., S. A. Eggland, and A. M. Gilley. 2002. *Principles of Human Resource Development.* New York: Basic Books.

Guthrie, H. 2010. "Professional Development in the Vocational Education and Training Workforce," National Centre for Vocational Education Research. http://www.ncver.edu.au/publications/2279.html (accessed November 10, 2010)

Hartl, M. "Technical and Vocational Education and Training (TVET) and Skills Development for Poverty Reduction—Do Rural Women Benefit?" Paper presented at the FAO-IFAD-ILO, Workshop on Gaps, trends and current research in gender dimensions of agricultural and rural employment: differentiated pathways out of poverty, International Fund for Agricultural Development, Rome, Italy, March 2009.

Hodkinson, P., A. C. Sparkes, and K. Hodkinson. 2004. "Career Decision Making and Culture in the Transition from School to Work," in *Sociology of Education: Major Themes,* (London: Routledge Falmer Taylor & Francis Group).

IIE Vietnam. 2004. "Higher Education in Vietnam Update—May 2004," Institute of International Education.

Johnson, D. 2005. "The Knowledge Economy and New Vocationalism: International and National Challenges for Mass Higher Education," *Supplement to UNESCO-UNEVOC Bulletin December 2005*, No. 11.

Lawrence, M., J. Bernstein, and S. Allegretto. 2007. *The State of Working America 2006/2007*. New York: ILR Press.

Mac Van Tien. 2008. "The Role of TVET Providers in Training for Employees in Vietnam," Paper presented at the APEC Forum on Human Resources Development, Chiba, Japan, November 2008.

Mounier, A., and P. Tangchuang. 2010a. "From Education to Work," in *Education and Knowledge in Thailand: The Quality Controversy*, (Chiang Mai: Silkworm Books).

—. 2010b. "Quality: The Major Issue in Thai Education," in *Education and Knowledge in Thailand: The Quality Controversy*, (Chiang Mai: Silkworm Books).

—. 2010c. *Education and Knowledge in Thailand: The Quality Controversy*. Chiang Mai: Silkworm Books.

Muller, W., and Y. Shavit. 2003. "The Institutional Embeddedness of the Stratification Process," in *From School to Work: A Comparative Study of Educational Qualifications and Occupational Destinations*, (Oxford: Clarendon Press).

Nguyen Thi Le Huong. "Vietnam Higher Education—Reform for the Nation's Development," www.unescobkk.org/.../ESD_AT_HANOI_UNIVERSITY_OF_EDUCATION_IN_VIETNAM_OUR_EFFORTS_AND_COMMITMENT, (accessed October 15, 2010).

Oudin, X. 2009. "Education Systems in Thailand and in Vietnam: A comparison," *Faculty of Education Journal* 36, No. 1-2.

—. 2010. "The Educational Progress of the Labour Force," in *Education and Knowledge in Thailand: The Quality Controversy*, (Chiang Mai: Silkworm Books).

Pauw, K., M. Oosthuizen, and C. Van der Westhuizen. "Graduate Unemployment in the Face of Skills Shortages: A Labour Market Paradox," DPRU Working Paper No. 06/114. http://papers.ssrn.com/sol3/papers.cfm?abstract_id=964899 (accessed November 13, 2010).

Pham Thi Thu Huyen. "Higher Education in Vietnam: A Look from Labour Market Angle," www.vdf.org.vn/Doc/2008/VDFConf_WIPHuyen.pdf (accessed November 11, 2010).

Pramono, W. 2005. "Summary on Vocational Education and Training (VET) for Youth Employability and Training," Symposium Resources, APEC Human Resource Development Working Group.

ReferNet Finland. 2009. *VET in Europe – Country Report*. Cedefop, 15.

Raggatt, P., and S. Williams. 2009. *Government, Markets and Vocational Qualifications: An Anatomy of Policy*. London: Falmer Press.

Sandrine, M. 2010. "The Burgeoning of Education in Thailand," in *Education and Knowledge in Thailand: The Quality Controversy* (Chiang Mai: Silkworm Books).

Supachai, S. "Economist Criticized Thai Education Get a Lot of Financial Support but Poor Quality," Bangkokbiznews.com, (accessed June 24, 2010).

Swanson, R. A., and E. F. Holton III. 2009. *Foundations of Human Resource Development*. San Francisco: Berrett-Koehler Publishers, Inc.

Tangchuang, P. 2001. "Concept and Practice of Knowledge-based Economies Promotions in Higher Education Institutes," *ASAIHL-Thailand Journal* 4, No. 2.

—. 2007. "Skills: Employers versus Higher Education," CELS Working Papers No. 4, Chiang Mai: Nopburee Press.

—. 2009. "Labour Capacity Preparation: Comparative Analysis of Thai and Vietnam 1980-2025," *Faculty of Education Journal* 36, No. 1-2.

—. 2010a. *Educational Personnel Development*. [in Thai]. Chiang Mai: Duang Kamol Publishing Company.

—. 2010b. "Credentialism and the Diploma Disease in Higher Education," in *Education and Knowledge in Thailand: The Quality Controversy,* (Chiang Mai: Silkworm Books).

—. 2010c. "Becoming a Reflexive Teacher: Intermediate Results of a Research Project," Paper presented at the 14th UNESCO-APEID International Conference Education for Human Resource Development, Bangkok, Thailand, October 2010.

Technical and Vocational Education and Training (TVET) in Vietnam. 2008. *Internal Working Material of Promotion of TVET in Vietnam*. TVET. http://www.tvet-vietnam.org/tvet%20in%20vietnam_brief%20 overview_080908.pdf (accessed October 20, 2010).

Teichler, U. 2000. "Higher Education and Graduate Employment in Europe," *New Perspective for Learning-Briefing Paper 10*. http://www.pjb.co.uk/npl/bp10.htm (accessed November 15, 2010).

Vallely, T. J., and B. Wilkinson. 2008. *Vietnamese Higher Education: Crisis and Response*. Hanoi: International Co-operation Department, Education Publishing House.

Weltz, G. H. 2005. "Youth Vocational Education and Training in the United States," Symposium Resources, APEC Human Resource Development Working Group.

Wood, S. 1992. "The Transformation of Work?" in *The Transformation of Work?: Skill, Flexibility and the Labour Process*, (London: Routledge).

CAREER SUPPORT IN UNIVERSITIES

MITSUKO UENISHI

1. Background to the Calling into Question of Current University Career Support[1]

Currently, what kind of career education and support should be offered to students is being questioned at Japanese universities. In order to understand why university career support is being called into question at this time, it is necessary to look at two significant background changes that have taken place in post-graduation employment. These are firstly, the increasing proportion of students who continue their education to university level and the decreasing ratio of graduate employment, and secondly, the changes that have taken place in the process of university graduate recruitment in corporations. These changes have led to calls for improvements in the way that universities provide career support.

1.1 Increasing University Entry and Decreasing Graduate Employment Rates

(1) Increasing University Entry: as shown in Fig.3-19 the proportion of students continuing education to university level was steady between the late 1970s and around 1990 at 24% to 27%.

Fig. 3-19. Trends in the Size of the 18-Year-Old Population and the Number and the Proportion of Entry into Higher Education Institutions[2]

---

[1] Uenishi, M. 2011. "Career support in universities," *Japan Labor Review* 8, No. 1,85-102. This issue of the Journal *Japan Labor Review* relates to "career education", but it is important that curriculum is implemented in conjunction with extra-curricular programmes implemented by staff organisations (excluding teaching staff) of the employment department/career centre. It is usual to refer to both of these activities together "career support" and in this paper, in the main, the phrase "career support" is used.
[2] The proportion of students continuing education to university level shown in Fig.

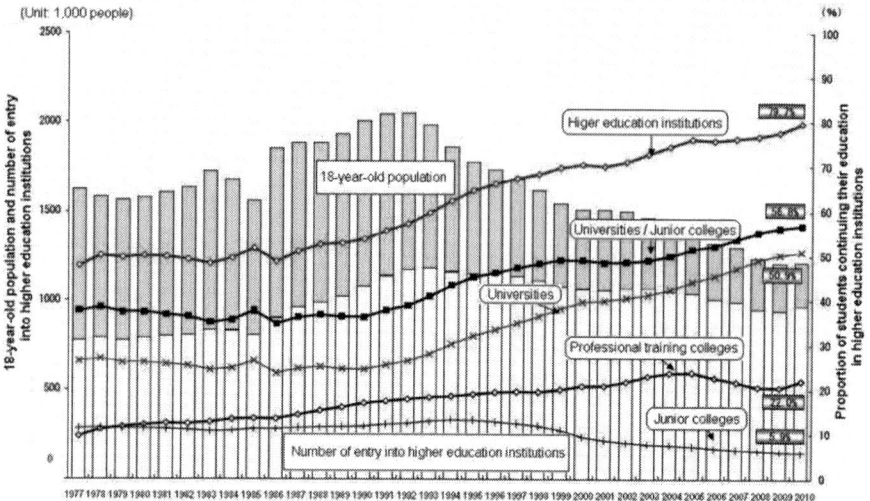

Source: Ministry of Education, Culture, Sports, Science and Technology, School Basic Survey.

This subsequently began to rise swiftly, exceeding 50% for the first time in spring 2009 (50.2%). There are three factors influencing this rise in the proportion of students continuing to university. The first was an expansion in student capacity at universities. During the 1990s, the trend towards the easing of regulations led to the relaxation of criteria for university foundation, leading to various junior colleges converting into universities, and a range of new university establishments, creating greater capacity for student entry. The second factor was a sudden worsening in employment opportunities for high school graduates. Subsequent to the bursting of the economic bubble in 1991, the ratio of jobs to applications

3-19 represents the proportion of students continuing education in each category of universities, junior colleges and professional training colleges to the 18-year-old proportion, including those students who graduated high school a year or more earlier. Using these figures means that the statistics include students who left high school but subsequently spent a period of time studying for entrance examinations before entering university. In fiscal 2007, 2.7% of university entrants were aged 25 or above, which is an extremely low proportion compared to other OECD countries: Central Education Council. 2008. *Gakushi katei kyoiku no kochiku ni mukete (toshin)* [Toward the Creation of Bachelor Education (report)]. Central Education Council, Ministry of Education, Culture, Sports, Science and Technology. http://www.mext.go.jp/b_menu/shingi/chukyo/chukyo0/tou-shin/1217067.htm (accessed November 30, 2010).

for high school graduates (as of end November in the third year of high school) dropped swiftly from its peak in 1992 of 3.3:1 to 1.74:1 in 1995, and subsequently maintained a low level of around 1:1 between 2000 and 2005. Alongside this, the number of high school graduates who neither continued education nor entered employment grew swiftly, and began to become a social problem. For this reason, families with even a small amount of spare economic capacity have begun to send their children to university, considering that being a university graduate would provide an advantage in recruitment, thereby strengthening the trend towards students continuing to higher education. The third reason is the decline in the size of the 18-year-old population, as can be seen in Fig. 3-19.

(2) Reduction in University Selection Function: the fact that universities' student capacity has increased at the same time as the 18-year-old population is decreasing means that the competition to acquire students among private universities, which make up around 80% of all institutions, has become severe. Many private universities have increased the proportion of students they attract through admission office entrance or referred entry, rather than through academic subject testing, so that now fewer than half of students (48.6%) enter university via standard entrance examinations.[3]

Standard entrance examinations at private universities have also reduced the number of test subjects. To sit general entrance for national and public universities, students are required to take first-stage tests in seven subjects, but conventionally, private universities only examine in three subjects, and an increasing number of universities and faculties now only examine in one or two subjects. Furthermore, in fiscal 2008, 47.1% of private universities (266 institutions) were under-enrolled, and in a certain number of universities where the number of students enrolled is significantly lower than the number of places available, it is true to say that the entrance tests are no longer playing a valid function in selecting students.

Conventionally, Japanese universities are said to be "difficult to enter, but easy to graduate from". The requirements for graduation may have been relatively relaxed, but the function of entrance tests to select students was highly effective. At present, however, other than a few top-level institutions, the situation has become one in which university is "easy to

---

[3] Central Education Council. 2008. *Gakushi katei kyoiku no kochiku ni mukete (toshin)* [Toward the Creation of Bachelor Education (report)]. Central Education Council, Ministry of Education, Culture, Sports, Science and Technology. http://www.mext.go.jp/b_menu/shingi/chukyo/chukyo0/tou-shin/1217067.htm (accessed November 30, 2010).

enter and easy to graduate from". This has led to a decreasing amount of study being done by high school students. According to research done by Motohisa Kaneko et. al., the time spent in studying by students at senior high school on weekdays during the autumn of their third year was, even in the case of those students who decided to continue their education to university level in March of their third year, reported as "up to 2 hours" by around half of them, which includes those studied "almost none" by around 20%.[4] As a result, universities are now accepting students who do not have enough basic academic abilities, and lack any desire to learn proactively.

(2)   Reduced Rate of University Graduate Employment: this vicious spiral has also been reflected in the situation regarding recruitment and employment of university graduates (Fig. 3-20). In a survey of students graduating in March 1990, in May of the same year (two months after graduation), 6.8% of students had carried on into graduate studies, 81.0% had found employment, and 5.6% had neither entered graduate studies nor found a job. The proportion of graduates finding employment fell drastically, however, to 55.0% by 2003, with 27.1% of students entering neither graduate education nor employment in the same year (including those entering temporary work).

Of course, the long-term period of recession following the bursting of the economic bubble, which caused a sudden decrease in job offers to graduates, is also a factor in the background to this decrease in employment rates (Fig. 3-21). As seen in Figure 2, however, during this period, the actual number of university graduates who began employment did not decrease particularly significantly. A bird's-eye view of the situation shows that the increase in number of university graduates in the 1990s may have manifested itself almost entirely in the increased number of graduates neither "continuing education" nor "entering employment".

---

[4] Centre for Research on University Management and Policy, Graduate School of Education, University of Tokyo. 2007. *Kokosei no shinro tsuiseki chosa, dai-ichi-ji hokokusho* [Survey Following the Career Path of High School Students: First Report]. Tokyo: CRUMP, Graduate School of Education, University of Tokyo. http://ump.p.u-tokyo.ac.jp/crump/resource/crumphsts.pdf (accessed November 30, 2010).

Fig 3-20. Progress by University Graduates[5]

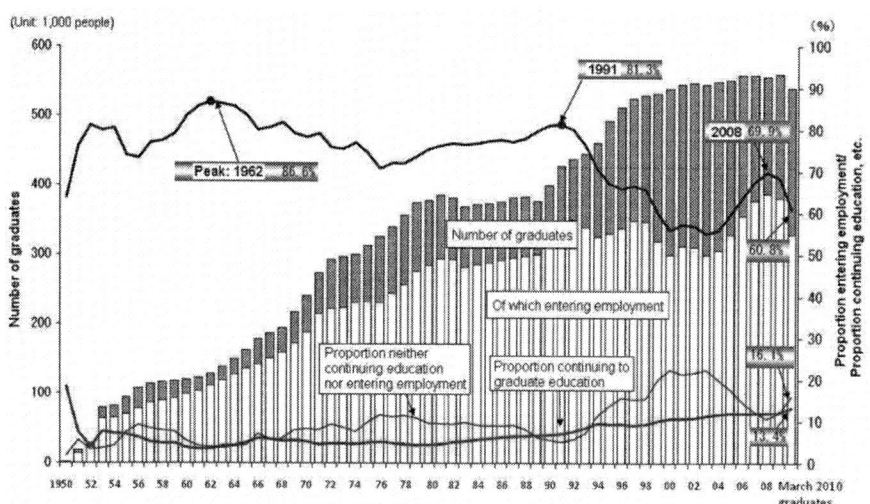

Source: Ministry of Education, Culture, Sports, Science and Technology, School Basic Survey.

Subsequently, as seen in Fig. 3-21, the number of job offers began to recover in the late 2000s, and as seen in Fig. 3-20, the proportion of students engaged in neither education nor employment began to fall. The global economic recession beginning in 2008, however, resulted in a significant depression in the number of job offers for graduates in March 2010, and the employment status of graduates has taken another sudden turn for the worse. As a result of an increase in university graduates, the proportion of graduates entering employment has become far more sensitive to prevailing economic trends.

---

[5] "Neither continuing education nor entering employment" indicates those clearly not engaged either in continuing education (graduate school, professional training college or study overseas) nor entering employment, but rather living at home and helping with chores, and so on. Of those people, figures for before 1987 include those who entered "temporary employment", and figures for before 2003 include those studying at "professional training college or overseas".

1.2 Changes to the Graduate Recruitment Process
in Corporations

Next, let us take a look at the changes that have taken place in the graduate recruitment process in corporations. To summarise, these changes have resulted in a switch from a situation where universities and corporations had semi-institutional linkages that provided strong and comparatively stable matching, to one in which students are uncertain and confused as they engage with a longer-term job search activities without any firm prospects for the future.

Mitsuko Uenishi

Fig. 3-21. Total Number of Job Offers, Number of People Looking for Employment in Private Companies, and Ratio of Offers to Applicants, in Regard to University Students and Graduate Students Expected to Graduate the Following Spring

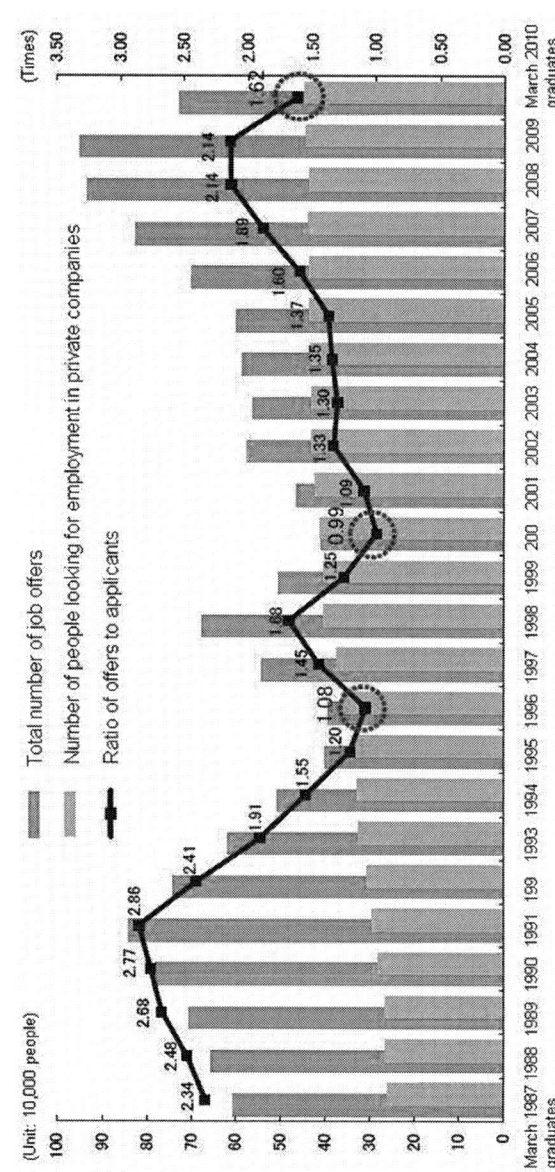

Source: Recruit Works Institute, *The 26th Survey on Ratio of Offers to Applicants for University Students*, news release, 13 April 2009. http://c.recruit.jp/library/job/J20090413/docfile.pdf.

(1)   The   Semi-Institutional   Linkages   between   Universities   and Corporations. Until the 1970s, a proportion of graduate recruitment was covered   by   corporations   that   recruited   only   from   their   preferred universities (the "reserved university").[1] Subsequent to this, the reserved university system for the recruitment of science graduates remained in place, but it became standard for universities not to contribute in a systematic way to job search activities by arts and humanities students, but rather let students and corporations engage in recruitment and job search activities in a freer way ("open recruitment").

Despite this, at the start of the 1990s, there were, in fact, a significant number of semi-institutional linkages between universities and corporations. An "information gap" existed, where recruitment information was sent only to students of their preferred universities,[2] and a system known as "Visit to Alumni", whereby current students visited their university graduates prior to recruitment selection processes and initiated informal contact, effectively played the function of connecting students of designated universities (particularly top-level institutions) with designated corporations.[3]

The fact that only students at relatively high-level universities had the opportunity to be recruited by top-level corporations presented some restrictions to individual students, but it is possible to think that the system has had the merit of facilitating relatively stable matching, allowing students who had been admitted to universities with high selection standards to be recruited by equivalent companies. With the growth of the Internet, however, in the late 1990s, "open recruitment" became more common, leading to greater individualisation, but also greater instability.

(2)   Increasingly Individualised, Complex and Long-Term Job Search Activities from 3rd Year Onwards. Nowadays, university students gradually begin activities related to job search from around the June of their third year. In June, internet sites that support third-year students in finding employment "pre-open", and begin to distribute information about companies that offer summer vacation internships.[4] In October, the

---

[1] Kariya, T., and Y. Honda, eds. 2010. *Daisotsu shushoku no shakaigaku* [The Sociology of Graduate Employment]. Tokyo: University of Tokyo Press.
[2] Toyoda, Y. 2007. "*Rikunabi* no tojo ga shinsotsu shijo ni motarashita hikari to kage," [Light and Shade Brought to the New Graduate Market by the Arrival of *Rikunavi* or Recruitment Information Websites] *The Japanese Journal of Labour Studies* 49, No. 4:62-64.
[3] Kariya, T., and Y. Honda, eds. 2010. *Daisotsu shushoku no shakaigaku* [The Sociology of Graduate Employment]. Tokyo: University of Tokyo Press.
[4] Internships began to be widely used in Japan at the end of the 1990s, but most of

Internet employment support websites open fully. There are three or four major sites, and it appears quite difficult to proceed subsequently with job search activities if a student does not register with one or more of these sites.

Students register their personal information on these sites, and can then search through companies wishing to hire university graduates. If they find a company in which they are interested, they can implement "entry" procedures, which notify the company in question of their interest. From the autumn of their third year, the companies hold corporation or industry explanatory meetings either at the university or at their offices. Subsequently, students select companies by which they wish to be screened, and from around December onwards during their third year, they begin submitting their entry sheets and résumés. If they pass the selection process involving entry sheets and résumés, they will next undertake written tests and be interviewed. Most interviews with major companies take place between March of the third year and April—June of the fourth year in several stages. Students who do not achieve a formal appointment during this time continue their job search during the summer holidays and from the autumn onwards.

In this way, if the internship in the summer vacation of the third year is included, students' job search activities nowadays begin in the early stages of the specialist study period of a university course, and continue over a long period of time, taking between a year to a year and a half.[5]

---

the internships on offer are not long-term internships to which the university contributes, which are linked to a student's faculty education. Rather, these internships are provided independently by corporations, and range from a few days to a week, or for only one day in some cases. The contents of internships are also less geared to allowing students to experience actual work, and in many cases consist more of implementing mock proposals, undertaking various miscellaneous tasks and visiting different departments. For students, even this type of internship, which is perhaps lacking in content, appears to offer advantages in job search, and most of them will try quite hard to experience some sort of internship.

[5] Around 1990, there existed "recruitment agreements", which detailed the schedule for employment selection, between universities and corporations. According to these, students would begin to visit companies from 20 August in their fourth year, and from 1 November, the companies were able to make formal appointments. In many cases, however, these "Recruitment agreements" were not abided by, and many companies in fact offered formal appointments to students at an earlier stage, leading to Keidanren, the leading economic organisation in Japan, to abolish the system in 1997. Subsequently, from 2004, Keidanren proposed an "Ethical constitution", aiming to introduce order to the recruitment process for newly graduating students, calling for it to be widely

The increasing use of the Internet has led to increasing levels of recruitment information from companies that students can access individually. It is extremely difficult, however, for students to determine which company they might like to work for, or by whom they may have the possibility of being employed, from that information. As a result, many students end up spending a large amount of time and effort in trying to make sense of their own job search.

At the same time as these processes become more complex and start to take place over a longer period, students are also increasingly required to implement them individually. Some corporations still implement company explanation meetings within universities, but students can also engage with individual companies through applying to explanation meetings, internet "entry", submitting entry sheets and résumés, taking written tests or interviews, and so on. For this reason, students are required to be highly proactive and have decision-making skills in a range of areas, in order to understand what industry or company they should apply to, how many companies they should engage in job search activities with, and how to balance job search activities with their university studies, and so on.

(3)   Recruitment Screening in Which Screening Criteria Are Unclear. Often, students are not sure what is required during screening processes, such as in document screening via entry sheets and résumés, written tests or interviews, and so on, as information relating to what they majored in, at what university is not clearly cited as an important part of the evaluation process. The selection criteria are often very difficult for them to understand. When applying to the screening process, students of the arts and humanities are not restricted by clear limits on what university they belong to and what they majored in the first place. Nevertheless, it appears that many companies merely implement first-stage screening by looking at the name of the university during entry sheet screening. Since this process happens behind closed doors, most applicants who do not make it through the entry sheet screening process never find out whether they were rejected because screening was done based on the name of their university or their major, or because the contents of their entry sheet were not evaluated highly enough.

In some cases, the questions asked on the entry sheet relate to areas such as "things you worked hard at while a student", "your strengths and

---

adopted by member corporations. The "Ethical constitution" published in October 2009 stipulates that no "interviews or other actual screening activities" are to be implemented during a student's third year. In fact, however, many companies that have signed up to the "Ethical constitution" still accept entry sheets and implement written tests, in order to select students for interview, during the third year.

weaknesses," "the reason you are applying to this company", and other issues, and nothing is asked relating to "the theme of your seminar class[6] and research". Many students tend to enter their experience in part-time jobs and club or group activities,[7] rather than in their studies, to questions relating to areas in which they have worked hard while in university, trying to show their "communication skills" and "independence", which corporations expect from them.

Other than for a small number of industries, such as the publishing industry, written tests tend not to be examining specialist knowledge required for the type or sector of work, but rather be weighted towards numerical problems examining a student's theoretical reasoning skills and/or calculation skills, reading comprehension skills or general knowledge, or (depending on the company) his or her English ability. In most cases, they do not test the knowledge a student has acquired from his or her major, but rather examine his or her basic academic abilities. They are often accompanied by personality tests.

At interview, students will be questioned on their motivation, and in addition, on the activities they focused on as students, and how they engaged with such activities. There is no particular restriction placed on the type of activity discussed. Regardless of the activity, students will be asked whether they engaged in it proactively, what role they played, what they thought about different aspects of the activity, and what efforts they made in regard to it. It is said that the company will try to assess a student's competency through these questions.

In this way, companies do not clearly state that their screening criteria include the university where students studied or their major, or even what they learned, but rather what sort of person they are, through a process of evaluating the whole person before making recruitment decisions. For this reason, while companies do include written tests, students do not see these as particularly assessing them on their academic abilities or specialism,

---

[6] The university seminar classes in Japan begin in a student's third year (second year in some universities). Most students belong to a seminar class operated by one particular member of the faculty, and the class involves proactive research by the students based on the specialisations of that faculty member. In some universities/departments, seminar classes may be restricted in numbers and therefore only a proportion of students may belong to certain seminar class.

[7] "Club" activities are official university groups, mainly based on sport, while "group" activities may include sports, cultural activities, volunteer activities, or activities designed to promote the social lives of students. "Group" activities may be officially approved by the university and in receipt of support for their activities, or they may be unofficial groups.

and there is a tendency to try to "play" the sort of person the student imagines a company wishes to hire, both in written submissions and at interview. In general, the sort of person a company is looking to hire is someone proactive and positive with high levels of communication skills. Some companies also emphasise theoretical reasoning skills, but many companies do not state clearly that this is important. In terms of the specialist knowledge required of students of arts and humanities, many companies state that "none is required, since we will train them once they enter the company",

If students try to perform in interview in such a way as to align themselves with the type of person they think the company wishes to hire, however, this can lead to the contents of the interview being very unoriginal. Many students find themselves discussing the aspects of their part-time work, club or group activities that emphasise how proactive and positive they are, or how they have communication skills. Manuals have even been published, which explain how to talk in this way. Despite the fact that the contents of their interviews are similar, one student may be dropped while another may progress to the next stage of the screening process. Students often struggle to understand where the difference between these two results lies. For this reason, many students become confused by fragmented information relating to what techniques may allow them to pass the interview. Since students who fail at the interview level are not told the reason why they did not succeed, it is difficult for them to learn from their failure, and they often lose confidence, since they feel that their personality has been rejected in a process that focuses mainly on personality.

(4)   Students at the Mercy of Job Search. Since the screening process is unclear to students, they often fear that they may end up with no formal appointments of employment, and as a result, become engaged in job search activities from an earlier point and over more time. Students are also applying to more and more companies for screening. As a result, they enter screening processes without spending sufficient time in researching either industries or companies, resulting in them either failing the screening process or being concerned that the company they are accepted by may not be the company they wanted to work for. On the other hand, as the job search process becomes more complicated, some students find it impossible to get going, and some give up at the early stages.

The extent to which the job search process has become so stressful is increasingly being identified as a problem. In 2008, a book was published under the title *"Shukatsu no Bakayaro* (stupid job search)".[8] It became a bestseller, and was widely read by many students. The title perfectly expressed the honest feeling that many students had about the stresses of the job search activities, and its subtitle ("The farce played out by companies, universities and students") expressed the distortion of the current job search/recruitment activities situation.

2. Measures by Universities to Support Student Careers

2.1 Switching over from Job Search Support to Career Support

(1) Measures by Universities That Are "Good at Employment". Finally, we are ready to discuss career support offered at universities. As stated above, the proportion of students continuing into further education is increasing, and the mere fact of being a graduate no longer provides a significant advantage within the youth labour market. Job search has become more complicated, it begins earlier and takes longer, and this means that there is a strong possibility that without career support from the university, many students may not be able to reach a formal appointment. In addition, since the bursting of the economic bubble, with employment restrictions in place with many companies, the reality is that there is now a significantly reduced rate of graduate employment.

Against this background, at the start of the 21st century, high school students and their parents began to look to universities that were "good at employment", in other words those universities that posted good graduate employment figures. Many universities also began activities to position themselves as "good at employment", seeing it as a way to survive the competition. So what makes a university "good at employment"?

The first thing that many universities have done is to introduce support activities that assist with the job search itself, such as giving guidance on writing entry sheets and taking interviews, offering individual guidance, creating and strengthening networks with alumni, corporations and the university, putting together internship and various other job search support programmes, supplying information regarding job offers, implementing job search guidance over a number of sessions, and so on.

As noted above, however, due to the individualisation and complexity of, early start to and long time spent in job search, universities have also identified a need to support students in becoming engaged in the job

[8] Ishiwatari, R., and H. Osawa. 2008. *Shukatsu no bakayaro* [Stupid Job Search]. Tokyo: Kobunsha.

search process itself. For this reason, some universities have begun implementing aptitude testing as early as in the first year, in order to consider what sort of job each student is suited to, and encouraging students to think about work from their first year, through implementing programmes under which human resources managers and young employees from corporations come to speak to students. Effectively this means that they are implementing "career support" from the first year onwards, not just "job search support" from the third year.

(2)   The Role of the Career Centre, and the Issue of Cooperation with Teaching Staff. In many cases, the measures introduced by universities to become "good at employment" have included a staff organisation known as the "career centre". Career centres are a restructured version of the "employment department" that has conventionally been found in most private universities.

Ritsumeikan University, which is a prestigious private university in the Kansai region, restructured its employment department into a career centre in November 1999. It was the first high-level university to implement these changes, and many other universities followed suit, changing their employment departments into career centres.

In this way, many universities sought to become "good at employment" through the leadership of their career centre, but encountered the problem of it being extremely difficult to implement changes to the curriculum, due to the fact that it required the agreement of the faculty council. The career centre may implement its own independent programmes, but this support will not reach the students unless they make their own way to the career centre, and for this reason, an increasing number of universities have now begun programmes in which career support has been introduced to the curriculum. These include programmes inviting human resources managers and young employees from companies as guests, to assist students in thinking specifically about the issues relating to work, programmes that seek to assist young people who will begin work in the future to understand the changes that are occurring in society, such as globalisation, diversification of employment formats, and so on and practical programmes that improve communication skills through group work, as well as internships that allow students to gain credits. Even if these programmes are, however, implemented as part of curricular education, they will still tend to exist as something of an "enclave" within the formal curriculum structure of the major subject implementing them, under the category of "career education courses", and since many of the classes are taught by external specialists, or by full-time teaching staff with a limited range, they tend not to link enough to the rest of the formal curriculum. In many cases, this has resulted in teaching staff in the rest of the department paying scant attention to what is being taught.

Here, I should like to introduce some data that allows us to consider this situation. In November 2005, the Japan Student Services Organisation (JASSO) implemented a "Survey into the state of student lifestyle support by universities".[9] According to this survey, whilst more than 70% of universities were implementing some sort of career support, only 41.4% of universities responded "Implementing systematically" when asked "Are you systematically implementing measures to support employment and career formation"?

Furthermore, when the author of this paper implemented a survey in March 2006 in regard to career support managers for higher education institutions, despite the fact that 85.1% of institutions responded that "It is desirable for elements of career support and career education to be integrated with the education offered in the major subject", only 47.5% responded that "Full-time teaching staff are proactively contributing to career support/career education".

2.2 Toward Integrated Career Support

(1)   Progressive Measures toward Integrated Career Support. As seen above, university career support has been led by efforts by career centres, which are staff organisations, and has not reached a state of being able to support student career activities throughout the whole curricular and extra-curricular programmes. It is not as if the need for integrated support had not been pointed out. In 2006, the Ministry of Education, Culture, Sports, Science and Technology (MEXT) defined "promotion of practical, integrated career education" as one of the themes of its "Support Programme for Contemporary Educational Needs (Contemporary Good Practice)", and MEXT is now engaged in a promotional strategy whereby universities that engage in excellent measures are selectively awarded subsidies. In many universities, however, it is a fact that involving the faculty and establishing the integrated career support cooperated with curriculum content have proved difficult.

Within this, however, there are some examples of situations in which the staff have been strong enough to influence the faculty in order to

---

[9] Japan Student Services Organization. 2006. *Daigakuto ni okeru gakusei seikatu shien no jittai chosa* [Survey on the State of Student Lifestyle Support by Universities]. Japan Student Services Organization. http://www.g-shiendb .jasso.go.jp/gsdb/main/tmp/contents/ab00141.html (accessed November 30, 2010).

ensure the inclusion of career support elements in curriculum. One representative of this movement is the aforementioned Ritsumeikan University, which took the lead in restructuring its employment department into a career centre, and where career education courses developed by the career centre were included in curriculum as early as 2000. Subsequently, students at Ritsumeikan have been encouraged to think about their own career paths from their first year, and career education courses have been gradually included into curriculum in order to improve their motivation to learn.[10]

Furthermore, the private Kyoto Sangyo University has been noted for its cooperative education measures, which involve the formation of an internship system as part of the curriculum. This programme, which received a subsidy from MEXT in fiscal 2004 as part of the "Support Programme for Contemporary Educational Needs", puts their students in small-group career-related lesson programmes from their first year onwards, as well as ensuring their participation in internships each year, resulting in the implementation of a sandwich-style programme of education that involves coordinated on-campus educational programmes and off-campus corporate and organisational internships.

(2)   Strengthening of Demand for Integrated Career Support. More recently, MEXT has strengthened its demands on universities to provide integrated career support. The criteria for university establishment was changed in February 2010 (to be enforced from 1 April 2011 onwards) requiring all universities to include "Guidance etc. relating to Social and Vocational Independence (Career Guidance)" both within and outside their educational courses. Furthermore, applications were invited in April 2010 for a subsidy programme entitled "Support for University Programmes Developing Employment Skills of University Students", demanding universities to proactively get engaged in measures, both within and outside of the curriculum, which facilitate students in developing their employability that assists them to social and vocational independence.

Subsequent to these demands, it appears that various universities are beginning to engage in a range of trial measures.

---

[10] Uenishi, M. 2007. "Daigaku ni okeru kyaria shien: Sono doko [Trends in University Career Support]," in *Daigaku no kyaria shien* [University career support], ed. Uenishi, M., (Tokyo: Keiei Shoin), ch. 1.

2.3 Curriculum Called into Question

(1) Developing Versatile Basic Abilities. These trial measures, however, have raised the question of what and how students should learn as a part of their university education.

The area on which various stakeholders are agreed is that students should learn "versatile basic abilities". In relation to this point, MEXT's advisory agency, the Central Education Council[11] defined in December 2008 some reference indicators for the "academic ability" required to obtain a bachelor's degree, which should be developed in all major courses focusing on learning outcomes. These were (i) knowledge/ understanding, (ii) versatile skills, (iii) attitudes/orientation, (iv) integrated learning experiences and comprehensive reasoning skills. The versatile skills required included i) communication skills, ii) quantitative skills, iii) information literacy, iv) theoretical reasoning skills, and v) problem solving abilities. The "attitudes/orientation" required included i) self-management, ii) teamwork and leadership, iii) ethical perspective, iv) social responsibility as a citizen, and v) ability to engage in lifelong learning.

The need for students to acquire these "learning outcomes" is unlikely to be disputed by anyone. The problem, however, is how to engage students in the process of acquiring such "learning outcomes".

(2) The Difficulty of Motivating Students to Acquire Versatile Basic Abilities. As stated in I above, many universities in Japan currently exist in a state of being "easy to enter and easy to graduate from". In this situation, outside of a certain number of top-level institutions, it appears to be easy to find students who may attend lectures, but have no real involvement in autonomous study. Motohisa Kaneko and his fellow researchers implemented surveys of university students, which showed that while attendance at lectures averaged 87.4%, more than 60% of students reported that they had "no interest or engagement with the lessons being taught", and that 70% of students considered that the statement "I attend lectures after implementing the required preparation or revision" either "did not apply at all" or "did not particularly apply" to them. Furthermore, 40% of students reported that they spent "0 hours" per week

---

[11] Central Education Council. 2008. *Gakushi katei kyoiku no kochiku ni mukete (toshin)* [Toward the Creation of Bachelor Education (report)]. Central Education Council, Ministry of Education, Culture, Sports, Science and Technology. http://www.mext.go.jp/b_menu/shingi/chukyo/chukyo0/tou- shin/1217067.htm (accessed November 30, 2010).

on study that "has no direct relationship to lectures" during the school term.[12]

Detailed guidance will be necessary for such students before they will be able to acquire the "learning outcomes" described above. Many universities have implemented their education via large-group lecture-style lessons, based on an assumption that students are self-motivated to study. The reality is that this system has continued to create graduates that leave university without ever achieving the "learning outcomes" above. These students are highly unlikely to achieve results in their job search. From the perspective of career support, therefore, they require not only job search support, but also support in acquiring basic academic skills.

(3) Measures Taken at Various Universities. This sort of learning support can take many forms. Universities that are "good at employment", such as the private Kanazawa Institute of Technology, implement academic abilities testing of students on entry, and where students do not demonstrate sufficient ability to undertake specialist education in areas such as mathematics, physics, chemistry, and so on, they are required to take lessons in basic mathematics. The institution also provides individual teaching, group guidance and e-learning systems, in order to ensure that individual students gain the basic academic abilities they require.

Some universities are providing training at even more basic levels. At the Kansai-based private university to which Igami[13] is affiliated, many students enter the university lacking basic techniques and abilities for study, and student opinions of university lectures includes honest expressions of lack of interest, describing teaching as "boring" and "meaningless". In general, many teaching staff merely complain about the attitude of students, but Igami and his colleagues are engaged in measures to correct the problems these students face, so as to ensure that they gain basic academic abilities they are lacking from primary education such as the concept of proportion, and that they establish good learning habits.

In other examples, one university has full-time teaching staff who teach first year students compulsory practical courses in small groups to

---

[12] Centre for Research on University Management and Policy, Graduate School of Education, University of Tokyo. 2008. *Zenkoku daigakusei chosha, dai-ichi-ji hokokusho* [Nationwide Survey of University Students: First Report]. Tokyo: CRUMP, Graduate School of Education, University of Tokyo. http://ump.p.u-tokyo.ac.jp/crump/ resource/ccs%20report1.pdf (accessed November 30, 2010).
[13] Igami, K. 2010. "Non erito daigakusei ni tsutaerubeki koto," [What Do We Have to Tell to Non-elite University Students?] *The Japanese Journal of Labour Studies* 52, No. 9:27-38.

ensure that students learn how to write reports, and another offers support for students acquiring official vocational qualifications as a method of ensuring they acquire learning habits and self-confidence. In another example, a university uses an information system to ascertain the individual learning status of students from their first year, in order to prevent students from dropping out or having to retake a year, and encourage systematic learning.

Of course, universities that only take students with higher levels of academic achievement are also engaging in practical programmes, such as project-based learning that aims to contribute to specific regional problems, or research themes in collaboration with corporations, which they anticipate will give good "learning outcomes". However, I should like to stress here that many universities are engaged not in highly progressive activities of this sort, but rather in much more gradual measures.

Furthermore, it is also important to draw attention to the fact that it is not always easy to engage students in such gradual measures. This is because, as mentioned in I-2-(3) above, many companies do not assess the actual study engaged in at university by students when recruiting, and that students feel that "even if they work hard at studying, this will not be appreciated in the process of recruitment selection". Additionally, as stated in I-2-(2) above, the increased complexity, early start and long duration of job search means that many students unavoidably spend a large proportion of their time in job search, and that once they become third year students, they quickly start to prioritize job search over and above study. It can be assumed that many companies do in fact include "academic achievement" as part of their evaluation of the "integrated whole person", but this in itself is too uncertain an objective to motivate students towards extending their abilities.

For this reason, some universities are now trying to guarantee an improvement in student abilities through making certain things obligatory, such as defining remedial education and basic education for academic skills as compulsory courses, or dictating that students who do not achieve a certain level of score in either TOEIC or TOEFL will not be able to move into the next academic year. At Hitotsubashi University, one of Japan's highest ranking national universities, students who enter after April 2010 are required to achieve a minimum GPA as part of the condition of their graduation. Up until recently, students were able to graduate from Japanese universities merely by achieving the required number of credits, even if the results achieved to gain those credits were barely acceptable, but this becomes impossible in cases where a particular

GPA is required for graduation. It remains to be seen whether other universities begin to adopt this same system.

(4) "Flexpeciality". In addition to "versatile basic abilities", should faculty education have more relevance to work? This topic is attracting attention as a significant area of discussion, but it appears to the author that no agreement has yet been reached among stakeholders.

Conventionally, with the exception of teacher training departments, it appears that arts and humanities departments at Japanese universities paid scant attention to the issue of providing an education that would equip students for a career in a designated sector of employment. This was partly due to the fact that many teaching staff were out of touch with business trends, but it was also to do with the fact that corporations hired new graduates with little or no attention to the specialist knowledge they possessed, and without restricting them to a particular post, subsequently engaging them in both on-the-job and off-the-job training that enabled them to acquire the required skills. Companies that would require a level of specialist knowledge from science graduates simply did not look for this among arts and humanities graduates. This situation has hardly changed today.

As stated above, however, since it is no longer possible to ignore the proportion of students who graduate from university without being engaged as full employees of a company, it appears unrealistic for universities to only count on post-employment training from the view point of ensuring students' interests. This highlights the issue of the relevance of education to work.

Yuki Honda is a leading figure in this debate. Stating that Japanese education is extremely lacking in vocational relevance when viewed from an international perspective, she coins the term "flexpeciality" (a combination of the words "flexible" and "speciality"), and states that this ought to be taught to students as part of their educational courses.[14] "Flexpeciality" is a specialism that is studied in order to act as a stepping-stone to broader related areas, and Honda states that such specialities are those that enable people to keep up with the changes in society. She recommends "flexpeciality" not only as a hedging of risk against the possibility of not being engaged as a full employee, but also as a means of protecting oneself against the trend in society that requires "versatile basic abilities" and excessive pressures of the recruitment screening process that evaluates the "whole person". While she accepts that communication skills

---

[14] Honda, Y. 2009. *Kyoiku no shokugyoteki igi* [The vocational relevance of education]. Tokyo: Chikuma Shobo.

and versatile basic abilities will be required in order to survive in the future, she criticises current career education, which she says does not provide direction or indicators for how to acquire these abilities.

These opinions of Honda's are becoming more and more influential, and as its name suggests, the Central Education Council's "Career Education/Vocational Education Special Working Group", which formed in December 2008 being consulted by MEXT, began to look seriously at the theme of "vocational education". Commissioned by MEXT, the Science Council of Japan also carried out a "Study of Quality Assurance by Sector of University Education"[15] the results of which[16] showed that there is currently no functioning link between universities and work, and that there is a need for this link to be recovered through improving the relevance of university education to work.

However, the concept of "flexpeciality" of this type and the current emphasis on vocational education, have so far been met with a cool reception within industry, and the future of this movement is unclear.

(5) "Application" and "Resistance". Another notable aspect of university career support is the need for students to learn the basic knowledge to protect themselves at work while still in school, such as gaining knowledge of labour law and labour unions. Honda[17] states that, in order to be prepared for the world of work, students need to be taught both methods to "apply themselves" and methods to "resist". "Flexpeciality" is a method for applying oneself, while basic knowledge of labour law provides a method for resistance when, for example, unreasonable demands are placed upon one at work. Nowadays many people encounter serious problems in the workplace, such as long working hours, unpaid overtime, unjust layoffs, mental imbalance such as depression, and so on, and the issue of "black companies", who force employees into indecent work practices, is also recognised as a social problem. Many young people, however, do not know what is illegal or unreasonable, and how to respond if they are placed in such a situation, because they have entered labour market with insufficient knowledge to deal with these situations.

---

[15] The committee who met to consider this issue was made up mainly of university researchers, with Yuki Honda playing a central leading role as director.
[16] Science Council of Japan. 2010. *Kaito: Daigaku kyoiku no bunyabetsu shitsuhosho no arikata ni tsuite* [Reply: Study of Quality Assurance by Sector of University Education]. Exploratory Committee of Science Council of Japan. http://www.scj.go.jp/ja/info/kohyo/pdf/kohyo-21-k100-1.pdf (accessed November 30, 2010).
[17] Honda, Y. 2009. *Kyoiku no shokugyoteki igi* [The vocational relevance of education]. Tokyo: Chikuma Shobo.

It would be difficult to say that university education has undertaken to provide training for "resistance". As Igami[18] states, however, there are some examples appearing where universities have begun to implement labour education as part of their career education programmes.

3. Conclusions

This paper introduced the situation surrounding university career support. A brief summary of the main discussion points is as below.

As increasing proportion of students choose to continue their education to university, the mere fact of being a graduate no longer provides a significant advantage within the youth labour market. In addition, with job search becoming more individualised, complex, starting earlier and taking longer to complete, universities are increasingly required to provide career support. This was initially considered to be supporting students through job search, but more recently demands have been increasing for curricular and extra-curricular educational activities to provide integrated career support for students. As part of this, the contents of curriculum have also been called into question, with the relevance of current university education to work being particularly under scrutiny. It could be said that universities are being called to answer the question of what exactly their significance is for young people in the first place.

While it is still unclear just how Japanese employment practices and human resources development will change in the future, it is not at all simple for universities and their staff to provide the answers to these questions. The problems of current job search and recruitment screening are currently shared broadly between universities, students and corporations, however, and it may be that this is increasing momentum for universities and corporations to work together in considering the role of universities, and recruitment methods.

References

Centre for Research on University Management and Policy, Graduate School of Education, University of Tokyo. 2007. *Kokosei no shinro tsuiseki chosa, dai-ichi-ji hokokusho* [Survey Following the Career Path of High School Students: First Report]. Tokyo: CRUMP, Graduate

---

[18] Igami, K. 2010. "Non erito daigakusei ni tsutaerubeki koto," [What Do We Have to Tell to Non-elite University Students?] *The Japanese Journal of Labour Studies* 52, No. 9:27-38.

School of Education, University of Tokyo. http://ump.p.u-tokyo.ac.jp/crump/resource/crumphsts.pdf   (accessed November 30, 2010).

—. 2008. *Zenkoku daigakusei chosha, dai-ichi-ji hokokusho* [Nationwide Survey of University Students: First Report]. Tokyo: CRUMP, Graduate School of Education, University of Tokyo. http://ump.p.u-tokyo.ac.jp/crump/ resource/ccs%20report1.pdf (accessed November 30, 2010).

Central Education Council. 2008. *Gakushi katei kyoiku no kochiku ni mukete (toshin)* [Toward the Creation of Bachelor Education (report)]. Central Education Council, Ministry of Education, Culture, Sports, Science and Technology. http://www.mext.go.jp/b_menu/shingi/chukyo/chukyo0/toushin/12170 67.htm (accessed November 30, 2010).

Honda, Y. 2009. *Kyoiku no shokugyoteki igi* [The vocational relevance of education]. Tokyo: Chikuma Shobo.

Igami, K. 2010. "Non erito daigakusei ni tsutaerubeki koto," [What Do We Have to Tell to Non-elite University Students?] *The Japanese Journal of Labour Studies* 52, No. 9:27-38.

Ishiwatari, R., and H. Osawa. 2008. *Shukatsu no bakayaro* [Stupid Job Search]. Tokyo: Kobunsha.

Japan Student Services Organization. 2006. *Daigakuto ni okeru gakusei seikatu shien no jittai chosa* [Survey on the State of Student Lifestyle Support by Universities]. Japan Student Services Organization. http://www.gshiendb.jasso.go.jp/gsdb/main/tmp/contents/ab00141.html (accessed November 30, 2010).

Kariya, T., and Y. Honda, eds. 2010. *Daisotsu shushoku no shakaigaku* [The Sociology of Graduate Employment]. Tokyo: University of Tokyo Press.

Science Council of Japan. 2010. *Kaito: Daigaku kyoiku no bunyabetsu shitsuhosho no arikata ni tsuite* [Reply: Study of Quality Assurance by Sector of University Education]. Exploratory Committee of Science Council of Japan. http://www.scj.go.jp/ja/info/kohyo/pdf/kohyo-21-k100-1.pdf (accessed November 30, 2010).

Toyoda, Y. 2007. "*Rikunabi* no tojo ga shinsotsu shijo ni motarashita hikari to kage," [Light and Shade Brought to the New Graduate Market by the Arrival of *Rikunavi* or Recruitment Information Websites] *The Japanese Journal of Labour Studies* 49, No. 4:62-64.

Uenishi, M. 2007. "Daigaku ni okeru kyaria shien: Sono doko [Trends in University Career Support]," in *Daigaku no kyaria shien* [University career support], ed. Uenishi, M., (Tokyo: Keiei Shoin), ch. 1.

READING INSTRUCTIONS

All issues of the *ADAPT LABOUR STUDIES Book-Series* comprise an online resources section, set up for documentary purposes and with the aim to implement and update the content of our publications on a regular basis.

The symbol 📖 within the text indicates a reference to the ADAPT website (*www.adapt.it*), where an embedded search engine and an A-Z index will enable to find the documentation cited within the book, notably:

a) sources of law,

b) relevant EU and international documentation,

c) memoranda of understanding, agreements and collective agreements,

d) monographic works,

e) studies and research reports.

ONLINE RESOURCES

1. APPRENTICESHIP 📖
(Apprendistato)

EU DOCUMENTS *(Documentazione comunitaria)*

European Parliament, 6 July 2010
Promoting Youth Access to the Labour Market, Strengthening Trainee, Internship and Apprenticeship Status

European Parliament, 14 June 2010
Report on Promoting Youth Access to the Labour Market, Strengthening Trainee, Internship and Apprenticeship Status (2009/2221(INI))

INTERNATIONAL DOCUMENTS *(Documentazione internazionale)*

Bundesagentur für Arbeit et al. (Germany), 26 October 2010
Nationaler Pakt für Ausbildung und Fachkräftenachwuchs in Deutschland 2010-2014

Bundesinstitut für Berufsbildung (Germany), 2010
Datenreport zum Berufsbildungsbericht 2010

Bundesinstitut für Berufsbildung (Germany), 2010
Ausbildung Plus

Swiss Confederation (Switzerland), 2010
Vocational and Professional Education in Switzerland

Fuller, A., and L. Unwin (United Kingdom), 2009
Towards Expansive Apprenticeships

REPORTS AND RESEARCH *(Studi e ricerche)*

ISFOL, XI Monitoring Report (Italy), March 2011
Monitoraggio sull'apprendistato

Association for Career and Education (U.S.A.), March 2011
Apprenticeships Techniques—American Journal on apprenticeship

Steedman, H. LSE, August 2010
The State of Apprenticeship in 2010
International Comparisons Australia Austria, England, France, Germany, Ireland, Sweden, Switzerland

Rauner, F., E. Smith, U. Hauschildt, and H. Zelloth, eds. 2009
Innovative Apprenticeships

Steedman, H. 2007
Adapting to Globalised Product and Labour Markets New Models For Apprenticeship In Europe

Steedman, H. 2005
December 2005 Apprenticeship in Europe: 'Fading' or Flourishing?

Leonardo Da Vinci – Dream Job (EU)
Analisi comparata dei sistemi di formazione dell'apprendistato nei paesi dell'Unione Europea (15) (Compared Analysis in the EU15)

2. EDUCATION, TRAINING AND LABOUR 📖
(*Istruzione, formazione, lavoro*)

EU DOCUMENTS (*Documentazione comunitaria*)

Communication of the European Commission, 31 January 2011
Tackling Early School Leaving: A Key Contribution to the Europe 2020
Agenda, COM(2011) 18 final

European Commission, November 2010
An Agenda for New Skills and Jobs: A European Contribution Towards
Full Employment, COM(2010) 682/3

**Council of The European Union, 3046th Education, Youth, Culture
and Sport Council meeting, 18-19 November 2010**
Priorities for Enhanced European Cooperation in Vocational Education
and Training for the Period 2011-2020

**A Report by the Expert Group on New Skills for New Jobs prepared
for the European Commission, February 2010**
New Skills for New Jobs: Action Now

European Commission, 23 November 2009
Key Competences for a Changing World. Draft 2010 Joint Progress
Report of the Council and the Commission on the Implementation of the
"Education & Training 2010 Work Programme"

European Commission, 23 November 2009
Accompanying Document to the Communication from the Commission:
Key Competences for a Changing World. Progress Towards the Lisbon
Objectives in Education and Training

European Commission, 16 December 2008
New skills for New Jobs. Anticipating and Matching Labour Market and
Skills Needs

European Commission, 16 December 2008
An Updated Strategic Framework for European Cooperation in Education
and Training, COM(2008) 865 final

INTERNATIONAL DOCUMENTS (*Documentazione internazionale*)

Sénat de la République Française (France), 14 October 2009
Projet de loi relatif à l'orientation et à la formation professionnelle tout au long de la vie

Sénat de la République Française (France), 16 September 2009
Rapport fait au nom de la commission spéciale sur le projet de loi, adopté par l'Assemblée nationale, relatif à l'orientation et à la formation professionnelle tout au long de la vie

United Kingdom, Employment and Skills Commission, 2009
Ambition 2020: World Class Skills and Jobs for the UK

Council of Economic Advisers—Report to President Barak Obama, July 2009
Preparing the Workers of Today for the Jobs of Tomorrow

REPORTS AND RESEARCH (*Studi e ricerche*)

Cedefop, 2010
Learning while Working. Success Stories on Workplace Learning in Europe

Cedefop, 2009
The Shift to Learning Outcomes. Policies and Practices in Europe

Cedefop, 2008
The Shift to Learning Outcomes. Conceptual, Political and Practical Developments in Europe

DATA AND STATISTICS (*Statistiche e note economiche*)

OECD, September 2010
Education at a Glance 2010

3. YOUNG WORKERS 📖
(*Lavoratori giovani*)

EU DOCUMENTS *(Documentazione comunitaria)*

European Commission, 15 September 2010
Youth on the Move, COM(2010) 477

EMCO—Ad Hoc Group - Report on the 2010 thematic review, 2010
Policies for Supporting Youth

European Commission, 2009
A EU Strategy for Youth—Investing and Empowering. A Renewed Open
Method of Coordination to Address Youth Challenges and Opportunities

INTERNATIONAL DOCUMENTS *(Documentazione internazionale)*

ILO, 1 September 2010
Promoting Job creation for Young People in Multinational Enterprises

**Resolution adopted by the General Assembly of United Nation, 3
February 2010**
Policies and Programmes Involving Youth

Afl Cio, September 2009
Young Workers: A Lost Decade

Eurofound, July 2009
Tackling the Increased Take-up of Incapacity Benefit by Young People in
the European Union

REPORTS AND RESEARCH *(Studi e ricerche)*

The Japanese Journal of Labour Studies September 2010, No. 602
The Labour Issue of Youth: Looking Back over 20 Years

Bell, D. N. F., and D. G. Blanchflower, January 2010
Youth Unemployment: Déjà Vu?

Scarpetta, S., A. Sonnet, and T. Manfredi, OECD, 14 April 2010
Rising Youth Unemployment During the Crisis: How to Prevent Negative Long-term Consequences on a Generation?

Contini, B., IZA, January 2010
Youth Employment in Europe: Institutions and Social Capital Explain Better than Mainstream Economics

Stampini M., A. Verdier-Chouchane, 2010
Labor Market Dynamics in Tunisia: The Issue of Youth Unemployment

Martin, G., International Bureau of Labor Statistics, July 2009
A Portrait of the Youth Labor Market in 13 Countries, 1980-2007

DATA AND STATISTICS (*Statistiche e note economiche*)

ILO, August 2010
Global Employment Trends for Youth

International Institute for Labour Studies, 2010
Youth Employment in Crisis

Eurostat, 10 December 2009
Youth in Europe

---

4. SCHOOL-TO-WORK TRANSITION 📖
(Transizione scuola lavoro)

INTERNATIONAL DOCUMENTS *(Documentazione internazionale)*

ILO (Matsumoto, M., and S. Elder), 2 June 2010
Characterizing the School-to-work Transitions of Young Men and Women: Evidence from the ILO School-to-work Transition Surveys, Employment Working Paper No. 51

OECD, October 2009
Learning for Jobs. OECD Policy Review of Vocational Education and Training

OECD, 20 August 2009
Going Separate Ways? School-to-work Transitions in the United States and Europe. School-to-work Transition Pathways in the United States and Europe between the Late 1990s and the Early 2000s

OECD, 1999
Preparing Youth for the 21st Century. The Transition from Education to the Labour Market, 1999

REPORTS AND RESEARCH *(Studi e ricerche)*

Quintini G., J. P. Martin, and S. Martin, January 2007
The Changing Nature of the School-to-work Transition Process in OECD Countries

Ryan P., 2000
The School-to-work Transition: a Cross-national Perspective

Ryan P., 1999
The School-to-work Transition: Issues for Further Investigation, Prepared for Education and Training Division, DEELSA, OECD

O'Higgins N., 1997
The Challenges of Youth Unemployment, ILO Employment and Training Papers, 1997, n. 7

CONTRIBUTORS

Thayyullathil Asokan, Professor and Head, School of Commerce and Management Studies, Kannur University, India.

Lilli Casano, Doctoral Student in European Labour Law, University of Catania, Italy.

Ludger Deitmer, Senior Research Fellow and Lecturer, Institute Technology and Education, University of Bremen, Germany.

Tayo Fashoyin, Former Director, Industrial and Employment Relations Department, ILO.

Franz J. Gellert, Lecturer and Researcher, Hanze University of Applied Sciences, Groningen, Netherlands.

Barbara Grandi, Doctoral Student in Labour Law, University of Rome "Sapienza", Italy.

Léna Krichewsky, Research Assistant, University of Magdeburg, Germany.

Attila Kun, Associate Professor, Faculty of Law, Department of Labour Law and Social Security. Károli Gáspár University of Budapest, Hungary.

Pietro Manzella, ADAPT Language Editor.

Enrico Marelli Full Professor of Economic Policy, University of Brescia.

Benjamin Ogwo, Coordinator, Occupational Competency Assessment Program, State University of New York, USA.

Mohammed R. Parakandi, Research Coordinator, Abu Dhabi University, United Arab Emirates.

Balazs Rossu, Assistant Research Fellow, Faculty of Law and Political Sciences, Department of Labour Law and Social Security. University of Szeged, Hungary.

Lisa Rustico, Head of ADAPT International Relations.

Malcolm Sargeant, Full Professor of Labour Law, Middlesex University, UK.

René Schalk, Full Professor, Faculty of Social and Behavioral Sciences, Human Resource Studies, Tilburg University, Netherlands.

Marcello Signorelli, Associate Professor of Economic Policy, University of Perugia, Italy.

Salma Khaled Slama, Associate Professor of Private Law, University of Tunis, Tunisia.

Erica Smith, Professor of Education, University of Ballarat, Australia.

Phasina Tangchuang, Associate Professor, JEAI CELS, Coordinator for PhD program on HRD, Faculty of Education, Chiang Mai University, Thailand.

Satomi Terasaki, Lecturer, Faculty of Humanities Department of Education and Clinical Psychology, Fukuoka University, Japan.

Michele Tiraboschi, Full Professor of Labour Law, University of Modena and Reggio Emilia, Italy.

Mitsuko Uenishi, Associate Professor at the Faculty of Lifelong Learning and Career Studies, Hosei University, Japan.

INDEX